OVER THE HILL AND 'ROUND THE BEND

or Gullible's Travels

GAIL LUCAS

For Amy,
Enjoy the journey!
♡
Gail Lucas

Artwork by Gail Lucas.

Photos by Gail Lucas and Terence Geoghegan.

Published by Gail Lucas.
Santa Barbara, California.

ISBN-13: 978-1981738007

ISBN-10: 1981738002

TWO MOTORCYCLES, FIVE YEARS, AND A THOUSAND PATHS.

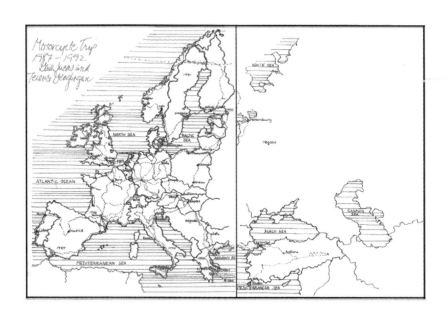

Chapter One

THE IDEA AND THE PLAN

ON MAY, 4, 1986, for my forty-ninth birthday I was given my first motor-cycle. Not that I'd asked for one, you understand...nor did I, even in my hearts of hearts, have the slightest wish for one. But then, you had to know Terence.

Terence Geoghegan was just twenty-nine when we met; a gray-eyed, dark-haired and bearded wild man living on a mountain-top above Santa Barbara, who rode fast motorcycles, championed strange causes, played the viola, had a black-belt in Taekwon-Do and worked as a sheet-metal construction worker to pay for his excesses which were many. Still reeling from a painfully broken marriage and taken to abusing too many things--alcohol, acquaintances and worse of all, himself, he tells me he was very close to giving up, and riding off to that Big Biker Rally in the Sky.

At the same point in time, around March of 1985, I was wondering what I was going to be doing with the rest of my life. I had been single for about ten years, with a daughter finishing college and a son about to enter one. I was working as a manager of a small dress shop--selling high-priced frocks to ladies by day, and singing and acting in local amateur productions at night. I seemed to be rather stuck in limbo, facing an empty nest and a lonely middle age.

It was as Phyllis, in Gilbert and Sullivan's "Iolanthe," that I spotted the handsome young hunk smiling at me over his viola in the orchestra pit, and within a week, we were turning each others' lives around, and Terence

1

began planning for our future. I say Terence planned, because although I was flattered and charmed, I was not, shall we say, "born yesterday," and the thought that this young and dashing savage was going to stay around a woman eighteen years his senior for very long was simply too fantastic to be true. But what a great time we were having! Overnight, I became a Biker Chick. Whipping over mountain passes on the back of his Suzuki GS 1100E, with my arms around his leather-jacket, my hair snapping against my helmet and the delicious roar of the engine in my ears, it seemed to be just about as good as life gets. He moved off the mountain and in with me.

After discovering how well we got along on a three-week biker-camping trip to Canada in July, Terence suggested that we go around the world together. On motorcycles. I blissfully ignored the plural of "motor-cycle" and said, "Why not?" He talked of learning several languages along the way and that he would be taking a correspondence Law School course that would enable him, after four and a half years, to take the California Bar exam when we returned. Also, he thought it might be the best way to get his higher degrees in Taekwon-Do in that he could practice with different studios in each country. Even teach their classes, after he learned their languages. I smiled. What an adorable dreamer he was. "Why not?," I said again. "You could even play your viola in the best orchestras of Europe and learn the language that way too!" He thought that was a great idea.

We saved. We scrimped. Terence signed up with the only correspon-dence Law school he could find, the University of Newport Law School in Orange County, California. He worked as a sheet-metal worker until the last minute and sold off various rusting vehicles and machine parts with which he had been decorating my driveway and yard. I gave notice at my job and cleaned out my attic and garage and held yard sales and started looking for a nice family to rent my house. We found a cheap leather jacket for me and some used rain gear at the swap meet for both of us. Terence said it was imperative that we look for sponsors for the trip, and he gave me a list of companies to write to or call. I have to confess I was terrible at it; how could I convince heads of companies who get these calls all the time that they should sponsor two wanna-be adventurers in a five-year trip around the world when I didn't really believe we'd last a month? You could say I was of little faith.

My birthday present was waiting in the living room when I came home from work that May day. Terence met me at the front door and put a bandanna around my head and led me to something metal, cold, and very big. I pushed up the blindfold. It was a used Kawasaki 305. To practice on, he said. My doom was sealed. I began to realize the man was serious about me riding my own motorcycle in Europe. I wondered how to tell him the whole idea was impossible; that at forty-eight, I was as likely to learn to ride a motorcycle as be a fighter pilot. Moreover, the only reason I had climbed on one and ridden behind him was because it was a thinly-veiled excuse to put my arms around a gorgeous hunk and nuzzle his neck in public without anybody thinking it strange...I might be killed in a grisly accident, but what a way to go.

Watching my expression after the blindfold was off, his grin reached his ears. He was as happy and excited as a three-year old. How could I disappoint him? Maybe if I just pretended to try to ride it and fell off once at slow speed, he'd realize how much he treasured me and how unsafe it would be to have me at the helm of such a dangerous toy that was, after all, designed particularly for wild young men who wanted to fling themselves off cliffs or through fiery hoops. Not for middle-aged housewives whose idea of danger was trying to extricate a fork from a turned-off garbage disposal.

"It's beyond anything I've ever imagined," I said truthfully.

I have blissfully forgotten most of my days of training. I remember I did fall off somewhere around the neighborhood. Hit a curb and went flying and landed, luckily, in a nice soft flower-bed. Terence never laughed at my failures, though he must have been appalled. It was inconceivable to him that someone wouldn't grab the chance to ride a motorcycle with all the zest he had himself for such things. Frankly, as a teacher, he made a better rider. His idea of teaching someone to swim was to hold them under, if that tells you anything.

But I learned. Even stayed upright long enough to pass the test at the DMV for my motorcycle license, although the young Hispanic woman testing me didn't seem all that happy to pass me. We sold the Kawasaki and found a bigger bike for me. A 1984 Honda Ascot 550. A shaft drive, not too big, and I could sit up straight. Terence finally located a used Gold Wing 1200 that could pull the thousand-pound trailer we'd bought at cost from some very generous people in the mid-west that Terence had talked into being sponsors. He and some pals welded strong sheet-metal boxes to the sides of our motorcycles and another much bigger one on the back of his Gold Wing. He would be keeping his most precious possessions within reach at all times. His viola and violin, his typewriter and his cameras.

We found some nice folks to rent my home. Denver and Donna Mills and three children promised to love the house as if it were their own. I wrote my will and whispered to my son and daughter not to worry--I'd probably be back before they knew it.

We had a stupendous Bon Voyage party, with bikers bringing the beer and members of the Gilbert and Sullivan Company orchestra--still in their tuxedos from the matinee of "The Mikado"--bringing the champagne. The cast dropped by later, make-up still clinging to their ears. Fishermen and surfers and everybody else we knew in Santa Barbara, mingled and shook their heads in disbelief as they studied the big maps we'd taped to the walls--our PLAN OF ACTION for the next five years--winters in the southern European countries, summers in the northern ones...and home by way of Russia and Alaska.

ALL YOUR FRIENDS WILL WANT TO BE "HELPFUL"....

Chapter Two

ACROSS THE SOUTHERN STATES

FEBRUARY 21, 1987 was a warm, sunny morning. The Millses helped us put the final touches on our preparations for departure. Donna performed a native American ceremony, complete with burning sticks and incantations in front of the wheels of our motorcycles and the heavily loaded trailer for our good fortune or maybe just for theirs as they were finally getting rid of us and could soon relax in my house, undisturbed by our land-lording over them.

It was dark before we got to our friends Carol and Dorian's in Fullerton. I remember getting stuck going up their hill, I couldn't get the bike in gear, and maddened traffic all around honking. Terence wondering what the hell--behind me--and having to stop with that heavy trailer. It was simply a matter of my inexperience, and after a few terrible minutes I had it figured out and got the machine going but it was no fun at all and just the beginning of what would be a long list of such occurrences with what always seemed to be the same formula: mistake, panic, denial, more panic, slow acceptance, then control and an attempt at a solution to the problem. I was not thrilled at this new role, but there was no turning back.

Our second morning on the road was lots colder. We headed for San Diego and our good friends Paul and Ella H'son. Terence had been on some memorable sheet-metal jobs with both of them and they were Gold-Wingers. Ella tried to help me get organized while the guys did some more last minute shopping for the trip. Paul and Terence decided I needed a sheepskin so I wouldn't be too uncomfortable for the long hauls. I was so naïve I thought they were just trying to make me feel more like a real biker with the thing on my seat. I was sure it was going to slide off or flap itself into the wheels and kill me at high speed so I was angry at their insistence that I use it. Five years later, tattered and filthy, it was stolen by Russian thieves in a campground in St. Petersburg and I was heartbroken and hated climbing on the bike's cold hard seat without it.

Leaving San Diego on February 26, we were amazed to discover snow as we climbed the pass over to the desert. Paul rode with us to the top of the mountains. We all wished he was coming too. As he waved good-bye and we started down the slippery road, it started to snow again. Terence slipped and slid around the narrowing street and I was paralyzed with terror. The men had outfitted me with everything possible for my safety and warmth, and I could barely move. I felt like the Bride of Frankenstein. Stiff all-weather gloves, a size too large, covered my hands so that I could barely feel the levers on the motorcycle. Electric wires traveled from the gloves and up through my vest and back down to a temperature control thing in my pocket. It had been set at too high a heat and I was sweating and uncomfortable but turning it down would have necessitated stopping the motorcycle and there was no place to drive off the snowy road and also I didn't dare get out of my place in line. Other wires ran under my bright yellow rain slicker, connecting the intercom which I hadn't learned to use yet. Terence was trying to communicate using his, and I was hanging on to the bike's handles for dear life instead of pushing the little red button on the little talk box he had so carefully installed for me to use. Concentrating so hard on staying upright, I barely heard his voice in my helmet, calling me to please confirm and answer...

Nobody had told me it could be this scary. Nobody expected it to snow in this part of the state at all, and certainly nobody expected anyone to be so foolish as to try to traverse it on a motorcycle!

Somewhere deep in the mountains, a motel appeared. We turned in. We parked the bikes where they could go no farther in the snow bank and went in and paid about thirty-five bucks and found our way through the falling snow to a tiny A-frame cottage to take hot showers and change into dry clothes. Terence was gently solicitous to this madwoman who appeared to be displaying early signs of a nervous breakdown. He helped me get out of the frozen yellow space suit, and hugged me and cooed about how brave he thought I was, and how proud he felt to have me with him. It did the trick. After a nap and a return to sanity where I was at last breathing easier again, Terence announced that he'd heard on the radio that the storm was going to get much worse and might last a week, and if we had any hopes about making it to New Orleans in time for Mardi Gras we'd have to get back on the bikes and head out! No! No!, every fiber of my being pleaded. But what chance had I against a Biker from Hell who wanted to see the Mardi Gras? We packed up and he once again wired me for sound and turned up my heat system and strapped and locked and plugged me into my rocket ship and we took off into the blizzard. My numbness was not due to the cold.

I thought he was crazy. I knew he was crazy. But I was not about to be left behind and he knew it. Incredibly, the snowfall let up after a couple of hours and bright blue patches appeared in the sky and we began hitting drier road. The whole world around me seemed to turn from nightmare to dream until I could feel the fear subside and a kind of euphoria take its place. The landscape on either side of me was sparkling and gorgeous. Once I could relax my death grip on the controls and lean back in my seat and look around, I realized the view was sensational. A Christmas card scene covered in pure white sugar. Nobody else on the road, and the smell of pine on the wind. I began to get an idea of what this trip was supposed to be about.

Down the mountain and into the eastern Californian desert. A night in a campground, a morning with frost thick on our bikes and gear, and then the long rides on endless highways began. I was glad to finally have the opportunity to reflect and get used to the feel of riding a motorcycle. It had all been such a mad rush. Renting the house. What a horror. All the cleaning, the storing of precious things, the paperwork. Yecch. The faces of my friends and children reflecting disbelief and something else. Was it pity? Learning to ride a motorcycle properly had been way down on my list of priorities. Now I realize it was simply fear. Listening to the drone of the machine under me as hour after hour passed on those highways going east, I began to understand something about that fear. Well, sure I had some to start with, let's face it. A forty-nine year-old woman with all the usual hang-ups about learning to ride a motorcycle in the first place--let alone her own! I mean I still hadn't gotten around to erasing the old wives tale stuff about bikers in general. I'd never even known a biker until Terence!

Arizona and New Mexico zipped past. Campgrounds and rest areas with stucco teepees and neon Indians. Texas. Long, hot flat rides for days. We stopped in Palestine to visit our good friend Chris's folks, then on toward St. Augustine in a frantic dash to get to New Orleans in time for the Mardi Gras. It was already dark when we pulled into a liquor store parking lot to ask somebody if they knew of a spot where we could camp for the night. No help there--in fact we were warned about certain lawless characters roaming the land or something, maybe he meant that we were the lawless characters and had better get out of town if we knew what was good for us. Back in the parking lot, a couple of good ol' boys leaned out of their truck and told Terence they'd overheard him talking to the guy behind the counter and they wanted us to follow them because they knew of a place to camp. Not at all sure if we really wanted to follow those guys in the pick-up, we talked it over and realized we really didn't have much choice. We boarded the bikes and took off after them. They led us to a picnic area off the road about five miles out of town. After we pulled in, the guys got out and one of them set a trash can on fire. He said that ought to keep us warm until he got back with the rest of the party! Then they hopped into their truck and took off into the night, leaving us in a thick cloud of dust and wondering what we'd gotten ourselves into.

About fifteen minutes later, the "party" arrived; our boys and an old Cadillac full of fun-seekers and a big bag of food. They told us they wanted to introduce us to the local fare which turned out to be some "head cheese"--a pressed meat and intestines thing that I found I could get down only if I didn't look at it too closely. Terence and I dug around in our tiny refrigerator for something we'd been saving for a special occasion: a cheese made with salmon that we'd found in a San Diego deli the week before. We thought our Texan friends would be much impressed. Instead, they turned up their noses and said they preferred their jellied innards. Oh well. We all drank a lot of beer and told stories and had a grand time. One of the young women had a small child on her shoulder who soon fell asleep and the lady didn't even bother to put the child down all evening. She just walked around and ate, drank and smoked as if the sleeping baby was a kind of shoulder pad!

The trash can blazed merrily. About three in the morning the folks in the Cadillac took off for home--said they were sorry but had to go to work in the morning, but the two from the truck hung around and asked Terence if he could play the violin they'd seen in the big metal box on the back of his motorcycle. He was delighted and took out his viola first and played a few snatches of things and got such encouragement from the guys, he pulled out the violin and proceeded to play that too. They were entranced. They told us they had never seen an orchestra play and this all was a mighty fine experience. For us too.

After they went home and we crawled into our little bed over the trailer, we noticed that we'd somehow burned a big hole in our nice new tent flap. Five years later that flap resembled Swiss cheese from all the times it had melted against the light bulb Terence had put in there so we could read in bed. Good thing it was fireproof or we'd have gone up in smoke many times over!

Well, the boys had broken it to us gently the proceeding night that we were just a slight bit off on our calculations as to what day Mardi Gras was, and instead of making it by the skin of our teeth the next day it seems we had already celebrated the occasion with the good ol' boys--eating head cheese to fiddle music and dancing around a burning trash-can somewhere in southern Texas! Still, Terence wanted to be in New Orleans in time to perhaps catch folks still partying, if possible, so we hopped on the bikes and rode like maniacs to make up for lost time. The ugly truth was, that no matter how hard we rode, no matter how many short-cuts we attempted, the distance to New Orleans through the swamps and detours of Louisiana was just too far, and by mid-afternoon we realized that no way were we going to make it to the city in time for partying and carousing with whomever was left from the bash of the day before. Tired and discouraged, we pulled up to a sort of diner. Paint peeling and ugly, the place was downright creepy, but we were so hungry by that time it hardly mattered and anyway, the smells wafting from its kitchen had us in its spell before we could get off the bikes! I couldn't tell you what we ordered except it had to do with rice and beans and peppers, but I do know that sitting at that splintery picnic table that afternoon, the Spanish moss swaying above us and the day's hot sun slipping red between the trees, we realized we'd just been blessed with our first Cajun cooking and we were converts !

Back on the road, just a couple of hours out of New Orleans, we encountered our first "roundabout." There must have been six roads-all converging in the center like spokes to a wheel's hub. We were to become old hands at them in Europe in a few weeks, but this one was something new and terrifying. A huge one and rush-hour to boot, and although Terence with his usual This-looks-like-fun attitude, dove right in and emerged grinning on the other side, I did the worst possible thing and slowed down and wobbled and prayed that the people in the cars swirling around me would be kind and understanding as I edged my way to the center where I thought I'd be safer while I figured out which road Terence had taken off the monster. So much for prayers made in hell. It was bumper-car time and the little woman on the motorcycle with the Cal-ee-for-nee license plate was fair game, Everybody was honking and screeching their brakes as I veered around in front of them in my confusion. Like I wanted to be scared and lost, I'm sure!

I finally saw Terence waving frantically from one of the off-ramps, so I headed for him and threaded my way to the edge of the whirlpool of traffic and pulled up behind him. The look he gave me was a mixture of disbelief and anger, but thank God he decided against saying anything just then because I was in no mood for a lecture. I was near tears and dizzy from going around in circles so many times and we still had a way to go before we could rest and think about it.

It was almost midnight when we found ourselves driving around the dark streets of New Orleans looking for a place to stay. The only campground within miles was closed to the likes of us, we found out. We knocked on the door to the manager's trailer there and a woman in a frizzy-haired wig and a dirty slip pulled herself away long enough from her television set to inform us, after seeing the motorcycles over our shoulders, that she didn't take "our kind" in her trailer park. Peering at our mud splattered boots through the smoke from the cigarette in her mouth, she sniffed and suggested we try some of the...uh...cheaper hotels down the road. We did. But the Ladies of the Evening pretty much had the rooms booked for the night. It seemed it was a great week for business. Around midnight we gave up and opted for a Ramada Inn near the airport. Horrible on the budget, but it had been a rough day and they at least seemed happy to see us--splattered boots and all!

The party was indeed pretty much over down in the French Quarter where we rode our bikes the next morning. Tons of trash and a few tired-looking tourists poking around the rubble of what must have been another great celebration for the city. Perhaps we'd catch it another year. We now had to run on to Florida--for the Daytona Bike Festival!

Over long bridges and through the swamps. March isn't the prettiest time of year for the Deep South. Sticky air around us and muddy roads and a lot of rain, soggy clothes and moldy motel rooms. We were relieved to see the sun begin to poke out of the clouds as we rode into the campground near Daytona. It was a comfy-looking place. Tall old trees provided a lace-work pattern against the sky and it had a rather homey atmosphere in that it served as a retiree mobile home park during the rest of the year when the Bike Festival wasn't in progress. A sign on the Community room door said "WELCOME BIKERS!" Then way down at the bottom it announced: "Blood pressure tests--tomorrow at 8:30 a.m.!" We had a laugh and got off our bikes to look around. The Louisiana Belle in the trailer back in New Orleans would have swallowed her cigarette if she'd seen what was going on at the moment in this RV park! Bikers were everywhere. And not sedate, well-heeled fellows on touristers nor even yuppies on BMWs, but her worst nightmare; gen-u-ine Hell's Angeles types--Wild Ones on Easy Riders, revving and raving and turning up their bad music and stomping to the rhythm with their heavy (and yes, mud-splattered) boots, a beer in each hand and a biker's bitch on each lap. Terence was in Hog heaven. The swimming pool was full of naked revelers, and he lost no time in grabbing his camera and joining the happy throng and getting some shots before the boobs, I mean beer ran out. I set up camp and wandered over to take a look myself. Those people were having fun. Terence wasn't the only guy with a camera, either. Several of the permanent residents of the park were having a field day watching the goings-on in the pool. Elderly gents leaning on the wire mesh fence hid behind their view-finders with mischievous smiles curling up the sides of their faces. Their wives stood at their sides with pinched looks. Other gray heads watched from a distance with eyes wide--yet I noticed they didn't leave until the last person was handed a towel! Most of the gang in the pool wanted their picture taken--and with their own cameras, too. Lots of strutting and showing tits and splashing and yelling. The ol' swimmin' hole. I was interested to see there was little or no --you know--tough stuff. I guess I expected to see somebody pushed around a little, if not actually knifed on the spot. So disappointing. Could it be that I'd seen too many movies?

Later that night we decided to see what would happen if we put an opera tape in the player and turned it up as high as our neighbor's rock music. I think we had Montserrat Caballé doing Mimi when one of the Hog riders walked over to our campsite and asked us politely to turn it down! Hey, sure Buddy. Sorry.

Downtown Daytona proved to be fairly tame in comparison the next day. Still, there was the earth-trembling rumble of the Harleys as they passed us in the street so everybody'd know who owned the place this week, and there was the famous bike exhibit--calling the faithful to come and worship at the Shrine of the Holy Hog Trough. Of course there were other bikes than Harleys. We loved looking at the new Gold Wings, and Terence and I were burning up the film. Some of the paint jobs on the motorcycles absolutely defied description, and quite a few of the bikers themselves were simply not to be believed. The "uniform" was jeans and leather, of course. But there were some fascinating variants on the theme. Patches--rude and/or commemorative, were popular, and covered whole outfits. Biker chicks of all ages had hand-embroidered everything they could stick a needle into, from the saddle-bags to the tiny purses on long leather thongs, to their own skimpy boob-covers. Also pins of every description. Pins from other biker rallies, pins that told a thousand stories. Older riders wore their collection of pins head to toe, looking like coats of mail. Terence bought me one. It was a big red heart with a sort of scroll across it like a tattoo. It said "#1 OLD LADY."

The week-end over, we rode up the east coast and stopped to visit Terence's friend Kendall Wilson in West Salem, North Carolina. Kendall was playing his bassoon in the symphony that night and he said we could probably sneak in if we wore our black formal clothes and carried Terence's viola and violin. It worked, and we were such a success we were able to also attend the reception for the orchestra members later--a dandy affair with lots of wonderful things to eat that Terence and I knew we wouldn't be seeing again for some time to come. I had to laugh as I stood there with a glass of champagne in my hand, taking tiny bites out of fragrant canapés and looking around the room at my fellow music lovers; beautiful people in gems and silk who might have been surprised to know they had a couple of sneaky, motorcyclin' gypsies in their midst!

On through the drizzle to Newport News, Virginia, where we had heard we could get our rig on a ship to England. Wrong information. We wasted the whole afternoon first trying to find someone who knew what we were talking about and then being shunted back and forth at the harbor there between shipping offices only to discover that they wanted no part of us. Moreover, they couldn't be bothered to suggest an alternative. As the clouds overhead opened up to pour further insults upon our heads, we slunk across the bridges again to head for the nearest campground in Williamsburg. Ah well, we had lots of alternatives, we thought innocently.

That night it rained so hard our month-old tent began to leak. I woke about 3 a.m., to discover my head was lying in a puddle of ice water! The next morning Terence dragged out his typewriter to complain to the people who sold us the trailer but of course it was a matter of talking to a wall. The company never imagined their trailer tents would have to endure such abuse as we had subjected it to, in just five weeks. We'd have to buy a tarp. Until then, we'd simply have to stay in cheap motels if it kept raining.

And it did. All the way up the east coast. Somewhere on the way we bought me some rain boots. Boy's fishing boots, actually, because boots with a sole that could grip the oil slicked road as the bike came to a stop, simply did not exist for women. Of course they were much too wide, so I had to wear two thick socks on each foot to keep the boot from falling off, but how lovely to have warm, dry feet again! When I thought about it, almost none of my outer clothing was made for a woman anyway, so why break the pattern?

We spent two weeks at Terence's family's house in West Hartford, Connecticut. As the rain came down in buckets around us, Terence stayed on the phone each day, trying to find an inexpensive way to ship everything to Europe. A lesser man would have given up. A saner man would have given up. But he kept after every lead...every operator who said maybe, until he found our savior--the United Parcel Service.

UPS promised us that if we could get both bikes and the trailer onto one pallet, the cost would be exactly eleven hundred dollars. They only flew into Cologne, Germany, so we would have to find another way to get ourselves there. Fair enough. On the twentieth of April we headed to the airport at Newark, New Jersey. On the way down from West Hartford that early morning, I had my first experience with rush-hour traffic heading for Manhattan. Not entirely a novice, having lived near Los Angeles most of my adult life, still the sheer number of cars snaking their way to the city from towns way up on the map was simply mind-blowing. I thought of those poor souls behind the wheel. What kind of life was that?--adding several hours each day to what was probably a tough day at the office. Here I was, fortunate among women indeed, just beginning what would seem to them a trip of a lifetime. Life is rarely fair.

Unfortunately, we had to go into New York City ourselves, because Terence wanted to buy a lot of film from a special discount house he knew about, so we joined the lava-flow of hot tempered madness over the bridge and into the heart of what surely must be the roughest test there is for the faint of heart driver--not to mention motorcyclist--in the whole U.S. of A. Again, ol' Terence is yanking that trailer over trolley tracks and greasy man-holes and racing to beat the red lights like he was born to it, while I'm hyperventilating with my heart stopping at every near brush with taxi drivers and delivery trucks and pedestrians who loved to call my bluff and run out in front of me, and scary kids who wanted to wash my windscreen every time I stop. We had to get tough with the little dears on that score...any wipe with their filthy rags or squeegees on the plastic of our fairings would cause permanent scratching. Terence yelled. I yelled too. "No! No! I don't need that! I don't WANT that! GET AWAY FROM THE MOTORCYCLE!! Grins full of teeth, they'd keep coming. We learned fast how to act like New Yorkers in traffic. Shove 'em off and leave 'em in the dust.

Alas, all that extra effort through Madhattern was for naught. The little slip of paper taped to the front door of the huge discount place read "Closed for Religious Holiday." I think Terence came close to throwing a brick through the window.

I was so bummed out about the wild goose chase, I hardly noticed the remaining rigors of the ride through Brooklyn and up to Newark. Finally we arrived at the UPS terminal. Got the rig on the plane...well, Terence got it on...by removing several parts and pieces and tying it all down himself while the amused cargo loaders stood around in their orange jumpsuits with silly grins on their faces because they knew if we couldn't get it onto one pallet, we'd have to pay another 1100 bucks to use another one. I believe Terence would have taken the rig apart to fit into a shoe box if that's what he had to do. Everybody cheered when it was all on. When we asked the guy in charge how much we owed, he slapped Terence on the back. "For you, an even thousand will do it," he said. A couple of the guys took us over to the passenger terminal to look for a cheap flight and we finally found one going to London on Virgin Air Lines and leaving immediately. We hopped aboard and slept like babies from the fatigue--even with crying infants and noisy movies and a swirl and press of humanity not seen since the days of steerage.

Chapter Three

THE BRITISH ISLES

ONCE WE LANDED AT HEATHROW, we found another cheap flight to Maastricht, Holland, and sometime after customs there (thrilled at our first passport stamp), we boarded a bus out of the airport and into downtown Maastricht where we located a rather seedy but friendly hotel across the tracks from the train station. As an introduction to Europe we seemed to have made an excellent choice. It was dusk when we ventured out into the narrow streets of that dear old Dutch city. Everything seemed to be in shades of purple--the stone bridge, the river sliding under it, the cobblestones, the cats. We were in a state of euphoria anyway because we had finally made it to that side of the Atlantic more or less in one piece. Now all we had to do was retrieve our rig from the Germans!

A generous Dutch-style breakfast of cold meats and cheeses and lots of fresh bread the next morning sent us happily on our way by train to Cologne. Unfortunately there was no time to see the sights of that magnificent city. We grabbed a bus to the airport and then spent a lot of time trying to locate the UPS hanger. Where were all those people who were supposed to be able to speak English? At long last we found ourselves in an office--standing in front of a huge desk upon which the paperwork for the importing of our motorcycles lay scattered like pieces of a difficult puzzle. Several men in too-tight collars and ties and with the dark green pants of the airport's security police stood around frowning. A very large man with pink jowls and watery eyes tapped pudgy fingers on what looked like the manifest--listing our two bikes and one trailer among lots of other stuff we didn't know about that UPS had brought over. We waited. A circular fan like something out of "Casablanca" slowly spun overhead. The great one spoke: "Und zo. You vant to take two motorcycles und an anhanger from der aeroport." "Yes sir," we said. "O.K.," said the boss brightly and handed us some paperwork. What a guy! We were going to like Germany.

Down at the hanger the men had taken our dismembered machines off of the pallet and disappeared. It was up to Terence to put it all back together again. We opened up our trailer and he got out his tools and went to work. I, as usual, proved myself indispensable, handing him the odd wrench and smiling at the German fellows whose curiosity had got the better of them. They couldn't help themselves from sneaking a peek now and then over at the strange Americans with the enormous trailer that they knew was completely illegal on the roads of their country.

It was late afternoon when he finished. The kind Germans had even supplied us with gasoline to fill our tanks for the road and wouldn't accept payment. Terence thought it would be neat to get a picture of the completed rig all ready to go off the tarmac, so he handed me one of the cameras and I climbed a funny sort of hill nearby to get a shot. I'd snapped one or two when we heard sirens coming our way, and a police car skidded to a stop right in front of me and two cops got out and shouted to me in German. I could tell they were very upset and it wasn't hard to guess that I had made a boo-boo taking pictures of their precious hangers or something. I was pretty sure they wanted the camera or at least the film, and decided to pretend that I simply couldn't understand a word and adopted a very dippy American tourist air. After much gesticulating and realizing they were getting nowhere with the stupid Yankee Frau, they talked among themselves and decided to go get an interpreter (I could understand that much). They bolted back into their little squad car and roared off. I ran down the hill and tossed the camera to Terence to pack into his side box, and jumped onto the Ascot and jammed my helmet on my head and we were outta there.

We found out later that little hill was an Israeli bunker--left over from that nasty time of the Munich Olympics. Oops. And after we looked at the slides I'd taken, it seemed that the big plane behind Terence and the rig was from Libya and maybe the things that were being unloaded or loaded was not for us to know about, who knows? Anyway, nobody followed us out of there and they were probably just as glad to get rid of us.

Everybody at home had warned me about the dreaded German Auto-bahn. "But don't worry," they all had said, "You'll have lots of practice riding around in Europe before you get to Germany and maybe by then it won't be so terrifying." And what do I face as my first ever road--coming out of the Cologne Airport? Das Killer Road itself.

Icy terror clawed at my throat as I gazed up at the road signs marking the entrance to the autobahn. Terence was barreling up the on-ramp in happy anticipation of zooming as fast as his bike could go with absolutely no speed limit. A biker's dream. "O.K., Gail," I said to myself, "Don't think. Just get on the damn thing and ride!" By the time I had taken the plunge and was trying to gain speed, Terence was way ahead, and I was furious at his lack of understanding about how frightened I might be, and then of course I was realizing how stupid I was being at the same time. What was I going to do, pull over and have a good cry? I took a deep breath and twisted the accelerator hard--OHMYGOD I'm going to have to pass a German! I'm really not ready for this! There, I did it and it didn't seem to make him too angry after all. OH SHIT! There's a car behind me blinking his lights. I'm sure he wasn't there a second ago! ALL RIGHT, ALREADY. I'M MOVING OVER ! Where on earth did he appear from? Good Lord, where has he gone already?!! Wow...that is f-a-s-t! Terence still far ahead... O.K. I think I've got it now. Stay in the slow lane until the very last second when you have to pass. Amazingly, there really are some people in Germany who drive slowly. Check your side mirror once more before you pull out. If there is absolutely no teensy, weensy speck on the horizon behind you in the fast lane, whip your machine to the left around the slower vehicle at the greatest possible speed and without hesitation of any sort, get back into the safety of the right lane. That way, the life you save may be your own. After a while I had caught up to Terence and we were going about 80 miles an hour. Even though my small motorcycle was making a sound I'd never heard before, it wasn't entirely unpleasant. As a matter of fact, it was probably saying, "Thanks babe. Now you're riding!"

That evening we stayed with Gerhard and Carolyn Vetter, friends of friends who spoke English and took us in as if they considered it a rare privilege--a situation that was to happen over and over during our journey and was to teach us a lot about kindness and generosity beyond the call of duty in this world. We four went into the town of Bergisch-Glade Aachen, and shared a pizza and got to know each other a bit before returning to their small apartment where our hosts moved their living-room furniture to make room for our sleeping bags. We were so tired, the hard floor was no problem at all.

The next morning we were given coffee and rolls and waved on our way with promises all around to keep in touch and we were soon back on the autobahn heading for the ferry at Oostend that would take us to England where our journey would officially begin.

After a long but not unpleasant ride from Germany to Belgium, we still hadn't a clue as to where we would be spending the night. We were as yet inexperienced at locating official campgrounds and a long way from knowing how to camp "wild." Somewhere in Belgium as it was beginning to get dark, we decided to eat in a small French restaurant and ask the folks there if they knew of a place where we might camp. Nobody spoke English, but we got along pretty well with our college French and although they said there was no sort of campground in the area, they would be happy to allow us to sleep in our trailer in their driveway, which was protected by a large gate. We explained that we would like to be able to get away as soon as it was light as we had a long way to go to the ferry and sure enough, maman arose at dawn and unlocked the gate for us without disturbing us as we were yanking on our boots in the tent. We left a note of thanks in what we hoped was correct French on the gate, and sped away into the pink mist of dawn.

The early spring fog lay like an ocean of cotton candy under the slowly rising sun. Trees with no trunks and cows with no legs floated past my peripheral vision as I concentrated on keeping up with Terence who was again seeing how fast his rig could go on that lonely highway. It was very cold, but we had electric vests and gloves, and when they worked, it was heaven. Later when the fog had burned off and other cars began to appear on the road, Terence slowed up a bit and I relaxed and checked out the countryside around me. There seemed to be a pattern in the homes we were passing in this countryside of Belgium. Shutters covered every ground floor window as if no one were home. Yet on the floor above, windows were flung open to the morning sunlight and piled on each sill were thick comforters and pillows and blankets and now and then I saw a whole carpet hanging out of the window. Keeping things damp-free. It was a strange sight to me and yet it certainly made sense in this part of the world.

It was sunny and warm when we rolled into the harbor at Oostend. We drove to our place in the long line of vehicles waiting to get on and were told we'd have a two hour wait, so we locked everything up and took a walk around the Belgian shops and streets of the popular sea-side destination. It was great to feel the sun again on our backs and smell the sea air. We treated ourselves to croissants and coffee and complimented each other on making it thus far--through snow, rainstorms and the German autobahn!

My thin veneer of confidence dissipated a little later when I faced my first on-ramp, entering the interior of the ferryboat. Even Terence was not thrilled for once at the danger. The thing was metal, slippery from diesel fuel, steep and rolling with the waves. The men waved Terence on with unsmiling faces. Our trailer was illegal in their country, too. He gunned the engine and took off at high speed. If he'd had to stop, he'd be over the side and into the sea. But he made it. Next, it was my turn and I felt faint. The men were all standing around watching me, and I had to go for it. I just concentrated on the black hole where Terence had disappeared and roared up after him; no doubt far faster than I needed to. A couple of big bumps and I was in there; pulling up short behind the black trailer and skidding to a stop. Terence was shaking his head in annoyance about how designers of such things never think about motorcycle riders and couldn't care less, but I was just damn glad we made it and hoped I might have a chance to practice a bit before the next one.

The Channel crossing was a delight; we tried not to dwell on the fact that a sister ship of our Ferry Line had had a rather nasty accident the week before. Apparently, someone had forgotten to shut the crucial doors as the boat pulled out of the harbor and the sea rushed in to claim seats. Not a pretty episode.

We rolled off the slippery ramp without a hitch and the lovely English customs waved us through as if they were happy to see us, and after a turn or two around the harbor and a quick chat with the sweet young thing behind the Tourist Info counter, we rode up among the famous cliffs of Dover to find the campground. All too easy. Even the weather behaved as we got our bearings. We poured over our maps and geared up for the big push into the City of London. We met some fellow campers who seemed very impressed with our rig. It was lovely to be speaking the same language, and we began to look forward to meeting many more people in the British Isles.

April in the southern county of Kent was exactly what we'd dreamed about. Blossoms from the trees bordering the country roads covered the way like a pink carpet of welcome as we rode into villages right out of children's books. At first we stopped at every half-timbered cottage on the way to take pictures and then realized we'd never make it around the world that way, so we attempted to control ourselves and just stop for the really spectacular ones; such as those complete with picket fence and gardens that were so typically English you'd swear you'd seen it on a post-card; thatched roofs above leaded windows, crooked chimneys, trailing vines and rose arbors-- did real people actually live in those gingerbread houses? Munchkins, probably...

Lunch was juicy apples and crusty fresh bread in an enormous field of yellow mustard blossoms. The powdery scent was almost overwhelming and I really began to feel like Dorothy in the poppy field at Oz. We lay on our backs and relaxed. I could feel the tension of all that riding on the left side of the road and getting stuck behind lorry trucks and stuff, ebb away, like the edges of the clouds high above me as the wind pushed great chunks of them around a bright blue sky. Ah, it was splendid to be in England.

And then, what a contrast it was to ride around its capital city! Actu-ally, I fared pretty well. I had expected the worst, but it couldn't possibly be as bad an experience as that "roundabout" in Louisiana! Oh, it was as congested and crazy as you'd expect a large city to be, but even though I could sense the impatience of the poor drivers behind us as we wound our way timidly around the strange streets and stopped to look at the map, or leaned over to ask a driver directions, everyone was terribly polite. Real gentlemen and ladies, yer mawt sahy, Gov.!

We found the Camping and Caravanning Club office and joined up immediately. Being members of that awesome club meant free maps and discounts to most of the camping grounds in the British Isles for a whole year besides all sorts of other benefits. Nice. I don't think the United States had anything like it at the time. For me, just knowing I could find a spot on the map where I would be able to lay my weary head at night was a great relief. Somehow, I don't share with hardier adventurers the tremendous thrill of not knowing where to find a place to sleep after a hard day's ride. Call me a wimp, I don't care.

Attempting to crawl out of London at rush hour like rats in a maze proved a bit harder than earlier in the day, but still folks were darned decent compared to say, New York City, certainly, and the signs were easy to read and made sense--never something to sniff at, you can believe.

We rode south; heading for Hastings on the coast and stopped at a campground on our map called Stansted which was located on a grassy knoll in front of a small wood between some rather large cow pastures.

The smell was so strong of cow droppings that we weren't sure we wanted to stay there, but after I made dinner and our little patch of grass began to look like home, the odor ceased to bother us, and as a light rain began to fall, we crawled into our little tent over the trailer and we were just glad to be cozy and dry.

The next morning was cold and very damp. We woke up to a sort of shuffling and snorting sound and when we poked our heads our of our tent, we were facing an entire herd of curious cows standing in the fog and sniffing and staring at us from over a wire fence about four feet away! Reach for the cameras!

It rained for three days. Terence curled up with his law books on the trailer bed while I tried to stay out of his way by taking walks and visiting the other campsites. A kind and most generous English couple in a van down the path brought over an extra tent they swore they had no use for, and our gratitude knew no bounds. Cooking and the other chores were becoming no fun at all in the rain and the luxury of the cast-off tent improved our outlook on life immeasurably!

Somewhere in those three days, I discovered I was 50 years old. I was determined not to let the event faze me and Lord knows I didn't want Terence thinking about it, so the morning of my birthday I heartily encouraged him to go by himself to the motorcycle races at Brands Hatch race track nearby. I really wasn't very interested and anyway it cost five pounds to get in and we just didn't have that kind of money to throw around. I settled down to write letters and then took a walk through the little wood behind us; a quite magical place with bluebells covering the forest floor and the songs of birds I'd never heard before and I contemplated how lucky I was to have my health and this great trip and my precious companion and then I went back to the tent and started to cry. I decided I was lonely and missing my children and presents and even one card would have been nice, thank you very much, and why wasn't there any mail for me in London and didn't anybody miss me and what the hell was I doing all the way over here without a roof over my head or enough money to even buy myself a bloody beer for Krissakes?! I thought I might feel better if I joined Terence at the races, so I boarded my black beast and bumped down the rocky road to the highway and remembered to ride on the left, but drifted too far over and hit the curb and the bike fell over! I couldn't believe it. I hadn't fallen on that motorcycle for the whole trip-- when there were some really terrifying moments--and here I fell over trying to stay out of everybody's way and keep left! How cruel. Cars screeched to a halt all around me to come to my aid. So nice of them but very embarrassing for me. I thanked them all and after a couple of men picked up the Ascot I got back on and forced myself to proceed to the races. As I entered the gates I slowed to read the signs and hitting a pot-hole --just a little one--promptly fell over again! I knew I was in trouble then. It had to be the birthday. I no longer wanted to see the races. Maybe the best thing was to try to make it back to the campsite and hang myself from a tree limb above some friendly cows. Just then, a rather emaciated young man with purple and green hair spikes and metal objects dangling from various body areas, came over to help me pick up the motorcycle. I believe he said "Y'aw raight, man?" I was wearing my helmet. I hoped he hadn't said "mum," I just couldn't stand it.

I thanked him for his help, gritted my teeth, and concentrated on getting home safely. Later, when Terence came back, I gave him an abridged history of the day and he decided I needed, yea, deserved a dinner at a restaurant--the budget be hanged. Better it than I, we agreed. It took some doing, but we finally found a very nice restaurant in the vicinity and after some peas and pot-roast, I was ready to get back on the trail with my man.

The next day, after touring Hastings and environs, we rode up to Avebury and walked around that mysterious ring of stones in awe of the whole idea of how they got there and what exactly they were used for. Not as famous as Stonehenge in the south, Avebury is still largely untouched, so sheep and tourists alike can feel free to ponder the mysteries of the hallowed spot without fences or ticket-takers.

We spent too much time taking pictures and exploring because it was almost evening when we climbed onto our motorcycles and we knew we weren't going to make it to the next campground shown on our map. As we drove slowly down the dark and narrow country lanes, an English gentleman passed us on the right and waved us over. "Need a place to camp?", the fellow shouted. "Follow me!" After a bit he turned into a sort of parking lot and stopped. "Now you two can just follow that path beyond the hedge and park and I'm sure no one will bother you." We thanked him and he was off into the night; leaving Terence and me to glance at each other and wonder if we ought to follow his directions or head out onto the road again. No contest. We gave it a go, as our British friend might have said and, with me bringing up the rear, Terence dragged the bumping trailer around the trees and down the muddy path for a ways and then he stopped. The path was getting slipperier and we figured we couldn't be seen from the road so we decided it was a good enough spot to set up camp. It wasn't raining, but there must have been clouds covering the sky because it was very dark around us. No lights from farmhouses nor sounds of barking dogs... not even passing cars anymore as it was getting late and we really were out in the country. We lit our lantern and ate some dinner I had thrown together after opening some cans, and later huddled in our tiny bedroom like a couple of rabbits in a burrow. We laughed because we thought it would be the perfect time to tell each other ghost stories but we couldn't think of any!

Early, after the first light, we woke to a faraway sound of tinkling bells and the baa-baaing of lambs. Terence looked out and said he couldn't see anything in the fog and they were probably a long way away, so we snuggled back down into the blankets and went back to sleep.

The first cars whizzing past on the highway woke us up again a while later.

The fog had disappeared and what we saw made us gasp. A bit farther down the road from where we had camped was a fence encircling a huge, perfectly round hill upon which was a large flock of sheep. Every ewe seemed to have at least one darling baby lamb at her side or leaping all over the rich green grass around her. Where is Walt Disney when you need him? We ate breakfast and took pictures and congratulated our English host in absentia for a dashedly good choice in camping spots and then, pulling the rig back onto the parking lot, we noticed a large information tablet near the entrance. It seems we had spent the night at the base of Silbury Hill, one of England's largest and most famous prehistoric mounds. To keep the curious off but the grass shorn, the clever English take a flock of sheep past the fence several times a year. Burial ground? Temple for human sacrifice? Nobody really knows today, but we really hadn't needed to tell each other ghost stories. They were all around us!

West to Rodney Stokes, Somerset, at the base of the Mendip Hills, where we had read of a campground costing only one pound per night--a bargain we couldn't refuse. Terence needed someplace to settle in and catch up on his law studies and the location of the campground would make it fairly easy to make day trips to places of interest such as Wells Cathedral to the east, and Bath to the west.

The campground consisted of a rather small field--full of weeds and sloping down to a nettle-covered creek at the bottom. No electricity, no water, no hook-ups. A concrete block house near the road containing toilet, sink and shower qualified the place to be included on the C.&C. list, but one glance from someone in a caravan (R.V.) would send them on down the road in disgust, which suited Terence and me just fine. In the two weeks we were there we had very few fellow campers and they were definitely more "our sort" anyway. Three young people from London arrived to pick onions in the fields nearby. We joined them one night in the local pub for a beer and the next Sunday we five hiked around the fascinating Cheddar Gorge nearby.

The wealth of local points of interest was inexhaustible. Terence had a tough time keeping his nose in the books. One day we rode the Gold Wing to Bath and there was so much to see it was overwhelming. There was the Baths themselves of course, with the famous Pump Room where the well-heeled still take tea at four--exactly as did the Bronte sisters with their mum all those years ago.

The Cathedral, a delightful mix of severity and good humor--with its jolly facade of angels attempting to climb the ladders to heaven only to lose one of their number here and there--slipping off the rung to Hell in ungainly descent... The shops and stalls smack up against that temple of holiness were doing a brisk business in post-cards and ash-trays. A hot day--everybody with an ice-cream cone and hyper kids everywhere. We were happy to get back on the bike and tool around the rest of that fascinating town. The Romans certainly knew what they were doing making it their number one choice for R and R in the seventh century!

Another day was spent checking out the fishing villages in the Bristol Channel. Sea Gulls and the sun setting into the ocean reminded us of home. The weather didn't. The wind whipped at us so mercilessly we could barely hear each other scream over it and the tide coming in looked dirty and terribly cold. It was hard to imagine a man making a living pushing a fishing boat into that unfriendly surf day after day. Hardy folk, those Devon fishermen. Again the English and their ice-cream cones. Terence and I got a real kick watching people in their cars on holidays--the whole family inside with the windows rolled up, slurping ice-cream cones and looking out at the weather. "An Englishman's car is his castle," Terence said.

The best, saved for last, was the fabulous cathedral in Wells, only six kilometers from our campsite in Rodney Stoke. After thrilling to almost every famous cathedral in Europe, I must confess Wells is still my favorite...probably because its gothic architects and builders did so much in so small a space. Before several of the carvings fell out from age and neglect, there was once over two hundred saints in niches on the intricately carved west facade of the structure. And the surface is small--nothing like the gigantic facades of say Chartres or Reims. The interior is such a treat I don't know where to start to talk about it. It truly has to be seen to be believed. I still feel a tingling when I look at our pictures we took of the rare high arch, carved into a figure eight, or the soft worn stone steps leading to the timbered meeting rooms above. If any European cathedral from the middle ages can be considered cozy, this one is it. We went back again and again during the two weeks of our stay in Somerset. We both agreed the best time to be inside the marvelous old church was a rainy day--sitting on the hard pews with our heads thrown back looking at the sweet carved figures or the gothic tracery or the warm red and blue stained glass windows. Somebody was usually practicing the organ and the faithful had plenty of cheery candles lit all around the nave so one felt warm there. If not in body, certainly in spirit. On the hour, the ancient clock would come alive; knights on horseback jousting with devils amid much chiming and whirring. The old abbey ruin was next door, partially surrounded by a pond. The swans of the pond had been trained to paddle up to a bell that hung from a narrow window in the abbey wall and pull it to summon a swan-feeding person who would open the window just a crack and toss out a few crusts of bread. A sensational act that delighted the tourists no end.

Chapter Four

IRELAND

AFTER TWO WEEKS, we gathered up the bits and pieces we called home and yanked the last of the drying laundry from the tree branches and rode back onto the road for Wales. We were heading for Ireland to make a sweep around the isle and then over to Scotland from the north and back down to England again. We took the ferry at Fishguard in Wales to Rosslare Harbor in southern Ireland, county Wexford. Stayed on someone's lawn that first night--it seemed that everybody had a CAMPING sign out who lived within miles of the harbor -- in fact we were never at loss for a place to set up camp in Ireland. We might have braved camping "wild," but the best places always seemed to be taken by the "Travelin' folk," and as a matter of fact, those same gypsies were our main reason for making the decision to spend the money and have the protection of a legitimate campground. We were beginning to discover the real nuisance the gypsies could be in that part of the world. We were so naïve at first, that when we saw them frantically waving us over to the side of the road, we actually stopped! It didn't take too long to learn that we were just going to be hit up for something. Walking down a village street, our arms would be clutched by women seemingly mad with worry over their "sick" infants and if we could help with a coin or two they might live to see another day. (Or another sucker). The kids sure did look sick; dark circles under their tightly shut eyes, rashes that made our own skin crawl and each with a whimper designed to soften the heart of the meanest skinflint. It's amazing what a little stage make-up and direction can do. We were impressed. And then, when there were too many everywhere we went, we got mad and snappish. They began to back off.

It began to rain again soon after our arrival in Ireland and, except for three measly days of sunshine, every day for six weeks had rain in it! Terence had some addresses of fellow Taekwon-Do martial artists to look up in Wicklow and we were kinda hoping we could stay under their roofs a bit until the incessant rain let up. Miles Howell was a young construction worker with prematurely gray hair and the air of a true recluse. His surprise must have been boundless when he opened the door to the likes of us two bedraggled and dripping bikers from across the sea, but he barely showed it. He showed us in and told us to make ourselves at home, then disappeared until evening when he walked into the front room where we'd thrown our bags, carrying several bottles of Guinness in his arms and we all settled down before the fire and had a fine chat. He must have felt he could trust us in his home because when we woke the next morning he had gone to work and left instructions on how to use the cantankerous old washing machine in the kitchen.

We stayed for eight days at Miles's "Ballinvalley House"--with side trips to Dublin and environs and a few work-outs in the Taekwon-Do studios in the not too nearby villages. The sport is very popular in Ireland and Miles was a black belt himself. However, except for one evening at a local pub with our host introducing us to his favorite colleen and a brisk game of billiards, we almost never saw him and by the time we rolled down the muddy path for good, we could only hope he enjoyed our stay as much as we did. Terence had got quite a bit of Law School work done in the freezing dining room while the rain lashed at the windowpanes, and I managed to catch up on my ink drawings and do some laundry which could only seem to get dry by being draped over the chairs and lamps of the front room where we kept a fire going in the grate. We had a laugh about that washing machine. I would put the dirty clothes in it around 8 a.m. and it would fill after a fashion, then it would flip the clothes around behind the tiny round window in front for about a minute or two, then everything came to a halt while it rested, I guess, for maybe five or more minutes before it would repeat its short tossing cycle. The whole event took all day--we couldn't believe it. It was just fine for himself, Miles told us. He could put things in in the morning and they'd be finished by the time he returned home in the evening. "Do y'need else?" he asked.

The day we were able to visit Dublin and take a look at that famous tome, the Book of Kells, it had been taken away to be cleaned! And would that be Murphy's Law, do y'think? At least I found all sorts of letters from home waiting for me at the Poste Restante. Even a birthday card from my daughter Meredith. Hoo-ray!

Another black belt and good friend of Miles was Jim Doyle, who with his charming fiancee, had us to dinner in her home near Dublin. We spent a couple of nights there so Terence could help Jim with some classes and seminars related to Taekwon-Do, and then we were off across the country to County Leitrim to visit with Terence's relatives. His father and two aunts from Connecticut were going to meet us there at the Geoghegan farm along with several descendants of the clan who had never left the old sod. Everybody had a fine time drinking little glasses of whiskey and water and trying to attach limbs to a family tree that was firmly rooted in this green land. I got the feeling that not enough information had been written down in the family bible and far too many children had the same first names, and too many of the ones who had emigrated to America hadn't bothered to write home for too many generations, but no matter; we're all related somehow, aren't we? Pearse Geoghegan and his wife and daughter drove us out to look at the old cemetery where all the Geoghe-gans from those parts were buried for centuries and Terence and I found it fascinating. It resembled a set from a Halloween movie, with its great tombstones askew and lichen obliterating the carved names and every-thing under creepy vines and gnarly trees. Apparently there had been an especially hard rain recently (we knew, we rode in it!), and some of the older graves were becoming, well...unearthed. No one seemed particularly surprised when I discovered an actual skull wedged under a newly exposed root of one of the rebel trees that had grown from the top of some-body's grave! Unfortunately, we couldn't find anyone's names we'd heard about, so we moved on.

We were taken to have a look at the parish's pride and joy, their new church, a concrete and stucco box with eyeless windows and a kind of Danish modern interior. It looked positively Californian. Across the street was the old church which the parishioners were happy to put behind them and forget. Built a couple of hundred years ago of stone and wood and loving care, it was not about to crumble to dust for another couple of hundred years or so. Yet the Irish would not be tearing it down. Aban-doned structures are always left to their own fate in Ireland. For a couple of good reasons. First of all, who knows but what some group of folks just might need the place--maybe fix it up and bring it to life again. Also, there are those who sincerely believe certain spirits dwell in such places and shouldn't be disturbed. Not to mention the trouble of it all--pulling down such a well-built place..it's not as if one needed the rocks! Let it be and think no more upon it.

Our hosts watched from the ivy covered wall as Terence and I walked through the tall weeds around the sweet old church. As we came to the east side, we noticed bits of colored glass in the dirt. Looking up, we saw what had been a magnificent stained-glass window--half gone now, and lying at our feet, broken shards of what was once a radiant depiction of the Virgin Mary holding the Babe. It must have been something to see for the faithful--gathered for mass on a cold winter Sunday morning- -all that color in a world of unrelenting granite gray. We called to the Geoghegans to come look. They looked at each other and nodded and said it was a shame indeed...and perhaps we would like to take the pieces home for a souvenir? T. and I looked at each other. Some things are hard to understand.

But our tour-guides had begun to get the idea, now. No more new stuff for the Americans. We were shown every ruin and ancient pile of rocks for miles around after that, and of course that was fine with us. Terence and I got some of our best pictures that day. Even the weather gave us a break between downpours. Huge white clouds would pull apart dramatically--exposing blinding sun for the odd shot among tombstones and broken walls. At one gorgeous site, Terence climbed to the top edges of an old abbey's walls to take pictures, and I love the photographs I have now of his silhouette against the stormy clouds that day--cameras swinging from his neck, and clomping around up there in heavy motorcycle boots like some kind of pirate in the rigging. It was a very long way to the ground and he seemed far more intent on his shot than his safety. Priorities he holds to this day. I'm sure the relatives thought him daft as they come, but I could tell they were proud too. The branch that got away.

Crossing the border into Northern Ireland was interesting. Our bikes and unlawfully large trailer attracted the usual stares as we pulled up at the guard station but it was Terence's dark beard, leather jacket and a face that looks like the map of Ireland itself that brought the guns close. Important looking men in officer's uniforms circled his Gold Wing and intently studied his passport. They asked him to get off the bike and they whispered among themselves. Soldiers with pink cheeks and very blue eyes forgot their rifles were pointed at us as they checked out the Hondas from Outer Space. I was shocked at how young they looked. They're recruiting babies now, I thought. More of them tumbled out of the bunkers on both sides of the street to have a look-see at the big motor bikes. Finally we were waved on. A newspaper headline we spotted at the first town explained a lot. Terrorists had murdered some people at a funeral in that border town just the day before!

Terence needed a dry place to study again. It didn't look promising. We spent a soggy night at the Archdale Castle campground and got up early to try to ride out of the weather. On and on--peering through fogged-up helmets and mud-splattered windshields. There's no such thing as a windshield wiper on a motorcycle. I found myself standing up in my seat to peer at the road ahead. This can't be the way it's done, I told myself.

By afternoon, we were somewhere in Donegal and the storm was just getting meaner. I could feel a nasty sore throat coming on and wondered if I were growing gills. Still, Terence had it much worse ahead of me. The roads were poor and so narrow he had to scrunch the trailer way over to the left for the oncoming traffic. Luckily, there weren't many people on the road. Still, I cringed as I watched him narrowly missing the ditch at the side of the road which was now full of rushing water. Most of the country roads in the British isles were built with a kind of hump in the center--O.K. for vehicles with four wheels but a real pain for the motorcyclist trying to stay upright and out of that ditch.

We were both getting too tired to drive sanely and were mighty glad to see the campground at the end of the day even though it was hardly what you'd call attractive. It seemed to be a huge parking lot surrounded by sand dunes. The wind was fierce and we had to keep our helmet visors down as we looked around so that the rain and sand wouldn't get in our eyes. The stench from the small toilet building in the middle of the lot was overpowering, and the thought that I might have to prepare our dinner in there because it had a roof did not fill me with delight. There was one other camper--a VW van with German license plates, and several caravans (trailers) parked on one side which seemed unoccupied. As we stood rather forlornly in the wind, a small car skidded to a sandy stop in front of us. A kerchiefed head leaned out the driver's window. "Would ye be wantin' to stay awhile?," it said. Terence walked over and asked if there might be a spot with a bit more shelter...say parked between the empty caravans? "Sure, and I could be rentin' one of the caravans to ye," the lady answered brightly. Terence looked over at me. My throat was worse and the aspect of dinner preparation in the latrine had given me a look as if I just might have swallowed something truly unpleasant. He haggled a bit as I remember and the price seemed extremely fair to us at that moment, and with joy bordering on hysteria, we entered a caravan that probably hadn't seen a lodger in years. The nice lady manager told us she thought the propane tank still held gas and proceeded to show us how to light the heater and stove. We couldn't wait to get her out the door so we could whoop and dance around our warm and dry new home! Sheer heaven.

We stayed there in Tullagh Bay for nine wonderful days. No matter what the weather was doing, my wash dried nicely inside that rectangular palace. Terence finished a large part of his studies, I got some nice drawings done and took long walks over the wind-flattened dunes, and we even managed to race out and see some sights when the weather cleared once in a while. We rode through tiny villages to the northernmost tip of Donegal and climbed up stony towers and down wind-bashed cliffs to the sea. Rarely did we see a soul to wave to up there. It would be a hard life. The fierce wind never stopped blowing.

Lusk, Ireland

One of the best things that could have happened to us there was meeting Norbert Schupp, a young German hiker whom our saintly land-lady put into the caravan next to us one stormy afternoon. A giant of a man, Norbert looked several years older than his mere 21, and yet was so much fun the three of us did everything together when Terence wasn't studying. He was taking a couple of weeks off from a rather depressing job as a prison guard, to photograph bits of the Green Isle. We ate together, drank together, giggled together, and if we could have found him a motorcycle, we'd have probably seen the rest of Ireland together, but then he did have to go back to his job before too long, and it was a tearful farewell when our big pal put on his backpack and disappeared down the road. We promised to meet again when we got to Germany in the next year.

Rolling down the west side of Ireland should have been glorious, but the weather gods simply refused to cooperate. All the campgrounds looked the same in the rain, and the dark road just went on and on. We knew there were places to explore out there, but with cold water trickling down your back and miles to cover before even a cup of tea could be brewed at the side of the road, most days simply passed in a blur of gray. The sights had to come to us. Twisting and turning along the crest of the mountains of Connemara one wet morning we came across a lovely old ruin of what was once someone's thatched cottage high on a bleak cliff in a sea of mud. It was occupied by a herd of spotted cows! We stopped to get a better look. Peering out each window and chewing their cuds were some of the happiest bovine faces you can imagine. It was quite a houseful. Everybody that could fit was inside with more trying to squeeze through the open front door. It was nice to know some of god's creatures had the sense to get out of the rain!

Farther down the road we saw signs for a dolmen, one of the thousands of pre-historic stone formations that Ireland has dotting its rocky landscape. Terence and I couldn't ever seem to get enough of them. Like many of the sites, this one was not easy to get to. Understandably, the farmers try to discourage the curious from tramping over their land even though such places of special interest are open to all by law. Signs and markers put up by the Preservation people are torn down by the locals who would rather not be disturbed. Who can blame them? Sour faces greeted us as we walked with muddy boots over cow paths and fields looking for the way to the ancient spot.

Suddenly we saw it. High on a rock-strewn knoll stood two mammoth slabs holding up another placed horizontally across like the Greek letter . It was a huge structure; again the question begged as to how mere mortals could manage such engineering without benefit of the most rudimentary tools. There must have been much more of it once; great clones of the monument were lying all around. A woolly-looking cow was relieving her boredom by rubbing heavily against the one of the standing stones and we wondered if that sort of thing played a part in hastening the demise of such jewels of prehistory in this country. Surely the farmer would be glad to see the thing topple at last and have done with the bloody foreigners!

The day cleared and just as we began to cheer about being dry and warm, Terence's allergies started to flare up. He had had a history of very bad reactions to pollens back home. I remembered him giving himself shots on our trip to Canada in '86 and we carried Epinephrine in the trailer for a dire breathing problem. But that was only to be used for an emergency. He had known he'd be in trouble during the pollen seasons on our trip, but hoped he could find some relief off the counter of the local druggist wherever we were when it got bad. We never thought we'd be glad for the rain, but it was definitely easier on his sinuses. Coughing and sneezing, he pushed on.

We came out of the mountains to the peat-bogs of County Munster; endless stretches of dark earth--often with just a lone figure working the land. The thatched cottages were more numerous now and sometimes we could see a woman hanging up the flapping laundry behind the house; children playing in the grass and mud. We waved at each other and children and dogs would run behind us for a time until they got tired. We must have brightened their day a bit, it didn't look like they had much diversion out there in those bogs. So few trees, too. I tried not to think about the stories we'd heard about the land being denuded of forests for gain of the very few.

We poked around a couple of interesting-looking cemeteries in the Ring of Kerry, that particular stretch of inlets in the southwest of Ireland much loved by tour buses and dotted with tourist traps happy to be of service. By late afternoon we had reached Sneem, halfway to Cork from the Ring.

The village of Sneem was a child's paint box of color. The shops and houses on the main street sported fresh coats of red, yellow, purple, kelly green, orange and whatever other bright color some mad leprechaun must have stolen from the rainbows. The tourists in the buses loved it and the streets were crowded although there was only one store that seemed to have anything much to buy and if there were any restaurants that could have accommodated a bus load of hungry travelers, they sure kept them well hidden. But eating in restaurants was not something Terence and I had to think about. We were thrilled to discover an official place to camp by the river near the town bridge. The rumor was that salmon were in that icy stream, so while Terence studied, I got out our fishing gear and attempted to catch us some dinner. A row of Irish faces studied me from the bridge, amused, while I got my line caught on one rock after another out in that fast-moving current and after losing a bunch of nice flies and lures to the naughty wee folk who lived on the river bottom, I gave it up and made spaghetti again for dinner.

The city of Cork was a great feast for our tired eyes the next day. Centuries of history made for a layer cake of architectural styles; the oldest beginning down at the harbor and creeping up the narrow streets through Georgian, then Victorian and Beaux Arts, up the steep hills with the facades going to Art Nouveau and Deco until the last layer at the top suggested a frosting of much modern design and the caprices of the well-to-do. As the sun beamed down through the clouds like a spotlight on the hills of the city, it was like a grand lesson in a city's individuality. When a man's ship did come in to Cork harbor, he was allowed to build a monument to his success any way he chose. Compared to all the poverty of spirit we'd just rode through to get here, it was a pleasure to see some flamboyance for a change.

I had been hoping along the way to make an ink drawing of the quintessential Irish thatched-roof cottage, but for all our miles of looking at the dear little things--each one sweeter than the other--I still hadn't found the one that, well..spoke to me. It was in a small town in County Waterford that I finally spied it. We had only been on the road for an hour or so that morning, but the rain had come down so hard we were already as wet as we could get and when I signaled Terence to stop so I could get a picture we both looked like something from the Black Lagoon. The house was much larger than any "thatchie" we'd seen--low and long and although the thatch had been recently restored, the house itself looked very old. An overgrown rose garden fought for space along the curving path from the gate and two enormous Irish Wolfhounds were wagging their tails and barking from the doorstep. We must have looked so terrifying in our helmets and space-suits looking through the iron gate the poor dogs decided not to get any closer!

We were struggling with our cameras --trying to wiggle them through the separations in the gate and keep them dry at the same time when a frail-looking elderly lady came out to see what the dogs were going on about. "Halloo!," she shouted. "Would you like to come in to tea?" Terence and I froze. "She must be mad," I whispered. The woman turned into the house and came back out with a large umbrella. Leading the two hounds who were delirious at all the excitement, she walked down the puddle-wet path to open the heavy gate. "You poor dears," she cooed. "How can you get decent pictures through this old gate? Do come in and let me pour you a nice cup of tea. I believe I just might have an old biscuit around too!" She had said the magic word. I was not leaving until I'd had a cookie, even if her beautiful old house turned out to be made of sugar candy and she had an oven in the back for bikers! As we walked back to the house with her, we began to try to explain what we were doing in the rain and on motorcycles and going around the world and all and our little hostess smiled and nodded and we began to get the distinct impression she'd heard it all before.

Over dainty china cups of steaming tea, the dogs happily curled at our feet and a fire in a hearth so charming it made us gasp, Mrs. Hughes told us all about the magnificent house and herself. Built in the seventeen hundreds, it had been owned by gentry for several generations and had then been sold to another family who loved and respected it for a couple more generations and finally on down the line to when she and her husband, on holiday, saw it and decided to give up their jobs and life in England, buy the place and turn it into a Bed and Breakfast. Aha! Our glances said to each other. That's why the warm welcome at the gate. She'd had lots of practice. After her husband died, she told us, she felt she just wasn't up to such a big job all by herself. It had been four years now, and she did get lonely sometimes. She wanted us to believe we were doing her a great service in appearing on such a mournful day and would we like another biscuit?

Pulling on our heavy boots at the front door, we noticed the sun was shining again. With her kind permission we trod through the wet foliage around the house and took shots from every angle we could think of. It was a thoroughly satisfying morning. (I finished my drawing a few weeks later and sent Mrs. Hughes a copy. I was not surprised to receive a perfectly gracious note of thanks soon after.)

We picked our way slowly back up the eastern coast of the country; stopping to camp for Terence to catch up on his studies now and then. Under a bungee line of drying underwear and socks in the sagging old tent we'd been given in Stansted, he would type on his little electric typewriter that was plugged into the battery of his motorcycle. When the sun would dry off the leather seats of our bikes once and awhile, we'd grab the opportunity to fly off to someplace unpronounceable in Gaelic and get ourselves joyfully lost among the ruins and relics of that haunted land.

Our border-crossing back into Northern Ireland was a piece of cake this time. Things must have been calm for once on the eastern front. We rode around the city of Belfast and treated ourselves to tea in a tea-shop near the splendid-looking Opera House (blown up in 1993, by the way).

Walking back to our rig through the large park in downtown Belfast, we were accosted by a gaunt young fellow in what appeared to be a sort of leopard-skin Tarzan costume. He wore sandals on his feet and a wool cap and was carrying a large tube such as carpets are rolled around--as a kind of lance. He said his name was Andrew and that he had seen us on our motorcycles and thought it all so marvelous that we must have come from heaven, and in that he was Christ's "man," he would be our official greeter and guide for the sights of Belfast. He seemed harmless enough and in fact very entertaining, so Terence got him to remove his cap and put on a helmet. He climbed onto the passenger seat of the Gold Wing with his lance at the ready and a rather large plastic shopping bag in his other hand which I suspected contained all his worldly goods, and off we went, looking like a circus parade--with the Jungle boy waving to one and all. A lot of people seemed to know him. After a while, Terence must have realized Andrew was far more interested in being seen on the motorcycle than in showing us anything of Belfast, so he let him down gently back at the park and we bravely carried on without him.

Northern Ireland has few holiday-makers nowadays and therefore camping spots are almost non-existent. At the town of Antrim, as night fell, we were directed to a large playing-field to camp, with the assurance that we could feel safe and would not be disturbed. They were right on both counts and at dawn the next morning, T. and I packed up and boarded our bikes for the long ride to the ferry at Larne, for the crossing to Scotland.

Chapter Five

SCOTLAND

A<small>FTER A FAIRLY SHORT</small> float across the water, a long day's ride up from Stranraer brought us to a village named Stonehouse, Strathclyde, where we were told of a campground just north on the way to Glasgow. This "campground" was little more than a parking lot but Mr. Gilbert Thomson, who owned the land, showed us a patch of grass where we could pitch our tent, and what the heck, the price was right--only a pound a night, so we settled in.

We had just finished dinner when we heard the most unearthly sound coming at us from around the main house. It sounded like bagpipes but with no discernible melody--just an ear-piercing cacophony of shrill blasts that were about as pleasing as an on-coming fire truck. We looked out of the tent to see a young boy--straight from a hundred Saturday Evening

Post covers by Norman Rockwell--red-haired, freckled face and bare-footed. Except, instead of a fishing pole over his shoulder, this child had bag-pipes slung over his, and he was marching back and forth in front of our tent, wheezing and blowing and growing very red in the face. After way too long he stopped playing. "What was that?," Terence asked me. Beaming, the boy answered, "Tha was yer wee WELCOME!"

And Glasgow was like that too. T. and I made several day visits to that fair city from our farm site. So long quite the "poor sister" to glamorous Edinburgh in the east, Glasgow in 1987 was still way behind in the popularity polls of places to visit for most tourists. Yet we thought her perfectly wonderful. The architecture of the last century has been spruced up and restored and stands proudly reminiscent of those heady days when her shipping industry made her one of the richest cities in the U.K. The brogue is thick, the people delightful and the many fine art museums rival several of the best anywhere. A couple of times, I left Terence in camp to study, and returned to the University of Glasgow Art museum to sort of steep myself in the richness of the paintings there. There is still a lot of money in Glasgow and much of it is going to the Arts of all persuasions. We saw posters for some marvelous things as we walked through town--operas, ballets, exhibits, and we caught a good many of the free ones. It was nice to have copy machines and especially Laundromats again too. The wearin' o' the green had lost its appeal!

I was getting good at "sink baths" by this time, although I can't say I enjoyed them. Happily, we were told about an indoor public swimming pool in the next town where the showers were hot, and for the low price one could have a swim as well! In that same little village, we discovered fish and chips the way it's supposed to be made; thick white fillets surrounded by a batter whose grease came through the cone of layered newspaper in great spreading splotches as we ate standing on the sidewalk with the rest of the patrons. Salted and vinegared fat fingers of potatoes we called fries lay on top of the fish, and on a cold, wet day, putting one's nose into the top of that greasy newspaper feed-bag must be a Britisher's bit of heaven. It certainly was for us.

We weren't the only folks staying at Canderwood, our little parking-lot campground. While we were there, several caravans came and went and one of our best memories of Scotland was meeting Bob and Bet Murdoch, a couple from Edinburgh who were on their way home from a holiday in France. They were in their late 60s or early 70s and were seasoned travelers who had lots of good advice for us about where we were going, which we soaked up eagerly. Bet had been born on an island west of the highlands, so she was a gold-mine of information for our pending trip up the west coast. We couldn't wait to get started.

Leaving my bike behind, we pulled out from Canderwood early one morning, planning to travel up through the northern part of Scotland and then over to the east coast and on down to Edinburgh to visit the Murdochs and then back to camp. There was a light rain but by this time we had found ways to keep ourselves drier. I had disposed of my torn and smelly old yellow slicker and acquired a new rain jacket made just for motorcyclists (men, of course), and we were very excited to think we were going to actually see the battlefields of Glencoe and Glenshiels and the rugged Highlands that Mrs. Murdoch had gone on so about.

She was right when she had said it is very hard to describe such places. And like going to your first opera, it helps to have some knowledge of the cast of characters and the plot. Imagine being a child in Scotland and hearing of the great clan wars and the battles against the English King. Bonnie Prince Charlie and Robert the Bruce. Maybe it's howling outside at night and you're sitting at your granny's knee and the only light is from the hearth and the crackling of the fire sounds like the distant clash of swords and shields. You hear of the river going red from the blood of the ambushed MacKenzies and the betrayal of the MacDonalds by the Campbells that dreadful night when the chiefs of the clan and their women were invited to a banquet only to have their throats cut when the wine ran out. Ah, other countries have their stories, but in the Highlands of Scotland, the moaning of the wind and the silhouette of the lone tree on the rock-strewn hill beg you to listen over and over to the great tales of woe and revenge. Heady stuff.

However, settling in next to big families of summer campers at Glencoe, with their folding lawn-chairs and ghetto blasters and children who wanted to be taken for a ride on the big motorbike and older kids throwing stones and logs into the river, we found it dang near impossible to you know, like, get in touch with the ghosts...

We had much better luck at Glenshiels, although I almost joined the dear departed myself--after slipping in the mud trying to help Terence pull the heavy trailer out of a ditch. The trailer wheel barely missed me as I fell under the heavy thing. It would have been a cute trick trying to find a hospital up there. I tried not to think about it. Anyway, the valley of the Glensheils massacre was sufficiently devoid of holiday-makers to allow the imagination full rein. In fact the sheer quiet was so astonishing that we found ourselves listening for something familiar. It seems we had left even the sound of the wind at the entrance to the valley and after I washed our dinner dishes in the grass and rinsed them in the quick-flowing stream, I couldn't help thinking about the women of the clans, coming down from the hills and hearing the cries--not of battle--but of the dying men, and then their own terrible sounds of sorrow and despair; perhaps kneeling at this same stream to get water to wash wounds and give drinks to the thirsty wounded ones. Wow. Scotland does that to you!

The Isle of Skye was certainly dramatic in its way, also. Again few trees. There were great forests once, they told us. But what the massive shipping industry didn't take, the people themselves did. Trying to keep warm in this harsh climate was a full-time job before natural gas and, as in Ireland, there was never any money for re-planting. So behold the stern and rock-bound land. Streets of stone, houses of stone, walls of stone.

But not the hearts. Somewhere on the west coast of Scotland we met John and Joan Hills, and on a Gold Wing, too! They were a handsome couple, closer to my age than Terence's. They had on all the very latest duds for bike-touring in cold weather. I had to admit envy in my heart for Joan's insulated sleeveless jump-suit under the jacket that matched John's--comfy, warm and still feminine. Attached to their gleaming motorcycle was a small, regulation trailer painted to match. The two were highly amused to see what our Wing was pulling. We went with them to a pub, and over a foamy brew or two got to know each other. Their kids were grown up and gone, they worked hard all week and really enjoyed flying away on the Wing on week-ends. They told us all about the Gold Wing Club of Great Britain and encouraged us to attend the next big International Rally...or Treffen, as it was called in Europe. As they lived near the Scottish border in Yorkshire, their local club was called the Border Wings and they told us they'd be delighted to have us as honorary members and that we absolutely must stop at their home and let them show us their part of the country. After they left us for home, we pushed on to the north; missing our new friends already and excited at the prospect of meeting many more Gold Wingers when we would be joining them at the Treffen in Nottingham in three weeks.

The treeless, wind-slapped land became more inhospitable by the hour.

Terence had to guide the big motorcycle slowly and carefully up the wet and narrow roads and then just as carefully down again, avoiding the many holes and mud slides in his path. It was slow going. With me on the back and the heavy trailer to add to the difficulty, I didn't envy the man. At one point, a trio of German bikers roared up behind us and buzzed like hornets impatient to get to the hive--waiting to get an opening big enough to pass us on the cliff-bordered curves. When they finally broke free I could sense Terence's envy to be among them instead of pulling this chuck wagon of ours. Unable to control himself, he twisted the accelerator and tried to catch up. Incredibly, he managed it for a bit. I shut my eyes as we tore around the curves; the trailer banging and bouncing in back. I did understand how he felt, but I did not want to die. I asked him to please slow down. After another spurt and also realizing the Germans were pulling away anyway, Terence relaxed his grip on the gas. With my arms tightly around him, I could feel the fire was contained, but not out. Just as well.

Little vegetation now. A few clumps of dry grass between the rocks in the fields on each side of us. Suddenly, I saw something extraordinary up ahead. "Terence, look! What are they?" He pulled us over and stopped. They were two very large mounds of long, dark red hair. Four great big brown cow eyes studied first the rig then the humans. Highland cattle, a male and a female, lying upon the rocks with nothing much better to do than ogle the tourists. We were enchanted. I'd seen pictures of such beautiful beasts, but this close up was dynamite! We got out the camera gear. They were wonderfully docile for such big animals. Terence walked very close to the nearest one, and she didn't bat an eye. The bull was long-horned and must have been enormous when he stood up so we thought it prudent not to get too close to him.

IN SCOTLAND,
WE INVITED ALL THE LOCALS TO TERENCE'S BIRTHDAY PARTY....

We were told later that only a few of the gorgeous creatures are left in Scotland now. Cattle-raisers discovered there were more efficient breeds for milk and meat production. One hopes that this magnificent species will not be allowed to become extinct.

August third. In two days it would be Terence's birthday and he suddenly decided he'd like to spend it in more civilized society than cows and sheep, so, with the blessing of the rest of the committee, he turned the motorcycle around and headed south, for Inverness.

Stashing our gear and rig at the nearest campground outside that city, we celebrated his special day by splurging on two movies and a steak house. The next day, perhaps feeling slightly guilty at needing such an American-style fix, we rode to Black Island and took in an Air Show and a kind of county fair where local farmers showed off their livestock and new tractors and things. Except for the brogue, we'd have thought we were in Iowa.

Back at the campground, we met two couples from Italy and France who begged us to stay with them when we got to their country. Oh, twist our arms!

Traveling south past intriguing ruins, castles and more old battlefields, we found once again the urge to linger was slowing us up dangerously if we expected to make it to the Gold Wing Treffen as promised. But who can drive past the haunted church of Elgin or the white granite city of Aberdeen without stopping to explore or admire? How foolish we were to think five years in Europe would be enough! We could only wade when we wanted to wallow! And when you think about it, a lifetime isn't enough to see everything this world has to offer. We had to be grateful for the time we had!

On our way down to Edinburgh and the Murdochs, Terence's allergies were becoming so bad that breathing was a major chore and even thinking clearly required more energy than he wanted to expend. After a short walking tour with the folks, we all came to the conclusion that he was in trouble. Before we had left California, we had joined IAMAT, the insurance people with a list of doctors all over Europe who were supposed to help traveling members get help in an emergency. I looked up the Doctor in Edinburgh on the list and the Murdochs drove us to the address and Terence was able to get a cortisone shot that afternoon. By the next morning he was much improved and we went back to sight-seeing. That evening we were treated to a delicious rich, thick lamb stew at our friends's apartment.

Bet Murdoch had, several years before, made an attempt at learning Esperanto, the universal language. She had sent in for lessons through the post and was eager to give it a try, but without support of family and friends who told her, in essence, that it was a pointless exercise, she soon gave up and put the lessons on the shelf. Hearing about how interested Terence was in learning all the languages he could while he was in Europe, gave her the idea of giving him her Esperanto Postal Course. He was delighted. We read that Esperanto is a constructed language, in that its basic grammar and vocabulary were created specifically to serve as an easy-to-learn second language. It sounded like the perfect solution to the world's language problems, and so that night we embarked upon a course of study that was to open many doors and introduce us to some of the nicest people on this planet.

We headed back to Canderwood to pick up my motorcycle. Jonathan's bagpipe playing had improved enormously...or maybe three weeks in the Scottish highlands had attuned our ears. In any case, when he played "Scotland the Brave" as we pulled out of the lane, I had tears in my eyes.

Chapter Six

ENGLAND

THE HILLS LIVED in Darlington--at the edge of the North York Moors. They seemed delighted to have a couple fellow Gold-Wingers come for a visit. The four of us on the two big motorbikes spent a sunny Sunday, roller-coasting gently over the grassy moors to the sea coast; visiting cozy Yorkshire villages on the way and mingling with other tourists--the English themselves, doing what they love best on holiday, taking pictures of each other and lapping ice-cream cones inside their cars.

Traffic was heavy in Scarborough, that sea-side tourist trap made so famous by poem and song. But Joan and I could enjoy the sights, perched like squaws behind the men who were doing all the work. I loved sitting back there, the weather lovely for once, and sights of people enjoying themselves all around us. The narrow beach was crammed with humanity in various stages of attire--from string bikinis to over-coats--one never knows when the English weather could become inclement--brightly colored beach balls being tossed over the patient heads of folks trying to soak up some sun in their tiny claimed spaces. I couldn't help thinking about the roominess of beaches at home in California. Would anybody stand for a beach ball being thrown over them there?! We parked the Wings and walked into some of stores along the promenade. Delightfully tacky and smelling wonderful of salt-water taffy and popcorn, it seemed about as far away from someplace like the valley of Glenshiels that one could get.

Back on the bikes, the Hills showed us where the famous Victorian hotel of Scarborough was beginning to slide down the cliff. So sad. Build thee not on sand...

Up the coast a bit we went, to Whitby, a sea-town clinging to its own precarious cliffs; a spot perhaps not as popular as Scarborough with tourists, but fabulous for our own particular taste in picture-taking. Yet another ruined Abbey graced its highest hill and the sun, be-coming low now, had turned the cliffs to a rose-gold ; the whole town slowly changing into a piece of Victorian jewelry. We fell in love with it. Too soon we had to push on. It was a long ride through the moors to home. Hardly the stuff from which English mystery stories were written, the vast and "danger-ous" Yorkshire moors simply provides today's traveler--who is lucky enough to be on a motorcycle--with some of the best riding there is. The long, lonely roads bend and swoop, and Terence and John finally got rewarded for all that bumper-to-fairing traffic during the day. An almost full moon lit up the scene as we sped through the cold evening. The men cracked the throttle and the metal beasts responded like hounds after a fox; unfettered at last and ecstatic to be doing what they were built to do. Joan and I hung on and enjoyed ourselves thoroughly. We spent the night snug in their sweet cottage; thrilled to have met such like souls and very happy to realize that we'd see them again.

Promising to meet at the Treffen in just a few days, we were off to visit Allison Redmayne in Chesterfield. We had met Allison and her boyfriend Peter Wooller in the Stansted campground in May, and planned to take her up on her offer to let us stay at her folks' home. She may not have realized we might make it happen, or perhaps she forgot to clue in her poor parents, but when we arrived after dark at their door, Bill and Marion Redmayne seemed slightly less than pleased. They told Allison to make us up a bed in the attic. That was fine with us. The next morning the three of us went to Derby Castle and toured the grounds and later rode to Sheffield and Allison's hometown of Chesterfield with its amazing twisted steeple. Allison explained that the story was that the steeple had been built many years ago by a crew that had been too impatient to let the wood "cure." As the green wood began to dry, the tall steeple shrank into its present twisted, very odd shape and well, there's probably no other on earth quite like it.

Allison's parents never warmed to us. There could have been a hundred reasons. We were beginning to learn that for all the warm accep-tance of most human beings, there will always be the chill of distrust in others. Perhaps they saw us as a bad influence on her daughter. Perhaps we were.

Soon we were back on the road and in the rain again. Our first destination was Theakston's Brewery, where Terence's favorite beer, Old Peculiar, was born. At first we were told all the tours were full, but as we walked back to the bikes, a tour bus full of Americans rolled into the parking lot, so we joined them. It was a great tour. Terence was in pig heaven because he was given lots of free samples. I can't say I minded them, myself. In fact, if anyone wants our opinion, Terence and I have to say, the best beer in the world is made in the small breweries of England. Don't ask how we managed to ride ourselves to the next campground. Even bikers must have guardian angels.

The International Gold Wing Treffen at Nottingham was nothing short of a shock for us. We had no idea that that particular motorcycle was so popular in Europe. There must have been five or six hundred and from several European countries crowding the huge field--and on a rainy weekend, even! T. and I marveled at the different customizing and paint-jobs and the sheer expense people had incurred with their motorcycles. This was no Daytona biker bunch, either. The Honda Gold Wing is a tourister--built for leisure and comfort. And in Europe one has to be fairly well-off to afford one in the first place. Eschewing the dirty leathers, fringe and metal studs which the Harley riders seem to find indispensable, the European rider prefers threads which compliment if not match his ride. And of course his pillion passenger wears a twin outfit. British riders seem to like metallic colors, like gold and silver. Germans often sport black and red or white and red--in futuristic racing designs, and one sensational outfit was often seen at these Treffens--Pure white leathers and helmet, matching her white Gold Wing! I think the most unusual ensemble, however, was one we later saw in France--Helmet, motorcycle, boots, gloves and total leathers--completely in lavender! Must have cost him a pretty franc!

I looked at what we had on--jeans and swap-meet leather jackets. Terence's huge leather boots were at least made for motorcycle riding, but my boy's size rubber fishing boots almost coming up to my knee made me feel like a clown! I got out my Swiss army knife and hacked off about four inches from the top. I felt much better.

What a great bunch of people! Each district club came roaring in together, and when the Border Wings rode slowly in preceded by a Piper in a kilt, we got all misty--this was our clan!! Such a thrill! And they made us feel so welcome. One Border Winner literally gave me the shirt off her back--that's the one I was wearing when I was almost shot at in Turkey! Whoops, that's a later chapter...

There was lots of good beer and a giant bonfire and a dance the first night. It was not raining the next morning, so a few of the revelers who could get out of bed checked out the motorcycle accessories sales in the big tent, and tried their luck at the games for which prizes were to be awarded that evening. Terence joined the sports at the archery contest and became one of the finalists--not bad on Robin Hood's very own turf! He never made it to the finals because he got uh..busy..in town.

John and Joan and a couple of other Wingers had asked us along that afternoon to visit the castle and go to a famous pub in Nottingham called the "Trip to Jerusalem." The story is that the early crusaders, including King Richard himself, drank a pint there before embarking on the Big Trip. Whether that is true or not does not take points from its reputation as Britain's oldest pub, which, by the look of things inside the place, was more than likely true. Low ceilings and uneven floors gave you the impression that you'd had too much to drink before you had even got to the bar. Tiny windows in very thick walls added little enough light and the density of smoke from cigarettes made seeing one another a job for Super-man. Terence feels the same way about secondary smoke as I do, only more so of course because of his allergies, and we couldn't wait for an excuse to escape from the polluted pub and into the outside air. Alas, our new friends were simply the vanguard of a larger segment of the world's population to appear on this sojourn-- men and women with cigarettes perpetually in their hands.

Saturday night on the Treffen grounds was a bigger party than before; it was my guess that most of these folks had fairly dull jobs and looked forward to this once a year bash with not a little impatience and anticipa-tion. I was astounded at how much booze these people could put away... and then get back in the saddle to ride all the way home for work again on Monday morning. Heroic, that's what it was. Sunday morning was raining buckets! The Hills who didn't have that far to go, stuck around awhile and we four drank coffee in their tent, hoping the rain would lighten up. The poor Wingers from across the English Channel didn't have that luxury. They had ferries to catch and by noon, the whole field was deserted except for us. We hugged our pals for the last time and parted company, they to Yorkshire and we to Wales by way of Liverpool. We all wished they could ride along with us.

We didn't stop long in Liverpool; there was no campground, and we were anxious to get to Wales before nightfall. I made a stop in St. Helens to visit a friend and his mum whom I had met in California years ago, and Terence got some business taken care of in Liverpool proper and then we met outside the city and battled horrendous rush-hour traffic practically all the way to our destination.

Chapter Seven

WALES

PENNY PERRIN WAS A LIVELY young lass we had the good fortune to meet in Bristol when we were there last May. She had told us to be sure to look her up when we got to Wales and didn't seem to mind a bit when we moved into the old caravan permanently parked at the bottom of her garden. She lived in a small cottage at the end of a long row of Welsh "worker" cottages; each painted white and lined up next to a bright green field and within hearing distance of a lively stream. Very much a set from "How Green Was My Valley". Penny was quite proud of her home and her Welsh heritage and her home reflected it. Warm-colored weavings softened the whitewashed walls and handmade furniture and dishes added a home-spun beauty as comforting as a lullaby. While Terence studied and Penny was at work, I moved big pieces of slate that had been leaning against the garden wall--to make a path through the garden instead of the existing muddy one. It was a big project but very satisfying and I hope Penny liked it when I was finished. She pretended to, at least. After a couple of days she said we could have the house to ourselves for the rest of the week because she had to go to Ireland to visit a boyfriend for awhile and would Terence mind taking her to the airport? He was delighted. We chose to stay in the caravan because we had all our things strewn around it, but we were honored to be allowed to watch over her precious domain and genuinely moved by her generosity and trust in us.

At the end of the week, after some delightful short excursions around the dark and dramatic terrain of the hills and Cambrian mountains, we were on our way to Birmingham. We checked out the famous motorcycle museum there and Terence got to test-ride some snappy new BMWs that had been brought to the museum parking lot as a publicity stunt. Terence thought I should hop on one myself, but the vision of dumping one of their pristine new machines on a rain-slicked curve persuaded me to decline the offer. No such silly notions get in the way of some people's good time, however, and the men from BMW and I were treated to a great display of Terence's dust as he tore away on the new bike, and out of sight. When he brought it back, he had a smile that lit up the whole parking lot and part of upper Birmingham, and then they let us both get on the tourister model and we spun away on the same course.

I like to joke about Terence's yee-ha! mentality on a motorcycle, but the truth is he doesn't have accidents. That is to say, the bike may crash and burn, but it is not T. who causes the accident. I remember one of our first dates in Santa Barbara. We were coming home very late from some concert or other. I seem to remember his viola case slung across his back and I in high heels! Anyway, we were tearing along the dark freeway on his Suzuki GS 1100E at around 80 miles an hour when the back tire blew--I thought it was all over, but Terence held us on to the road until he could reduce speed enough for control and we made it to the side safely. I've never worried about riding behind him since.

So our ride there around Birmingham's wet countryside was sheer pleasure; a new motorcycle, hardly anyone else on the road, and a man who knew what he was doing at the controls. Lovely.

The next night found us near Ivinghoe, in a farmer's field that was mostly water from the recent storms..a real mud hole of a place but we'd run out of choices when we finally found a farmer to ask, so it would have to do. Terence pulled the heavy trailer onto the thick soggy weeds, and took my bike to look for a food store. I was setting up camp when I heard shouts from over a ridge to my right. Curious, I walked up the grassy slope and discovered to my delight, a family working the locks on the canal so their boat could slip through. I talked awhile with the man who told me they had just rented it and weren't very good at these things yet. Everybody seemed to be good-humoredly shouting directions at everybody else and it looked like great good fun. The barge was painted shiny black with all sorts of gypsy wagon floral designs on the sides. There was a lace curtain in the tiny porthole and flowers in bowls and the British flag fluttered gaily in the breeze at the stern and I thought what a great idea for a holiday!

After they glided away down the canal waving to me, I heard the strangest sound overhead--rather like a Bunsen burner or welding torch. I looked up to see a hot-air balloon drifting over me! All this and Terence not here to see it. A bit of rotten luck for the poor chap!

Bourton-on-the-Water

It was already September. Giddy from a spirited week-end in Hogsbarn for the Kent Wings' "Wing Ding" where we saw many of our English buddies from the Nottingham Treffen, we rolled back up to London to finally spend some time there. We couldn't have afforded to stay long in the pricey campground near the city, but as luck would have it, I had an ex-cousin in-law living in Dulwich, south London who, along with her husband and his brother and his wife and their children, turned out to be absolute saints of mercy to two wandering waifs from America. The Jolys not only gave us the beautiful apartment on the third floor to live in like Kings, but they appeared even to enjoy our company for the seventeen days we were upon them. Quite a feat for a busy family.

Terence got all sorts of studying done in the Jolys' top rooms and I finished a few drawings and some paperwork that had been nagging and then we were ready to go to France! Our good friend Chris Liles flew in from his job with the U.S. Navy in Saudi Arabia to join us for a short time exploring London and then to sit behind Terence on the Wing and see a bit of France with us. Chris had lived with us for a time in 1986 in Santa Barbara when we were all performing in the local Gilbert and Sullivan Company; Chris and I acting and singing on stage (one of my handsomest leading men with a honey-baritone voice to match), and Terence in the orchestra pit with his viola. We three had celebrated Christmas, Opening Nights, Birthdays, wine labels and each other's ups and downs together, and if it weren't for Uncle Sam's pressing need to have Chris teaching our Arab friends how to stay friends with us and each other, we'd have had him with us for the whole trip. Or at least until he couldn't stand the sort of Pilgrim's life of poverty that our trip was soon to become.

But for the moment, we three were riding high. The money was sufficient for us to stay in nice campgrounds, go to museums, take tea and buy booze. Our hearts were young and gay. This time, at Devon, we took the hydrofoil across. In a mere 45 minutes we were across the Channel and riding into Boulogne-sur-Mer, France. The French border guards advanced upon Terence's rather rough appearance but backed off quickly after Chris flashed his Diplomatic passport. We wondered how we would cross another border without him.

Chapter Eight

FRANCE: PARIS TO TOULOUSE

We headed toward Paris. A serge of excitement rose up to meet my smile behind my face plate. In France, at last. My first country where I wouldn't understand what was being said. Or nearly. I was hoping my couple of years in school memorizing all those verb tenses would not be in vain. Hoping it hadn't been too long...

After a couple of hours, we stopped for coffee. How nice to have the men in charge. Both Chris and Terence knew more French than I and everything went smoothly. We passed the strange-looking coins around to get used to handling them but we were all surprised at how much the bill was. So much for the "old days" in foreign travel. Terence and I would have to tighten our belts; no more drinking coffee in restaurants. Somewhere along the way, we found a market and bought provisions and the guys found a cheap bottle of wine. After we'd settled in at the campground at Loeuilly, Terence put up the extra tent for Chris, and I made dinner and we all congratulated ourselves on how clever we were to make it thus far.

The next morning I felt awful. Richelieu's revenge. We all decided it was the cheap wine even though the men felt fine. I would have liked to hand over the Ascot's controls to Chris but he hadn't learned to ride a motorcycle yet and would be staying on as Terence's passenger. I climbed dizzily onto my bike and followed the guys onto the road. We stopped at a pharmacy somewhere around noon and I was given some pills for what we hoped I was suffering from, and then kept riding.

Late afternoon I was much worse and we were heading for the rush hour traffic of downtown Paris. I remember being far too sick for fear; I was simply concentrating on staying upright and trying not to vomit. Up ahead Chris was turning around in his seat to look anxiously at me. It seemed to me I was about to explode--the inner part of me wanting to leave the outer part of me through every orifice. Not a pretty picture. As if on automatic pilot--I don't remember actually maneuvering the bike through the congested streets--I found myself parked behind the trailer at our destination. Chris needed to check in at the U.S. Armed Forces Officer's Club and then he'd stay in a hotel while we found a campground outside of the city. I slid off the bike and promptly sat down on the curb and was horribly sick in the gutter. A beautifully dressed French lady asked me (in English!) if she could help. I shall never forget that. I must have looked like some drug addict who crawled out of the sewer to die in the street and she still came forward. If I'd been in New York, I'd probably have been robbed. I told her no, that I was fine (a lie) and thank you. Then Chris, who no doubt wanted me in his pristine officer's club in that condition as much as he wanted a large wart on his nose, asked me to come in to get cleaned up and I had no choice but to go with him. Later, after much hot water and soap and a change of clothes, I smiled weakly at the charming young officers who were staring and probably thinking I was Chris's grandmother as I found my way to the door and out. Oo-la-la, my first day in Paree!

We left Chris in the city; planning to pick him up in two days, and Terence, all heart as always in these situations, told me that I'd have to get tough and just ride--so that we could somehow get out of the city and to our campground. And of course we got lost several times on the way. I was actually past caring. Back on automatic pilot, I dizzily followed the funny little setting sun printed behind the word California on the trailer's license plate, careening around cars and across dividing lines and under green lights and through the smog and noise. I remember faintly hearing him cursing in the distance, trying to read the map each time we'd come to a stop, but I had my head lying on the handlebars and was drifting into blissful sleep. Poor Terence. My timing in getting sick was inexcusable.

I got well. Whatever it was gone by morning. I awoke to a neat and clean campsite bordering the Seine, which was bustling with loaded barges and shouting men on the river. Terence was handing me a cup of coffee and the sun was flashing its smile at me between the poplar branches at the water's edge. We were in an eastern suburb of Paris known as Maison Laffitte and although expensive, as campgrounds go--about ten dollars a night, it was certainly the nicest location and best run one we'd seen thus far.

After a day spent gasping at all the riches in the Louvre, we picked up Chris and rode up to Abbeville, where the French Gold-Wingers were having a (National) Treffen. Everybody seemed glad to see us and our French was improving and at the banquet I was asked to sing, and by the end of the week-end party, we Gold Wingers were just one big happy family. On Saturday, everybody gathered in front of the funny old glass-fronted hotel and revved engines and slipped their favorite tapes into their machines, and treating the local Abbevillers to a rare good noise, the big bikes pulled out--one by one--onto the road for the long ride up into the hills and around the area of Picardy. There must have been close to a hundred Gold Wings on the tour. Because riding any bike other than a Gold Wing was a no-no, I rode pillion behind a fellow from England whom we'd met at the Nottingham Treffen so that Chris could ride with Terence. As the long line of bikes snaked up around the vineyards and villages, everybody smiled and waved and we felt like conquerors! We toured a castle and had a banquet, and by Sunday morning felt we were truly getting the hang of this Treffen business! That afternoon, the three of us left Abbeville to see how far we could get on the way to our next destination, Mont St. Michel, in Brittany.

After a long ride, the sky was growing dark and we realized that the only possible campsite was somewhere in the heart of the port city of Caen. We were very hungry by this time, and rode hard to get to the site before gate-closing time--around 11 p.m. The three of us were trying to make some sense out of a bad map under a sickly pink street-light when two young motorcyclists pulled up next to us and told us to follow them. It was a complicated route; through industrial areas and dark alleys but they seemed to know where they were going and we followed like duck-lings--until the lights of the campground appeared and I wanted to cry with relief. Before we could properly thank them, the two bikers were off. Having never taken off their full-face helmets, I had the strange sensation of having been guided by spacemen to a friendly planet. After some food, we put up the leaky old English tent and made a bed for Chris with our extra blankets, and then the heavens opened. None of us slept very much and the next morning, a very wet Chris confessed he missed his up-scale hotel in Paris. Yet it could have been worse. A look at the map of Caen the next morning told us that we probably never would have found that campground by ourselves.

How many things can equal the purely heart-stopping thrill of the sight of Mont St. Michel rising from the mist? It's the magic castle of Disneyland--for adults. It's a memory of a favorite illustration from a beloved book in childhood. It's theatrical and it's pure corn and absolutely perfect for the incurable romantic. We put up the tents on the nearby shore in the little deserted campground among trees turning bronze and gold. The autumn afternoon was warm and inviting and the three of us explored the village and shot rolls and rolls of film and were awed by the magnifi-cence of the cathedral on top of the hill and properly disgusted and appalled by the sleaze in the tourist shops below. Heaven and Hell on one little isle.

It was now October. The days were definitely colder. Our camping spot was carpeted by fallen leaves, and the dusty smell when I walked on them spoke deliciously of Fall, my favorite season. Between the tall trees we could catch a glimpse of the Mont, and the orange glow from the setting sun bathed the isle in gold and turned the figure of St. Michael at the top into a beacon of light. I had to go back and explore it again. After dinner, with the men occupied with brandy and cigars in the drawing room, (sit-ting on stumps sharing a jug of mystery hooch doesn't quite sound the same, somehow), I decided to walk the two or three miles on the marsh road to the isle. I asked them if they'd like to join me, but they were deep in conversation and weren't much interested in such a long trek in the dark.

Ah, but it wasn't really dark. The rain clouds from the day had all dissipated and the wide night sky was preparing a big welcome for a giant harvest moon rising at my back. Mont St. Michel shown blue-white against the dark of the sea behind it. Tiny lights from the houses leading up to the cathedral at the top indicated there was life there somewhere but the scene was so picture-perfect that I half expected to discover only a giant, painted stage set at the water's edge. The tide was out. I was able to walk across the sand to the isle. In the moonlight, I could see the fluttering of the flags on the embankment. It was very quiet. Because there are almost no tourist accommodations out there, the visitors are all gone by night-fall; leaving the locals to close their shops and climb the stairs to dinner and have the evening to themselves. The sea curls around their village like a massive moat, keeping the hordes of strangers at bay until the next morning, when they can look forward to opening their doors and relieving the poor creatures of the burden of their purses!

I walked around as far as I could go on the path that runs along the top of the wall, then down some narrow steps to the cobbled road that leads to the cathedral. The town cats greeted me as I padded around and I confess to stopping in the shadows once in awhile to listen to Monsieur and Madame behind the shutters--I couldn't understand a word--I was just listening to the lilt and music of it. The streets that just a few hours before had swarmed with humanity and rung with the cacophony of a crowd on a holiday; these streets that had not so much resembled a French village on the ocean as the pier at Santa Monica or perhaps Coney Island, had been transformed somehow into not just a sweet little town in France, but a sweet little medieval town in France. I was enchanted. How long had it been since I could walk down a street at night--unafraid and unobserved? I walked slowly, listening beneath small-paned windows to the sound of dishes clattering and murmured words and laughter. No cars in the street, no dogs barking. (Mouse-catchers would definitely be the wisest choice of pets here.) There was something else that bespoke of another time...what was it? Of course. No television! The cozy familial strains floating on the night air was devoid of canned laughter and commercial pause. I looked up. I could make out the stark contrast of the old half-timbers against antique bricks and white plaster. Not an antenna in sight. The slate roofs angled sharply to points like hands in prayer.

I had spent about an hour on the Mont and was returning to the little door at the side of the entrance gate when a policeman stepped out of the shadows and asked what I was up to. He was not unfriendly and I wasn't in the least frightened after I got over the initial shock of seeing him appear in front of me. My French must have been awful but I was so obviously moonstruck and harmless; not to mention the important fact that I was going out the door so he didn't have to care about me anymore anyway, that he simply tipped his hat and wished me a safe walk home. "Merci beaucoup" I hoped I said.

Chris had to be in Paris the next day, so we dropped him off at the train station in Rennes on our way south. As we headed for La Rochelle, we realized we'd have to take the long bridge over the Loire river at St. Nazaire. The wind was fierce as we stopped for groceries in that port city and by the time we came out, wind and rain had joined forces and it was beginning to feel like a small hurricane. As we pulled on our heavy rain gear, I told Terence I thought maybe we should try to find shelter somewhere in St. Nazaire, but he assured me it really wasn't that bad and we'd feel it less riding through it.

It got worse fast. We looked at the map. There was really no choice but to cross the huge suspension bridge in St. Nazaire and as we drove up to it, the sight of the gigantic thing was enough to turn me into a quaking blob of jelly. Still, it was in use; cars were going back and forth on it so we decided it must not be too dangerous or they would have shut it down.

We were a quarter of the way across when I realized we'd made a big mistake. Never in my life have I seen such a storm, except in movies. The wind was blowing horizontally and was full of water. You couldn't tell if it was from the sea below or the sky above--I just knew that everything was combining to push us off the bridge. Annoyed drivers behind me honked as I slid around in front of them, desperately trying to stay upright and in my own lane. I honked my horn too--to get Terence's attention to beg him to stop because I knew I couldn't hold my motorcycle up anymore. He screamed through the gale back at me that I had to keep going because it was only going to get worse and he couldn't leave his rig to help because it was being pushed over too! My mind took a leave of absence. Then the mixture of my panic and all that water killed my engine and I couldn't get it started again. Angry and frightened drivers managed to swerve around me from both directions, as I had landed in the middle somewhere and was using all my strength to hold the bike upright. I could barely see through the storm that Terence had stopped too. I put the kick-stand down and hung on to the bike and waited to die.

After my whole life had passed before my eyes and was well into the second showing, a Rescue van pulled up alongside and the driver shouted something at me and took off again. I had a bizarre impression that he had ordered me off his bridge! But then I saw him stop for Terence and realized that because Terence was closer to the middle and had that (very illegal) huge trailer, he was, in their opinion, in much worse trouble than I. While the van shielded the Gold Wing from the terrible force of the storm, Terence ran back to me, and prying the handlebars from my death-grip, yelled at me to grab the railing and inch my way to the Rescue team. He then got on my bike and got it started and managed to come up to where we were. The only way we could save our bikes as well as ourselves, it was decided, was for him to ride the Ascot off first, with the van driving alongside for protection, shielding him from the wind--while I held up his bike in the middle of the bridge until they could get back to me. After what seemed like years, the van brought him back and I climbed, shaking, into the cabin with the driver while Terence got on his bike and rode--with us protecting him on the right side--slowly through the hurricane to the other side.

After we stammered our thanks, the fellow who had been left to guard my bike on shore got back in the van and they turned around to go to the aid of others, whose cars were now slipping around and stuck just as we had been on that Scream Machine of a bridge. Terence said they had cheerily told him that this was always a busy time of year!

That night, on the road to La Rochelle, after driving through pouring rain for hours, passing "CLOSED FOR THE SEASON" campgrounds that the book had said should be open, we were very close to giving up and blowing money on a hotel. Exhausted and drained from the scary experience earlier in the day, we were relieved to find an open campground near the ocean called Sables D'Olonne.

The rain had stopped but the wind was still gale-force and if we'd been a little smarter and not so tired, we would have gone to a hotel anyway. But hey, we were tough, right? So while the few "campers" in caravans lifted their curtains to watch the crazy Americans, we attempted to set up camp in the dark. And in a sandstorm! Our French wasn't quite good enough at the time to translate "sables" to mean sand or maybe we'd have known what we were getting in for. As it was, we felt we really had no choice at that point and I was starving--always a problem, because although Terence can function without food for days, I tend to grind to a halt very quickly if I miss a meal and am about as much help as a zombie with a blindfold if it gets much longer than that.

Cooking in the blowing sand was completely out of the question, so we snuck into the ladies' restroom to light our little one-burner and heat up a can of soup. Of course some cranky woman came in and yelled and pointed to the sign listing things you're not supposed to do in there and we presumed cooking was on it but then again, we couldn't imagine gendarmes coming through that storm to throw us out--at least until we finished the soup.

Terence had parked the trailer as close to a wall as possible, hoping for a little protection from the sandstorm. As it happened, it was right next to the men's toilets but as that was the only wall around; it had to do. We spent a memorable night in the hours left of darkness--holding on to our flimsy tent as the stinging wind tried its best to snatch it away. We could hear the great thumps and thwangs of the metal trash cans as they were pushed over and then rolled back and forth to divest themselves of their contents--which the wind playfully picked up and tossed into to air--a lot of it splattering against the shuddering tent and no doubt adding to the strong perfume from an open drainage ditch out of the men's room. We were both too sickened by the odor to get much sleep.

Needless to say, at the first light of dawn, we crawled out to pack up and get out of there. The wind was gentler; almost sandless as we surveyed the devastation of several can-loads of garbage covering our motorcycles and trailer-tent. We looked at our neighbor's spotless camp-sites and realized that it was our wall that had attracted and stopped every scrap of trash for miles around. It was tempting to withhold the fee from the pay-box on the office door.

The port of La Rochelle was used by the Germans as their Atlantic submarine base during WWII and the huge concrete-covered slips were fascinating to see. We tooled around on my bike and had our bread and cheese and beer sitting on a bunker near the wharf. No doubt the French would love to clear the whole mess from the area, but the sheer expense, even if they could find a way to break up all that concrete, would no doubt be astronomical. Fortunately, a lot of the port's architectural treasures survived the war. The towers and fortress walls by the harbor gave us some wonderful moments of picture-taking and the covered arcades in the "old town" served as a rare example of what must have been malls for the Middle Ages--and still full of shoppers!

Farther south on the road, the weather once again turned nasty. After driving around in the vast environs of the big city of Bordeaux, looking for an open campground, we decided to wait out the downpour under the over-hang of an abandoned gas station. As we hunched over in our soaked rain clothes, we heard giggles and looked around. Behind the gas station stood a tall old house. Three little girls were watching us from a second-floor window as if we were members of some mime-troupe there for their amusement. We waved and said "Bonjour!" and they shyly disappeared. A few seconds later, the door opened below and their father asked if we'd like to have tea with the family.

Oh, would we! I tried to appear casual as I dashed through the door and made for the furnace in their living room. Happily, Monsieur Lavalette spoke English beautifully, and we all had a lovely time sipping coffee and munching tea-cakes. One would have thought we were expected, they were so gracious. The young ladies, their elegant mother, and the pretty young au pair girl from Germany draped themselves about the floral covered furniture like a painting by John Singer Sargent. Like so many homes in French cities, the drab exterior belied the beauty and pride of the interior and the Lavalettes lived in a comfortable yet stunning environment; with high white ceilings and rich draperies and scattered with lovely antiques and other objects of obvious good taste. We were very impressed.

As evening approached, T. and I said good-bye to the charming Lavalette family and less than eagerly got back on the cold saddles to resume our search for a campground. The fourth and last one listed in our book was indeed open but charging enough to make up for all the other three! We were incensed at the rip-off and even though we had nowhere else to go, we turned around and roared out of there in a snit. Later, after we'd cooled off, we decided that what the hell, who was going to bother us in the rain if we just set up camp in the nearest vacant lot, which we did. The storm was so strong that night that I found myself wondering if it might be nicer anyway to be in some local police station for the night. At least it'd be drier.

Nobody arrested us for trespassing. The next morning we rode east; planning to visit our new acquaintance Jean Michel Leloup, whom we had met in the campground at Inverness, Scotland. Jean Michel had written us that he'd love to have us stay awhile with him in Cesseras, in the south of France, so he could improve his American English, and it sounded like an invitation too good to be true--especially as he had promised warmer weather where he lived. As it was, the rain just kept following us, and we were getting tired of hearing how unusual it was to have so much of the stuff this time of year, etc. The campsites through the famous Dordogne region were little more than soggy bogs as we passed through, and we were beginning to hope Jean Michele knew what he was talking about when suddenly the landscape changed and with it the weather, and before we could even peel off our heavy all-weather gear, it seemed that we had been yanked back to the deserts of California!

I couldn't believe what I was experiencing. We passed through couple of mountain villages, ancient and clinging to rocks, then down into a stretch of treeless, dry, even hot terrain. We pulled over to open a can of sardines for lunch and could feel our muscles relaxing in the sun. I pulled off my big boots and wiggled my toes in the dry air. What bliss. We could spend the winter here.

Jean Michel Leloup was a young man who had recently graduated from college and was in the throes of finding his first important job. He was living all by himself in a very old village named Cesseras--way out among the straggling vineyards and small olive groves that dot the arid landscape of the south-east region between Toulouse and Montpellier on the Mediterranean. His house was as ancient as the village itself. It opened out onto a narrow cobbled street that had gutters stained purple from the wine his neighbors pressed each year for their own use and perhaps a bit left over to take to the district Co-operative. The whole town was supported by the grape. There was never enough rain in this part of France to grow enough grass to feed sheep or even goats. It was a dusty, sad and abandoned little town. The only people who had not left for a better place were the very old and the occasional descendent like Jean Michel, who came to check on the family holdings once and a while. The little church and its brood of tile-roofed houses were built of stones and clay from the very earth around it and were slowly crumbling back to the clods from which they came.

We were all happy to meet again. Jean Michel lead us past the large olive barrels on the ground floor and up the stairs to a sort of family room. There was a large hearth at one end and a (definitely modernized) kitchen along the side. Great black beams held up the next floor which no one had explored in years and we certainly weren't about to. J.M. was not a house-keeper, and after warning us about the scorpions, he pretty much left us to ourselves in a room down the hall which rather made you not want to inspect too scrupulously. The truth is, of course, we were extremely grateful to have a warm place to stay, and complaining or balking at anything was simply not something we were about to do.

While staying there, we explored the whole region of the Languedoc and heard marvelous stories of battles and fervent religious movements and stories told from one generation to the next about why things were the way they were since as far back as anyone can remember. We loved these French people of the land, and we grew to respect their rougher ways. But after a few weeks, Terence and I and Jean Michel too, knew that we could not spend the whole winter in Cesseras. It was time to move on. But to where?

Terence felt our best bet for a job would be in a big city. We had just missed the grape harvest and all the kids who had come to France to pick grapes and learn the language had gone home and back to school. The next idea was music. Maybe he could get a job playing the viola or violin in an orchestra...

Chapter Nine

WE WINTER IN FRANCE

TOULOUSE WAS A NOISY, congested, University town. Sitting on my motor-cycle while T. was in the Information Office, I felt extremely out-of-place, and decided we ought to keep looking somewhere else. After the quiet of Cesseras, the din was frightening. But then Terence came out with a big grin on his face and told me that Toulouse had three orchestras and two of them paid, and one of them was actually interested in hiring him as a violist! An offer we couldn't refuse. Apparently they had just lost their violist to Army duty and they were about to perform Offenbach's "La Belle Hélène" in a matter of a couple of weeks and then take it on the road. Finding violists not working at the time was hard enough, but finding one who didn't mind being on tour through Christmas and New Year's would be tres im-po-seeb-bleh!

December first, and still no working papers. Terence had reported for rehearsals while I stayed in the freezing campground and took long walks around the bare countryside. It began to snow. We started looking for a cheap flat in the city. Being a University town, the students pretty well had them all sewn up. Mary Horvath, a kind and most generous American violinist from Chicago whom Terence had met in the orchestra, let us move in with her until we could find a place. Finally, in the Algerian section of town, we located a tiny walk-up studio apartment we could afford and moved in. Divine smells from the Algerian and Pakistani restaurants in the street floated into our unshuttered windows. Looking over the tile roofs below us we were thrilled to spot the colossal six-sided brick tower of St. Sernin--only a couple of blocks away! Some architectural buffs believe the church to be the finest example of southern French Romanesque in the world. Terence at last had his papers. We were settled for the winter. The heater worked, the toilet worked, the mousetrap worked...who could ask for anything more?

Terence was in seventh heaven; playing in the Opera orchestra and meeting other musicians and learning the language, and I was quite content myself. I got a lot of drawing done and sketched the old city of Toulouse to my heart's content. It became very dear to me as I walked all over its ancient streets.

The French are very proud of their architectural heritage; they don't willy-nilly mow down an old building for a parking lot the way we Americans do. They don't mind a bit living in something medieval if they can modernize the interior enough for comfort. They wouldn't dream of changing a roof-line or widening a window if that's the way it's been for centuries. Sacre bleu! What an idea! Therefore, buildings lean, they crumble, they disappear under moss and ivy, and the whole character of the neighborhood is retained--soft and charming--and tourists from all over the world come to admire and wish they lived in such places.

View from our Toulouse apartment (St. Sernin tower in distance)

Of course that means there are no parking places in the city. So everyone has to park on the sidewalk because the streets are too narrow and practically all of Toulouse is one-way streets which are never going the way you need them to go, but C'est la guerre, I say!

I learned to shop for our food in the morning street markets. Not so easy at first for a woman trained to be polite and of the "You first, please" and "After you, I insist" school of shopping. With Terence along, it was a swell adventure; I could walk behind him and not panic while he pushed through the noisy crowds and dealt with the food sellers. He was speaking French very well by this time, and I'm ashamed to admit I had adopted the lazy habit of letting him do all the talking. After he left for his first tour with the orchestra, I had to face the crowds and the vendors alone and I almost starved before I got the courage to elbow my way through the mob of French and Algerian housewives, trying to buy something. The sellers have very sharp eyes and if I spent too long deciding, they'd shout "Madame?!" I learned to grab the fruit and vegetables and wave it in front of the seller's nose with the correct change in the palm of my hand and then wiggle my way out to freedom. It took a while before my heart stopped pounding in my ears. I got better at it, but even months later I never could hear that "Madame?!" without flinching.

Window-shopping in Toulouse was another matter. I adored it. The sheer pride in the shopkeepers's windows was something to see. One offering would be devoted all to cheese--goat, cow, sheep, whatever--in the most imaginative displays. Another would be an ode to sweets... There was a store that sold nothing but honey! Its window included old-fashioned hives, and strange shaped jars, and bottles, and then all the things that can be done with honey, and odd little utensils Madame must use to get the honey out of the container. Bookstores, florists...I enjoyed them all and one day, when Terence was on tour with the Opera, I was sloshing around on some popular shopper's street when it started to snow. Great white globs of the stuff were dropping out of the sky like wet feathers. This southern Californian was enchanted; I reached out to catch one of the funny things and a woman, swathed in furs and carrying exquisitely wrapped Christmas presents placed a franc in my hand! I stood there mystified for a moment, then I looked into the nearest shop window to see my reflection. Oh wow, no wonder. Amid all the carefully coifed and sartorially aware passers-by, stood this frump in tattered jeans and a stained leather jacket and boy's rubber fishing boots. "Gee," I thought. "Maybe if I kept my hand out I could make more money than Terence!"

Terence was on the road with the Blagnac orchestra over the holidays, so Christmas came and went and I kept busy and didn't mind being alone. I fashioned tiny village scenes as gifts for my new friends in Toulouse from wild and weird things I found in trash cans behind the city's better shops, and wrote nice long letters to people who probably thought I'd fallen off the edge of the earth. It was a happy time.

In January, Terence had a two-week vacation from the Opera, so we decided to dash to the Italian border to get our passports stamped because of France's silly idea at the time of allowing foreigners only 90 days at a time in their precious country. We packed a small tent and some cooking utensils into the big metal box on the back of the Gold Wing and headed for the Mediterranean! We spent a night with our pal Jean Michel in Cesseras, and then found ourselves in Marseilles the next evening roaming the streets with Misha Horton, a wild young cellist from Santa Barbara who was living in a garret with an opera singer. As she was gone for the week on tour, there was room for us! We shared a bottle of wine and I threw together something for dinner while Misha spoke of the difficulties of trying to make a living as a musician in France. Once, he said, he was playing on the street corner in that port city and some man threw a fish into his cello case. Things were so bad that Misha took it home and cooked it and considered himself lucky! Terence and I felt very grateful for the job in Toulouse.

We rode through the rain to Menton, where our English friend Martyn Murphy had a flat, but unfortunately Martyn wasn't home and as there were no campgrounds open, we had to stay in a small hotel near the railroad station. After sneaking the camp stove and my frying pan and a couple sacks of food stuff up the back stairs, I made dinner and prayed no one noticed the smell of frying onions wafting down the hall. French hotels frown on such things.

Our quick run into Italy was not exactly satisfying. All we had time for was San Remo, which resembles more a suburb of Las Vegas than a quaint Italian seaside resort. We bought some truly hideous day-glow colored postcards of the town and mailed them and rode back across the border. This time our pal Martyn was home in Menton and we were able to spend the night in our sleeping bags on his floor. Martyn had a bad cold and was no doubt feeling cranky when he said, "The trouble with the French is that they are all so hostile!" We had heard that before from British and American travelers who hadn't bothered to learn the language.

On our way to Nice the next morning, a man in a car honked and waved for us to follow him. We had no idea why, but Terence was game, so that's what we did; snaking around the downtown streets of Nice in hot pursuit of our hot-rodder. I began to think he just wanted to show us off for his friends and neighbors, when the man pulled up in front of a restaurant and told us to take chairs at a table outside and then he disappeared. We obeyed. We were definitely puzzled when a waiter brought us beers and a large tray of divinely-smelling oysters fried in bread crumbs. We thought the guy must have been awfully hard up for business and were wondering how to get out of the trap when the waiter explained it was all free and welcome to the country. We wished Martyn had been with us.

A long couple of rides through some really spectacular grottoes and mountain villages along the south edge of the Massif Central and we were back home.

Chapter Ten

THE THREE MUSKETEERS IN ESPANA

AFTER "LA BELLE HÉLÈNE", Terence rehearsed and performed "Carmen" for the Opera Orchestra, and in April, Chris got another leave from duty in the desert and so he came to Toulouse and the three of us decided to visit Spain!

Chris had made up his mind to learn to ride a motorcycle so, after a few short lessons, he was riding the Ascot and I was behind T. on the Gold Wing. He really did splendidly, considering how little practice he'd had, but once we got up into the Pyrenees and the roads were slick from snow, he began to have big problems so I took over and he took my place behind Terence on the Gold Wing.

We stopped in Andorra--that tiny province that has no tax on liquor and chocolate--and stocked up. Then on down the mountain past groves of pink and white almond blossoms and the first hint of Spring green among the steep and rocky slopes. We were definitely in another country. You could feel it in the air. España! Later, over our lunch of wine and cheese, Chris and I couldn't help but break into some corny song or other. It was probably "The Rain in Spain" and as I recall, Terence added some disgusting lyrics of his own. We rolled onto the grass, giggling like eight year-olds.

Somewhere out of Barcelona, my motorcycle developed gear trouble and, as Chris and I stood helpless at the side of the road, our Mr. Good-wrench set to work. But it didn't fix, and exasperated, Terence told us in no uncertain terms how useless we both were and that we were going to have to accept the fact that we were all stuck in the hinterlands of Spain for maybe two weeks until he could get some part to fix the damn thing! A sobering thought. Suddenly, we weren't having fun anymore. But it was all just a silly ruse; if I learned anything on this crazy trip, it was that Terence can fix anything, anytime, anywhere. Sometimes he just takes a longer time bitching about it first. And of course he was right. In this particular instance, Chris and I were useless.

Slamming open the trailer top, Terence rummaged around our pathetic belongings and found a wire hanger. Chris and I didn't dare look at each other. We just kept quiet. After several minutes of cursing and messing with the clutch cable, the bike was rideable again and we, thanks to Zorro here, had been snatched from the jaws of our enemies way out in nowhere and would live to see the bright lights of Barthelona!

We found a little room six floors up near the old Cathedral and stayed three days. Ogled the amazing Sagrada Familia church by Gaudí and walked along the pier, stopping to snap pictures of ourselves in front of the replica of one of Columbus's tiny ships that carried the famous explorer to our own shores. We walked through the magnificent gothic cathedral and rambled on the Ramblas--arm in arm, the three Caballeros!

We traveled back by way of the Costa Brava, not a very interesting area at this time of year. What is not industrial is built up for tourists and it was too early in the season for holiday-makers, so we passed a lot of empty concrete apartment buildings and shops boarded up against the wind. After a night in a rather sleazy Perpignan hotel, we climbed onto the bikes for a long day's riding back to Toulouse, with just one stop for the awesome castle at Carcassonne off the main road. There are worse ways to break up a long ride--the three of us used up the rest of our film on that exquisite fortress with the village inside. What had been damaged during countless battles or the ravages of the ages has been restored so lovingly here that you really feel transported back in time as you walk the dusty cobblestone alley-ways through dark archways and by not-so-straight-walls. During the height of the season, I understand, many of the locals who live inside the walls dress up in period costumes to delight the tourists and there are concerts and other sorts of entertainment and of course a light show every evening; illuminating the famous towers and historical spots. France loves to show off its antiquities; from sacred relics to crumbling towers--every other town seems to have something and they light them up every summer for the tourists. Not a bad idea for local revenue, certainly.

Riding into Toulouse, Chris went somewhere with a friend he'd met before we all left for Spain, and Terence and I rode out to Gers to meet some pals who rode mostly Gold Wings and who had sort of taken us under their wings after meeting us in Toulouse last November. Pascal and Marie. Jean Michel and his brother. Tin-Tin. Alex Boudrin. They were a rollicking, fun-loving bunch who, although they all had different jobs during the day, came together to ride their big bad bikes on weekends and work in each other's garages at night. In other words, Terence's favorite kind of cat. I became very fond of them too.

We had been invited to have dinner at Tin-Tin's house here, and then spend the night and ride with the gang in the morning zooming around the hills and dales about 45 miles west of Toulouse, where the land is wrapped in yellow from the fields of sunflowers and mustard. Terence and I were pretty tired from the day's ride from Perpignan and quite hungry, so when the big plate of shrimp came to the table, as our French friends discussed the correct wine to accompany it, we set about making pigs of ourselves--there was a lot and it was so good And so was the fresh bread. We were sated and happy when a giant bowl of salad was brought. Terence loves salad and so took a plateful--we never did get used to the French way of serving the salad anywhere but first--and I took some so no one's feelings would be hurt. We were leaning back thinking what great cooks these French bikers were when the steaks appeared! Apparently the main course! All that other food had been the appetizers! Terence and I had one tough time making it through to the end of dinner and of course we were expected to comment upon the choice of cheeses after the what-ever it was after the meat and before the fruit! Groan. Let there be no mistake. The French are very serious about their food. A meal without at least five courses is no meal at all...just a snack. We were learning.

During our stay in Toulouse, we joined the France/Etats Unis Club which promotes greater understanding between the countries and is a great way to meet the French as well as other Americans and study the language. It was discovered that Terence and I were performers, and we were soon hired to sing and play for their next event, a wine and cheese-tasting party held at a sort of Country Club just outside of the city. We were delighted to be making money of course, but the opportunity to taste the real stuff of France made the evening an exceptional treat.

After we were seated at a long damask-covered table among dozens of other such tables, the different wines flowed so fast and so freely along with the most incredible cheeses I had ever had the good fortune to nibble, that before it came our time to perform, we had had at least a couple of bottles each, and the two of us were floating in a rose-colored fog of the most amazing well-being...

These were not the wino-wines he and I fortified ourselves with on a cold night on the trail. These were the veritable pride of the French harvest, and their doting fathers and mothers were right there to see how they were received. At first, T. and I made serious attempts to look like we knew what we were looking for (and discovering). We swirled and sniffed and introduced the precious nectar to our mouths with furrowed brows and quizzical expressions. I think we all had note pads and vaguely remember writing some sort of bogus evaluations on it, but after several glasses of different sensational vintages, the whole table--French and Americans--were snickering and making rude comments on things like the well, smellier cheeses or the silly hat on the matron at the next table--All in all, having a perfect Bacchanal of a good time. When the moment to perform came along, I was in extremely good spirits, as I said, and Terence and I gave a perfectly splendid show, or at least we felt as if we had. Luckily for us, we were chauffeured home later, or the ending to the evening might not have been as pleasant.

Chapter Eleven

GAIL GOES IT ALONE

In May, Terence had to return to the States to take the Baby Bar exam, a nasty little test given to all Law students who are not attending an "accredited" Law School, so that the powers that be can determine if such students have the stuff of which California lawyers are made. Or something. Anyway, we had to move all our belongings back into the trailer and yank it to Pascal's house west of the city. Then Terence, with three huge boxes of old and spent law books and various items he needed in California; his blessed viola, of course, his typewriter, some clothes, cameras and bits and pieces that added up to enough to get him thrown off the plane, heaved and shoved himself into a train bound for Paris where he would try to find a cheap flight home. Meanwhile, I stayed in the apartment just long enough to clean it cleaner than it had ever been before, so that Madame Dufarge, our landlady, would have no problem giving back the hefty deposit we had to hand her to get into the place. She had the problem, anyway, but that's a story for Terence to tell...

Friends in Toulouse had found me a job house-sitting, while my man was away. The place was a somewhat-renovated farm house in a forest near Limoges, in the heart of France. On May 29th, a Sunday, I had just finished cleaning the refrigerator in our apartment. It was 1:30 on a dark afternoon. I was supposed to meet the man that owned the house in the Limoges countryside in about five hours, so I bungeed down the last things onto the bike and headed north out of town.

It was raining softly, but I was so excited and nervous about traveling such a long distance without Terence and the big trailer's reassuring red lights in front of me, that I hardly noticed it. It was the Fête de Mères (Mother's Day) and a lot of people were on the road so I took my time. Somewhere around Cahors, the bulging heavens opened and the deluge began and the going got rough. I pulled over under a tree and changed to my full-face helmet and put on the cumbersome rain gear. The mud was swirling down from the tall banks at the sides of the road and the white lines were obliterated. I needed gas but all the stations I'd seen were closed for Mother's Day. On and on I pushed, with panic beginning to crawl up my back like a spider.

I almost lost control of the motorcycle on a particularly slimy curve and wound up shaking on the shoulder, weak and in a cold sweat but thankfully, still upright. It was a while before I had the courage to get back on the road and by this time it was getting dark and I was soaked through. Fortunately a tiny filling station was just around the bend. I filled up and followed the signs around Limoges to the forest Le Menudier. The rain was lighter, but I was achingly tired and beginning to lose hope of ever reaching my destination. Dead hedge-hogs and flattened slugs littered the forest road as I drove through the dark woods. It was about 8 p.m. when my headlight picked out the crumbling stone building that was to be my home for the next two months.

I had been warned that it was no palace, but because it was free and had a roof, I had had little choice but to accept the job. The landlord, Monsieur Charles Levy, was a young man from Paris who had bought the property as a get-away from the crowded city, but in that it was a good six-hour drive from Paris, he couldn't get down as often as he liked and the place had been broken-into a couple of times so he needed a house sitter.

He was relieved to see me finally arrive, I'm sure, but my drenched and frazzled appearance obviously unnerved him and I could imagine him wondering if he ought to take the chance of leaving his precious property in the hands of this frightening apparition emerging from the night. He understood English pretty well though, so after having a cup of tea together, I think I was able to make a somewhat better impression and so he left me the key and departed for Paris. I rolled myself up in my sleeping bag and gratefully welcomed sleep.

The next morning I surveyed my new surroundings. I had to laugh. We do ask for what we get sometimes, don't we? I found myself in a three-story stone box with tiny windows and cold and dark as a cave. The ground floor was the kitchen-family room. The only window was over the sink and Charles had put some heavy plastic sheeting over it to keep out potential squatters so the light coming through from the rainy day outside just served to make the place gloomier. An enormous fire place covered most of one wall, and the blackened stone all around it and the black rafters overhead indicated that it no doubt had served as the stove, furnace, and clothes-dryer for the household in ages past. Very efficient, probably. As I sat on the little wooden chair I'd pulled up and warmed my toes by the tiny fire I'd lit in its great belly, I could imagine a farming family gathered around this hearth. There were places for hanging pots over the fire and poles sticking out from the stained old mantel where one could string lines of wet clothes. A heavy iron door at the side opened onto the baking oven and I thought, with a little practice I could learn to live like that. Lining another wall was a fairly modern refrigerator and on a table, a two-burner gas stove. I could heat water for a cup of coffee! Warming my cold fingers around the mug, I climbed the narrow stairs to check out the upper rooms.

They weren't much to look at. Just cold empty rooms with only one tiny window at the front. I'd slept in the middle one and because it had a light bulb hanging from the ceiling that actually worked, I decided that would be where I'd read and draw. There was a bathroom of sorts; that is to say a small enclosure on the third floor that had a bathtub in it. A drain-pipe had been hooked up to the hole in its bottom and it extended through the wall to the outside where the used water simply poured out and onto the ground! The tub faucets were not attached to anything; the only water supply being at the sink downstairs. Cold only, of course. So for a bath, I had to heat the water in pots on the two-burner, carry them up two flights of stairs and pour them into the tub which I'd stoppered with a sock, get in, wash myself and pull out the sock and listen to the music of the drain water cascading upon the rocks three flights below! Actually, in that I was alone, it was not an unpleasant experience. I certainly didn't have to worry about what the neighbors thought. I sang and made as many rude and wacky noises as I pleased--in every room. Not a bad life, really.

The fact that there was no toilet facilities was a little unsettling at first, but I soon got used to using the great outdoors. After all, we had been "on the trail" for some time now, and the lack of that sort of plumbing was no big deal anymore.

After a couple of days, I thought I'd better get some provisions and also was hoping for some mail at the Poste Restante (General Delivery). The closest post-office and market was in Sauviat-sur-Vige, a village about six kilometers away. I wiped some of the mud from the bike and rode through my forest slowly, looking at the neatly planted rows of pines. Not exactly a story-book forest, I noted. Every tree was numbered and destined for the wood needs of the country, but still dense enough and hilly for a nice feeling of wilderness.

The whole village of Sauviat had closed for lunch. Oh rats. I'd forgotten about the three hour break they insist upon in so many of the European countries; in order to eat their main meal of the day and then sleep it off or have an affair or whatever. It's so annoying to us Americans who find it truly hard to believe how one can keep a business going or simply get things done when everyone disappears behind closed doors in the heart of the day! I mean, doesn't the baker, for instance, want to sell bread to folks who might realize they need some between one and four? Terence and I were often stuck without a crust when we couldn't get to a village in time for the blasted midday curfew. If we did manage to walk in, as a grocer was about to lock his door (us begging for stale food from his shelf he probably had lost all hope of selling to his neighbors), we'd often get a look that made us feel about as welcome as two great maggots in his moldy flour bin!

I drove on to the next and larger town, St. Leonard de Noblat. Still the curse of the closed doors, so I settled myself at an outdoor café (they stay open everywhere) with a cup of coffee to wait for the grocery store to open. At four o'clock, le Super Marche honored me with a sort of readiness for business and I was able to buy all kinds of goodies to lift the spirits. Passing through Sauviat on my way home, I discovered there was no mail for me and dejectedly rolled on home.

Later that afternoon, weather at

last permitting, I was able to look around my "farm." It must have been a rather large holding, with many stone buildings attached to the main house. Now only the house remained; the rest nothing more than some leaning walls and fallen beams--a pile of rubble that Charles had said would have to be removed soon for the sake of safety.

I took the three kilometer walk one morning to Auriat, the nearest village at the edge of the forest. I imagined it must have once been a cluster of pretty homes with a church in the middle with busy people inside them and lots of noisy children running around, but now Auriat was all but abandoned; with just a few old folks peeking out at me from behind their upstairs window shutters as I passed. I walked the small hill to the cemetery at the edge of town. An obelisk to the two World Wars rather said it all. No less than twenty-eight of their sons had been lost to those wars--and this awful toll from a village with only about ten houses and a church! The sun came out as I stood before that sad monument; lighting up the roof tiles of the little village below me like embers. Life goes on.

In the evenings under my little light bulb, I studied French, but with no one to talk to, I wasn't getting very far. Some animal lived in the walls and after I got over being afraid of the scurrying and crunching sounds it made, it became a kind of pet; although it was much too shy to come out and shake paws. Once, on my way to the tub, lugging the two heavy pots of hot water up the stairs, I caught a glimpse of it peeking through a space in the rock wall. It looked something like a lemur or very exotic squirrel. Weeks later I would be informed that it was called a Loire, like the river.

I was writing a letter one afternoon when I was startled out of my wits by a pounding on the door downstairs. I rushed downstairs and opened it and standing on the doorstep were two of the best-looking men I'd seen in some time! Of course, they were the only men I'd seen for some time but never mind... They were uniformed policemen and had wondered what the strange-looking motorcycle was doing parked upon Monsieur Levy's property. No English spoken here, now was the chance to practice my

French. I was so nervous I forgot to ask them in, but simply kept saying attendez, wait, and ran up the stairs to get my passport which was pretty stupid because I really was able to explain myself without it if I could just calm down.

I gave them the "blurb" we'd written about our trip that Terence had translated into French and that explained enough to make them smile and everybody relaxed. Then I was able to put together enough French to tell them about house-sitting for Charles until August and that I was writing and drawing and oui, quite content to be here toute seule, thank you. They tipped their hats and departed and I stood there saying to myself, "If only I knew more French...."

One cold, wet day, I was tired of studying and reading and was hungry for a real live homemade cookie. I went down to the kitchen and stirred up a concoction I called "no-bake" cookies, for of course that's what they were. I stirred in some oats and some cocoa and milk and threw in a Hershey's kiss I'd been saving since my daughter had sent it to me in my birthday card in May. I heated the mess over a low flame for awhile until everything melted together more or less and pretended I was eating chocolate Truffles. It might not have been close, but it wasn't as far away as say, corn-on-the-cob. "I do believe I am becoming rather adept at this gypsy cooking scene," I told my friend in the wall. "The masterpieces I've produced from one pot would boggle your furry little mind. All I ask is that you should be starving."

One day at the Post Office in Sauviat, I received a letter from an old friend and ex-college room-mate Lynn Price, who said she was coming past Limoges on a trip through France and could we get together? Could we ever! I wrote a post-card to her hotel in Paris and when the day came to meet her at the train station, I was so happy to think I'd have someone to talk to after all these weeks I didn't even mind the traffic jams getting into the city. We shrieked and clutched other as if we were meeting on the moon.

We had a marvelous time; she sat on the back of the motorcycle and I (very carefully--I'd never had a passenger before) rode us around that old city, We explored the cathedral and the museums and she treated me to tea and a cake in some glorious paneled and mirrored tea room among the fine ladies of Limoges and their poodles. We shared a hotel room, talking into the night like the twenty-year old room-mates we once were-- comparing notes on our men and telling each other how clever our children were and what we were hoping for them...blah..blah. A great time. After putting her on the train the next day, I rode back happily to the forest, refreshed and eager to receive my next visitor, my son Lucas, who was supposed to be arriving on a bicycle with his friend Eric from Paris but he hadn't been able to tell me when...

A couple of days later I rode into Sauviat to find the church bells tolling mournfully. I got off the bike at the Post Office and watched as a small sad procession in black walked behind a slow moving hearse going up the main street from the little church. As usual it was drizzling and with the gray of the shabby houses and forever closed shops matching the color of the mud in the streets, I couldn't help thinking this had to be the gloomiest place I'd seen in all of France. I turned into the P.O. and felt a lot better after finding not only lots of jolly mail, but two great big fat books from my good friend Judy Bysshe in California. I flew home to start reading.

June 16th turned into an amazingly hot day. I was feeling smug that I'd caught enough hours to dry some clothes for once. In the afternoon, as I picked some things off the line I'd rigged between a couple of trees, I noticed how jungle-like the forest was acting. The air seemed thicker and sticky and the insects seemed to have changed keys. I looked at the sky and watched while the gray clouds swallowed up the white ones--chasing them around the sky in a kind of feeding frenzy. Thunder began to bounce around the hills and I hoped it would get nearer and liven things up. Amazed at an almost black sky growing behind a rich green stand of pines to the south, I went inside to get the camera. The air had suddenly turned cold so I thought I'd better also get a sweater.

Pulling on a sweat-shirt, I heard a slow plunk-plunk as if someone were throwing rocks at the house. I yanked open the front door and stood in shock as hail stones of all sizes smacked onto the grass in front of me. The plunking sounds came from the roof and grew so loud I was sure they must be breaking the tiles! At that moment, a tremendous wind turned the frozen downpour to slants and the thunder I had been hoping would come nearer only minutes before, seemed to be right on top of me--in great crashing explosions! What sensational theater it was! I felt completely safe--surrounded by my stone house--and shrieked with glee! Through the squall-like waves of water and ice, I could just barely make out the old fir trees on the hill across the road. They were bending way over and from side to side like a geriatric exercise class.

After a while it was just rain I was watching and I realized I was getting wet standing in the doorway, so I closed the heavy door and started to make dinner. About a half-hour later, as I stood with a sizzling pan in my hand, the lights went out. Irritated but grateful that it was still light enough to see outside, I put down the pan and turned off the burner and with a big black umbrella I found under the stairs, I went in search of the electric box. All I found was the meter which told me there was no juice flowing. Oh really? No circuit-breaker or fuse box. I gave up. As I sloshed back to the front door, I was surprised by several tiny frogs jumping out of my way. I wondered if this was that phenomenon when things like fish and frogs get snatched from their watery homes by invisible forces in gales and deposited miles away. Wouldn't it be nice to have a few trout on my doorstep? But it seemed I was not to be so blessed. I went in and, after a quick search, found a short candle that I put in my pocket for later. There was still some light coming in eerily and green through the plastic sheeting on the kitchen window. I pulled the chair over to it and sat with the pan of food keeping my knees warm.

I thought about the young Parisian owner who was so valiantly trying to transform this ancient ruin in the woods into a restful country retreat--with the forest, selfish as a spoiled child, snatching it back every time he turned his back. It hadn't been three weeks since he'd mowed down the wild growth around the house and already, with all this rain, the weeds were up to my knees! Visions of young Charles bringing guests down from the city for a weekend brought all sorts of delightful scenarios to my mind as I munched away in the twilight. "He probably doesn't tell them there's no plumbing other than the cold water tap over the kitchen sink. He waits until they're 450 miles from the city to break the news!", I chortled. "And those insects out there in the night are voracious," I'd tell the new arrivals. "Of course Charles will hand you a pair of boots to walk on snakes with if you must answer the call of nature. He keeps plenty of boots around. The perfect host. And the mice, my dears!" I pictured myself addressing assorted sweet young Parisiennes. "These old walls made of rock and sand are veritable mousie condominiums! They squeak and play and snatch food right from your plate when you're not looking. Better keep it on your knees, ladies. And during the night here, when it's as quiet as a tomb and the tall black trees block out the stars overhead (on those rare nights when it doesn't rain), one is often awakened by something that drags or rolls objects overhead and seems to spend endless moments chewing something that sounds like bones. Charles will tell you it's quite harmless; probably a cute little hedge-hog or adorable furry Loire. I, however, think it may be a... troll!"

I had been hearing the hum all the morning of June 24th but had simply ignored it. By noon, though, it was so noisy above me that I went outside to take a look. What I saw chilled me to the bone. Part of the underside of the roof tiles was covered with bees--the queen must have found her way into the attic space to take up housekeeping, and her devoted subjects were trying to follow her.

I ran into the house and up the three flights of stairs to the top room where my worst fears were realized. Bees were everywhere, looking for mama in the ceiling. Whatever signals they were following fell short of getting the poor creatures to the right passageways to the center of things. Instead, it seemed cruel mother nature had supplied them with just enough homing devices to get them close, but no cigar. They were seeping in through all the cracks in the old walls and in the open windows and then of course, lost, they'd fly around in circles; desperately trying to find the way out so they could start all over again. The queen had to be somewhere on the roof under the tiles.

I don't know whom I was feeling sorrier for--them or me--but I knew I had to do something to get them to leave. I closed all of the windows in the room after shooing most of the existing bees out, only to watch in horror as the poor little things began bashing their tiny bodies against the window panes to get in again! I turned away and closed the door tightly to the room and went down to the next floor to shut all of the other windows. The buzzing sound was ominous and when I went outside again to look up, I saw the upper part of the house literally crawling with the insects, and I knew I had to get help. I ran into the kitchen to get my keys, and ran out again and jumped on the motorcycle and drove to Auriat to use the public telephone I'd seen standing at the edge of the village. I thought that perhaps the best thing to do was call Charles in Paris and pray he'd think of someone to call nearby to come to my rescue. Of course he wasn't home. I had to think of something else. I walked down empty streets. People were home. I could actually hear television sets and dinner preparations, so I mentally rehearsed my story and plea for help in my shaky French and started knocking on doors. The furtive movement of curtains and behind half-closed shutters indicated that I was being observed, but nobody answered.

Riding back to the house, I thought of a neighbor way up the mountain; a family who hung out wash on the line every day with lovely noisy children who used to grow silent and run for the house when I'd go by on one of my walks. What choice did I have? I rode past my house without daring to look at it, and up the mountain and surprised maman in her vegetable garden before she had a chance to run into the house. Once I had her attention--with much gesturing and awful French, the rest of the family began coming out of the house to see what was going on. It was the teenaged son, Artur, who understood first and offered to call the firemen-- les Pompiers--for me. What a relief! We all went in. He phoned and told me they would be by in two or three hours (!) and so I calmed down. It was probably dinnertime at the station house, I thought, and one does not ask a Frenchman to cut short his repast. Mon Dieu!

Papa poured me a lovely glass of Port while I answered their many questions about the crazy trip I was taking and how my companion had had to return to the States for awhile so that I had to house-sit in their forest for two months. They told me about how they had been forced to leave their native Portugal to find work and that papa was a forestier here and that they were living in a house loaned to them by the people who owned the forest. They confessed that they thought of little else but the day when they could return home.

They loaded me up with produce from their garden and I was so grateful for their kindness that I promised to return and paint them a picture of their house and garden soon and we all waved good-bye and I returned to what was by now more a hive than a home, to wait for the firemen.

I was sitting in the kitchen, staring at a page in my French grammar book and trying to concentrate over the bee's Hitchcockian buzzing and bashing when I heard the stomping of heavy boots on the stone steps. I opened the front door. They were three men in blue jump-suits. A rather wine-sotted looking older guy, a dashing young brave, and a lad so young

I figured it had to be a summer job for him between school terms. He was laden down with hoses and tool-boxes and metal canisters. The sight of these three musketeers picked up my spirits considerably. I led them up the stairs--they'd already seen the swarm on the walls outside--and into the top bedroom where now, dozens of bees were trapped. The two older men poked around the ceiling and discussed the situation, speaking far too fast for me to follow, while the kid stood in the doorway, out of breath--having lugged all that stuff of three flights of stairs with no help. I felt sorry for him and wished I could have talked to him.

The men explained to me that the only solution, Madame, was to cut a large hole in the roof to let the bees out! Alas, it would be très cher... I said thanks very much but that would be out of the question--at least until I had spoken with the owner of the house, who lived in Paris and couldn't be reached at this time. More conferring in a French spoken too quick for me to grasp.

Monsieur Le Brave turned to me smiling, came very close and squeezing my arm with rather too much warmth and understanding, suggested I learn to live with the bees. "Because les bees, Madame," he explained, "are very domestique. One is lucky to have them nearby for the honey they produce!" My jaw dropped. Booze-breath attempted to illustrate how harmless the little buzzers were by opening the window and herding the frenzied insects out by waving his hands and even picking up some that had fallen below the sill--and tossing them out. I felt a little feminine appreciation was called for at such bravery, so I gave what I hoped was appropriate gasps of admiration and girlish pleas for him to be careful and damn if he didn't get stung by one! And he howled! I was enjoying myself immensely.

Angry now, and maybe deciding it might be nice to get even, the wounded chief was struck by a new idea. He could, he told me, attempt to spray this room with something that would certainly kill the ones that were still in the room and probably discourage the rest under the tiles so that in due course, they might leave. I was all for it and so the poor little rookie was told to run down the stairs and get such-and-such from the truck--which he did in record time--and while we underlings went down to the kitchen for a cup of tea, our fearless leader got the job done upstairs.

Happily, it went as he had predicted. Following orders, I did not open the door to that room for three days and each day there were less and less bees on the outside walls and roof until one morning I realized that they had all disappeared. I was glad to see there were very few little bodies to sweep up in the top room when I finally peeked in. The tiny buzzers had, after all, provided me with some very welcome moments of high entertainment and a chance to meet my neighbors. I hope they found someplace more hospitable not too far away.

By June 30th, I had all but given up hope for my son's visit when one cold morning around six a.m. I heard a faint knock on the door downstairs. I hurriedly threw on some clothes and ran down to peek through the small dirty pane. There on the doorstep, white, wet and hunched over, stood something that looked like the ghost of Hamlet's father emerging from the morning fog. It croaked: "Mom?" I pulled him inside and we hugged a long time. I could tell he was in a bad way; dehydrated and close to losing consciousness from extreme fatigue. He slipped down onto the chair by the fireplace while I rushed to give him water and heat some tea. I built a fire and then helped him off with his rain gear and was very relieved to see the color come into his face. At first he could just whisper but as the tea took effect, I learned the whole story of his crazy journey from Los Angeles to my hut in the forest.

It had been planned carefully enough, but at the last minute his friend, who was to be bicycling with him, couldn't make it and a series of mishaps and just plain inexperience in traveling led my young son on a trip that almost proved fatal, and I found myself both grateful he was safe, and furious at what seemed like dangerous stupidity in trusting the fates or whatever, instead of using his head...not providing himself with enough water, not reading the directions in my letter carefully, not having the courage to ask the people along the way for help or directions because he didn't feel his command of the language was good enough, etc. Even though it occurred to me that I might have done exactly the same foolish thing at 22, I wanted to smack him one for frightening me so much!

Apparently, after finally locating the right train from Paris, he'd landed in Limoges, and instead of flopping in the Youth Hostel to wait for morning, he had decided to brave the night and just go for it. He had no idea how far I was from the city. Lost in the forested countryside and wandering around in circles, he had pulled over when the light on his bicycle failed. He curled up on some pine needles and tried to sleep, listening to the night sounds coming from the pitch black woods. At the first light of dawn, he got up and pushed on; finally coming to the signs I'd written about in my letter. He had a sore throat and an earache and I put him to bed. Just like old times.

A couple of days later he'd completely recovered. We went sightseeing. He rode the Ascot--with me on the back--past Limoges to the ruined village of Oradour-sur-Glane. I had read the macabre story about the village in my handy Rough Guides to France, and wanted to be sure Lucas saw it. To most American young people today, WWII is ancient history. I didn't think it would hurt to have him see some of the realities of war.

The sad story is that on June 10, 1944, the soldiers of the SS das Reich Division rounded up everyone in the village and locked them into their little church and set fire to it. 500 men women and children were burnt alive in reprisal for attacks by French Resistance fighters in trying to protect their homeland. The rest of the village was burned too and the whole thing was so terrible that the French decided to leave it exactly as it was for the world to see. The sign on the entrance gate says: "Souviens-toi." Remember.

Lucas and I walked around with tears in our eyes. The village streets are littered with gutted pre-war cars and twisted telegraph poles and gray and rusted bicycles. Each sad shell of a house makes you gasp as you spot a charred sewing machine or a child's melted toy. It's powerful stuff and even though a sign asks for "Silence," one would be hard put to speak a word in this dreadful place anyway. The memorial cemetery contains the awful list of names and many tiny framed pictures of the victims in life--dark, serious faces...collars too tight and hair pulled back in no-nonsense attitudes. A hard life at best in this small village, yet all they knew. A large family of tourists were peering into a burned-out bakery on the corner. They were a handsome group; blond, tanned and healthy. They were speaking German.

Lucas stayed a week with me. We toured Limoges and walked around the Cathedral there before I waved good-bye to him at the train station. I supposed he was bored out of his skull staying with his mother in the middle of Nowhere, and by the end of the week he'd been chomping at the bit to be off and to meet up with an ex-school chum whose family's summer home was a chateau in Varax, north of Lyon. They had been kind enough to ask me to drop by also, for a couple of days, and although it was a long way for me to go on a motorcycle alone, I decided to do it anyway. I felt I could use a break from all that peace and quiet in the forest. So a couple of days later, I packed up and locked the door and began the drive over the mountains cutting right across France's middle. I passed Aubusson with its famous tapestries and up the lofty lava walls to the "black city" of Clermont-Ferrand. The trip took me much longer than I thought and the heat was fierce, so I decided to stay in a tiny hotel by the train station and start out fresh in the morning. I was glad I did because it gave me a chance to visit one of the most unusual gothic cathedrals I'd seen. Built of lava from nearby Volvic, and standing on a worn-away volcanic peak, the 13th century structure looms high over the city. I walked from the afternoon heat into the cool and dark of the nave. The rich reds and blues of the tall stained glass windows saved the interior from being too gloomy. Black and strong and yet strangely delicate, I thought it an incredibly beautiful place.

The next morning promised another scorcher, so I left early and zoomed at a pretty steady speed--past volcanic puys and down into valleys of sunflower fields and maize. About three o'clock I found the turn-off for the chateau. My leather jacket was sticking to me as if it'd been soldered to my back. I roared up past manicured lawns and flourishing gardens and up to what looked to me like a movie set for a truly drippy romance.

Chapter Twelve

LE CHATEAU DE VARAX

DATING FROM THE 15TH CENTURY, the Chateau de Varax is a happy medley of styles in stone and brick--carved arches over doorways, Renaissance gables and a splendid square tower and everything covered in ivy and flowers. Two elderly people were standing in the drive. They'd probably felt the vibrations of the motorcycle loosening a few bricks and had come out to greet me. I thought they were Clementine's parents--what do I know about servants? After a rather clumsy beginning, I made an effort to observe more and talk less. It seemed the family and my son were in Lyon until dinner, so I was led up a spiral stone staircase to my room and handed a great fluffy towel and was shown the shower chamber so I could freshen up. Unbelievable luxury. The first hot-water I'd seen come out of a tap in weeks! So when everybody tumbled out of the cars later in the grand drove, I was clean and in a dress and had had time to get over the first shock of the place.

The Berards were absolutely wonderful people. Unstuffy and warm and generous and kind. They also spoke perfect English. The whole chateau reflected their personalities. Doors and windows stayed open for air and comings and goings. The interiors were faded and fabulous. Magnificent oriental rugs--warn to shreds here and there--disappeared under heavy, carved wooden furniture that Beverly Hills decorators would give their souls for. I floated from room to room, disembodied, as all sense of time dissolved in that heady atmosphere. I asked about certain fascinating old paintings and sculpture tossed about the place and was told that they'd been on the walls or lying about for so long no one knew about them anymore!

My room was in the newer wing (18th century). I could look out of the leaded panes of the windows to the older part, with its romantic tower and beyond to the private lake at the end of the drive. There was a tiny island in the middle one could row out to. The moat was filled in, alas. The view out the rear of the castle was just your usual ho-hum panorama of a long half-timbered medieval barn on an endless expanse of thick green grass upon which three snow-white horses--perhaps they were unicorns--nibbled and tail-swished.

The Camelot-like rain would appear in the afternoon around nap time to freshen the air and insure the lushness of the garden. A rainbow would appear after that, then a spectacular color and light show, starring the clouds and the lake; ending in a sunset that outdid itself every time. I always suspected the rich live differently.

Clementine, the Berard's beautiful daughter, had been an exchange student and living with the Schneiders and my son while he was attending UCLA. Steve and Shari Schneider had been friends of ours since my former husband and Steve attended UCLA law school together years ago, and I hadn't seen them for 12 years. They were here visiting the Bernards and so was their daughter Stacy, who was studying French at the university in Montpellier. We were all enjoying the reunion hugely and the next night decided to go out for dinner.

I must mention that I had been corresponding with Jean Michel Leloup, our host in Cesseras, who now had a job very near Lyon and when he heard that I would be there, he wrote to me in my forest at Le Menudier in June, to beg me to join him for dinner at the Paul Bocuse restaurant. Knowing this charming young Frenchman to be a closet chef-de-cuisine and also aware we would each be paying for our own dinner, I did some checking up on the place and discovered to my horror, that it was known as almost the most expensive restaurant in France--Paris's Tour d'Argent just edging it out for that dubious distinction. Apparently, Monsieur Paul Bocuse is the father of Nouvelle Cuisine, and not so stupid a businessman either, as he zips around the world; the golden medal of the Legion of Honor swinging from his ample neck, while he stirs a sauce here and opens another restaurant there... It seems Terence and I just missed him in one of them at Florida's Disneyworld. A pity.

Anyway, I had written Jean Michel and had wiggled out of it; pleading not only poverty but the fact that I had no idea what the group at the castle might have planned and that certainly was the truth.

Back at the castle. The Berards and the Schneiders were warring over restaurants. The Schneiders wanted to take the Berards somewhere special to thank them for their hospitality, and the Berards wanted to show their immense appreciation for housing and being a family to their daughter in Los Angeles. The young people had already gone somewhere chic to do their thing, and everybody was insisting I must join them, when all of a sudden I had this terrible realization about what was going to happen and I wanted to simply disappear. There seemed to be only one way the War of the Most Gracious Lords of Generosity and One-Upmanship could be won. Nothing would do but Le Paul Bocuse!

I made an attempt at excusing myself from the party but everyone agreed it would be unthinkable to leave me home with the servants (no matter how much more comfortable I might have been in their company). So resigned, I asked Shari if I could borrow a necklace to dress up my dear old cotton frock that's seen about as much mileage as the body it covers, and I became determined to carry it off.

I was sweeping into the foyer of the restaurant in my role of the eccentric aunt and thinking I might be getting away with it too, when I noticed the ashen expression of the maitre d' as he helped me off with my cheap gray motorcycle jacket. Grasping the frayed collar with the tips of two manicured fingers, he held it aloft as he took it away; things dropping out of the many pockets all the way to the cloakroom. Waiters scurried to pick up my Swiss Army knife and my lucky ivory camel Chris gave me from Saudi Arabia, and returned them to me with a slight bow. My cover was blown.

College French had not prepared me for the clever disguising on certain menus of what is actually offered in such places. Nowhere could I find the words I knew for chicken or fish, for instance. Everybody chuckled behind their menus when I asked for help. So I tried choosing from the prices, where it seemed they had moved the decimal point... Surely, I thought, they can't be asking twenty-seven dollars for a side dish of greasy green beans? That was one I could read. Salade de haricots verts a foie gras--160 francs. Things began to swim around the page. I finally settled on something that looked interesting for a mere 370 francs (about $64) while some of the company chose menus at 500 F plus and the sneaky Schneiders found one I didn't see at 510 F for two. (It turned out to be boiled chicken). Naturally the wine was extra and it never stopped coming. Later, a dessert wagon rolled by and I discovered one of the nicest things about Nouvelle Cuisine is that it doesn't make you too full to have to pass up dessert. The display was heavenly. I was encouraged to sample several..don't ask me if they were included in the price. Nobody was about to tell me and anyway, I had my eccentric aunt act going in full swing by then, largely due to all that wine, no doubt, and it seemed to me I was the life of the party.

The great chef himself made an appearance at our table and the Schneiders snapped a picture as he leaned over to whisper sweet recipes or something in my ear...probably trying to get a close look for himself after hearing the rumor in the kitchen that the American frump was really Linda Evans in disguise.

I have to hand it to the establishment, though. As we left, that same maitre d' placed my ghastly old jacket around my shoulders as if it were sables. I understand better now what one is paying for in such places. I try not to think how many days Terence and I could have stretched the cost of that dinner. Or worse, thoughts of starving millions, etc. I guess life will never be fair.

The next day, as I got off my motorcycle to rest a bit on the long journey home, I put my hand in the pocket of my jacket and found three chocolate truffles I'd put there to save for later. Somebody had handed them to me off the dessert cart the night before when I was too full to eat them. I thought about having them bronzed but yielded to temptation instead and munched down all three there at the side of the road in one great chocolatey binge.

I made it back to Le Menudier by early evening...out of the heat, into the cold gray fog of the forest. Sliding off the bike, it seemed as if I'd stepped out of a time machine. The ghostly quiet again. I missed Terence. I wondered how much longer it'd be before he could leave California and get back on the road with me.

Chapter Thirteen

TERENCE RETURNS

ON JULY 31ST, I left my little home in the woods to return to Toulouse. Wonderful Mary Horvath was going home on her month-long vacation from the Orchestra to see her parents in Chicago and she was letting me stay in her apartment for the whole month of August! Of course, there's a very good reason why everyone leaves Toulouse in August. It's largely the same reason everyone who can gets out of New York City in the summer...the unrelenting heat and pollution. But sometimes one cannot be choosy and I tried to make the time pass by reading and writing in the heat of the day and taking long walks at night. My friend Martyn Murphy came through for a couple of days and we enjoyed ourselves visiting the museums and churches and art galleries.

Terence didn't make it back until October 15th! I had had to move out of Mary's place and take up temporary residence in a small village called Villemur-sur-Tarn to wait for him. It wasn't a bad stay, actually, my French was getting better and I was now brave enough on the motorcycle to take long trips by myself into the surrounding countryside; sketching old barns and pigeonniers and smelling marvelous autumn smells from the dried fields of corn and sunflowers. It would have been a completely enchanting time if things were going as well back home.

My daughter Meredith had written that she'd been very ill and in the hospital but was better now and she didn't want me to think of trying to get home. Guilt and concern made me frantic. I called everybody I could think of in California and got only answering machines! I finally got some straight answers from her step-mother who told me there was nothing to worry about and Meredith was fine, but it didn't exactly quell my anxiety. I was becoming a nervous wreck. It hadn't been easy for Terence, either. He had had to find new renters for our house again because the Mills family had to move and as he also had the examination to study for and take, plus work as a sheet-metal construction worker for the money needed to buy his ticket back to France. The whole thing was a nightmare. But he finally found a nice family whose breadwinner was a union carpenter and after he got them settled, he quit his job, grabbed his viola and typewriter and flew back.

Chapter Fourteen

OCTOBER, 1988. BACK ON THE ROAD

To say I was glad to see him would be an gross understatement. A couple of days getting the bikes ready in Pascal's garage, and we were once again ready to move on to the next country, Spain! Well, not quite to Spain. First, we had to pick up a giant load of stuff Terence had sent from California to Cologne by our old pals, the United Parcel Service. The plan was to take just the Gold Wing with the trailer--leaving my bike behind-- and dash up to the airport in Germany, grab the goods and be back to Toulouse to pick up my motorcycle before the frost hit the pumpkin. That's the way T. saw it and it sounded good to me. I was just glad to have us back on the road again.

But the Gold Wing had other ideas. The alternator burned out just as we left Toulouse, and the bike had to be pushed to start--every time he turned off the engine. I could see this was going to be a very long trip. By nightfall, we had only traveled as far as Uzerche, where we made camp near a swollen river. It was a public campground but out-of-season, so we had it to ourselves--free of charge.

We waddled through the rain to Orleans where we were to meet with Alex Boudrin, one of our Gold Winging pals from Toulouse. All the way up, when the bike wasn't causing us problems, the painted scenery of a French autumn was glorious to observe. Red and gold leaves dropped around us like a massive ticker-tape parade.

We stopped in a small village named Chauvigny to ask the owner of a

little outdoor café if we could recharge the bike for awhile, using his electricity. He was kind enough to show us the plug behind the bar. While we
waited for the transfusion to bring life back to the old girl, we walked up
the cobbled street to look at the tiny 12th century church of St. Pierre that
our precious guide book had glowingly recommended. We were thrilled to
see the marvelously graphic paintings there, of monsters and men and sin
and redemption. So much imagination and skill and in a time when most
people could neither read nor write! Afterward, we felt we ought to order
some coffee and pastries from the generous cafe-owner after using his electricity even though it was not in our budget. He not only would not hear
of payment for the electricity, he wouldn't even let us pay for the eats,
insisting the pleasure was all his and if we would allow him to take a
picture of us that he might show his friends, it would be all the payment
he needed. Who was it that said the French were hostile?

We spent two days at Azay le Rideau, a very pretty campground sheltered by trees, and just beyond a leaf-strewn pond at its border was a small
but trés elegant chateau. The fog had rolled in...quiet and eerie. I cooked us
breakfast with icy hands. Gray trees against white sky. The Gold Wing had
been giving us fits. The day before, eight miles out of the campground, the
battery simply gave up. Terence parked the bike onto the shoulder and
with the heavy battery under his arm, angrily strode on down the poplar-
lined road to hitch-hike to a garage. As the sun sank beyond the row of
poplars, I forlornly stood guard by the rig to wait for him. After a little
while I heard that strange blow-torch sound again and rising over the
poplar trees was a huge hot-air balloon with giant tulips and daisies
printed all over it and a jolly French flag fluttering from the ropes. As the
people in the basket leaned over to take pictures of me, I grabbed my
camera and snapped pictures of them! I think we both got shots to
remember.

Terence was in no mood to hear about the balloon when he got back. It
was dark and he had to wire the battery onto the bike and hope it would
stay connected long enough. He then ordered me to hold the whole thing
on my lap while he rode us into town to get to the garage. I was very
nervous at the prospect of being unpleasantly shocked as I held the damn
thing together against the bouncing of the motorcycle ride, but as usual, I
had little choice if I wanted to get to somewhere safe for the night.

The same problem happened over and over as we limped our way
toward Germany. We did stop to visit Alex in Orleans and in his company,
enjoyed the luxury of a pizza in that town where Joan of Arc had rallied

the troops. That determined young woman might have crossed the very bridge next to our campground by the river, for all we knew.

After walking in awe through Chartres cathedral the next day, we camped in an apple grove that night and as the wind swayed the laden branches, our dreams were punctuated with the plopping of falling apples all around and over-head. A bountiful harvest, but a perfect bitch to try to push a heavy motorcycle over the next morning!

We rolled past Versailles. "Oh Jeeze, Terence, it's not just any place, it's Versailles!" I pleaded. But there was no time to linger. It was a Sunday and we just had enough time to see the Musée d'Orsay as we passed through Paris--which has free admission on Sundays. Oh well. Maybe on the way back. At least I wasn't going to be violently sick on this visit to Paris.

We parked on the sidewalk, and looking like tramps--no showers for days--we shared a beer and munched an old baguette that had been squashed in the saddlebag all day. Street musicians played string quartets and jugglers performed amazing feats for our pleasure. Ah, Paris. Inside the museum there were beautifully written brochures in many languages-- including Esperanto. They were free and Terence collected one of each to compare and study later. Then, as we looked at some of the best Impressionist Art the world has to offer, we were transported. It was a true forget-your-dead-batteries and-muddy-clothes kind of experience, and the lovely high lasted all the way through the Parisian traffic to the campground on the east side of the city. The place may not have been the most pleasant of campgrounds nor the cheapest, but the blessed showers were hot and turned us into human beings once again.

Then up to Reims after taking a delightful detour at the Mercier Champagne winery. The tour and tasting event made us late getting into the city of Reims and so our look at the cathedral there was hardly satisfying, and yet we managed to see the last rays of the sun through the splendid windows of Chagall, and even though scaffolding all but obliterated our view of the smiling angel we'd some so far to see, she was waiting there in the dusk; seeming to forgive these two errant children who preferred loitering over a glass of champagne to coming to visit the house of God at a decent hour. We grinned back.

I pushed the Gold Wing out of Reims. I pushed it again after we had stopped to discover the municipal campground was closed. Dark was closing in and we couldn't use the headlight because the battery didn't have enough power. Seeing a battered gas station emerge from the fog, we brazenly asked if we could use their electrical outlet and did they have any drinking water. Two fellows in oily overalls were so surprised to see the big trailer behind the bike, they didn't bother to answer. They just waved us into the warmth of the garage while they circled the rig scratching their heads. Terence quickly unrolled the extension wire to the outlet--he was getting very skilled at it by this time, and I elbowed an elderly man out of the way at the mechanic's filthy sink to fill our coffee pot. Terence asked if there was a spot we could set up camp, and the men waved in the direction of the fog and said something about a stadium. We never found it; we were lucky just to stay on the road out there with no headlight and no street lights to see by. Terence gave up looking for it and turned onto a dirt road that seemed to border a newly plowed field. We were so tired from battling that sick motorcycle all day that we didn't even care where we were. Let the farmer try to remove us!

Seven or eight in the morning and we couldn't see the road for the fog. Bitterly cold. I made coffee and we clutched the mugs tightly to warm our fingers. I pushed the bike to the street and hopped on behind Terence, and we picked up speed in the direction of Luxembourg. The scene along the road was eerie in the fog. Signs told us we were passing by cemeteries for the dead of WWI and WWII. This area must have been a real hot spot. We stopped to give some horses the rest of the rotting apples we had picked from the ground three nights ago in the orchard. Fixing Terence in my camera sights as he fed the horses, I saw a large bunker loom out of the fog behind them. Life and death, juxtapositioned.

At the German border, Terence decided he needed to send some business letters while we were still in France, only he hadn't written them yet. So he pulled the heavy rig into a large parking lot and promptly sat down with his typewriter on the asphalt and began typing. The parking area must have belonged to a school because soon children of all ages with colorful little book-packs on their backs began to surround us--very excited and convinced we had stopped there for their amusement. To help T. concentrate, I did my best fielding their questions and they all thought my accent so funny, not to mention my idea of French, that I soon had quite a following and I have to admit I was enjoying myself and flattered that they seemed to understand what I was saying back to them. Darn! Here I was going into another country just when I was getting the hang of it here! After a while their school bus rolled in and they all disappeared into it and after waving good-bye to the little kiddies and observing that Terence was going to be at it a bit longer, I opened up the trailer and dragged out our moldy sheets and wet towels and decorously draped them all over the bike and trailer to get some drying time from the sun which had just shown its face as the bus pulled away. I was fast learning gypsy ways.

The municipal campground near the capital city of Luxembourg was open that night, mercifully, and even though fog covered the ground, I could see the full moon shining through the mist the same way the sun had all day through the fog--making everything on the ground look ghostly and white. We put up the extra tent and turned the little stove up full blast to warm it up in there, and I once again draped the same socks and underwear that I'd been trying to dry all week--over bungee cords tied to the top of the tent. I tried not to think how hot and dry October is in Santa Barbara. Apparently the campground perched on top of a sort of rabbit warren. Bunnies were everywhere; I practically fell over some of them on my way down the hill to the women's loo. It felt like something out of Watership Down.

Back in Cologne again, we took time to walk around that famous city and even pulled out all the stops and bought a bratwurst at the train station. Ah, the juicy thing--smothered in hot mustard! We felt like a couple of Oliver Twists about to break into a chorus of "Food, Glorious Food!"

Dieter Willecke of the UPS was very nice to us at the airport. No trouble getting our shipment this time. I was aghast at how much Terence had sent over; although knowing him, it shouldn't have surprised me. Apparently he planned to affix two huge sheet-metal boxes to the trailer-- one on each side. One was to be my kitchen, he explained brightly, and the other would be his tool-box. And then there were several other large boxes full of things ready to go in them. He said we could stop at Norbert Schupp's place to get them on. I thought about the legality of such appendages. Shoot, they wouldn't even be legal in the States! He stacked everything onto the trailer and roped them down. We were about to roll onto the German Autobahn looking like something out of a circus parade. I hoped the German police had a sense of humor.

Norbert, the amiable young fellow we had met in Ireland, lived in a small apartment in Wiesbaden, West Germany. we'd told him we were coming and although his neighbors might not have been thrilled, he found us a place to park the rig in the back of the building and then proceeded to help Terence bend, shove and screw the big boxes onto the trailer's sides. It took three days with Norbert being the perfect host. He showed us around that charming city and took us to some sweet little hamlets in the surrounding countryside and we sampled the local wine of the Rhine's famous vineyards and learned some history and began to really appreciate his country. Still, we were losing the war with time, and we were all relieved to have us finally drive away with the funny-looking motorcycle with the gross load.

The way back to France was fraught with fits and starts and the icy weather didn't help. One morning, still in Germany, after spending the night in the road in front of a "CLOSED FOR THE SEASON" Campground sign, the heavy bike fell over on the frosty shoulder because it had slipped into neutral while we were packing the trailer. Terence screamed at me to kill the engine but I panicked and pushed the high-beam button instead. He swore at me and I felt stupid and, desperate to help, ran into the woods to find something to use as leverage to get the motorcycle upright again. Pulling a limb from a pile of leaves, a small branch smacked me hard in the left eye. Blinded and in pain, I began to cry. Terence, never good with the frailties of mere mortals, stood by the downed bike and wondered if I'd be any help now with one eye. He managed to push the damn thing up all by himself and then sat on it and waited. After a while I felt better; the tears sort of serving to wash the wound, I guess. I blew my nose and resumed my usual place behind the trailer, to push with all my strength, such as it was, and help get the rig on the slippery road.

We crawled at a snail's pace all morning; every tree or house blocking the weak sunlight made a band of ice across the road. By afternoon the sun had dried the roads, but the wind remained and was like a knife slicing through our damp clothes. Over the border now, in France, I was so cold I developed a kind of palsy. I couldn't stop shaking or keep my teeth from chattering. Terence pulled into a supermarket parking lot and while I sat on some nearby grass with a blanket from the trailer over my shoulders, he went into the store and bought some food and wine which he forced me to eat and I began to feel better. Of course I ought to have known better about how weak I get without food for too long, and should have asked him to stop earlier so that I could eat something. But we had both wanted to make it to Nancy and the hot shower promised in the book.

The Campground at Nancy was closed, not surprisingly, but Terence found someone in charge and sweet-talked him into opening the gate and letting us not only stay the night, but using the electricity in the rest-rooms to re-charge the battery. The next morning, the three of us--Terence, the bike and I, felt strong enough to go the distance, and by nightfall we were all the way to Dijon, where we stayed for three days and were able to spend the nights in that good city's muni-campground.

We spent November 5 at our buddy Jean Michel's new apartment in Bourgoin-Jallieu near Grenoble. He was very happy to see us and treated us to our first "raclette," a melted Swiss cheese and ham and potato treat that really made our tummies sing his praises. Didn't I mention that Jean Michel was a closet chef? We agreed that he ought to think seriously about opening a restaurant.

We were doing fine on the motorcycle...zooming along with the Rhone river at our side. We stopped to gape and shudder at the giant nuclear reactors at Debieres and after a quick bite of bread and cheese, we were making very good time for once, through the stunning gorges of the Ardeche, when we hit a tram track hard and something broke. Terence held the shimmying motorcycle upright until he could bring it to a stop in the oncoming lane. He pulled off quickly to the shoulder. Several drivers in a hurry pulled around him without a glance, but a couple on a motor-cycle stopped farther down the road and offered to help. The four of us got the rig to the right side shoulder and Terence found that the trailer hitch was broken clean through. After much cursing, a chain was found and T. wound it around the rig and then we very carefully rode into the next town. We stayed overnight in a vacant lot and Terence was able to find somebody to weld the thing together so that we could continue on our way.

So we continued, pushing and nursing the poor machine along with its ridiculous load past the treeless plains and gorges of southern France. More nights in the rain; now instead of frost, gummy yellow mud around the tires of the rig. Fears of flash floods. We hear Nimes is flooded; its famous Roman ruins battered and bruised. All of France wants to come to its rescue. As soon as the rains stop, of course.

At last we reached Toulouse, and we yanked everything into the camp-ground. Terence called his Gold-Winging pals and one of them offered a garage he could work in to fix the alternator.

As we pulled the rig onto the highway to head for someplace nearer to our friend's house in Montgiscard, a well-dressed Frenchwoman waved us over and asked if we spoke French. But of course, Terence answered. She then invited us to ride to her house a couple of miles away so that we could stay with her and her family and have a good French meal and a nice clean bed. We had no idea what we were in for, but it turned out the lady was a true philanthropist. She could tell that we'd been on the road a long time, and reading our USA country sticker, she remembered that people in the States had been kind to her daughter when the young lady had visited a couple of summers ago, so she just decided to do a good deed in turn. We followed her into a wide driveway in front of a nice-looking suburban home in the south-eastern community of Toulouse called Ramonville. They were the Michel Daudet family. Eliette, the daughter, came out and greeted us in American English as if she'd been expecting us. Later the father, who was not quite as sure of us at first, seemed to overcome his bewilderment and treated us like honored guests; serving us sherry and Pastis before dinner and asking all the usual questions about what we were doing in France, and then we had a dinner that could have been Michelin-rated, with all the courses, rich and perfect. Monsieur served the dessert liqueurs. Everybody seemed to enjoy themselves enormously until bedtime which was fairly early because all three of them had to go to work in the morning. Suzanne showed us to our room. The guest bedroom cracked me up. It was all in white; bedspread, rug, furniture, curtains, everything. And here we were, all in dirt! Fortunately, there was a large bathroom adjoining with a nice big tiled shower with a glass door, unusual in France--and we scraped off a lot of road before crawling between the snow-white sheets and sleeping the sleep of the truly pampered.

A light tap on the door told us it was seven thirty and coffee was waiting. Eliette knew from her travels that Americans usually need a bit more to get going in the morning, so she made us toast. The whole family's kindness touched us very deeply.

Chapter Fifteen

SPAIN

THE REPAIR of the Gold Wing took a week, with Terence and good buddy Jean Michel Proust-Boucle cursing and getting greasy together in the garage. I was beginning to think they were never going to finish the ghastly project the way they were acting, but one should never underestimate true bikers. Even though I suspect a few mistakes were made that made the complicated procedure last much longer than it should have, I have great admiration for both men the way they stuck to it when everything seems to go against them. The Honda people should have heard what they thought of their useless "How-To" book, and making some parts so hard to reach, or stuff that would need a special tool only somebody in the factory in Japan had heard of. Horribly frustrating for the men, and of course they had no one to put the odd question to. It took real courage to take apart an engine in a small town in France--that was devised in Japan and made in the United States, and then try to fix it and put it back together again. That's probably why the guys needed all the beer. And also why they needed to make up all the new shock words in several different languages that sent them into fits of laughter that could be heard all over the neighborhood...

We were almost ready to ride to Spain. As useless as I was while the motorcycle was being repaired, it seems I could be trusted to spend a few hours cleaning and waxing and chrome-polishing the two bikes. Ugh. At last it was finished and our rig looked almost new again. With Michel, we had a party and said good-by to all our Toulousaine friends. It was already November 21st, almost too late to be toddling over the Pyrennes, but with the repairing to do on the motorcycle, there was simply no choice.

The ride over the mountains was indeed as bone-chilling as we'd been warned it would be. The steady hard wind had a chill factor I'd never experienced before--only the warmth from my electric vest and gloves kept me on the road. We stopped to eat lunch next to a couple of bare trees bending way over in the wind. We didn't take off our helmets or gloves, and felt like Spacemen.

Crossing into Spain, we took the road for Figueras, where Salvadore Dali lived and built his museum. It was dark when we rolled in to the main square, and because we felt so cold and dirty and also because the Tourist Office was closed for the night--making it difficult for us to find a place to camp, we opted for a cheap hotel. While Terence was down the street trying to ask someone where we might stay, I removed my helmet and tried not to look too strange to the nicely-dressed folks taking their evening stroll along the square. An elderly man selling hot-chestnuts glanced at me a few times and I wondered if he thought I looked as silly as I felt in my man's attire and sitting alone on a muddy motorcycle. He walked over and with a smile, placed two of the lovely warm chest-nuts in my icy paw and then walked back to his cart! I had no Spanish money to buy more but I could say muchas gracias and when T. came back I persuaded him to buy us a whole sack (a dollar) to celebrate being in Spain!

The hotel was in a rather creepy part of town but the room was clean and nobody bothered me while I cooked our dinner on the floor, and once more, blessed hot showers gave us a happier outlook on life.

The exterior of the Dali museum was a delight, promising more inside than one actually got for the hefty entrance price. I began to feel that it was pretty obvious that his best works were elsewhere. It seemed that several lesser artists had put up the exhibits in the famous Dali style--all very theatrical and rather silly. Presumably Dali over-saw what went on...we were told he lived in Figueras. It just came across, in my opinion, as some-thing of an ode to self-indulgence, but then Dali was like that, wasn't he? Laughing all the way to the bank.

A couple of hours ride south took us to the nightmare of city traffic in Barcelona. Terence went in to the Information Office and got us maps and a list of camping sites. We were shocked to discover that the price of legal camping was about three-times that in France! Hey, we thought Spain was supposed to be cheaper! We were going to have to find jobs. We rode out of town. It was a good thing we had seen a lot of Barcelona with Chris in April, because we couldn't afford to stay in the beautiful Catalan city this time. We pushed our way past the mass of evening drivers and up into the mountains looking for a place to camp. Still in the city suburbs, Terence decided to yank the rig out of the crush of traffic in order to read a map. Unfortunately, the driveway he chose to enter turned out to belong to the Gendarmeria! He damn near rolled over the toes of a policeman just coming out the door. The cop was so surprised and then alarmed by the size of the rig bearing down on him he reacted by blowing his top at Terence. A perfectly reasonable reaction, I thought. He asked for our papers, trying to compose himself, and after shuffling them back and forth without reading anything, he told us the rig was completely illegal in Spain (Oh, really?), and we would either have to dump it or immediately get out of the country. "Funny you should mention that," said my companion. "As it happens, we were just trying to find the fastest route to Portugal." He was happy to show us.

A full moon came over the trees and illuminated a kind of cement quarry around us where we had pulled in to "wild" camp. We were becoming less fearful of camping illegally--the thought of saving ten bucks here and there certainly made me braver, in any case. Also we had noticed a lot of gypsies doing the same--even in plain view--so if we could find spots hidden from the road, who would care? Anyway, if anyone asked, we could always say we were on our way to Portugal!

By morning our covered wagon and bikes were under an inch of cement dust! We'd been listening sleepily to heavy trucks roll by since dawn but didn't worry about it because nobody stopped. Of course there was no water around to clean things with, so we simply brushed off what we could and packed things away as they were. Cement Loaders were passing in earnest now, and the air was white with the stuff. Pulling onto the main road we could see last night's full moon just dropping over a pink mountain in the west.

We had a nice ride down a Spanish mountainside while our families at home were celebrating Thanksgiving. Near Tarragona, we spotted a billboard that glorified the charms and low prices of Caledonia, a cheap campground just up ahead and we pulled in. Amiable Senior Jose showed us around and we decided to stay. It was a large place; dotted with scruffy pines and too close to a railroad, but the price was right and Terence needed to study for a few days to catch up. The weather was warm and dry and there was almost no one else around. We could feel our moods warming up along with our backs in the bright sun as we unpacked.

We stayed in that cozy spot about two weeks. One afternoon we discovered a "Supermercado" on the other side of Tarragona that had everything and more that we could buy in France, and the prices were lower! At last! So we ate well and rested, and the time spent there would have been perfect except that both of us got bad colds from somewhere. I suspect it was that freezing ride in the Pyrenees three days before. Anyway, T. got over his quickly and then it was my turn. We had planned to visit three Cistercian Abbeys in the mountains the day I woke up totally congested. Terence said not to worry, I could pop a few aspirin and we'd take the Gold Wing and I could just sit behind him and doze. But of course the weather turned mean that day and the wind came up cold as Siberia and although I stuffed paper towels into every pocket and my gloves, I was sneezing explosively inside my full-face helmet and shivering from fever and I'd used up my paltry store of paper by the time we got to Poblet, the first monastery. I dragged myself around the tours, bundled up like an Eskimo while other tourists were in shirt-sleeves and sandals. I felt so awful at one point during a walk around a nunnery I almost asked the good sisters if I might stay in their infirmary a couple of days...someplace where Terence wouldn't be allowed in and I could be left in peace to blow my nose and take a nap. But after a glance at what they were getting to eat in the dining hall, I decided to stick with my man. Apparently, he guessed my earlier mood, because he actually stopped the motorcycle in the village and guided me out of the wind and into a taberna for a luxurious cup of hot coffee which did wonders for my disposition if not my cold. I was lots better the next day.

The owner of the campground, Sr. Henriques Parmirs, stopped by one evening while Terence was typing his Law study homework. He asked to be shown the rig and how everything worked and then graciously asked us if we would accompany him to the bodega owned by friends in the near-by village of Altafulla. He was Spanish, with family in England and Scotland. He spoke the king's English with the barest accent. We had a smashing good time. The proprietress in the bar was from Liverpool and sat with us. We all drank champagne and discussed languages. Henrique told us that his native language, Catalan, is so close to Occitan in France (We heard some of it while living in Toulouse), that he swore every peasant in France could understand him. Knowing him made it tougher for us to leave La Caledonia, but after a couple more days we had to pack up and roll south.

The celebrated city of Valencia holds few happy memories for us, I'm afraid. A tire on the trailer waited to go flat until we were parked right in front of the cathedral in the old center of town. With Valencia's famous white pigeons swirling around his head, Terence got down on his hands and knees and pumped it up again. The populace, gathered around the rig thought it highly entertaining and applauded when it was done. It held until we could get to a garage where they scalped us (Terence used another word) to fix it. Barely back on the road, two policemen in a car pulled us over and wanted to see our passports and all other papers concerning the ownership of the rig. They were not friendly. They let us know that because we were foreigners and therefore just passing through, they would let us go. But we should expect to be stopped many times before reaching the border to Portugal. Not a pleasant thought. Terence was stung (and scared) and wanted to kill something. He also wanted to write scathing letters and get out of this #&*^@! country! No way after that experience were we going to try to see more of the city. We headed out as darkness surrounded us, and started to look for a place to camp.

The street lights had disappeared, and our head-lights seemed to show nothing but swamp and rice-paddies on both sides. Mile after mile. I got very hungry and tired of it all and honked for Terence to pull over. He agreed to look for any road off at this point, and so we pulled into the nearest orange grove. It was a long dirt track with deep holes and when he pulled the trailer over a small ditch to get to a clearing something snapped under the trailer. Ay yi yi! We voted to just leave the heavy thing where it lay and eat some dinner before we dropped. We were so tired and disgusted, we crawled into the crippled trailer and slept like stones.

~ A BREAKFAST STILL LIFE ~

We were awakened by a huge explosion. Poking our noses out of the tent, we saw men in the distance blasting holes in the cliff-face at the end of the long rows of orange trees. Close to the blasting site was a large white manor house with people walking around and looking busy. We wondered if they might send the dogs if they caught sight of us plowed into their ditch. In the other direction we noted a group of orange-pickers just getting off a truck and setting up their empty cartons at the side of the grove. Terence got dressed and while I put the coffee on, he walked down to the men to ask if they knew of a garage near-by where we could get the trailer fixed. Nobody knew of one. But they wanted to be helpful and told him he shouldn't bother because today was a holiday and no garage would be open anyway! He came disconsolately back to the campfire. As we prepared to eat breakfast, one of them walked up and asked if he could join us. We said sure, and the man took out some bread and cheese and a beer from his pack and began to eat. He told us the grove was not owned by the people in the Manor house so we didn't have to worry about what they thought of our camping there. That was a relief. After his meal he took from his pocket a plug of hashish which he called "chocolate" and offered some to Terence who declined. We three sat back on the clover carpet and looked out to sea. Our grove was up on a hill that sloped up from the beach. We hadn't realized how beautiful the area was until that moment. It was as the whole coast of Spain must have looked before the English-speaking invasion began. So little of it left. There was a long white sand spit stretching out into the Mediterranean directly below us. We didn't need hashish to be enchanted. A little later, our new friend went back to join the others and we went back to trying to decide what to do with our broken trailer.

Terence was on his back underneath it when a car drove up the road and a distinguished-looking gentleman got out. It was the owner of the orange grove. Talk about luck! Mr. Desmond White McNamara had been born and raised in Ireland, had moved to Spain thirteen years ago, married and became a teacher and somehow had acquired quite a bit of property on the coast here below Valencia. Once he got over his surprise at the strange contraption that had landed in his orange grove, we all had a fine chat and Mr. McNamara offered to take Terence to a garage to get the necessary parts for the trailer. I poured Mr. McNamara a cup of coffee and he told us about his exciting plans for building hotels and restaurants across his land and down to the beach and across the spit. Terence and I couldn't look at each other.

I stayed with the rig while the men drove off in Mr. McNamara's car. The sea and sand sparkled blue and white. Someday, from this hill, one would only see the dead grayness of concrete and glass. And Mr. McNamara was such a nice man.

Terence was able to repair the trailer with a new U-bolt and jack for which he was gouged once again so ruthlessly that Mr. McNamara felt he ought to try to make up for his countryman's avarice and insisted we come home to dinner and meet the family. Mrs. McNamara was a delightful lady and the children thought we had dropped from heaven when they saw the motorcycles. Dinner was a small meal because of course the Spanish, like the French, eat the main meal in the middle of the day, but a very tasty treat for us because we hadn't had such wonderful fried potatoes since the Fish and Chips place in Scotland. They were accompanied by a small fresh salad of tomatoes and cucumbers. Rosé wine was poured from a paper carton. Senora McNamara seemed a little embarrassed that it wasn't fancier, but Terence and I were thrilled to get a genuine taste of Spanish life and quite happy that she hadn't had a chance to run around "picking-up" and cooking something "special" for guests. How lovely to feel like part of the family! Later, Terence rode the teenagers around the village square where they made sure all their friends saw them on the motorcycle. So cute.

We were on the way to Granada. We stopped for lunch next to an old cemetery to eat our cheese and bread under the shade of a few olive trees. A car drove up to the gates and a middle-aged man helped a very old lady dressed all in black, from the passenger seat and opened the gate for her. I hoped we weren't being disrespectful by dining on sacred ground. The man sat in the car for awhile then went back to the gate to give his arm to the woman who had returned from inside. They looked over at us and then he reached into the back seat for something. Finding it, he walked over to where we were sitting and with a grin, handed us a sack of big, juicy oranges!

That night was spent on top of a mountain. Turn-off roads were scarce and the one we chose was probably used for maintenance of a kind of radio-TV antenna, we guessed. Up too high for trees, the wind was strong and very cold. We drank a lot of wine to keep warm and I burned a hole in my sock from holding my feet too close to the lantern. We crawled into bed at nine to keep warm and soon fell asleep and slept for twelve hours like hibernating bears!

Slid down the mountain the next morning under a cloudless sky, but it didn't warm up until we were on the plains to Alicante. Just outside of Granada, we found an abandoned building that we were able to drive the whole rig into. There are many such structures in Spain--some of them fairly new. It seems that someone optimistically begins building a structure and then the money runs out. Or maybe the builders are shot. Or there's a plague. Qui sabe? They stand forlornly in fields and by the roads in Spain, a concrete floor, walls made of cement blocks sloppily mortared together and covered by a tile roof. Gypsies and other traveling people such as ourselves find them very convenient and as evidenced by the floor in that night's shelter, shepherds often bring their whole flocks in for the night. By this time, we had grown used to certain uh...seamier aspects of wild camping and were quite cozy as the wind whipped the sand around outside.

The Spanish poor have come up with some imaginative answers to the housing shortage. Even these abandoned places are do doubt owned by someone, so a family couldn't actually move in permanently and take up residence. And all the tillable land is generally owned by an hildago, or gentry, probably for generations, so the rest of the people who don't work for him have to find shelter in places that can't be worked, which isn't easy because even the fields that consist almost entirely of solid rock can sustain olive or almond trees.

So the Spanish peasants went to the cliffs and found caves to live in, and most curious of all, others even burrowed into the arid piles of dirt of the desert! Not like rabbits or prairie dogs exactly, but in mounds and hillets with windows and chimneys and front doors and steps. Whole communities, built not from the mud, but into the mud. Many were white-washed and some had tiles placed on the earth roof; and with the laundry flapping on the lines, and gaily painted pots of geraniums on the sills, the overall effect was absolutely inviting.

Up, up we rode, into the Sierra Nevada mountains. The original Sierra Nevada mountains! White, sugar-topped peaks with brave little villages perched on the crests. Over the other side, Granada lay below us like an enchanted city; a sea of tile roofs and church spires and, on its own special hill, the famous Moorish castle of the Alhambra. But the campgrounds were very expensive, and Terence and I knew we could not stay this time; maybe we could come back if we would be able to find jobs farther south.

I was extremely fortunate to have an aunt living on the Costa del Sol, and she had invited us to stay a while with her while we looked for jobs or regrouped or whatever, and we were on the way to her house in Fuen-girola. We had one day to go. That night, as we pulled the trailer and bikes into an olive grove, we celebrated our progress with meat for dinner for a change and some fruit drinks made with vodka left over from the Super-marcado in Tarragona. We were listening to the Allman Bros. playing lustily from the cassette on the Gold Wing and sipping our strong drinks like a couple of Plantation owners on the verandah, when somebody banged on the upturned roof of the trailer. Frightened, I put my mug down on the grass and Terence reached over to turn down the volume on the bike. Three elderly men, whom Terence was later to call the Polizia Pensionare, emerged from the shadows and demanded our passports. Terence's Spanish was pretty good by now, so he explained carefully about who we were and why we needed to spend the night in their olive grove. When they saw that we were Americans, they warmed up fast and turned out to be really sweet guys. Apparently they lived nearby and heard the music and were probably just curious as to what the hell had dropped into their neighborhood. I had visions of their wives pushing them down the road to find out. We really didn't have enough Spanish to sit around and chat with them, and they left laughing and waving good-bye soon after.

Chapter Sixteen

AN EXPERIENCE WE COULD HAVE DONE WITHOUT

WE WERE 8 kilometers out of Malaga when a spring broke under the trailer. We had been traveling at a good clip--maybe 50 mph-- and had just come onto a bridge; along with a few cars and a couple large trucks. Riding behind Terence as usual, I saw the trailer suddenly lean heavily to one side as if it had a flat tire and in the same instant, I could see the Gold Wing shaking out of control and Terence trying desperately to keep it from flipping over but the momentum and the weight of the rig was too much even for him, and with a horrible metallic scraping sound, I saw him disappear from my sight as the huge trailer rose over him and did a flip in the air before it fell heavily onto the pavement ahead. Terrified, I pulled my bike to the side of the bridge and ran to where Terence was lying with the massive, still-running motorcycle on top of him. Other drivers stopped all around us and people came running up to help. I seem to remember debris and bits of our trailer's contents still floating down from the sky as I knelt beside the Gold Wing. From somewhere under the machine, Terence ordered me to turn off the motor and get the bike off him. I was able to do the first and then a couple of men helped me with the Wing and no sooner was Terence standing than he was ordering all able-bodied hands to help him get the trailer off the road. The men told him it couldn't be done. It was a gigantic twisted piece of metal and plastic and we would have to wait for the Polizia. Terence seemed to check to see if his body was still intact and then he went down the street to the trailer and while we all thought he'd lost his mind in the accident, he moved that sucker all by himself over to the side of the bridge. The Spaniards looked at each other and shook their heads and turned back to their cars. At this point, I realized that all sorts of people had been silently coming up to me and tossing things at my feet. When I focused on the pile, I noticed it was a heap of small-sized shreds and pieces of our two years on the road. Stamps, coins, photographs, clothes, books--Whatever the wind was trying to blow off the bridge and into the river below. Larger things that the trailer had regurgitated, the kind folks had stacked at the sides of the road.

An English couple stopped and offered to call my aunt Daphne when they reached a phone. I took them up on it and told them to tell her to bring a trailer. Then suddenly everybody was gone. Swift passing traffic was crunching our last bits and pieces to powder or blowing things off the bridge to disappear over the edge. Terence was hurt after all; he thought something might be broken but we forced ourselves to think clearly. Two motorcycle policemen stopped and looked around at the mess and assessed the situation. They walked slowly to Terence, looking him over carefully. Terence told them brightly that no one was hurt and that there were no other people involved, and they appeared satisfied and left.

Three and a half hours later, Aunt Daphne appeared, bringing food and drink, but no trailer. Still it was wonderful to see her and things seemed to be looking up, when the dreaded Guarda Civil drove up in a patrol car. Terence swings into his "Everything is fine" act, and even tells them we're just waiting for the truck and they buy it and leave. We were very surprised that they weren't as scary as we'd heard, but decide perhaps they simply don't want to have to write a report. T. said he bet they could get plenty mean if they had a lot of paperwork to finish, especially for the American Consulate. While I stood guard over our pitiful possessions, Terence and Daphne drove off to find a phone to call a tow-truck.

Eleven hours after the time of the accident, a Spanish Gold-Winger appeared with a van. He was the only person in that part of Spain whose name appeared in our Gold Wing Owner's book and Terence had called him out of sheer desperation. His name was Angel Fernandez Sanchez. He came right from work and although he was expected home for dinner, he couldn't let his family know he would be hours late on this mission of mercy because they had no phone. Angel spoke both French and Spanish so we were able to converse and he went right to work helping us get the ruined trailer into the van. Then the men worked on the Gold Wing by the light of the van's headlights and miraculously were able to get it running so that Terence could ride it to the safe harbor at Daphne's home in Fuengirola.

We were a strange little convoy that dark night--Daphne in the lead, Angel in the Van, Terence hunched over, willing his battered bike to keep going, and me bringing up the rear on my trusty Ascot, the only piece of our little Gypsy train unscathed, purring along happily as if nothing had happened at all. We made it to Daphne's around one in the morning. The Gold Wing died a few times on the way and had to be resuscitated at the side of the road. The numbing shock Terence had experienced at the onset had worn off and he was in a lot of pain from various complaining areas, so Angel and I did most of the carrying of the torn pieces into Aunt Daphne's patio. When the last bit was dropped on the pile, we offered to pay Angel, but he would not accept payment, and because he was so eager to get home to his worried family, he also said no to Daphne's offer of food. We were almost speechless with gratitude and hugged him and promised to visit him soon in Malaga, where he lived. Indeed, the young man was well-named.

Our days of healing, sorting, jettisoning and repairing began. Terence decided he had nothing broken and the mean-looking bruises on his body turned from black to green and then faded away. Aunt Daphne was (and is) one of the kindest and most gracious people on earth. Realizing we were going to have to stay under her roof awhile if we were going to be able to get back on the road and finish the trip, she saw to it that we not only felt welcome, but absolutely indispensable to her well-being.

She found all sorts of little things that needed to be done or fixed around the house so that we could feel helpful, and when she left to visit her daughter in England for the Christmas holidays (The same Gigi Joly who had been so good to us when we were in London), she tossed us the keys to the place so that we could "house-sit" for her! A great lady.

While she was gone, Terence started studying again and I busied myself painting some french doors and sewing and repairing what I could from the accident. On Christmas day, we had been invited to a dinner party of Daphne's friends in Marbella. A sumptuous affair, in a home full of good cheer and surrounded by a very large golf course. We felt a little out of place, but everybody was nice to us and it certainly felt as if we'd never left the U.S.

Terence was beginning to show signs of despair about learning the Spanish language among all these Americans and British and when we returned to Daphne's house that night, he announced that if I wasn't going to speak only Spanish to him, he'd rather I didn't speak to him at all.

It was to be the first of many such declarations on the subject and because learning languages is very difficult for me, I really didn't know how to handle the situation. It occurred to me that even though I believed his great quest for knowledge of different languages was admirable, I wasn't sure how long I could last as his Sancho Panza. I stayed mute for a couple of days and then on New Year's Eve, we had it out and came to some sort of agreement, but it seemed a fragile truce at best...

Daphne was still in England, so T. and I thought it might be fun to see how the locals celebrate the coming of the New Year. We walked to the village square and Terence was delighted to see that there were few English speakers there for once. Free champagne was being passed out to anyone who could push their way through the dense crowd to the table and fireworks were going off all the time so the noise was deafening. Police stood at the edges of the square talking to each other and I wondered if they planned to do anything about the setting off of fire-crackers so near the revelers, but they seemed extremely relaxed about the mayhem. Perhaps they felt outnumbered. Later, a still-smoldering bit fell from the sky onto my hand; scaring the hell out of me for a moment, but I poured champagne on it and it stopped burning and soon I forgot all about it.

The clock on the tower showed midnight and we merry-makers kissed and hugged and cheered and went back for more champagne. The fellows manning the table earlier had disappeared and the cops had taken over-- big smiles on their faces and having a ball! The cute blonde lady cop posed amiably for my camera as she poured the bubbly into Terence's paper cup. Heaven is where the bartenders are Spanish police!

We were invited to a nearby Discotheque by a couple of Dutch folks and one Spaniard. Terence was thrilled to be at last talking Spanish, and the Dutch couple spoke English so I was enjoying myself too, as we pushed with the crowd into what seemed like a ghastly cacophony of electronic noise, sweeping searchlights and smoke--with everything painted in black, the walls, floor and furniture--and as if you weren't disoriented enough by the massive attack on your senses as you walked in, the diabolical designers had also raised or lowered the floor levels here and there in the darkness so that the mob could be further entertained by watching their friends and fellows trip and crash into the arms of strangers-- a great way to meet people, no doubt--and when it was my turn, those nearby must have been highly amused at my flailing and crashing as I tripped on the black stair to the black dance-floor. Only the hardy survive in such places. Or the very young. Certainly not the claustrophobic. By the time we'd had a couple of very odd drinks our new friends had generously bought for us, we were ready to go home. It was the smoke that got to Terence.

Chapter Seventeen

1989: SOUTH OF SPAIN

A FEW WEEKS LATER, we were still in Fuengirola, trying to repair the rig. Things had become more desperate as frustration and helplessness set in. Everything had to be done by hand. There was no money to buy new parts or pay body shop mechanics to fix old ones. Terence and I rode around the area looking for whatever--in junk-yards and used auto lots. Taking advantage of the Spanish habit of leaving cars in the ditch where they had died, so to speak, we picked them over for something he could use to rebuild the trailer. Of course, we were never the first to the scene. But we could use everything. We ripped out wires, horns, odd pieces of iron, springs, even tires when T. decided the ones on the trailer were too small for the monster it was becoming. He finally found someone who was willing to loan him a welding machine, but it turned out to be too weak for the job and he had to try to find another. Time whizzes by and so little was getting done. Every other day seems to be a holiday in Spain and I find myself wondering again how the nation's economy can stand it. The shops are closed every day from noon to four in the afternoon. Everything is wait, wait, and then it's not what we needed after all. In his frustration, Terence turned on me again, snarling about my lack of progress in learning Spanish along with him. We both said things we hadn't had time to think out beforehand. The problems were clear but the solutions not so. We felt trapped. Some painful truths were aired and we separated for awhile. I walked to the harbor; past the Fish and Chip joints we couldn't even afford to go into, and I hated the ugly little tourist town and felt very sorry for myself. Later we took a walk together and tried to act more grown-up. We reminded each other of the good things, and how much we both wanted this trip to work and how we needed each other in order to finish it. We realized that life isn't a script--written by somebody clever enough to make both of us say the right things at the same time and resolve our differences and arguments to perfection. All we could do, we decided, was try harder. Listen. Think. Talk. And listen again. Hug. Try harder.

After Daphne came home, it was another whirlwind of social events-- teas with British folks, cocktails with expatriate Americans and lavish parties with the International set. We celebrated Robert Burns's birthday with Daphne's Scottish friend and neighbor, Shelia, and the highlight of the afternoon was hearing the Selkirk Prayer softly spoken by a true Scot: "Some hae meat and canna eat...." Everyone seemed perishing for details about our trip. We told the same story over and over while being stuffed with the choicest tapas and finest wines and liqueurs. Not a bad life. We began gaining weight. Terence couldn't really complain. Although the language he was so desperate to learn was almost never heard, we did have fun at those things, and who knew how long it would be before we'd be so feted and fussed over again once we got back on the road. Thanks again to Daphne, I got some paying drawing jobs, and slowly the trailer began to take shape as well. A very LARGE shape. If it was illegal to pull in that country before, well....

It was almost February. We'd been in Fuengirola for a month and a half. We were anxious to get on the road. We packed up the Gold Wing for a look-see at the interior of the country. We left my bike and the monster trailer behind; just taking the pup-tent and some basics along. Who knew? We might even be lucky enough to meet some Spanish people along the way who might love to have us stay with them a night or two. We also figured that Daphne could use some peace and quiet for a bit...

We headed into the cold wind up past Mijas and over the ridge to the white mountain top village of Alora. Terence had to twist the motorcycle around several times trying to find the right road through the narrow maze to the top where the old Moorish castle ruins had been turned into the village cemetery--with the interesting scheme of stacking the coffins in the walls instead of putting them into the ground. A method, I understand, that came from the Romans. One or two old women were tending the graves; their black scarves whipping in the wind like the feathers of crows.

The road going back down through the village was little more than wet round rocks placed close together, and every other turn was a hair-pin; forcing poor Terence to use his feet as well as the brakes, to avoid crashing into several small children crowding the open doorways along the labyrinthine alleyways. At the bottom we emerged from the whitewashed shadows into a pastel sea of almond, orange and lemon groves. The glorious sight and smells filled us with a kind of bubble-bath euphoria. We both realized at that moment that we'd been too long away from the open road. This was why we'd come. Ahh yes!

Mossy aqueducts, crumbling farmhouses, goats in the road, and suddenly we found ourselves looking up at the amazing Charro Gorge; a dizzying collection of enormous rock slabs sometimes called the Eighth Wonder of the World (by the Spanish). We zig-zagged up the side of the huge rock pile and followed the little wooden signs to the "Ruinas" at the top, which turned out to be little more than some rocks lying around in no particular order that we could see. But the moon was rising and the light was fading and we pretended that the scattered stones may have indeed been a castle once, or maybe just a nice monastery whose ghosts might be tickled to have us pitch our tent on their holy turf as we sought protection from the night wind.

It was difficult to wake up the next morning. We'd grown soft at Daphne's. Aching cold and wind kept us awake most of the night and it wasn't until we were surrounded by the tinkling of tiny collar-bells that we stretched our necks from the tent flap to look around.

A profusion of goat faces greeted our astonished looks. Some of their jolly band had found our garbage bag with the orange peels inside and were gaily ripping it to shreds. We yanked on our boots and started shouting to scare them away and except for the lucky few still devouring the contents of the trash, most of the animals realized they were not welcome and took off.

I had just poured the last of the coffee when the Goatherd appeared. He was ancient and toothless and extremely dirty--even compared to the goats--and as he came toward our camp stove, he made a gesture that seemed to say we were to share our breakfast with him. All I had left was some chocolate which I gave him, but as he turned slowly to look at the motorcycle and then back at us, he made it fairly clear that he expected more from two rich Americans. It was not a pleasant moment. Just then I noticed a couple of his goats had gotten inside the tent and as I angrily shooed them out, the old man turned and followed them and T. and I breathed a great sigh of relief.

For the next few days, we rode through the almond groves and white towns, the pueblos blancos of Andalusia. It was still February and blustery and cold. There were no shops in the small villages; we learned to ask someone in the street to point out the bakery--usually just an unmarked doorway--and they always seemed to have one or two loaves left. Terence and I agreed that it was the best bread in Spain. At night there seemed to be plenty of abandoned and crumbling farmhouses with enough roof left to shelter us from the rain and wind. Sometimes the ruins of the stables looked better than the ruins of the houses, but always, whether in house or stable, the same sort of signs appeared that other folks and other flocks had been there before us.

Surreal landscape rolled by as we traveled from Grazalema to Ubrique. Rock formations so vast around us that I felt we'd shrunk to half size. Few trees, but the winter rains had caused little waterfalls to trickle from the moonscape and form icy pools and tiny silver streams below us. I sat on the back of the big motorcycle and wondered at what a perfect serendipity Spain was. And to think that many visitors never get beyond the Costa del Sol! No wonder people at home have the wrong idea of this country. The beauty that lies within!

Nearing Jimena de la Frontera we could see the first glimmer of spring in the bright blue crocuses between the cracks of the stones. Soon they were joined by purple wild irises and now and then a clump of fragrant white narcissus. Euridice had come back to earth from Hades. We passed an abandoned and rusted old automobile and Terence pulled over for picture-taking. Two black goats were inside; one of them was peering out of the passenger window, looking for all the world like he was ready to be chauffeured somewhere. We had seen goats so often on this trip; not only as herds to be passed in the road, but on roofs, munching the weeds growing between the tiles, on balconies, on door-steps. No doubt very important members of the family.

The sun came out as we rode into Jimena de la Frontera but the streets were still slippery from the mud, so Terence rode cautiously up the grade to yet another Moorish fortress at the top. This one was largely intact and it was a pretty picture indeed, with a very white donkey tethered to an almond tree in bloom on the grass in

front of the castle. After so many
gray days, the sunshine was new to our camera's eye, and the blaze of
white, pink and green caused us to rather over-do the donkey shots, I'm
afraid, but we were to be forgiven as we were so starved for color in the
last few days.

We were able to buy beer and some canned food in a shop before
leaving town. Riding through the dusk, we noticed the land on both sides
of the road was largely under water from the recent rains and even though
we passed an occasional cork tree grove, there were no cozy ruins to camp
in. We were getting close to the crowded Costa del Sol again and although
we had learned that the Spanish were extremely tolerant of people
spending the night on their land, privacy was what we sought more than
anything. Someplace away from the stares of little boys, and where I could
bend over the camp stove and not feel gawked at by the women who
seemed to be wondering what someone dressed as oddly as I could
possibly be feeding my man.

It had grown dark. Terence decided to take a steep dirt road to a cork
tree grove at the crest of a soggy hill. I hung on for dear life as the bike
lurched over some railroad tracks and slid its way up the slimy hill and
into the trees. We'd have never made that distance with the trailer! At least
we'd be safe from the flood below if it rained all night. Groping about in
the blackness, we set up the little tent and crawled in.

As we looked around our camp site the next morning, we discovered
we were in a beautiful spot. Cork trees look a lot like California Scrub
Oaks and I felt right at home. The cork bark is harvested just to the
"elbows" of the trees, and the exposed area becomes sepia brown so that
the shapes around us resembled dark-skinned beings struggling into thick
gray-green sweaters. A comical and comforting sight.

I had read that the dictator General Franco, in his infinite wisdom, had
moved people completely out of their villages in several areas of Spain and
relocated them into newly built housing--for reasons perhaps beneficial to
the people, perhaps not. You'd have to ask the people. In any case, the
mountain village of Castellar de la Frontera is one such place and because
of its gorgeous location--a pine-clad mountain-top stroked lovingly by
Mediterranean breezes, it was not long after Franco's demise that word
spread--especially among the foreign hippie population; mostly from
Germany--that digs could be had for free and no one would be around to
bother them. So the more enterprising of the lot--primarily artist types--
took up residence there; leaving their psychedelicly painted vans scattered

around the outskirts of town like so many Peter Max posters, and blazed their colorful trail into town with drug-induced graffiti along the once pure-white walls of the village and on up to their lofts, where they probably shared checks from home along with their smokes and wine until some of them actually began producing some sellable stuff to the tourists who began to hear about another Place to See.

After a while, some of the original owners came back and things weren't free anymore, and then rich folks decided to get in on it and I understand from Aunt Daphne, even Lew Hoad had a place up there. Oh well. It's still far enough away from Gibraltar and the coast that most foreigners wouldn't be interested. After all, how can one put a golf course on a mountain top?

Terence and I got a real kick out of it. A lot of imagination was shown by those kids. It was a true culture shock to see a modern stained-glass window, for instance, glowing from an ancient stucco wall, or several large metal sculptures with, shall we say, truly secular themes placed along the pathways. Some of the mural paintings were pretty awful and must have embarrassed the natives, but I can imagine, as a painter myself, how tempting all those white walls must have been to the squatters on a boring afternoon... Of course, with the infusion of serious money, the village will no doubt begin cleaning up its act and become more respectable. Too bad.

Heading for Gibraltar, we spotted our first storks, which made us screech to a halt to take pictures. They were two handsome adults setting up house-keeping on a giant nest atop a chimney. The white stucco farmhouse below them seemed empty and the nest looked old, so we guessed they knew what they were doing. How beautiful they were. Snowy white and black, they danced around the nest and clacked to each other. The sound they make is very much like two sticks being struck together. When one flew from the nest, it might have been the Concorde, we were so thrilled by its sheer size and grace. We felt honored to have witnessed such a sight.

Gibraltar was crowded and noisy and took awhile getting used to, after the peace and quiet of the Spanish countryside. We crawled along with all the other tourist traffic; adding our own nasty bit of noise and pollution between the tightly-packed shops and houses that bordered the main street of the little British enclave. The signs were in both languages and the faces were a colorful mix of races; reminding us that this was a major stopping-off place for North Africa as well as the great gate between the Atlantic and the Mediterranean Sea, and it occurred to me that it was a terribly small place to have all that history and notoriety, and naturally everybody wants a piece of that particular "rock," and the Spanish, upon whose land it clings, must be properly pissed that it's not theirs.

We bought fish and chips..YUM..and then indulged in over-spending in the supermarket; buying cheddar cheese and dark beer and ground beef and all sorts of English things we'd been longing for, and then we hauled some large boxes we'd put together the night before, to the post office. We knew the mailing prices would be much lower here on Gibraltar than in Spain, and so we were getting rid of lots of heavy things like T's early law books and our two-year collection of photographs and slides, plus most of my ink drawings to keep them safe at my sister's house in California.

After a nightmare at the post office, of going back and forth to different windows and standing in long lines and then having to sit on the floor and cut up our boxes with our Swiss Army knives and take things out because the weight wasn't right--I felt sure we had to be on "Candid Camera"--we finally were able to get rid of the blasted things and walk back to the motorcycle.

Terence looked for the "beeper" he always sets when we had to leave the machine for any length of time, and he couldn't find it. It was his security system for the bike. If anyone tried to break into the big metal box on the back (where he always carried his viola) or the bike itself, an alarm would sound on the beeper he carried with him. And he had left it somewhere! If he had left it by mistake--and armed--inside one of the metal boxes on the bike, and we unlocked them to look for it, it would automatically go off, which would be O.K. if it was indeed on the bike somewhere. But if (and this was the unthinkable), the beeper had been left at the Post Office and went off, all hell would break loose. Just the last week, the British had shot three members of the Irish Republican Army right down the street from where we were standing because they suspected them of planning a bomb attack! And here we were looking to all the world like a couple of motley members of some leather-jacketed clan who would leave a bomb at the Post as sure as we'd drop one in the lap of our poor old mum! OHMYGOD! If the damn thing went off inside one of our packages, we could be sure they'd be thrown--slides, drawings and all--into the nearest vat of water for that very purpose!

While I stood shaking by the bike, Terence ran with all haste back to the Post Office. I remember wondering if he'd come back alive and if not, how the heck could I get the monster bike out of Gibraltar by myself?

No shots nor sirens later, himself jogs down the road with a big grin on his face and the crisis is averted. One of the postal clerks had seen it on the counter and deciding it was not a bomb (Saints be praised), put it under the counter to wait for its owner. Luckily, we hadn't set it off!

February 21st, our two-year anniversary away from home! We were back at Aunt Daphne's. Terence woke me up with champagne, flowers, and a wonderful card in Esperanto. Feeling rather beholden, I sat still for a long study-session led by Professor Geoghegan, because we were to ride to Malaga in the evening for our first Esperanto class. Actually, the classes were rather a pleasant experience. Apparently the Spanish Railroad people believed Esperanto was the answer to the language problems they were having as their trains crossed borders, and of course they were right. So they were giving classes and anybody was welcome. Naturally, no English was spoken so it was a little tricky for me, but Terence just zoomed, and then at home he would drill me and to my horror, I began to realize I was thicker than I thought when it came to language. For some reason, although I could recite Shakespeare learned in High School thirty years before, or sing all the lyrics to a patter song by Danny Kaye I had heard when I was ten, I couldn't remember a verb tense for Terence three minutes after he'd repeated it for me. I began to feel old and stupid and panicky. Terence began to lose his temper. I tried not to think of him as Torquemada, but it was hard.

Meanwhile, we were waiting for the rain to stop again. This time we were going to give the rebuilt trailer a test run behind the Gold Wing--and pull it to Granada. To save money on gas, I would again be leaving my bike at Daphne's and riding pillion behind Terence. Finally, the sky cleared and although the cold wind was fierce, he said the trailer felt good behind him, so off we rode. We took a slightly different route than the one on which we had our accident, and going through Malaga, we stopped to visit our Angel at work. He seemed a little embarrassed at our fawning over him and presenting him with a couple of small gifts, but good Lord, what would we have done without him that day? He said he'd do it for any Gold Winger!

On the hills behind Malaga we looked back to view the panorama of high-rise bunker-type apartments marching to the Mediterranean. It looked as if it might have been Miami...or Chicago...

The wind became mean. We ate our bread and cheese standing behind the trailer for shelter as tiny drops of rain began to sting our faces. On a ridge high above two valleys, we found a gas station and were, for a few minutes, sheltered from the gale. So long in the lap of luxury at Daphne's,

I'd become soft and, to use one of Terence's favorite terms, wimpy, and wanted to stay at the little gas station until the wind died down. I'd noticed that the trailer was much higher now with the bigger tires T. had found on some abandoned car weeks before, and it just seemed a lot more dangerous. Silly me. Terence said he felt comfortable pulling it, and anyway the wind wasn't going to die down for days and so end of discussion...

As we veered around the narrow road, I wondered why in the world didn't the Spanish harness this incredible gift of nature. Surely its force could provide enough electricity to light up the whole city of Malaga at least. Maybe the whole coast. Fortunately, when we curved down the north side of the mountain into the valley, the gusts weren't nearly so scary, and we both began to relax and enjoy the scenery. And what scenery it was! The almonds were in full bloom. And all sorts of other fruit trees, too. Pink, white and with a delicate scent of apple blossoms. The petals blew across the road like snow flurries and when the view wasn't of endless hills of flowering orchards, it was the gray-green of olive trees, polka-dotting the landscape--sometimes standing in brick-red earth, or twisting in uneven rows and pushing from the inhospitable white marble where nothing else could grow. Way to go, olive trees!

We camped in a small, man-planted pine forest whose floor was covered with pine needles and the trash of previous wayfarers. The storm raged, but the trees protected us enough so that we could manage putting up our tent, and we lashed everything we could around the trunks so that we wouldn't blow away in the night. The thin walls of our tent sucked inward and slapped outward and stretched until we thought something would tear for sure, and then all four sides would billow out like a balloon and we hugged each other and laughed and wondered if it was ever going to stop.

It kept up all night and into the morning. Braving the storm for the call of nature, I marveled at the drama of it all. The tops of the trees swayed and swished and between the even rows I could see the low clouds bounce around and once in a while they'd part company and let the glorious sun shine through; spots of molten gold on the limbs and in puddles at my feet. I ran back to the tent to tell Terence to look. "Look how nice it can be!," I cried. "Maybe in Scandinavia," he said.

We spent two days in Granada. As we sloshed around the magnificent Moorish fortresses and gardens of the Alhambra, the weather was still being theatrical--dark, rainy and cold for a bit and then teasing as soon as we'd put away our cameras. Now and then, the emerging sun lit up the Alcazaba spectacularly. A lavish Opera set--arches and mosaics and tiled pools glistening in the capricious sunlight, and high above, the sheer mind-bending beauty of the Sierra Nevada mountains, turning gold and rose-red when the heavenly spotlight beamed on their snowy slopes. Then, as if God had left the light booth, they would immediately become just a somber gray backdrop again, for the ongoing spectacle of the amazing Alhambra.

On the way out of the city to Cordoba, we visited the Cartuja, a Carthusian monastery highly recommended by our faithful Rough Guides book. A well-kept secret from most visitors to the city, the chapel holds some of the most decorated interiors of the Baroque period in the world. The twisted and carved marble columns around the altar are worth the visit alone, and Terence was happy as a kid in a sandbox as he rolled around the cold marble floors shooting rolls of film of the fantastically ornate ceilings and writhing carved angels and fat putti and worshipping marble monks below.

No sooner did I put black and white film in my camera than the sun came out to stay awhile! Rolling into the municipal campsite of Cordoba, we realized we'd have to put a balm on our new sunburn! While we set up camp, we met a nice young British couple who were standing and eating their lunch which had been spread on the seat of their BMW motorcycle. They told us they too, were seeing the world, and had been gone from England for about a year and planned to keep on the road until their money finally ran out. We looked behind them to the tiny pup-tent that was their home. And we had thought we were roughing it!

We got some wild and wonderful shots of things Moorish and Christian in the Mezquita, the grandest mosque ever constructed by the Moors in Spain. Very, very sad to see the results of mindless destruction of all that splendid Moorish architecture--in favor of a misdirected attempt to bring the "true" faith to the citizens of Cordoba by yanking down the minarets and towers and many of the splendidly carved and mosaic arches. And then planting a squatty cathedral in the center, and draping morose carved images everywhere, which gaze forlornly at the heavens or weep or hang on the cross forever dying. Fat plaster cherubs now cover some once-proud and exquisite Moorish tracery over the arches. Just obese brats--defying the law of gravity.

We visited the old Jewish quarter. More cruelty and stupidity on the part of the majority. Stories it's hard to read about, but important to know because we wanted to learn everything about this country that we could possibly soak up in our short time here.

We walked over the bridge built on Roman foundations--so many vistas begging to be filmed. We ate our lunch by a crumbled old mill next to the river. A gypsy family ate theirs across the road from us. The sun baked us all and it felt wonderful.

In the garden of the Alcazar, we watched as a group of rather well-endowed matrons stopped their walk on the path, put down their shopping bags and began to clap. Someone began to sing in a kind of high-pitched flamenco wail and one by one they would hand their purse to another and take off a sweater or jacket and began to dance! Not a fast dance, but arms up and heads down or to the side...snapping fingers and stamping high-heels..twirl around and yelp! Wonderful stuff! We were enchanted. Proud faces flushed and shiny, ample bodies twisting in tight blouses and skirts. After a bit they stopped, and laughing, picked up their wraps and purses and carried on down the path, all talking at once. Enjoying life.

We came back to Fuengirola and Aunt Daphne's for one more week to put ourselves together for the big push out of Spain and into Portugal. Our generous hostess was on a cruise, teaching bridge classes, so there was nobody to say good-bye to as we locked the door behind us and pulled away from the safest harbor we'd ever had.

In no hurry, we wound our way slowly up the mountains out of Marbella and stopped at the base of Casares, another pueblo blanco muy famosa for its weathered charm, and yet another ruined castle at the top. We left the Gold Wing and trailer in a sort of lay-by and packed our bread and cheese into my bike's saddle-bags and rode to the top of the village where what was left of the castle stood in the wind. The view of the valley below took our breath away. We sat in the rubble to carve ourselves a piece of cheese and checked out the strange structures around us. At one time in the long ago of this village's colorful past, a small but sturdy church had been erected over the ruins of what was probably originally a Moorish fortress, and now the church itself was going the way of all flesh. Two of its walls had caved in and it looked unsafe to enter--even for goats! High at the top was an odd-looking cross, we thought, until on further inspection, we realized it was not a cross at all but a big TV antenna! It probably served the whole little village. Terence, munching on a hunk of bread, said "It must be the Church of the Immaculate Reception."

For the next two days as we rode west, I seem to remember a blur of white villages and waving people. Women stopped hanging the wash on the line on top of their roofs to stare down at us, tiny old widows in black stood in their doorways and smiled toothless grins, and men and children waved and cheered. Their eyes grew wide as they realized the bike following Terence had a female driver. They'd laugh and shout encouragement. So friendly. Always a feeling that we were welcome, and that our passing-by just might be giving them the same joy as we were receiving.

In between the villages were great expanses of lush green. No orchards, almost no trees at all--just rolling hills of what looked like unripened grain--the bread belt. About an hour before we'd be in Seville, we spotted a huge cathedral rising out of the mist. A small sad-looking village needed to be threaded through to get to it. We drove around a maze of narrow streets between sand-colored houses to try to find it but just kept getting hopelessly lost. The old men sitting in front of the hovels chuckled at our predicament. Finally we found the right road and we were parking the two bikes when a tour bus stopped a few feet away and disgorged its passengers, who were all carrying bouquets of flowers. They seemed to be a mixture of nationalities, and a German lady who spoke English explained to us that their destination was not the huge old church but a new chapel which had just been built beyond it. They were pilgrims of a sort, and today they were going to consecrate the new chapel and expected none less than Christ himself and his mother, Mary, to appear! Wow. That's faith.

Terence and I figured we really weren't dressed for such an occasion, so we simply tried to find a way into the big old Baroque building which had apparently been the pilgrims' previous place of worship for centuries, but we couldn't get anybody to let us in. An elderly gentlemen who was part of the group walking to the new chapel told us in Spanish that the story was that the last priest of the cathedral had been de-frocked--because he had become a "seer" who had gone wrong. And so now, apparently, his church was no longer "hallowed ground," and no one was allowed to go in to worship anymore. So, we supposed, the grand old building would be left to stand alone for a few more centuries, desecrated and ignored, until some earth tremor or other force of nature leveled it to the ground. Dust unto dust.

We adored Sevilla. Who wouldn't? It was getting close to the marvelous madness of Easter Holy Week (Semana Santa) and the stores were showing off how beautiful the Fiesta dresses would be and there were flowers everywhere and the excitement was infectious. Handsomely dressed and coifed women whistled and called to Terence without embarrassment--all in good fun--and he thought he'd died and gone to heaven. We were in the city of Bizet's Carmen, and the air was full of castanets.

The real gypsies, however, were slightly less wonderful. Accosted by fat and frightening-looking gypsy women selling carnations outside the cathedral, Terence came close to socking one hefty dame right in the kisser. They were not friendly, they did not sing, and their aggressiveness was unbelievable. We must have looked like the perfect "marks" with our cameras swinging from our necks, and one of the larger women simply would not take "no" for an answer. After she had shoved her wilted flower into his chest for the umpteenth time, he drew back and I think really meant to slug her. At least she thought so and it seemed to be something she could understand, because she finally turned away and sat on the steps glaring like a doused cat.

Another day was spent visiting the Plaza de Espana and Maria Luisa park, where the swirl of green and blue tiles were all hand-painted, and the small boys in their designer-jogging suits all decided at once to dance to the same beat as their female cousins in the park in Cordoba. I would have loved to see the faces of American children as they watched these eight year-olds twirl and stamp and clap their small hands to the beat. They knew we were standing a few feet away with our cameras pointed rudely in their direction and they simply didn't care. We were very impressed.

Leaving such a fabulous place wasn't easy and we felt ashamed not giving it the time it deserved, but a whole new country was waiting for us at the end of the day and so after sharing our breakfast coffee with a charming young French biker named Jacques, we pulled our little wagon train out of the campground and headed toward the border.

Chapter Eighteen

PORTUGAL

THE TRAILER SWAYED BACK and forth in front of me in the wind and I hung back on my bike, wondering if it was going to break free and come flying back toward me. It looked enormous. I became aware of what looked like strawberries, lying in heaps all over the side of the road. They must have fallen off some donkey or truck and would be marvelous for dessert if I could find a place to clean them. I stopped and put some gently into my tank-bag and then made tracks to catch up with the wobbling trailer.

We caught the ferry at the river border that afternoon. Nobody seemed to mind how much space we took with the rig; even though we seemed to be rather forcing folks to hang on the rails. The fare was cheap and the Spanish ferrymen friendly, so we were a little surprised to see the dour looks of the custom officers at the Portuguese dock. Maybe the Spanish were just happy to get rid of us and get that beast off their roads! And the Portuguese police were now facing the uncomfortable decision about letting us in or not to muck up their lives with that ridiculously large monstrosity we were rolling off the boat.

The stiff, uniformed fellow in charge waved me through after our passports were checked, and then told Terence to stop and open the trailer side boxes for inspection. It was obvious he was looking for drugs. The one he pointed to first was my "kitchen," and Terence obliged, feeling a little uncomfortable because he hadn't learned any Portuguese yet and his

Spanish was being met with complete disgust by the surrounding uniforms.

The Inspector General peered at my cooking utensils without touching them. I was fairly certain I had flunked the white glove test, and then he spotted the box of seasonings. Aha! The old cocaine-in-the-curry-jar trick! Now he had us! He straightened up, looked at each of his men as if to say, "Now watch this," and proceeded to put his nose in the jar and inhaled vigorously. They had to peel him from the ceiling. Fortunately, for us, an underling waved for us to get the hell out of there while he was occupied coughing and sneezing, and we took his advice and sped into the street and outta town!

We arrived in the late afternoon at the Monte Gordo Campground, Portugal. I made a superb entrance as usual, as my right food dropped into a hole I didn't see and the Ascot and I fell over right in front of the Registration Office. So much for the ol' "Born and Bred on a Motorcycle" act I always try to aspire to when we first get to a campground and everybody is gawking. Terence had to come over of course and help me pick up the damn thing. One wants to die...

The strawberries I'd found by the side of the road were divine that evening. A last taste of one of the most beautiful countries in the world. And one we were swearing we'd see again. The camping "Park" at Monte Gordo was full of northern Europeans who seemed to live there at least several months of the year. I could see why. The people were tan and relaxed and they had lots of their countrymen around. The local stores were cheap beyond belief, although there wasn't much in the way of variety. Someone sold marvelous fresh bread and rolls in a shop on the premises each morning and the Atlantic Ocean lapped gently on the white sandy beach just across the road. Terence studied, I read and drew and took walks and one afternoon we took a look at a local fortress ruin that had a stork as a mascot; a very pompous and self-important bird, and obviously well-loved.

Time to move on and the next stop was Faro, an island-sand spit sort of campground with no trees to buffet the wind and therefore not too popular and therefore super-cheap, so it got no complaints from us. Well, none at least until we'd been there a couple of nights and the heavens opened and I though we were going to be swept away in the night!

We had had a lovely dinner with Desmond and Irene Tamaki, an American couple in a minivan whom we had had the very good fortune to meet that afternoon and discovered to our complete delight, that we had practically everything in common and best yet, we were probably going to be able to meet up with them again in Lisbon. I have to say...rarely did we meet two people on the road that we felt so close to so fast. Well, I was talking about the storm.

Terence had partied heartily with our new friends. A volatile mix of rum, beer and wine had pretty much rendered him unconscious for the duration of the night. As the wind howled around the quaking tent and the rain fell like bullets, I tried several times to waken him to help me batten down the hatches, but without success. I slipped and sloshed my way around the trailer trying to tie down the flapping tarp and prop up the bikes well enough so we wouldn't find them on their sides in the morning--their life's blood trickling away into the sand and no gasoline for miles. After chasing my tail in panic for awhile, I decided there was nothing more I could do. If the wind tore our puny shelter to shreds, so be it. I crawled soaking wet into our bed next to old Rip Van Winkle and dozed off.

We awoke to a blinding sun against a cobalt blue sky. Hard to believe. Terence was properly apologetic about being no help during the storm. We got up and bailed out and hung up everything that was wet--and that was everything--to dry in the warm and welcome sunshine and went over to the Tamaki's for coffee. They kept house in a nice VW van they'd bought in Amsterdam and planned to sell when their two-year trip was finished. They also had a puppy with them that kept them busy. As we four sipped and swapped stories--they'd been on the road for several months--the dark clouds began to gather once more and the wind picked up. The Tamakis decided to pack up and move inland to a less windy campground, but as we didn't fancy riding in the storm, we opted for spending another night on the island. We had time to tie things down properly this time and the gale that night didn't bother us much. In the morning we grabbed what we could between squalls and rode off the island to try our luck at Portomao.

We should have known. A very popular seaside resort for tourists, the camping prices were astronomical and we had to move inland, where few tourists dare to roam.

The journey up to Lisbon was slow going. We found it difficult to believe we were using the main road to Lisbon. Very few other vehicles, mostly families. Papa would be driving a three-wheeled sort of motor-scooter, with mom and the kids squished into a tiny box behind him. At one point, the road went into an eucalyptus forest and became little better than a muddy trail. If a car came from the opposite direction, someone would have to pull off the road and into the trees to let the other pass. Guess who usually did the honors. Spanish drivers had been perfect gentlemen and ladies compared to these Portuguese machismos behind the wheel.

At one point along the way, we had just taken a turn on a nice wide part of the highway, when we were suddenly faced with a sight that made us both brake sharply and pull over to the shoulder. Twelve-foot long logs were strewn all over the road like Jack Straws! If Terence had been day-dreaming, he might not have been able to avoid them. We were both shaking when we climbed off the bikes. We ran to roll and lift them off the road as quickly as we were able so that motorists coming around that bend at high speed wouldn't kill themselves. We had just made a narrow path through the logs when the first car came from the opposite direction. The driver looked out his window. He slowed to watch us for awhile. Then he drove on. So did the next guy. And the next. No smiles. No help. A few miles on, we passed the truck that had dropped the logs. The driver was standing on the shoulder looking helpless. Our Portuguese was not suffi-cient to tell him what we were thinking.

Sines, a fishing village but savvy about tourists, boasted a super-clean campground among the pines and while the sun shone, we rested and repaired things. Terence worked out with his Taekwon-Do patterns and played his viola among the pine trees and it was all very pleasant. But we were beginning to wonder what was going on in the world. Newspapers were all in Portuguese and even they didn't seem to have much news beyond Portugal. We felt as if we were on another planet. I had had so little news from home in so long I was beginning to suspect something was wrong. Terence told me I worried too much, and of course the worrying didn't change anything so I tried to put it out of my mind.

The long day's journey north from Sines included a stop at a Honda motorcycle place in Setubal, a fairly large city a few miles south of Lisbon. My bike needed a bulb and Terence's needed fuses. We were so relieved to see all the motorcycles outside. Civilization at last. Dream on! The apolo-getic mechanic said the bulbs were on order (for how long?), and as for Terence's fuse problem, the man grabbed the scotch tape and went out to the Gold Wing, his entourage of wanna-be great mechanics--following close behind. As he bent down to tape something, I noticed his cigarette coming dangerously close to T's gas tank and moved far away. That gesture seemed to make the guys more comfortable, I noticed, and as

Terence was practicing his Portuguese, he was in no hurry to leave the company of his macho brothers. I began to realize rather sadly, that Portuguese men were certainly not like the Spanish, who would have welcomed me warmly in their greasy garages and introduced me to their wives and children as an interesting person to know.

Trying to find an open campground near Lisbon was an exhausting exercise in futility. Our Portuguese book on campgrounds was absolutely useless because every one mentioned, was either closed or had disappeared without a trace. We were hungry, tired and desperate. Trying to find one near the river Tejo across from the city, we missed the turn-off and found ourselves being sucked into the rush-hour traffic going onto to the huge suspension bridge over the river to the city. Realizing his mistake, Terence pulled over into the center divider to stop and think while I, with the panic of Bambi in the forest fire, wobbled over two fast-moving lanes and stopped traffic in trying to follow him. Horns honked from all around me and the angry drivers cursed and spat at me and of course they had good reason. To this day I do not know how I survived the experience. All I could think of at the moment was that if I stayed in the lane I was in, I would be swept over the bridge without Terence and if I made it without being killed, he would never find me. I had no business being on a motorcycle at that time; I should have been in a padded cell. And the drivers of Lisbon would agree.

Terence was furious. Of course seeing my death dance across the stream of traffic must have taken its toll on his nerves, too. After he cursed me for my stupidity, I believe I gave him an appropriate gesture with one gloved finger which caused him to turn around and start his engine and take off across the bridge without another word which was just fine with me except there I was, stopped in the middle; with the maddened motorists going both ways past me with hostile glares that seemed to say "Don't even think about it, woman!" I had to think about it, though. I bent my head to listen to my heart beat and breathed deeply. Then I looked at my instrument panel to remind myself I was indeed in command of a machine that was simply waiting to be told what to do, and then I did it. I waited for a sympathetic driver to slow up after I signaled and went for it and onto the swaying bridge. Ah yes. I hadn't had so much fun since that thrilling hurricane on the suspension bridge over the Loire in '87. The road surface on the bridge consisted of slippery metal slats that moved noisily as my tires bumped over them. There were spaces between each slat and I could see the river way down below through them. The wind coming up through the spaces made a moaning sound that made me feel as though I was riding over graves! I felt my stomach knotting and to avoid nausea I tried to concentrate on the car in front of me. The turbulent wind on the high bridge was very cold and as I was shaking uncontrollably anyway, staying upright in the bumper to bumper traffic took tremendous effort, but I had no choice.

I saw Terence too late through the exhaust fumes--waiting for me on the first off-ramp--and I pulled over to a screeching halt just past the turn off. He left the rig and walked over to me and decided to push me back to the ramp. No easy task because I was facing downhill and was still numb with fear, but we made it and with a break in the traffic I was able to maneuver the bike to a spot behind the trailer and while horns blew in annoyance, we tried to decide what to do next. Against my fervent prayers, T. announced that we had to go back and look for that campground! Oh well, at least I'd be behind him this time and with him running interference, it wouldn't be too bad. We finally found a place to turn around in downtown Lisbon(!) and got back on the moaning wind machine. Still no picnic, I felt better when I thought about how it must have been for Terence--pulling our unwieldy trailer over that ghastly surface in the high wind. Noo thanks! Heading south, we had to pay a toll at the end! One hundred and twenty escudos for risking our lives!! Criminal.

The campground was closed for the season...

Back over the bridge. Never mind that it seemed to be getting easier. I decided the whole thing was a vicious plot and SOMEONE WOULD PAY FOR THIS!!!

The Lisboa municipal campground was expensive--compared to all the other ones listed in the book, but it did have the distinct advantage of being the only one open. It was huge and full of campers from everywhere. We pulled our rig under some pines and still badly shaken from the bridge experience, I drank too much cheap wine and ruined the dinner by mistaking ginger for garlic powder in the dark and couldn't eat it. Terence however, was full of compliments about the gingery dinner, but then he's crazy.

Sometime in the night I became very sick. I crawled over Terence and noticed that my right arm was completely numb. No amount of shaking could wake it up and I had the thought that I might be dying. Crouched out there in the light rain, I began to think maybe somebody ought to call a doctor and wished I'd written a will. After I had sullied more than a few pine needles, I felt OK enough to crawl back into bed with one arm. As I lay there, the possibility of a Portuguese doctor coming to the campground in the middle of the night and taking my pulse through the tent flaps seemed remote as hell. So I went back to sleep, dreaming of gory accidents.

Felt much improved in the morning. After a ride into the city--the two of us on the small bike, we tried to get all sorts of things taken care of, but it wasn't easy. First T. tried to find a darkroom--even begged at the University and the city newspaper offices, but there was none to be had, so our black and white film had to stay undeveloped. Then it was other things-- electronic parts, information, maps, unleaded gas for the camp stove--we had a long list and each item was met with failure. And this was the nation's capital! We knew there would be no other place in Portugal where we could do any better. Very frustrating. At least we found the Taekwon-Do studio active. While he worked out with the guys and dutifully studied the language, I found the American Library in the center of town and gobbled up the latest newspapers and magazines in English.

I picked him up at eight o'clock, and he'd made a new friend named Jose who spoke English pretty well and wanted to take us for a beer and then home for dinner! Sounded good to us, so after Jose and another guy got in a taxi, we got on my bike and followed. It seemed they either wanted to show off by showing us how fast their taxis could go, or they just wanted to see how fast the Ascot could go, or maybe they were simply on a testosterone high from the studio work-out, but Terence was definitely put to the test in keeping up with the racing cab. My poor motorcycle screamed under us as we flew over the ruts and tram tracks and cobblestones of the congested streets to keep up. I was hardly amused as I hung on for dear life and once, as the taxi--with us on its tail--sped through a red light, I decided it was all over and kept my eyes shut for the rest of the horrible ride. After an eternity, we hit the outskirts of the city and suddenly there were no more paved roads and the going was truly uncomfortable, and then all at once we were in front of Jose's apartment and amazingly still alive.

Not surprisingly, Jose's wife had not been informed of the two Americans coming to dinner and even without understanding the language, the meaning of her reaction was clear. No problem, Jose and a new friend, Carlos, would take us to the local restaurant. Backing out at this point seemed out of the question. The happy couple plus their four-year old daughter and Carlos and the other man from the studio led on through the mud-filled alleyways smelling of sewer, and T. and I, like sheep, followed.

It was eleven p.m. when we knocked on the door of the local Bar and Grill-type place, and the cook seemed about as thrilled to cook for us as the wife had been. She told Jose she hated the English and wouldn't serve them. Jose explained we were not English, but Americans. She scrutinized us, plainly not liking what she saw and said we sounded English and it was the same thing. I believe her husband, our host, may have said something to the effect that Americans have a reputation for being dumb enough to tip lavishly, because all of a sudden she was convinced, and if not any sweeter, at least able to come up with a very welcome dish of fried potatoes and eggs, and with the addition of a couple of bottles of the red "Tinto," we were all satisfied, indeed.

After dropping off the poor wife who hadn't looked very happy all evening (I wish I could have talked to her), the fellows wanted to take us to another bar down the street. Booze was delightfully cheap, so T. and I were able to buy a few rounds. During the course of the conversation, our friends became a bit maudlin and confessed about how much they wanted to be in America--the land of dreams. We were to hear the plaintive cry many times before returning home, but this was the first and it made us pretty uncomfortable. The men told us how they despised their poverty but didn't know what to do about it. I felt guilty when I thought about how much I possessed. Here I was, trotting around the world on a motorcycle I thought was a piece of junk, and to the young men, it was an incredible piece of machinery they could never hope to possess. And they thought it belonged to Terence. We didn't tell them about the Gold Wing back at the campsite. Somehow it seemed obscene.

We stayed about ten days in Lisbon. Terence taught some classes at the Taekwon-Do studio and I did a lot of walking around the various barrios and up to the castle and along the harbor. The museums were free on Sunday so we whipped around to the juiciest ones and saw some fabulous stuff. All the monuments around town seemed to be of Henry the Navigator. A big moment in their history. In fact, time seemed to have stopped altogether around the 16th century for the Portuguese, for some reason. But what a wealth before that time. The blue tile everywhere was a knock-out, too. From church facades to railroad stations, it turned the meanest spaces into works of art.

The Tamakis showed up at the campground and we had some more great times together. We promised to meet again in Madrid.

On April 20th we headed out for Porto. Terence was suffering from his allergies already and it was only April so it was a bad sign. Still it was a sensational day to ride. Cool but sunny and the traffic out of Lisbon not too bad, roads manageable--passed through a lot of small factory towns. At a campground by a river, we watched children catching fish with bread, so we dug out our rods from the trailer and baited them with everything we had but no fish wanted to be our dinner. I guess we spoke the wrong language.

On the road to Nazare, I got side-swiped in the rain by a van trying to pass us at a bend. Damn macho drivers. I fell into a wet grassy ditch and spat with anger and frustration, but I wasn't hurt physically. Terence turned around and came back and picked up the bike for me. Just into the fishing village of Nazare, Terence hit an oil slick in front of a gasoline pump at the side of the road and went down hard, but wasn't hurt, either. What a day!

Waiting for Terence to look up the Taekwon-Do studio in Nazare, I stood near the bikes and watched the parade of mostly women pass by. There seemed to be three styles of dress--depending on one's age and social status. Western-type jeans for the unmarried girls. The older ladies were in short, many-layered skirts with aprons. They wore long gray wool stockings just up to the knee and their feet were shoved into what looked like house slippers. Their upper bodies were wrapped in large woolen shawls so that they looked as

NAZARE, PORTUGAL

if they had no arms. Many of them balanced baskets on their heads. I marveled at the skill at holding the basket on the head without benefit of

142

hands. Several of the women I noticed, wore the identical costume in black. Even the apron was black. Widows. Yet so many of them were quite young. It was puzzling. Is making a living fishing still that dangerous for the men today? Later I learned from our hosts that a woman could wear widow's weeds if any male in the family died. A father, uncle, brother or even a son. Good lord, how depressing. A celebration of death! And does nobody mourn the passing of a female?

I stood there so long an old lady wanted to adopt me. Well, at least I didn't scare her. In some Portuguese towns when the men and boys would stand around and stare, I'd learned to whip out my Swiss Army knife and file my nails. They liked that. "Sim, Manuel, it is a woman!"

We next headed to the university town of Coimbra, Portugal's capital for over a century (1143-1255), and supposedly the third most important city in the country. We found the municipal campground on the stadium grounds and tried to find the right stores for things we needed. Forget it. The day was dark and wet and the people's moods seemed to match. Even the pretty young thing at the Tourist Information counter was snarly. We forced ourselves to tour the sunken cathedral of Se Velha. Actually, it wasn't really sunken, just flooded big time from the recent rains, and we had to walk on planks placed between the chapels. It had long been abandoned, the people having relinquished its squat Romanesque interior for a no doubt lighter, more decorative atmosphere in newer places of worship through the centuries. As the crypt and all the tombs of the various bishops that were supposed to be there were under water, I wondered if anything macabre might be floating up as we peered into the depths. I confess to some disappointment when nothing did.

More time wasted as we looked on the University campus for a student book-store so we could buy a good Portuguese/English dictionary. We weren't too surprised to find out there was no such thing as a student book-store. We Americans are so spoiled.

A small female cat joined us for warmth back at the campsite. We let her sleep with us to keep dry as it rained all night. I got little sleep, but didn't mind. It was nice having a furry purr around again.

On the third day of heavy rains, Terence had had it and wanted to pack up. I tried to convince him I had some sort of fever and should stay in bed, but I was overruled. Not knowing when I might get another shower, I braved the moldy women's shower room and after undressing and turning on the water, it became cold almost immediately. An English woman in the next stall had washed her hair and used up all the hot water.

She was very apologetic, but in my feverish state I felt like shoving her into my stall to see how it felt, but of course nice people don't do such things... I finished my shower in ice water and chattered my way back to the rig. Terence gave me some aspirin and we hit the trail.

It took us the whole day over cobble-stoned and pot-holed streets to get to the city of Porto. The Municipal campground in the center of the city was expensive, so we opted for the cheaper one a few miles away and then took an hour trying to find it--slipping in the mud and joining the line of other impatient motorists behind all sorts of slower road users. We watched as what had to be the family cow pulled a cart, its udders swing-ing, with papa walking at its side pulling it along and the rest of the family in the cart behind it. What a life for that poor cow. We found the camp-ground sometime after dark, and slept a very deep sleep.

When we awoke, we discovered ourselves on a pine-covered hill overlooking a white sandy beach. Not too bad, we said, congratulating ourselves. Terence found he could breath without sneezing as the sea breeze blew the pollens and dust inland. The sun was warm on my back as I lined up with the other ladies and scrubbed the dirt from our clothes at the trough. Not much has changed in laundry methods for the Portuguese in the last several centuries. The water was cold and the soap bar greasy and the only way to get the dirt out was muscle power.

At least we aren't bending over rocks in the river, I consoled myself. Besides, all that exercise had to be good for me.

The city of Porto was a treat, pastries so cheap we treated ourselves to two at a time. Still no book stores or dark rooms to be found, though. I was thrilled to find some letters waiting for me from my daughter at the Poste Restante. We stayed about a week. We took the tour offered at one of the Sherry factories across the Douro river and climbed the old Torre dos Clerigos to get our bearings, and went to museums and down to the colorful market along the river. Terence attended a couple of classes at the Taekwon-Do studio. The improved weather warmed our spirits considerably and by the time we were ready to get on the road again, we agreed this part of Portugal earned highest marks in our book!

For the next few days, we gloried in the warm spring sun. We rode leisurely over the countryside; heading once again for the Spanish border. The landscape was more hospitable for "wild" camping than it had been in the south and, even though it was harder to find food to buy and the natives were not overly friendly in that neck of the woods (the hostile stares of the men and boys in each village was really beginning to unnerve me), there was a lot of open land between with trees and streams and nobody around to bother us. We stopped for long lunches and siestas and Terence would take out his typewriter and do some homework or practice his Taekwon-Do patterns and I wrote in my journal, and one fine morning I even felt tough enough to wash my hair in the stream! Well, I actually washed it using our saucepan and pouring the stream water over my hear over the grassy banks. I was careful not to get soap into the current. Bloody cold, but such a lovely sun that the discomfort didn't last long. Wildflowers and new leaves all around. Those were some marvelous moments.

The days became hotter. Crossing the border into Spain near Vila Ponca de Aguiar was a simple matter that far north. We were probably the first Americans that had come through there all year and the Portuguese guards were so agape at the rig they forgot to stop us or even wave us through; they just stood at the gate with their eyes wide as we passed by the check-point. We were glad we had made the decision to use the back roads.

Chapter Nineteen

BACK IN SPAIN TO SOME BAD NEWS

MAY 4, 1989--my birthday--a celebration of storks. We jumped off the bikes in a small village on the way to Salamanca to burn up the film taking pictures of a stork family on top of a village church tower. Then, riding in the shimmering heat, we spotted the huge birds flying high above us and nesting among the tall poplars planted in rows by the fields. Lord, what a sight when they flew! Great skinny crosses in the sky--the long, long legs behind and the thin outstretched neck. And yet not one carried a tiny baby bundle. They must have just dropped them off... Terence and I both kept pointing sightings out to each other and cheering over the sounds of our engines. We were both so glad to be back in Spain!

The rolling fields of scarlet poppies turned the view into a Fauve painting. Here and there, blue and white and yellow wildflowers could be seen seeping into the red panorama or the bright green of new leaves. I had to stop and take pictures because I knew no one would ever believe me when I told them about that Spanish shawl of a landscape. I rode up to the side of the Gold Wing and waved T. over. He tried to join me in my enthusiasm, but his allergies were ganging up to ruin the moment. It was unfair.

We rolled into the sandstone city of Salamanca that afternoon. A row of poplars shaded our spot at the campground from the intense heat and we felt very much at home. We spent two days wandering around that beautiful old university town. The sight of the magic hour of dusk absolutely blew us away with the pinks and golds and shadows of purple against a cerulean blue sky. And still more storks--irreverently nesting and clacking on every Renaissance bell tower and Plateresque church spire.

We pushed our way through a covered market in the center of the old town that certainly took the prize for freshness and inventive display. After the rather sad offerings we had seen in Portugal, we may have just been dazzled by the abundance. Even in the meat department, the displays showed a sense of humor and a sort of joy in the job. Even if one wouldn't want to actually eat some of the items, the show was entertaining. Terence asked a vendor for permission to take pictures of several hanging animal heads; skinned and eyes bulging and the lady got right into the spirit by posing next to the grisly things--flashing a playful grin and holding something truly slimy in her hands for extra effect.

On to Toledo. Little open space. No place to camp. Finally, stopped by the river Tagus and looking up at the craggy mound upon which the famous town is perched, we decided to simply pull the rig over the sand and camp by the bridge--in full view of the main road. We were feeling very brazen after seeing so many gypsy families squatting wherever they felt like it all over Spain. At least we wouldn't be pan-handling and shaking down the tourists!

The spires of the magnificent cathedral glowed in the morning sunlight as we pulled the rig through the lumpy streets. It got hot fast and the narrow openings between the houses and shops were quickly filled with gawking tourists like ourselves. We found a place to chain the bikes together and walked to the center of the city to see as much as possible before everything closed for the dreaded three-hour siesta. We were eager--along with practically everyone else getting off the buses--to see the paintings of El Greco, of which Toledo has so many. One of his masterpieces, "The Burial of the Conde de Orgaz", was so outstanding we had a hard time leaving the tiny chapel that contained it. Toledo's other riches just couldn't seem to compare.

As we waited out the siesta, the air became hot and heavier, and noticing how full the restaurants were along the dusty sidewalks, the reason for the long break in the day became uncomfortably clear. Lots of money was to be made by quite a large sector of the city's population while those who couldn't afford to eat in restaurants simply had to cool their heels until the last cup of espresso was drunk and the tip paid before the museums and shops opened again. A nice idea for the local economy, a rotten deal for two budget-conscious bikers. Thirsty, hot and dirty, our moods became blacker as we walked around the city. The clever marketing of Toledo's great treasures began to rankle us further as we realized each famous painting, for instance, was placed in its own museum instead of a collection, so that one had to pay over and over to see them all. Not to mention the time it took to ferret them out in the city's labyrinthine alleyways.

It was four o'clock when we were finally allowed entrance to the cathedral. Even the paintings inside the church were sequestered into individual chapels that charged admission! I began to burn. We just couldn't afford to see any more. Caravaggio's "St. John the Baptist" was a painting I had very much wanted to see, but when we saw that the ticket for the privilege would have been three dollars each, we bought a slide instead, to study later. Then we wandered around the beautiful Baroque interior of the cathedral for awhile to cool off and, after a while, with a somewhat nasty taste in our mouths, we rode away from the place.

I understand that in the evening, with the crowds gone, it's a different city entirely. I am glad to hear it.

Tired and filthy on Sunday evening after our day of dragging around Toledo, we despaired of finding a place to hide and camp near Madrid. So Terence said f... it, we're camping here and I was too beat to put up much of a fight. "Here" was a dirt quarry behind a factory in a sort of industrial suburb of Spain's capital and, I can tell you, it ranks among the worst of the rather questionable locals we ever had to park in. I was nervous all night wondering if we were going to be awakened by a junk-yard dog or flashlights in our face from the factory's night watchman.

Around seven in the morning, the trucks began lumbering in, and we threw our stuff into the trailer and booked outta there and onto the highway, feeling all mossy and unwashed. Madrid lay in a brown haze of smog before us. From all around tall factory stacks belched smoke and pollution. We had to remind ourselves we were here because the Prado was here!

First a stop in the city at the Poste Restante, where the bad news from home leveled us like an eight-point earthquake. My friend and bookkeeper, Rochelle, had written that the people renting our house in California had stopped paying the rent! We were without funds.

In shock and indescribable gloom, we rode on to the main campground on the northside of the city. The Tamakis had been there for a couple of days before us and were full of good advice and provided their shoulders to cry on which I took them up on without a moment's hesitation, and then the four of us tried to think of a way for us to stay in Europe and finish the trip and somehow solve the disaster at home. In California,

Rochelle had done her best to keep the rent money coming in, but each month had become more difficult. The renters had decided we were too far away to get tough, and as we couldn't afford to hire someone Stateside to take care of the matter they were, shall we say, "home free...".

We would stay and see the Prado and then head for France; putting the northwest of Spain on hold, putting the Basque country on hold--putting our beautiful dream of making it around the world on hold.

We dragged ourselves to the great art museum the next morning. The sensational painting and unusual plethora of famous artists exhibited should have moved us to tears of joy, but the way we were feeling had left us with the urge to weep for a far different reason. The day was sweltering and even at four bucks a head, the Prado people hadn't bothered to put in air conditioning--and don't try to tell me the paintings do better in that heat! Hey, we suckers will break down the doors to see the things anyway, why go the extra expense? There were no signs to tell you where anything was, nor where you might find yourself--after being pushed from room to crowded room in the flow of sweating bodies. Obviously, the idea was that more money was to be extracted from the rich tourist by forcing them to buy the guides and floor plans being hawked at the door. If one was so lucky as to find a particular painting one was looking for, the mobs of students or bus tours would inevitably be standing in front of it blocking the view endlessly while the teacher or tour director took advantage of what they probably considered their "finest hour", spewing more than anyone ever wanted to hear, while the kids doodled in their notebooks and older tourists swiveled their heads around--vainly looking for a place to sit down.

We were surprised to note that there was nothing Italian or French after the 16th century and no sculpture at all. How can people compare such a museum to the Louvre? A delightful Bosch, "The Garden of Delights"--all in pinks--saved the day for us however, and the annex up the street with Picasso's "Guernica" and some Spanish impressionists put us in a much better frame of mind by the end of the afternoon.

In early May, while searching for a spot to camp on the outskirts of the town of Segovia, a Spanish gentleman walking along the country road must have read our minds. He waved us over to the side of the road and directed us to a place down a lane nearby where he was sure we would be comfortable and cozy. He was so right. A long green meadow swept and bowed before us about half a mile down the path. It must have been grove of olive trees a very long time ago, because a few of them remained, twisted and gnarly, with ancient trunks still sending tender Spring growth bursting with newborn life at the tips. Our hearts began to lighten. We would find a way...

Amazing Segovia, a place I could draw for weeks. Romanesque and Renaissance edifices so sweet to look at, Terence had to drag me away from the splendid Gothic cathedral at the top of the city with so much ornamentation still remaining it looked almost new. The Roman aqueduct still spanning the valley after all these centuries--and without a drop of mortar between its perfectly cut stones. Then, as if we weren't filled to bursting with all those riches, the fairy-tale castle jutted from the western cliffs like an ocean liner, the Great Segovian Love Boat!

We sat in the little park that fronts the entrance and ate our stale sandwiches in the cool shade when a tour bus pulled up at the curb and disgorged a group of American tourists. It was nice to hear the language of my fathers and I smiled over at them. Several of the folks broke away from the cluster and stood around us to chat as we munched our lunch. They asked us where they could get a sandwich like those we were eating, and I thought they had to be kidding. Apparently, they were sick of restaurant food and were drooling at our simple fare! With just a little advance warning I could have made them such a deal...

That night, riding on a long stretch of highway out of Pedraza, T. led me off the road and onto a newly tarred side road, partially hidden by some dry shrubbery. As we started to set up camp, the rig began to sink into the tar! Terence jumped onto the Gold Wing and I pushed and shoved and got his rig back on the road before we were swallowed up into the killer pavement! A bit later we found a dirt road that led us out to a cliff with just enough parking space for our machines and trailer and although rain threatened and the wind howled around us, the view of the rugged valley below was nothing short of sensational from our cliffside perch. We sat on our rickety camp chairs and ate out of the pan and passed the wine bottle and declared that we must have one of the finest four-star rated views in Spain for our dining pleasure.

The road to Pamplona was a checkerboard of brilliant yellow mustard and kelly green grain fields. A sight for sore eyes and worried souls. When I spied a picture-perfect village on the top of a rocky hill, its patchwork fields drawn up to its chin like a counterpane, I had to laugh out loud. Why anguish about what was happening in California? It would work itself out somehow and meanwhile I should let my senses O.D. on what we had left of the trip! We began to climb. Basque farmhouses and barns begged to be photographed and we weren't making very good time. But we were feeling a little frantic about the thought that it might be all over soon so we forgave ourselves and stopped anywhere we felt like it and sucked up the scenery like drowning sailors. In the mountains, the hamlets in the mist under the dark trees seemed worlds away from the heat and vivid color that had been Spain.

By evening, we had just made it into France, and were asking people in the street where we could find a campground. Someone told us the Municipal campground wasn't "officially" open yet but it would probably be all right if we pulled in there for one night. The gates were wide open and soft lights illuminated the paths in the dimming twilight. The layout resembled something out of the Tuilleries. Tall hedges marked perfect spaces of privacy for RVs. Others bordered neatly cut grass plots that were obviously for tents. The young trees were all clipped evenly and a gentle, well-bred river glided gracefully past, no doubt to provide a further sense of peace to the wayfarer. At this point, the two of us didn't need peace as much as a bath, and as rare good luck would have it, the nice clean shower stalls produced an unlimited supply of very hot water! Our gratitude knew no bounds. We had been left completely alone, and after we packed up the next morning and drove around to find someone to pay, we finally gave up and drove away, singing our praises to La Belle France.

It was a long day's ride to Toulouse, but the day was fine and we were looking forward to seeing our friends and getting the money problem solved. Found a huge stack of mail at Mary Horvath's and after several frantic calls to people in California, it seemed the renters were paying the rent again and Rochelle was not as worried as before, although there were outstanding bills for us to pay and the money had to come from somewhere. Terence and I had a long talk about whether he should return and work awhile and then I decided to cash a fund I was saving for my old age, so that we might be able to finish the trip after all. It really wasn't much of a difficult decision for me because the truth was, as long as I was with Terence, I would never know how old age felt, and it looked like we were going to be good friends for a very long time.

Chapter Twenty

NORTH TO THE GERMAN GOLD WING TREFFEN

TWO WEEKS LATER, after more repairs on the bikes and heavy partying with our Toulousaine pals, we bid them all a sad adieu and climbed aboard our space crafts for the next leg of our soujourn. Heading in the direction of Le Puy in central France, the days were perfect, hot but breezy. Not much traffic to share the roads with and the early summer's countryside had us mesmerized. Every bend in the road seemed to bring a new view of panoramic splendor. How can there be so much to see?! The landscapes were like faces--all the same and yet all different. We checked out a camp-ground at St. Sernin. It was crowded and as, there was still light in the sky, we went on. Nearing the famous Gorges du Tarn, we found a nice spot by the river in a small village. Our dining room was under rustling leafy trees and our dinner music the eventide bells from the old church across the stone bridge. Unfortunately, Terence's allergies made for a restless night. Something had to be done about them soon.

Another day of riding hard to get to Lyon so that T. could get a shot and some pills. On the way, we rode into the volcanic city of Le Puy. The narrow cobbled alleyways to the cathedral at the top were no joy for Terence pulling that ungainly trailer. Then, coming down the steep inclines was even less fun as we slipped on the sand between the cobblestones. I was hanging on to my handlebars for dear life trying to stay upright. Terence in front of me--his eyes swollen, his head completely stuffed up and breathing in gasps through his mouth--held up traffic as he yanked the big bike around corners and slipped on the steep incline and jack-knifed trying to stop for pedestrians who had no idea how difficult it was for him to stop, pulling a 1000 lb. trailer with no brakes. For traction, he had to stay in first gear and keep his heavily booted feet onto the street to help him wrestle the snarling beast to earth. And somehow he still had time for a grin and a nod to the pretty women who lined the sidewalks to giggle at his progress. Following him on my safe little motorcycle, I was filled with admiration. A fine madness. Down off the old volcano at last, we pulled over to assess the damage. All sorts of electrical things were glitching again, and Terence had to once more get out his tools and work on them while I stood there with my kick on my stand. So much patience. I wondered how he could bear it when he could barely breathe or even see! It took us the rest of the day in Lyon to locate a doctor who could under-stand what he needed and we felt so sticky and miserable that we knew we couldn't sight-see without a shower and to our horror learned that there was no campground at Lyon! We became so desperate, we even went into a police station to ask where it might be legal for us to spend the night. After some thought, the helpful gendarmes directed us to a large park outside of the city, but after circling the area, we found that there was no way to get into it with our large rig and so Terence, who was as yet feeling no beneficial effect from the shot given him that afternoon, simply pulled into a field between the freeways to die. If I could have, I'd have made him stay on the road a bit longer to find something else, even though I was starving and dead tired myself. But there was no budging him. He had pulled next to a pile of rocks and a couple of walls of what was once a small house--probably abandoned when the freeways were built close around it. Rubbish was everywhere and overhead thick cables bringing electricity to the big city hummed and buzzed ominously and I was thinking that a few hours underneath them would probably give us cancer. It was nine-thirty at night so there weren't too many cars on the freeways around us, but what about rush-hour in the morning? We'd be like road-kill out there! Terence was beyond caring. I gave in and heated up a can of beans. We shared it and then I tossed it on the pile around us and crawled into our flimsy tent where Terence had crashed and was snoring like a drunk. The sodium lights of the freeways made the interior of the tent sickly pink. I closed my eyes and tried to sleep. I hated being so dirty.

Surprisingly, the freeways had very few cars on them the next morning when we pulled out of our little trash heap by the side of the road. We were amazed that a city as big as Lyon didn't have snarls of traffic at this time of the morning right here on the edge of the city as it were. Could it be that someone built a few too many freeways for the present flow of traffic? We wouldn't know about such things in southern California... Returnez to the drawing-board!

Soon we were over the border to Switzerland. Having spotted Spain on our passports, the young Swiss border guards detained us for a while to make sure we had no drugs. "Uh..try Zurich if you want drugs," mumbled T.

While we waited for the go-ahead, some friendly Swiss truck-drivers came over to look at the trailer. They were shocked to see there were no brakes on it. They warned us we probably wouldn't get far without hassles from the Police.

We headed into Geneva to change money. Passers-by were extremely friendly. We left the rig for awhile and came back to find a note on the Gold Wing seat that said "Thanks for existing. Good Trip. Good luck. You are doing what we all dream to do!" And it had two tiny daisies placed above the words. We were very touched.

Rolling hills and waving seas of grain. Swiss houses and towns much too pretty. Cutsie, even. I began to get the feeling that the cows on the hillsides were washed each morning. Reminded me of a living-room I'd seen once--all in white. White walls, white carpet, white upholstery. Makes one afraid to sit down, for Chrissakes. At the campground among the scarlet poppies we were given a long list of rules and shown the exact place we were to be allowed to put ourselves and our muddy machines. The RV waiting to roll into the cubicle next to us was Swiss, and Papa jumped out to mow the grass before he drove over it! It wouldn't have been quite so astounding to us except that we had noted that it had been freshly mowed before he got there! The nice part was that the campground telephone not only worked, which was a first for us, but had complete instructions in four languages on how to use the thing. And no graffiti! In the bathroom we found clean toilet paper. Even clean toilets! It made a nice change.

The next campground in Switzerland was in Bern where the price was fair at seven dollars, but the manager was cranky. He stewed about whether we were a tent or a trailer, and finally gave us a spot he really wanted to put a genuine trailer into, but then we just wouldn't fit into one of the little tent places. We were sure it kept him up all night worrying about it. We stayed two days, probably causing him great mental stress. T. practiced his Taekwon-Do, feeling much better now that the shot had had time to have some effect. I washed clothes and hung them around the tent and slurped my coffee by the river and thought about how beautiful it all was.

Riding through the steep Heidi-like valleys the next morning, we guessed the Swiss must not like the quiet. Cow-bells, goat-bells, gate-bells. They'd probably put bells on the birds if they could catch them. In one village, on a Sunday, the church bells seemed to come from everywhere; bouncing off the mountainsides and drowning everything in their path in marvelous, reverberating sound.

BERN, SWITZERLAND

Somewhere, in a dark and dripping forest, we decided to pull over and have lunch. We had just opened a couple of beers when a police car pulled up. They seemed friendly enough, but we were waiting to be told how illegal the trailer was. One fellow started to take pictures of the rig and we thought we had had it. But then they both came over to help us pour over the map to find our next camping spot. Nothing said about the beers in our hand. Nothing about the rig except they thought it super and thanks for letting him take a picture to show to the kids. Hey, no problem... After a bit they popped back into their car and waved good-bye. Nice fellas.

We had met a Swiss biker named Lukas Boesinger when we had camped in Porto Gordo, Portugal. He had kindly asked us to visit him when we got to Switzerland. He lived in a small town outside Zurich and while it rained outside, we spent four days there catching up on studies and the laundry and taking trips to Zurich and environs. On the weekend, he invited us to go for a motorcycle ride with him that was to meet up with other bikers at some Gasthaus in the hills. It was a beautiful ride--up and up into green forests and farmland. We began to notice other motorcycles here and there on the road, and after a bit they were all around us; zooming happily back and forth to show off their stuff and gear to their friends and fellow bikers. We pulled into the meeting place--a Gasthaus parking lot. There were so many of us that everyone had to keep on the move--roaring in and out of the lot, showing off and sneaking peeks at the others. They came from France and Germany as well and the noise was deafening as clouds of them would arrive and have a beer or two and all the time someone was just leaving--joyfully revving their engines. Grateful for being alive and able to ride their bad machines on a splendid sunny day!

It was a warm June afternoon when we left Switzerland for Germany. I mused on my bike about the things that had impressed me there in that tiny country. Its neat-as-a-pin houses, many with a barn attached that you could bet was as clean as the house itself... Lots of bright paint on the shutters and trim, with geraniums leading the popularity poll on the porches and in long window boxes. Never a drooping flower nor brown leaf. No trash anywhere. No graffiti. How can so many people be so damned good? Lukas had told us that cars were taken off the road if they had any rust. As we passed some road workers dressed in immaculate orange jump-suits bending to plant tulips by the roadside, I realized they were senior citizens. Everyone has a duty. No telling what mischief those gramps and grannies might get into with time on their hands!

The rain began soon after we entered Germany. We ducked for shelter underneath the overpasses--along with several other bikers doing the same thing. The ever-natty German and his passenger would usually be enjoying a cigarette--decked out in matching leathers and helmets which, of course, also matched the shiny motorcycle they rode. Terence and I stood dripping in our torn and patched clothes and dirty scratched helmets. I guess we matched our rig, too. When the rain would let up a bit, we'd all strap on our helmets and head back out, hoping for the best. But that day it never let up. After stopping three or four times, we gave up trying to keep dry and just kept going. With any luck, the campground at Mannheim would have hot showers and we could put on something from the bottom of the trailer that might have stayed dry.

There was no one to take our money after we rolled in. So we located a camping spot by ourselves and as there were no showers, unfortunately, we just ate something and went to bed damp and were tired enough not to care. The next morning we were met by the manager who over-charged us or perhaps it was just a matter of sending one price-quote to the publisher of our Camping book and charging another when the hapless camper appeared. We were in no mood to argue and our German wasn't good enough yet anyway, so we paid up and then shoved our damp things together and rode off to check out Worms cathedral on the way up to Wiesbaden where we would visit Norbert again and his new woman, Berga.

After a couple of days with them showing us the sights along the Rhine and driving in Norbert's car to see things they thoughtfully thought we'd enjoy (we did!), we jumped on the bikes again to try to get to the Gold Wing at Diepholz in time for the German Treffen. Each campground along the way was full of German retirees who all seemed to want to talk about the war and how "sorry" they were. Terence and I were rather confused as to how to deal with all the guilt-trips and I in particular wished I'd studied a little harder in school on the subject. Mostly, all we had to go on was horror stories and movies about WWII and we both felt sadly uninformed. I have to confess that I was unprepared for the sort of unzipped friendliness the German people displayed in those campgrounds. Especially the older people. They just couldn't leave us alone. In the evenings they'd hand us bottles of beer. In the morning while I tried to get the coffee boiling, they'd walk over with sacks of brotchen--little bread rolls. At a service station, a man left his family in the truck and ran over to hand us a sack of black cherries they'd just picked. Good grief. Maybe it was because we were a little shabby compared to other Americans they'd seen touring their country, and they thought we were hungry. They all seemed to be dressed in the very latest garb for the leisure classes. Matching warm-up suits in that light material--what is that stuff? And colorful. Nobody I know at home wears such beautiful clothes to camp in. Purples and magenta and teal and celadon. And with expensive jogging or running shoes; the sort of shoes recommended by one's personal trainer, I thought. I'd seen what those outfits cost in the shop windows of Wiesbaden. This generation of Germans was doing all right. Well, that is, in the west of Germany they were doing all right.

Whizzing past giant houses of four floors each, I wondered why they needed all that room. Lots of farmland and lawns and neatly manicured gardens. As clean and neat as the Swiss, but so much bigger!

We received a warm welcome at the reception area of the Gold Wing Treffen in Diepholz. Saw where the British were staying and moseyed over. It was good to hear our language again.

Once more we were surrounded by a colorful pride of motorcycling lions from all over Europe. The German Treffens are popular and Diepholz was a locale even the Scandinavians could reach without having to miss a day of work (even if some of them did have to ride all night Sunday to get home for Monday morning), so for two days the roaring never stopped and neither did the drinking. Those northern folk sure knew how to party! It must have been a long winter.

Standing out among the Holland contingent was Dirk Kraaij, a lean, craggy guy who reminded us of a sort of Dutch "Marlboro man." After sliding off his great yellow-as-a-tulip steed, he proceeded to make himself comfortable by donning a black Greek mariner's cap and to our delight, changed from his riding boots to actual wooden shoes! His 1976 Gold Wing was fitted with two modes of fuel use. The standard, plus a propane tank lashed to the pillion seat! The rig caused quite a stir and for much of the week-end he was surrounded by the curious and adoring. Not all of his fans were simply interested in his novel use of gasoline intake. He also carried--draped on either side of the motorcycle--two containers of hooch; Jagermeister for the men, he said, and Apfelkorn liqueur for the women. Sexist? Absolutely, and we babes couldn't wait to be offered some of the delicious stuff!

We joined the traditional Treffen "Parade of Nations" the next afternoon. I counted over 400 Gold Wings in the line-up. Lots of bikers chose not to go. I guessed some were still hung-over from the previous night and sleeping it off. Terence and I loved going on those things. It was not only a chance for us to gawk at all the other bikes, but it was always such a hoot watching the countryfolk wave and drop their jaws as we passed by.

We were a long, noisy procession. German Polizei dressed in green and white leathers kept the traffic back at each intersection. I rather felt sorry for the people in the cars. It took us a good twenty to thirty minutes to roll slowly by while they were left cooling their heels. Most of them took it pretty well, getting out of their cars and sitting on the hoods and waving. Well, what else could they do? We rambled on through the countryside, smelling the young growing things in the fields and the flowers in the gardens and being charmed at the horses with their foals as they lifted their handsome heads at the growl of our engines. It was a perfect day for a ride, and for Terence and me, an outstanding opportunity to observe the German countryside and the people who live in it. At last the puzzle about the huge German homes was solved. The whole family lived in them. That was the answer. Unlike most American families who expect each generation to move out and start anew somewhere, the German nest was simply made bigger from the start to accommodate everybody--kids and grandparents and even aunts and uncles and cousins. I was fascinated to see certain people--whom we in Santa Barbara would have more than likely "put away" in some old-folks's home or asylum--lined up along with the rest of the family at the gate, waving and smiling, some of them supported by their loving kin, some of them drooling or sightless but no less a member of the family, and caught up in the excitement of it with all the rest of us.

By Sunday afternoon the last mean machine had rolled away and we found ourselves alone on the big playing field which had been covered with tents and bikes and bodies just a couple of hours before. We had helped the clean-up folks scoop up the last beer can from the grass and as nobody seemed to mind, we decided to stay another night on the field before riding up to Bremen--a good day's ride from Diepholz. Taking a stroll that evening in the balmy summer air, we met a sweet old lady whose English was pretty good and who insisted upon showing us the local summer produce gardens near the river. Moving among the cabbages and fragrant just-turned earth, the three of us chatted away like old friends and she told us that her son who had died tragically several years before would have been Terence's age. Further conversation divulged the death of her husband and how she managed and coped, etc., and T. and I wished we could think of something appropriate to say to let her know how sad we felt. Again the subject of the horrible war came up, and again we heard the plea for peace between people on this planet. When we parted, she hugged us both with a firm grip and I felt a little shaky.

As we finished packing the next morning, an elderly couple came out of that same garden to wordlessly hand us a huge sack of freshly picked strawberries. They spoke no English. Just the universal language of big smiles. We ate those strawberries at the side of the road that afternoon-- with some thick cream we found in a small grocery shop in the last village. Ambrosia of the Gods.

Our Bremen campground was quite a distance from the city, but inexpensive and bordered by a clean, sandy beach next to a very interesting river where cargo boats and ferries plied the waters up and down. Sleepy, warm days passed quickly with lots of birds singing in the trees and two nights with a pretty full moon and a young manager who insisted we come over to the campfire and drink his beer with what other campers he was able to rustle up. Gemuchlikeit all around. I sat there in the moonlight listening to German campfire songs and drinking my host's beer and pondered on what everyone outside of this country had said about the German "Industrial North." Even other Germans had warned us about the traffic, smog and especially the "humorless and bitter" inhabitants up here. So much for generalizing.

Bremen was picture-post-card perfect. We must have shot up four or five rolls between us on the exquisite medieval downtown architecture and the ultra modern stuff that borders it. The day was very hot and the sky so blue it felt more like Greece than Deutschland.

Bremen Musicians

Loving our campground, we spent a couple more days there while T. studied and I cleaned and mended and sketched and just soaked up the warm sun on the white beach by the river. It was so heavenly, it seemed like the flip side to some of the bad days in Portugal and Madrid.

Our weather luck ran out after driving all day to Kassel, on the way back south. Terence had heard of a large Taekwon Do studio there and so was determined to check it out. The first campground we found was terribly expensive so we rode out into the drizzle and into the countryside until we found a forested hill with a tractor path leading up into the trees.

We found a place hidden from the road and ate a quick dinner and went to bed early.

Trying to find the Taekwon Do studio the next morning, we drove around the city for an hour and needing to use the restroom, we pulled into the parking lot of the Bahnhof (train station). While Terence guarded the rig under a pretty obvious NO PARKING sign, I dashed to the Women's toilets with my 50p in my hand because by then I was familiar with the routine in Germany. At least I thought I was familiar with the routine. Instead of taking my money at a kiosk, the warden (male) followed me into the cubicle! As I prepared to inflict some bodily harm, he bent over and swabbed the seat! And then held out his hand for the money. Maybe he had figured me for a rich (though shabby) foreigner and thought the extra service would earn him something over and above the price of entry. I'm afraid I was not amused. First of all, I never quite sit in those places anyway. My dear Victorian mother made sure to lead me to believe public toilets were swarming with unbelievable germs, and secondly, the whole idea of paying to pee when the MEN in Europe get away scot-free burns me up.

Anyway, as I ran back to Terence, I saw the Polizei had indeed caught up with us. He was surrounded and I wondered how large a fine it was going to be to park illegally as well as drive around the city pulling a heavy trailer that had no brakes, when I realized they were helping T. find the studio on a map and were busy taking pictures for the guys back at the station "Who vill nefer beleef dis!"

I decided to stop worrying about Germany. "They love us!," I told myself. Later, we finally found the studio and discovered that neither Mr. Lee, the master, nor any of the students spoke any English. Terence, undaunted, taught two classes anyway, and we stayed in Kassel for three days in the municipal campground. The last day was spent checking out the delightful art gallery in the Schloss. I was beginning to develop a real taste for Van Dyke and there were several magnificent paintings by him there.

After a couple of nights camping wild, we once more pulled into Mainz to stay with Burga and Norbert while we packed a couple more boxes to mail. The first night, Burga made sauerbraten and knudel so that we could experience real German cooking, bless her heart! But the second night, unfortunately, all of us were sick with separate complaints--Terence was fighting a losing battle with a cold (maybe the from the kids in the studio in Kassel), I had a raging sore throat, Norbert came down with the stomach flu while we were there and poor Burga had some mean moments with complaints stemming from her diabetes! One big happy family! Unfortunately, Burga enjoys her cigarettes, and we who were accustomed to living in the great outdoors could hardly breathe in their small apartment when she lit up which was, well, constantly. Nothing could be done about it. They were very kind to allow us to sleep on their living room floor and I'm sure they were not thrilled to have us around when Norbert had the flu. So as soon as we were able, we got ready to go. Being the perfect hosts, they loaded us with food to take with us and gave me all sorts of throat remedies they swore they would never have a use for. As Terence was packing the trailer, Norbert stuffed three bottles of wine--from the rich slopes of Das Reineland, no less--under some towels I'd just washed. He said he was horrified at the cheap junk we'd been buying. What a sweetheart.

Winding our way down to Heidleberg, I still felt woozy, but it was great to be in a smoke-free environment again. The rain fell softly as we looked around that romantic city and after three nights in quiet, dripping forests, we were ready for a campground shower. A wine bottle had broken in my saddle bag again (a cheap bottle, thank God), and this time it had soaked both our pairs of tennis shoes!

Grumpy, sticky and hungry, we pulled into what the book had told us was a fairly low-priced camp next to the Ammersee, a way-too-popular resort near Munich. After discovering we couldn't afford it, we sat, glum, in the dripping evening--looking at a map to try to decide where to go next. We were startled when a young German couple walked over to us and asked if they could help. Five minutes later as the rain began to fall in earnest, they were asking us to come home with them and let them take us to a restaurant for dinner. Of course it would be unthinkable to accept. But we did. Terence rarely bows to the pressures of the social graces and I was in a weakened state. We threw on our helmets and roared onto the road to follow them. Once again we were saved by the kindness of total strangers.

Thomas Ziesecke and Evelyn Haala were one handsome couple. Tall and strong and healthy and with personalities to match, they were simply examples of the best people a country can produce. They swept us in out of the rain and fed us and took care of us and pampered us and while they went to their jobs during the day we rode around Munich getting parts for the bikes and generally sight-seeing and we'd come home in the evening to a luscious hot meal and more love and warmth than most people get from their families!

Thomas took us for long walks around the countryside and we spoke of the differences in freedoms between us--and especially about the suffocating restrictions his country imposed on young people trying to do their thing. The most obvious case in point was the simple fact that in his whole lifetime, Thomas could not possibly own such a rig as ours. So much of our machinery and the trailer was illegal by now in his country he couldn't believe how we were permitted to ride on their roads. But of course we were Americans. "Americans can do anything they want," he said bitterly. Before we left them, Terence insisted they take a long ride on the Gold Wing around the village. They were gone a long time.

Chapter Twenty-One

AUSTRIA

RIDING through the rain to Austria, Terence began to experience stomach cramps. We pulled into a small lay-by so that he could rest. As I got off my bike, Terence said softly, " Gail, you might be in their way." As I was mouthing "Whose?," I caught sight of about a dozen young soldiers lying in the bushes near my motorcycle with their rifles aimed across the road! I must have jumped a foot into the air before I ran to Terence screaming and acting like a total flake! The men didn't move. They reminded me strangely of a wax museum exhibit about WWII. We must have landed right in the middle of "maneuvers." A couple of them were losing the battle in keeping a straight face. I decided they were going to let us live. We got back on the bikes and even though Terence was now in worse stomach pain than before, we pushed on until we found a campground on the Austrian side of the border.

He was no better in the morning. Grudgingly, we both climbed aboard the Gold Wing and rode to Innsbruck, where we found a doctor who announced T. probably had food poisoning and would be better in time and then charged us thirty-five bucks for the helpful diagnosis. That gave me a stomach-ache! We dragged back to the campground and Terence went to bed while I pondered about what I was going to do if he died.

To my great relief and no doubt his as well, he was better the next day, and we took a fabulous ride on the Wing around the top of Austria, making our way through the adorable Tyrolean villages and back into

Germany to the famous Neuschwanstein castle. Eschewing the steep price of the entrance ticket to the castle, we opted instead to sit and eat our lunch on the great expanse of summer grass in the valley below the castle, and watch the hang-gliders float down from the mountain above. The day had suddenly become sunny and hot. The many pictures we took could never begin to capture the enchantment of that afternoon. It was as if a mighty rainbow had shattered, flinging its brilliant fragments in slow motion to the ground. And high above the pines, the white fairy tale castle stood--the colorful gliders crossing back and forth in the breeze like confetti...Old Mad Ludwig would have loved it!

In order to get around the mountains and over to Oberammagau, we had to cross into Austria first and then back into Germany. The Austrian border guards asked for papers which was unusual, and then we rode about two miles between the borders in a kind of No-Man's Land before coming up to the German crossing. Again we were asked for papers. This time the pompous old guard checked and rechecked and then went around to the back and discovered our California registration was out of date. Terence tried to explain that it wasn't necessary to update the registration because we weren't riding the motorcycle in California. No go. We were told we could not come into Germany! The fact that we had already been traveling in Germany for months only seemed to make the old man angrier. We weren't coming in at his border crossing! We had no choice but to turn back. What if the Austrians saw us coming back and realized we'd been turned away from Germany and maybe they had missed something and shouldn't let us in their country either? We'd have to spend the rest of our lives catching birds and small animals to eat in that two-mile stretch between the countries!

Terence didn't give the Austrians a chance to think about it. We sped through the opening in the gate before the guards could get out of the kiosk. By the time they rose from their chairs, we were past the wooded bend in the road and prayed they wouldn't bother to follow.

By this time the sun had disappeared behind some very dark clouds and our vast euphoria at the events of the morning had worn off. Trying to find our way home with a bad map, we got lost a couple of times and were beginning to get desperate to find gas for the Wing.

After narrowly avoiding a nasty accident by riding into a village on an unmarked one-way street, we finally located a gas station and thanked our lucky stars it wasn't another holiday. As we filled up, the sky to the west of us was turning black with a most peculiar green edge and the air became difficult to breathe. We sped for home as the lightning flashed. Terence pulled over at one point to take some pictures of a rather spectacular ruin on a hill, and while I cowered on the bike, it started to hail! Hard to believe that it was just three hours ago that we were munching bread and cheese on a warm lawn under a hot sun! Even wilder to imagine was the weather after we emerged from a long tunnel in a mountain. As serene and sunny again as one could wish! The contrast was astounding.

We stayed at our campground in Sharnitz about three days so Terence could catch up on his homework. Our little site had become so muddy I felt like a cow in a stable, wallowing and slipping around while I prepared meals and threw damp things on a line for the sporadic sun to dry--soon to slosh back in the next few minutes to yank them off again before the rain soaked them all over again. Still, the ever-changing view of the mountains around us was worth the minor inconvenience. One minute they were sparkling in a great sunbeam, then blue and brooding in shade, another swathed in fog and clouds curling like sea foam around their stony faces. I hated to leave.

Nor did the scenery disappoint as we rode through the Southern Tyrolean mountains the next day. Just so we wouldn't feel too smug though, the rain kept coming back and soaking us through between each incredible vista and ecstatic picture-taking. After pricing the pretty camp-grounds in the area, we looked for someplace wild to camp to save money, but all the roads led to houses and there was simply no place to turn off. Around nine o'clock in the evening, we gave up and rolled into a very popular and very wet site named Werfen and were immediately surrounded by the other campers who had probably just had their dinner and were eager for some entertainment. It was at such times that I longed for the privacy of my own house--even a nice van where I could shut the door, but alas, it was not to be. Faint with hunger, we fielded the usual questions and even signed autographs for some French children! It was about ten o'clock when I finally got some dinner on the table and the folks mercifully retreated to let us eat. Later, as I cleaned the dishes, they came back and we actually enjoyed their company. They were a very international group--we met a couple from Norway who were riding their own bikes. Very nice, very fast bikes, they were, too. They must have been amused at my old ride, but hey, it got me there, didn't it?

Salzburg, the city of Mozart. Expensive muni-campground, so Terence shared my coin-operated shower on the ladies's side to the shock of one or two passers-by. By this time in our journey we'd seen plenty of others do the same so I wasn't too worried about its propriety. Terence and I decided we liked the place even though it rained all day and night. While we waited out the weather and Terence studied, I deciphered the odd little centrifugal dryer thing sitting in the corner of the ladies's restroom and managed to get some clothes washed and dried which improved my mood considerably. Let it rain! I have something to wear!

The old town was a delight. Very Baroque and neat without being saccharine. So many of the Austrian smaller towns had been so sicken-ingly adorable. I still hadn't figured out if it was just for tourists, or if the people really liked to spend every waking hour cleaning and painting and trimming and shaping. It was really too much. I found myself counting geranium blossoms in window boxes just to see if it was always the same number.

The last afternoon in Salzburg was a treat. Warm sun spilled over the edges of the thick white clouds and everybody grabbed their cameras to catch the precious moments. There were mobs of tourists but the old city seemed to have enough to see for all. Mozart's birthplace was all yellow and white and nice enough for Mr. and Mrs. M to move back in any time. The "Old City" is a warren of charming boutiques now, but still retaining the distinctive flavor of the 18th century, with carefully restored storefronts and the quaint jumble of iron shop signs overhead--each depicting in fanciful figurative design what was to be had within. Perhaps in consider-ation of the non-reader among the potential customers in the street.

We rode away from Salzburg through dark green hills and forests and past some exquisite blue-green lakes that were so clear we could see the bottom. At Grossraming-Erkende, we were fortunate to discover an inexpensive campground on a little knoll overlooking a very slow-moving, avocado-colored river. A herd of bicyclists sharing our hill left early the next morning and the quiet was heavenly. I spent the day resting and reading while Terence slaved over the bikes's wiring, a constant headache for him because of all that rain. Our precious privacy was interrupted that evening by a middle-aged local who drove right up to our table on his mini tractor. I had just poured us our coffee when this fellow decided to make himself at home. We presumed him to be either simple-minded or drunk and neither of us could figure a way to get rid of him. Refusing a cup of coffee, he roared off with much display to fetch us all a large pitcher of what they'd called "Scampy" in England--that awful headache-producing cider made from over-ripe apples. He was very jolly, and carried on all by himself in some sort of rural Austrian German that we understood none of. The fact that we sat there mute and miserable didn't seem to bother him at all. Both of us were dying to read for awhile and it was hard to be kind. After a while we pretended that we were going to bed and he stumbled off into the dark.

Coming close to Vienna on July 17th, we decided to camp at Rossatzbach--on the Danube, no less. But Herr Strauss would have been shocked. It is now the Beautiful Brown Danube. "Progress" and pollution have taken their toll, I'm afraid.

Church restoration

We stayed at that crowded campground for three days while we tried to locate more permanent digs. Much had to be accomplished in Vienna plus the fact that the city was the perfect jumping off place for other destinations such as Hungary, Czechoslovakia and Italy. We were hoping to find a shed somewhere to leave my motorcycle and save gas money by using just the Wing.

While visiting with Mr. Tom McCallum at the Taekwon Do studio in the city, Terence learned that one could place a one-time ad on the English-speaking radio station called "The Blue Danube." He phoned the station and was immediately put on the air and incredibly, a family living in a suburb of Vienna heard his plea and responded, offering a room and a place in their backyard for the rig!

The Petz family could not have been more generous. They welcomed us with open arms--fourteen open arms to be exact! Alex Petz had met Patsy while working in South Africa. She already had one beautiful daughter when they met and married, and then they very soon had four more children: Michael, Lisa, Hildegard, and baby Andrew. Terence and I began learning about two new cultures at the same time--Austrian and African and it was a rich and wonderful two weeks. While Terence studied, I tried to make myself useful and the children, though shy at first (except for Hildegard, who is never shy), proved to be extremely friendly. We loved listening to their funny conversations in sing-songing Austrian mixed liberally with Afro-British. Alex worked at home and was a man of tremendous creative talents. When Terence saw his workshop and various inventions laying about, I think he believed he'd died and gone to heaven. The two of them got along famously. With Alex's help, T. was able to repair and fashion new things for the bikes that he had given up all hope for earlier because parts were so hard to locate.

Vienna seemed to be a huge, gray place for two Americans without funds. The famous coffee houses were beyond our budget and that rather put me into a funk from the beginning. It had been as long ago as Portugal when I had been allowed to stuff my face with pastries and wash them down with great gulps of creamy coffee. Truly one of life's greatest pleasures and I confess, a favorite vice of mine. Yet here we were in what was reputed to be the birthplace of the croissant and we had to save our pennies for gasoline. Too cruel.

The traffic snarls were horrendous. Fortunately for me, Terence rode me around on the Ascot when we went into the city. I bounced on the back and looked at the architecture of the marvelous old buildings to keep my mind off the mayhem of the streets. Vienna is certainly a city of the Beaux Arts. It was amusing to see so many naked stone bodies holding up the odd overhang. Always young maidens, young men, a few old men, and the ever-popular putti or naked fat babies--usually with wings. I have to say I o.d.'d in Vienna on those ghastly cherubs. What on earth could have been the attraction for artists? And what did they have against occasionally sculpting the image of say, a teenager, or--God forbid--an older woman? Nowhere to be found.

Chapter Twenty-Two

TALES OF THE VIENNA HOODS

ON THE WAY back to Obersdorf one afternoon after we had picked up our monthly allotment of cash at the American Express office in Vienna, we were waved over by two policemen who had been standing in the street. We were told that they had seen us pass a vehicle down the road and that this was a "no passing" zone. Surprised, Terence told them that we understood the presence of broken yellow lines was universally accepted as "permitted passing."

Ah, but there is a sign that says "NO PASSING" that you should have obeyed, the policeman said. It was soon clear enough that this was a "shake-down," with the older cop showing the younger how these things were done. We were asked for the equivalent of about $40 in Austrian schillings for the "fine." Terence told them we had no money, that we had tried to get some at the American Express office but that we had arrived too late and the office was closed for the day. I gulped. I am lousy at lying and in that it was I who had cashed the check in Vienna, it was I who was standing in front of the two officers with $300 bulging in the wallet that was peeking out of my jacket pocket. I was in mortal terror anticipating their questioning me and felt as if I were going to faint with fear. I put on my best blank look to have them believe I didn't know enough of the language to know what was going on.

They told Terence to show them his wallet. It was as empty as he'd said. I hadn't had time to share the money I'd received. I awaited my turn.

They asked Terence if we had money where we were staying in Obersdorf. He told them that if we had, we wouldn't have ridden all the way into Vienna to the American Express office. They looked at me. I looked blank. They were not pleased, and the older officer was looking bad in front of the rookie. He waved us away, disgusted.

Chapter Twenty-Three

BEHIND THE IRON CURTAIN

ONE OF THE reasons we were in Vienna was for Terence to prepare for his 3rd Dan level blackbelt at the Taekwon-Do studio there. A bonus for us was getting to know the MacCallums, who hailed from Scotland. Tom was a 6th Dan himself and Under Secretary General for the International Taekwon Do Federation whose European headquarters were located there in Vienna. His good wife Morag was in the throes of some culture shock as she was attempting to all at once settle in a foreign land, try to smooth the transition for their two young sons in Austrian schools and learn the difficult language herself. They were lovely people and I would have liked to stay to get to know them both much better....but the road was beckoning...and we had to be in Italy by September first, for the International Gold Wing Treffen at Castigliano del Lago.

Getting visas in Vienna at the embassies for Czechoslovakia and Hungary was no picnic. Both countries were still communist at the time and not overly friendly nor thrilled to have us visit. We arrived early and waited in long lines along with other hopefuls, while the clerks seemed to be filing their nails instead of dealing with the tired and hot petitioners. Yet finally one morning, I covered my little motorcycle in a corner of the Petz's garden, and climbed behind Terence and we were off to Hungary! The Petzes and another couple visiting them from Africa were to meet us in Pannonhalma in a couple of days, but our first stop in the new country was Györ, just over the border. As we passed the depressing concrete housing blocks on the outskirts of the city, we realized with a shock that we were indeed in our first Communist country. Innocents, we laughed at first at the backward way of life around us as we sped past factory towns with garages full of piles of manure or sugar beets instead of cars, leaning old telephone poles heavy with mangled and frayed wires and people dressed in styles from the 50's. It all seemed like a huge joke we Americans heard over and over at home--about the Communist countries: "Canvas industrial-strength underwear." But our smiles began to fade as it dawned on us that these were real people. There, but for the grace of God, were we, etc... I began to feel an awful anger that made my face hot. What a colossal dirty trick Communism was!

The heat was stifling. We pulled off for a beer and were dealt with (served would not be the right word) by an extremely surly waiter who first brought the incorrect amount of beer bottles, then later the incorrect change. Terence was trying out the Hungarian from the Berlitz book and had also used some German and Russian--none of which was appreciated in the least. We were beginning to get an introduction to life among the Communists.

The Györ campground was full of eastern Germans (DDR). The crowds who surrounded the Gold Wing were respectful and although not unfriendly, we felt a little like moon rocks. Fascinating but perhaps diseased. It was definitely a different audience than we were used to in the west. Mothers kept their young children away and many of the other campers simply watched from behind the shabby curtains of the rows of identical worker's cabins that circled the small tent field where we were allowed to set up camp. A few of the braver young men couldn't be kept back, however. Their wistful and hungry looks turned Terence into the perfect American ambassador, waving them over to chat and patiently telling them the same old story everybody always wanted to hear about our trip and our hopes to go around the world and of course, the guys' favorite part, how the machines worked and how fast they could go.

He spoke in German, my genius, and although he only been practicing it a few weeks and it was laced with a pretty strong French accent and no doubt further sprinkled with the seasoning of Alex's Austrian dialect, the men were captivated and so polite that not a glance was passed between them when he must have made mistakes in the language. I could catch enough words to note that he was modifying the tired old story of our trip to fit the audience. I heard him stress how hard we had worked to save and earn enough money to buy the (used) bikes, and how everyone had told us it couldn't be done. Their eyes grew wide at the thought that as Americans we weren't handed the whole thing on a silver platter. Oh, we all had a lot to learn about each other.

That evening we decided to ride into town and try a restaurant. Although the city of Györ is big, the only restaurant we could find was a small one right across from the Opera House in the center of town. We had dressed up; so if the huge Gold Wing hadn't been enough for the people of Györ to stare at, our clothes were, as we climbed from the motorcycle in front of the restaurant.

We seemed to be the only people in the dining room, and the "staff" seemed a bit surprised at having customers but quickly recovered after they realized we planned to stay. The waiter was very gracious and after a couple of drinks we were shown the menu. Not even Terence could decipher the Hungarian but the three of us chose the most expensive item on the menu at about six dollars...a kind of Hunter's Plate for two which consisted, as it turned out, of really tasty mystery meat under lots of paprika sauce with vegetables we could identify. There was salad and bread and desert and a bottle of very good Pinot Noir, and coffee with a Hungarian liqueur and the bill came to a whopping eleven dollars including tip. Terence and I decided to retire in Hungary.

The crew from the kitchen followed behind our waiter as Terence offered to show him the bike. In French, with many hand gestures, the whole story was told once again and I saw in the dark several more people craning to see and understand. It was nice to feel the initial hostility slip away from the crowd and I think, but I can't be certain, that when I smiled at faces in the dark gathering, someone smiled back.

Chapter Twenty-Four

THE IRON CURTAIN BEGINS TO PART

THE NEXT DAY we bought food in the state-run store--so inexpensive we felt as if we'd stolen it. We found the campground in Pannonhalma and set up camp and then rode the Gold Wing to the city of Vesprem to visit the local Taekwon Do instructor there that Tom McCallum in Vienna had told us about. Dr. Janos Somlai spoke little English but he and his wife were very kind and seemed thrilled to meet us. We were served tea and cookies. Unfortunately, the studio was closed for the summer and they hoped we could return in the fall....

Back at the Pannonhalma campground, the multitudes had gathered around the trailer and my motorcycle. Again, mostly East Germans, with a sprinkling of Italians and others. No Hungarians. As we gave the usual speeches about how everything was so available and cheap in America, it began to dawn on us that we needed to change the script radically. What could it mean to these eastern Europeans that our motorcycles only cost a couple of thousand dollars? That we got the trailer for half-price at another thousand because the company had decided to sponsor us? These people only earned about $100 a month! Even old motorcycles like ours didn't even exist in their country at any price. And their governments forbade them from traveling to countries where such things could be found. We decided to talk instead about what the people were like in the States. It soon became obvious to us that the brainwashing we'd heard about was sadly all too true. These folks were astounded to learn that there were people just like themselves in America. They'd been told all their lives that Americans were greedy, money-hungry monsters that hated their minorities and shot at anybody that got in their way. In other words, all the bad stuff in the news was played up and embellished and they were never given wind of the good things going on all the time...nor even just about regular folks going about their business and being nice to each other. "What sort of food do Americans eat?," they asked? We said, "Which Americans? The Japanese Americans, the Mexican Americans, the Swedish Americans?" Their eyes grew very round as understanding dawned.

The next morning we heard that over three hundred East Germans were using the easing of the Hungarian borders to try to dash to the west. Someone in the campground had seen a few that were caught, and the story went that the punishment wasn't pretty. We wondered what on earth that meant. By noon everyone was listening to the radios around us. The newscasters went too fast for Terence to understand much of it, but he was able to talk to the other campers who spoke German and it seemed to be all about the defections. Apparently people were making it across. We could feel the excitement around the camp.

After lunch we rode back to Györ to sightsee a bit. Tired of walking in the heat, we went inside a church to rest. It was a dark, cavernous place without chairs or pews but at least nice and cool so we walked around looking at the sooty paintings and peeling plaster. We were just remarking about how sad it was that there was no money to restore the church when we were surprised to see a huge hand-carved pulpit covered in gold and looking splendid. Time and neglect could not dim that giant bit of swirling Baroque and we hoped it would last at least until it could be appreciated again.

Walking back into the sunlight, we decided to do as the Hungarians were doing and get some ice cream. There seemed to be a stand on every street. I chose boring old vanilla by mistake because I couldn't read the sign, and for a second scoop, pointed to something green which turned out to be a very interesting apple flavor. Terence picked kiwi and banana--both very tasty. Four scoops plus a tip came to 34 cents. The "tip" was really just a keep-the-change affair because the silly money was really so worthless.

On the evening, August 21st, Alex Petz and the Gomezes finally showed up. Patricia and the children had elected to stay home. The folks were hot and starving because they hadn't had anything to eat but a cup of tea all day and they were kept two hours at the border waiting for visas. I handed out bread and jam to keep them from fainting and then we all took the short walk to the town's only restaurant.

Pannonhalma is renown in Hungary for its hilltop monastery--once the castle of Prince Geza and his son Stephan, who became Hungary's first Christian king. In better times, the small town must have been full of visitors--especially in the summer, but Communism changed all that, and they certainly weren't set up for foreign tourists the summer we arrived. The front door of the restaurant was closed, but we heard people dining somewhere and so we all walked around to the back where there was a sort of beer garden. We recognized a couple of other folks from the campground sitting at the tables, who waved at us. A waiter that looked as if he'd been double-dared to approach us tossed us some dirty menus. It was no surprise to discover that almost nothing on the menu was available, but after several glasses of a sort of green colored wine, we didn't really care what we got as long as it resembled food. Something came out of the kitchen on a platter that reminded me of the meal in Györ across from the Opera House. Again, thinly sliced meat without a name smothered in paprika sauce. Only this time it didn't look quite as good. Something about the color of the meat and the watery sauce made me wish I were back in Györ. Oh well, the wine cost practically nothing and there was plenty of that, at least. I finished the green stuff in my wine glass and helped myself liberally to the reds for the rest of the dinner. As I recall they were out of any sort of dessert and had no coffee either, but what the hell, the price of the meal for the five of us only came to about ten dollars. How could we argue with that? By the time we were walking home I was certainly feeling no pain and the fact that the dinner might not have earned any Michelin stars didn't really bother any of us at that point.

When we arrived at the campground, someone offered me a lemonade heavily laced with vodka, and I quaffed it down without thinking. Dropped into bed like a brass cloud and was unconscious to the world until about two A.M. when I awoke with a searing headache and realized I'd been poisoned. Made it to the restroom where I waited to die between dreadful episodes of being sick. To my amazement, out of the corner of my bloodshot eye, I noticed someone was cleaning the restroom without so much as a glance in my direction. At three in the morning! Perhaps she was used to such occurrences with foreigners who drank the local swill intemperately. I crawled back to the trailer with bits of red pepper still stuck in my burning nose and throat. No help for it. I was wondering why nobody else had joined me in the restroom. Could I really have been the only one who got sick?

The next morning everybody was sympathetic but infuriatingly healthy. They all wanted to see more of Hungary as we'd planned and I didn't want to be left behind, so they pulled me into Alex's van along with them and as I stretched out on the pillows under the back window, Alex drove to Györ, because of course Priscilla and Chris hadn't seen it yet. Mother Gail hadn't been well enough to make breakfast for everybody this morning so they had decided to find a place in Györ to get some eggs. In my weakened and cranky state, I let them know that they'd be lucky to find one of the ice-cream stands open. I was jealous that they felt good enough to actually eat again.

I fell asleep in the van and a couple of hours later they returned, complaining of the horrible service they'd received in trying to get some breakfast, but at least they were fed and soon we were on our way to the ancient city of Szekesfehervar. After we arrived, I was feeling almost human again and walked around with them into the open-air museum where we attempted to read the Hungarian signs telling of this city once being the seat of Kings and so forth (a bit of information I had read in English somewhere else). We found an apothecary and mimed our request for aspirin, which we received in a bottle of 10 for 3.60 florints or about 40 cents. They probably thought they'd gouged us.

Everybody but me was hungry again. Alex drove us to the very popular Lake Balaton in hopes of finding a public eatery. After almost despairing, as it became obvious the local holiday-makers had ported in their own food in baskets from home, we spotted a small outdoor restaurant with a parking lot full of foreign license plates and knew we'd found our watering-hole. The place was full--mostly folks from Holland and West Germany--and the few waiters looked as happy as if they were facing a firing squad, but we were handed a menu and told to sit down at table that looked like it hadn't been cleaned since the summer before. By this time we were all pros about ordering from a Hungarian menu. Without looking at it we asked what was available and we were happily surprised to discover that besides the usual sliced beast under paprika sauce, there was a fish soup and even a side order of rice for those who ordered (and paid for) the meat dish. Avoiding the red pepper sauce as best I could, I forced myself to poke about in the fish soup for things recognizable and had a couple of bites of my friends' rice and decided I was going to live. I tried not to care that the bottled water seemed a little cloudy and just fervently hoped they didn't fill the bottles from the lake behind the restaurant...

On a sort of porch near the kitchen, was a gen-u-ine gypsy trio at work entertaining us. I liked the guy on the zither, and the oom-pah oom-pah of the small bass viol was harmless, but the lead violinist was a joke! Luckily for us, he was kept from strolling our way by a tipsy fan who kept tipping him and asking for the same songs over and over so he could sing his favorite verses. The guy with the violin leaned over the old drunk and sawed and pizzicatoed and once in awhile slipped into snatches of things recognizable. But not for long. He never seemed to finish anything. Staring at the trio and not believing my ears, I began to wonder why they didn't throw the old guy out. Then it occurred to me that maybe the man wasn't drunk at all. Maybe he was part of the gypsy band and placed there to rescue our violinist from having to finish difficult cadenzas or say, the ending of the piece. The coins that flowed so freely were probably back in his pocket for the next set. The other diners didn't seem to mind the questionable musicianship and the bellowing of the supporter. Terence commented that if the gypsy violinist came near us, we should all pretend we were using sign language! I howled at the joke, but the rest of our party didn't seem to get it. Meanwhile, Priscilla and I got stung to death on our lady-like ankles by voracious lake mosquitoes.

Alex realized a little late that we probably wouldn't make it back to camp before the 10 o'clock curfew. Unlike our first campground experience in Hungary, where holiday revelers partied loudly until dawn, the Pannonhalma camp was run by a little Caligula. At precisely 10 p.m., the jerk first rang a bell to mark the hour, then, just in case he missed waking every poor sod who might have turned in early, he played a sort of Taps-plus-improv for several minutes afterward which had been recorded lovingly a few years back, we learned, by a Belgian who had stolen his heart, or something like that. Anyway, as Alex didn't want to miss the Belgian Taps and have the gate locked so that he and the Gomezes would have to spend the night parked in the street, he was determined to get us all home lickity-split--only his sense of direction was just a little worse than his..er..punctuality, and after some pretty strange turns, Terence grabbed the map and began shouting directions at him while the Gomezes and I bumped along in back and dozed. It was an eerie experience to travel at high speed over rough roads in the total dark. Even passing through villages not a light was to be seen. *Electricity is expensive, why waste it?*, I thought sleepily.

As Priscilla and I made breakfast together the next morning, we laughed about just making it past the gate as the bugle began to toot. The camp director must have been quite disappointed when he didn't get the chance to lock us all out and point to us as an example of Western decadence. As we ate, we realized this would be the last meal we friends would have together for awhile because Terence and I were going on to Budapest while the rest would be turning back to Austria. Chris and Priscilla begged us to visit their home in Zimbabwe one day and of course we invited them to California, but we all knew it was far more probable that we might never see them again and it hurt. I had become very fond of her and I knew she felt the same...

When we arrived at Camp Hars-Hegy, Budapest, the place was a madhouse. Mostly Germans with their kids--frantically taking advantage of the last week before they have to go back to school. We are pounced upon as the afternoon's entertainment while we ride around and around looking for a space left to camp in. We finally had to settle for a tiny spot between a large RV from France and the ladies's showers. Terence didn't seem to mind a bit when the sweet young mädchen paraded by in their towels and bathing suits, but any peace and quiet was out of the question. Hoping to find something Hungarian, we hurriedly ate dinner and locked up and took off for the city on the Gold Wing. Not quite into the main part of town, we were hit by a cloudburst! Terence ran the big bike up onto the sidewalk and we waited it out under a large awning marked Coca-Cola hanging from a Snack Bar that was closed for the night. People in the street under their umbrellas twisted to look at the odd picture we must have made, then turned on their heels and quickly walked away.

When the storm lifted, we rode downtown and tooled around the shiny wet streets admiring the beautiful old architecture. Eight bridges crossed the river Duna (still the Danube!), and on the Pest side, stood a great university-gothic style building with stone knights in niches and a huge dome that was lit by a spotlight. Where there must have once been a cross at the top was now a bright red star glowing against the night sky.

It began to rain again and we decided to head back to the campground except that we'd forgotten the way. After a few wrong turns in the bowels of Budapest, Terence spotted a couple of young men on motorbikes by the side of the street and we pulled up to them and he asked in German if they could point us in the direction of Camp Hars-Hegy. Their response was enthusiastic, to say the least. Several more fellows appeared out of the dark--many also with motorbikes. One of them explained in very good

French that we had had the good fortune to meet up with none other than the "Devils of Obuda," the local "biker gang." I had to smile when I noticed the various uniforms and emblems of these "Devils." At home in America, our rebel youths sport skulls and cross-bones, Nazi swastikas and tattoos and drape themselves in black. Here in Communist Hungary, the forbidden was none other than "Old Glory" itself, helmets and bikes painted with the stars and stripes! They were such bad boys!

Anyway, a bunch of them piled onto about eight of the little bikes, and with our energetic gang of Hell's Devils leading the way, we roared and clattered up and down the hills of Budapest heading for the campground. The little motorbikes were rickety single-cylinder things--MZ's...125's and 250's--and we all had to stop now and then while someone put his chain back on or ran down a street to pick up something that had fallen off. Terence was in hysterics at how those motorcycles were put together. It was funny and of course very sad too. It didn't look like those poor "dev-ils" would ever have the opportunity to even ride a real bike, let alone own one. We poured into camp like a scene from "The Wild One", and the administration was not amused. Still, nobody said anything to us about the disturbance and Terence and I and the Hungarians hugged and hand-shook and back-slapped and we were all friends for life and then suddenly they were gone and we began to miss them already.

The next day, while it rained on the beautiful old city, T. and I took advantage of the low museum admission prices, and took our time indulging ourselves among some of the most wonderful and rare artifacts in Europe. First we visited the State Ethnological Museum on the Pest side of the river. It was a massive building with a very ornate interior in marble and gold leaf that even Communism hadn't been able to destroy. We saw photos and objects from Transylvania and a huge exhibit of Gypsy life. There were black and white photographs of the gypsy faces and children that I know I shall never forget. There was also an exhibition of Nâif painters that some Beverly Hills galleries would love to get their hands on. And all that was just the temporary exhibits! Their permanent stuff included authentic Hungarian costumes in history, tools, jewelry and life-size tableaus of family life in the last century. Also a collection of carved pipes I thought rivaled the best of Japanese netsukes--maidens, stags, faces and several ribald themes.

Feeling hungry and reeling from trying to absorb all those roomfuls, we decided to find a nice quiet restaurant near the museum for lunch. Dreamers. At a "typical" Hungarian restaurant that seemed open for business, we discovered we could have anything we wanted as long a it was carp. Terence and I had noticed a small fish tank with two or three sad-looking fish swimming in the murky water as we walked into the restaurant and thought it was a strange way to decorate. Apparently they'd just been pulled from the beautiful brown Danube and were waiting to grace the table of some unwary tourist. No thanks, we said, and went to find a snack bar.

A couple of pieces of pizza later, we felt much better and strong enough to check out the Museum of Fine Art. A tad disappointing, this museum contained a lot of overly varnished or maybe just under-cleaned old masters. I suspected they hadn't been their best work. Also a collection of equally underwhelming works of lesser artists. But a terrific display of ancient Egyptian goodies. Lots of mummies--wrapped and unwrapped. By the time we made it back to camp we were so tired from standing and staring at rare and wondrous objects that we slept right through the squeals of the girls in the showers.

The Castle Museum on the Buda side was certainly an example of best saved for last. Each room seemed designed for the particular exhibit it held. It was very warm and I felt sorry for the elderly ladies plopped on chairs in every room who were fanning themselves with the translation sheets thoughtfully provided next to each doorway. The Glorious People's Party gives everybody a job whether one wants one or not and these women were stuck at their post all day--uncomplaining, even friendly as they guarded the masterpieces around them. I supposed they sat there until they died of old age. Well, there must be worse jobs. I'm just glad they were allowed a chair.

The place was so rich we had to give up after two hours. Never even made it to the second floor. We would have to come back the next day. That afternoon, while Terence was looking for a chicken in a likely grocery store, I was sitting on the back of the Gold Wing day-dreaming, when a young couple came up to talk to me. I was shaken out of my reverie by their eagerness to tell me their story. It seems she was from West Germany and he from East Germany and they had met in 1984, fell in love and were in despair because he was trapped in the DDR. Every year they timed their short vacations to meet in Hungary and now they were terrified that it would soon be off-limits to East Germans. I had an uncomfortable feeling that they thought I could do something about their plight because I was an American.

Terence came out of the store with the chicken under his arm and they told him the story over again. The whole thing was so theatrical I became really uncomfortable. The young man told us that he wanted to defect--we could see they had discussed it over and over--but he was terrified of prison. This was real, and Terence and I exchanged sickly glances. "Last week-end," the boy cried, "300 East Germans escaped into Austria from Hungary and 200 were caught! Lives destroyed without bullets!" We couldn't think of anything appropriate to say. They knew we couldn't help. Clinging to each other, they turned away, leaving us with gray faces.

Riding into camp we looked at all the people from the DDR differently. And they sensed it. Instead of the usual superficial questions about life in America and how fast could the bikes go, the heartbreaking stories of life in a fenced-in country began to pour out from each visitor until Terence couldn't bear any more and went to bed. It was early and I wanted to write in my journal. I presumed that because I knew so little German they'd go away but it was not to be. The tales of escape and woe turned into begging and before long I had given away the rest of the stove and lamp fuel and what food that could be carried in their jackets. After a while I realized that I was actually taking part in the mad dash for freedom that was making neurotics out of everyone in the campground.

Around three in the morning one of the East German youths was bumping around in the ladies' shower room, singing and shouting as only someone who had drunk too much bad booze could. We had noticed during our stay that a lot of the men had been fortifying themselves with something truly lethal that was made out of whatever could be found with the correct chemistry to render them senseless. Some of the young ones had not bothered to become sober for the whole time they were allowed to be away from home. And the stuff really was poison. The poor youth was raving drunk and was keeping everyone awake. I heard a West German try to quiet him from the doorway and then give up, muttering "Communist SWINE!" Well, well.

After a while even Terence woke up and, as the kid had by this time made it to his pup tent and was thrashing and screaming inside it, Terence walked over to it and knelt down and talked through the tent walls to the boy and after a while he got him to quiet down. Our hero.

On Monday, August 28, in pouring rain, we took down the trailer tent and stuffed it under the mattress and boarded the Wing for Yugoslavia. Sometime during the night, most of the East Germans had departed and we wondered if they had tried to cross the border to Austria. "Lives destroyed without bullets!," the boy had said.

Spent the next night all by ourselves in a small woodsy campground near the border and then early the next morning, crossed into Yugoslavia with no hassles. We changed money into more worthless paper and then rode into Zagreb. Terence looked up the local Taekwon Do instructor-- master Toni Nobilo--who was very friendly and took us out for a beer. Unfortunately, their studio was closed for the summer also, so Terence wouldn't get a chance to teach there either.

Still in Yugoslavia, we rolled into a campground that evening that was fast being inundated from all the recent rain. The long road into the site was full of puddles and soft mud and made our progress slow and dirty. It must have been a beautiful spot once--with a castle-turned hotel by the lake and tall trees all around. A van from England joined us on some higher ground and it was lovely to hear our language again. A swan with five cygnets paddled up to us as we ate our dinner by the swollen lake. We were sorry we had to leave for Italy the next day.

Chapter Twenty-Five

THE ITALIAN TREFFEN

HAPPILY, the morning shown bright and clear as we rode past the last of the onion-domed village churches and the funny little top-heavy wooden barns of Yugoslavia. We came into Italy near Triest and then rode until the sun set--frantically looking for a place to camp. A farmer's dirt road past a field of soy beans looked promising and Berlitz guide book in hand, Terence bravely asked the old man at the nearest house if we could spend the night there. The man looked very frightened at first, but soon understood that we were harmless and began to warm to us. Later, he passed a wine bottle with one glass over the fence so that we could taste his own vines and feel welcome. That made us very happy and we wished our Italian were better so we could have a nice chat and maybe meet the Missus, but at this point we had to make do. His dog barked at us all night from the yard, but we were so tired we didn't care. In the morning, I gave the old fella a copy of a cartoon I had drawn of the two of us, and waving to the shy wife in the doorway, we pulled away.

The Autostrada was fast, but the toll booths seemed to be run by hoods. They popped up every few miles, and they wanted to charge us as a car and trailer which was expensive and beyond our means, so after a few heated disputes between my driver and the Italians in the kiosks, we got off of the superhighway and headed for the smaller roads. It was a much more scenic route to be sure, but also much longer and requiring much stopping and map reading. We were relieved to arrive at last at our destination in the Umbrian hills: the International Gold Wing Treffen at Castigliano del Lago. It was dark and we were very tired, but the lights and the laughter and the noise of a couple hundred motorcycle engines really picked up our spirits. We felt that we were in the bosom of our family and the Italians running this particular show made us feel like royalty. Lots of our new friends from the other Treffens in England and Germany were there and as soon as we settled in, we joined them for beers in the main tent.

Our Italian Gold Winger hosts had worked hard to make this Treffen a success, but the weather wouldn't cooperate. Trips had been planned to Assisi and environs--even to the famous Lamborghini factory and Wine Cellars, and an interesting small motorcycle museum, but only the hardiest braved the rain storms that whipped off the lake and drenched the land for that Treffen weekend. Of course Terence and I took the tours. We were fairly used to riding in the rain by now, and we didn't want to miss anything. But a lot of the other bikers were softer, most of them worked all week, and the British especially had had their hearts set on a weekend in sunny Italy, and when the rain wouldn't let up, they chose to stay in their tents and drink beer or nap--waiting for the party in the main tent that would start in the evening. Terence and I felt sorry for the Italians. It was a rotten piece of luck.

About sixty motorcycles braved the long wet tour up the hills of Umbria to Asissi on Saturday. The rain came down in sheets and very soon we were all drenched and miserable. The Italians had planned little snack and wine stops along the way which helped considerably, and the ancient village of Asissi was enough to warm the heart of the most uncomfortable of the sufferers, but the long way home in the downpour simply served to remind us what we must be missing in spectacular views along the way and it was pretty hard to take.

Almost immediately after peeling ourselves off the bikes from the swim home, we were ordered to line up again for the (usually) very popular "Parade of Nations." Back into the rain again we went, but nobody minded much this time. This was the opportunity for everyone to show off his bike and fly his flag and as T. and I were the only Americans in the parade, we brought up the rear--in this case, a coveted spot. People leaned out of their windows; holding small children and shouting and waving. We all waved back and it felt so damn good--it's just hard to describe. The road wound up from the lake to the castle and the narrow-ness of the village streets amplified the din of the motors to a deafening sound and everybody loved it! Being the last couple and having our nation's flag tied to the aerial--wetly flapping in the breeze made us feel terribly important as we heard the children cry out Americani! Americani! Sometimes, in the twists of the tiny streets, the kids would run behind our bike to reach out and touch it as if we were some sort of holy relic. It was certainly some sort of relic, by this time.

Sunday dawned warm and clear! I grabbed a couple of things to wash at the basins and then draped them decorously on bungee cords between the bike and tent. The other Gold Wingers laughed to see the Americans act like gypsies, but they of course were going to be riding home later--to warm houses and dry clothes, and for us, home was a long way off. Gypsies we were.

We had a long way to go to get to the GW Treffen in Luxembourg by September 7th. We said Arrivederci to our friends and hosts in Castigliano, and rolled up into the hills to pick and find a way other than the expensive Autostrada which everyone else was taking to get home, the lucky stiffs. It took us about an hour to make thirty miles or so and as the afternoon got darker and the sun left us to go shine on more fortunate beings, we realized our pretty day was over already and we braced ourselves for more rain. On a mountain top somewhere out of Florence, the clouds began to dump their loads and by evening, with no hope of finding a campground up there, Terence pulled into a small parking lot next to what looked like a tiny village square and we covered the trailer-bed with our tarp and huddling together, ate some left-overs and listened to the thunder and lightning.

The next day was no better. When it wasn't raining, the fog was so thick and cold it might have been the Alps in January. Still with no trailer brakes, we slipped and slid up and down muddy mountain roads and past drab little villages that seemed deserted in the cruel weather. By midday I was flagging with hunger and soggy depression, so Terence finally pulled into an empty restaurant parking lot and as a large dog on a chain stared nervously at us from the corner of the building, he poured me a portion of rum we kept for such emergencies. We got out the stove and heated some water for our dry soup packets. The heat from our little stove was so lovely. I stuck a fork into a piece of bread I'd sliced and held it over the flame and the charred results with a little butter tasted a lot like toast. I was very pleased with my new discovery. We were in much better spirits as we boarded the bike again to crawl our way slowly north.

That evening, we had stopped for gas when Terence discovered he had somehow lost our petrol coupon book--which we had bought at the Yugoslavian border in order to save money. It was an awful blow to our budget. At the time gasoline was about $6.00 a gallon in Italy. I paid for the gas with the last of my Italian lira and as we pulled away from the station, the weather and the hardships and now this latest bit of ill luck all conspired to lay me low and I began to cry inside my helmet. Terence was very sad and sweet and I felt so bad for him too, yanking me and the giant trailer-with-no-brakes all over the Italian mountains for days in the freezing rain and fog. At least we had some coupons left for the Autostrada that we'd been saving for about this far north, and so as soon as he could find an on-ramp, T. pulled us onto the superhighway and after a couple of hours going at top speed, and the weather improving, we both felt much better.

Just before dark, we pulled off to find a place for the night. We were just north of Milano and had passed what looked like the last of the villages for awhile. The terrain was treeless, with no place for us to hide. We pulled up against a long high wall and got off the bike to look around. It was a cemetery, but unlike most cemeteries we'd seen in Italy, this one looked rather uncared for, if not forgotten, and so we decided to keep the dear-departed company. It had been a very long day.

As darkness fell and we were finishing dinner, thousands of tiny lights went on all over the tombs and gravesites, throwing an eerie glow over our wall and giving us a bit of a shock. We walked over to the entrance to have a better look but the iron gates were locked, which begged the question as to just for whom were the lights lit?

We packed it up early after a great night's sleep. There's certainly no quieter place than a nice graveyard to camp by! By noon we were at the Swiss border where we had a friendly chat with a young Swiss border guard about visiting California and how to camp free of hassles with (ha ha) cops. He was very appreciative.

Chapter Twenty-Six

THE TREFFEN IN LUXEMBOURG

THE SCENERY through the Italian Switzerland was far more appealing to my jaundiced eye than the other Switzerlands up north. The gardens had weeds in places and several chalets were unpainted and I even saw an occasional flower past its prime in the window boxes. Homes looked lived-in and cozy and I decided I would love to set up my easel there. We climbed past melting snow rivers with giant boulders and crumbling stone bridges. Dark brown chalets perched in the mist on cliffs between rolling soft green expanses, and the view began to be below us as well as above. The road suddenly became steeper and then cobbled and very narrow and slippery and Terence loved the challenge. "WA-HOO!," he yelled, as he yanked the heavy trailer up the mountain and around the sharp curves. I clung to him for dear life and tried not to show my definite lack of enthusiasm for the sport. "I'm going to pull over as soon as I can find a place, and take some pictures of this road-from-hell!" he shouted. "Better not stop now," I told him. "We've got a police car on our tail." Expletives from Terence. And the uniforms stayed right with us the whole tortuous way to the top of the notorious San Gottardo Pass. A great relief to see them drive away without giving us a ticket for being a hazard or something. We slid off the motorcycle and crumpled on some seats overlooking the Dreadful Ascent and took long breaths of the rarefied air. Little did I know at the time, that the only thing worse than riding up that slippery mountain on a motorcycle was riding under it, but that wasn't to happen for awhile yet.

In the town of Goldau, we stopped to ask directions from men sitting in a doorway, and one of them jumped up and greeted us and acted as if he'd been expecting us. He put two small glasses of something potent in our hands which turned out to be the local "white lightning", and talking in three languages at once, he led us into the shed to show us his pride and joy--three huge copper vats. He told us that we must come back later and get some good pictures of them--after he'd cleaned them. He poured something from another bottle into our glasses which turned out to be a sublime plum brandy. We would have liked to tell him how impressed we were with it, but try as we might, it seemed impossible to get a word in edgewise--in any language.

After the pear brandy, which definitely was our favorite, we begged him to let us go or we'd be unable to get back on the road and stay upright! He grinned and told us the campground was only two kilometers farther and would we be sure to come back tomorrow? Whatta guy. We all kissed each other on both cheeks several times and Terence and I managed to wobble our way into the night, singing the praises of the Italian-Swiss. Yodel-o-dee-hoo!

After visiting the Victorinox Swiss Army knife factory the next morning, we stopped at our friendly brandy maker's to get his picture standing next to the now super-clean and shiny copper distillers. He was pleased that we had come back and I gave him a few of our Castigliano del Lago stickers to join many others from everywhere on his walls. Hugs all around and we were off again.

I somehow lost the big map of Switzerland--probably flew off my lap in the wind when I was chalet-gazing. Of course the real reason I lost it, I decided, was to make Terence feel better about losing the gas coupons in Italy, but somehow, he didn't see it that way. Every time thereafter that we took a wrong road in Switzerland, I got blamed, and I decided that by the time we reached Germany by what might have been one or two perhaps curious routes, the man was not a gentleman.

The German autobahn is free, bless their Teutonic hearts, and we were able to make up precious time by staying on it all the way to the French border near Strasbourg. It looked like we were going to make it in time to the Luxembourg Gold Wing Treffen!

There were zillions of Gold Wings in the fields near the Knockelscheur campground. The little country is so centrally located to most of the Gold Wing owners in Europe and Scandinavia that it is always a very popular Treffen. As I may have mentioned before, Terence parties hearty. I try, but the truth is, I bore easily at such things. Luckily for me, Terence didn't care if I was at his side swilling warm beer or not. It was fine with him if I left him listening to the very loud quasi-rock bands with his mates--sinking in a sea of cigarette smoke and discussing motorcycle engines for the rest of the night. I retired to read. Curled up in our little trailer-tent bed listening to the familial hum of the swarms of my fellow fans of the Open Road around me in the night. I fell asleep early, comforted in sweet security.

For the Saturday Tour, we were led over hills of bronze and copper as the vineyards turned into the mantle of Autumn. The day was breezy and even sunny at times, and snaking our motorcycles through villages of waving arms and the smell of wood smoke and ripened grapes was a plea-sure tough to beat. Luxembourg is tiny but very beautiful, and we felt fortunate to experience it from a bike. We were taken to a big winery high above the Moselle river. So much free wine was handed out to us I began to wonder if everybody would make it back to camp. It seemed to me, for a country that's so very strict about driving under the influence it was an odd thing to do. Happily, we all made it back safely.

After the Treffen was over, Terence and I wandered slowly south through Germany. We visited Norbert and Berga and again they were the perfect hosts. Terence needed some concentrated study time for his Law School, so while he studied, I took long walks to look at the German archi-tecture in Mainz. After I washed some clothes, Berga showed me how to hang the laundry on long lines in the attic. Everybody in the apartment building dried their things that way. While it rained outside, the space under the roof was warm and dry and it only took a couple of days--and with the added advantage of not having unsightly wash lines draped from everybody's balcony. Very efficient. As soon as Terence was caught up with his studies, we rode to the Metzler tire factory on the way to the border and thanks to Gary Gallagher, our generous Metzler contact in Seattle, we got a free tire for the Gold Wing.

A couple of "wild" camps and then Nürnberg. The campground was a hefty $10 but well worth it because we really enjoyed seeing the infamous city. Lots of the medieval part of the old town was now restored completely after the bombing of '45. The reconstruction was so well done that it didn't look new. We toured the notorious courtroom where the war criminals were tried, and then the proud German History museum which is a true gem. We slowly rode past what was once Hitler's viewing box at the now deserted parade grounds. Tall trees had grown up through the stands where once people cheered for goose-stepping battalions of German soldiers, and weeds were flourishing all over the pavement where once hundreds of Panzer tanks rolled in formation.

Chapter Twenty-Seven

BACK BEHIND THE IRON CURTAIN

WE SPENT another night in a forest and then on to Czechoslovakia. We rode to the border through thick fog. The experience of once more entering a communist country was made even more creepy by the wet and cold. Tall guard towers loomed over the mist and the humorless guards with their great-coats buttoned to their chins again made us feel the eerie discomfort of feeling we were in some sort of second-rate spy novel.

We were forced to change fifteen dollars each into Czech money at the border. For each of the ten days we were planning to be in the country! That come to a whopping $300! Much more, of course, than we had planned to spend there and also eliminating any chance we might have had to take advantage of the famous "Black Market" change system, which was obviously why they were enforcing the nasty law. Very annoying. And even more so as we discovered later that there was nothing to buy in Czechoslovakia!

Riding deeper into the country that gray morning was a real study in gloom. Houses in terrible states of disrepair, gardens full of weeds and broken things. Nobody around--all must have been at their appointed tasks in the big factories that squatted and belched black smoke in the center of each mean little cluster of houses...the children in classrooms in grim little uniforms--sitting at grimy little desks. Everywhere, unfinished buildings stood, forlorn and waiting in vain for someone to do something with the ever-present mound of sand and cement and heaps of concrete blocks that lay in the yards. Gray, all gray. We didn't stop until we reached Prague. There were no campgrounds along the way and we couldn't camp "wild" because we had been told we were required to show an official stamp from a hotel or camp director for each night when we got to the Czechoslovakian border on the way out. If we should be so brazen as to spend the night in a private home, we were required to let the local Polizei know where we were staying. Sure, and then our hosts would disappear, we thought. We were relieved to at least see a gas station now and then--even though they all had long lines--but then we were shocked to learn the price per gallon was as bad as Italy! At least we knew how we were going to spend that $300. We reasoned that no one except the high officials and foreign tourists could possibly afford to own a car. Much later we discovered there was a different rate for the natives!

Officials at the first campground near Prague said they would allow us to spend one night, but that all the campgrounds in the city would be closing for the winter the next day. Their smirks were the nearest thing to a smile we'd seen in that country as they told us there was nothing anyone could do about it. Fortunately, they were wrong (or just mean), and we found another place on the south end of town the next day that wasn't going to close for another month. It was Camp Branik, lots nicer than the first, and situated right next to the Vltava River which was none other than Smetena's own "Moldau"!

Registering at the camp office was a new experience. Again, in the Communist attempt to keep every citizen employed, there were far too many chiefs at the desk, which made the simple process drag on into the afternoon with our patience fraying with each bureaucratic start and stop-page. Two rather elderly people at separate desks went over our papers and passports and filled out more forms for us. They seemed frightened. I tried to think why. One reason could have been the sight and noise of two big, black and filthy motorcycles and trailer bursting into their space where only swans and the occasional well-trained camper usually appeared. Another might have been our appearance. I knew I must have looked odd. A middle-aged motorcycle mama in a cheap, frayed Taiwanese leather jacket and dirty jeans. Ugh. I looked over at Terence. Dust in his beard, bugs in his teeth. Well, no wonder. It's American Bikers From Hell. Open your borders an inch, and the next thing you know, you've got a couple of Hell's Angels from America the Bruteful. A man in a shiny green business suit watched worriedly and offered suggestions and gave commands to the workers at the desks. Terence said he was speaking in Russian.

After we had been given more paperwork and labels and tags for the tent and bikes, we were issued an old gentleman whose job it was to "show us the best place for our particular needs." He turned out to be a wonderful guy who spoke six languages and even shared his loaf of bread when he heard we hadn't been able to find any. He had been treated by the others in the office like a bell-hop, and was obviously distrusted by his comrades because he could hold conversations with folks from the decadent West. If he hadn't been over eighty, they probably would have reported him and he'd be shipped off to Siberia as a subversive.

Shopping for groceries the next day was no fun at all. Prices weren't too bad, and would have been terrific if we could have taken advantage of the Black Market, but finding anything we needed was nearly impossible. I was determined to find something to send to my son for his birthday in October, but although I pushed and shoved my way through promising lines at better-looking stores in downtown Prague, the article for sale was always something equivalent to a jar of cabbage, and with a heavy heart I had to give up. We found it very strange how difficult it was to find bread. Bread, the staff of life! Candy and even sticky pastries appeared sometimes in the tiny shops that carried the cabbage jars, but no bread. No bakeries. No fresh fruit or vegetables. We bought a jar of cabbage. And when I mixed it with a can of tuna later for dinner, nobody complained.

Prague, however, had other charms. One of the very few cities in eastern Europe not touched by bombs in WWII the architecture of many centuries stood in all their glory. T. and I spent a week slowly drinking it all in; the Old Town and the New, the fabulous Charles Bridge and the castle on the hill. Countless spires and towers dominated the landscape and the Vltava flowed gently under the bridges to deposit swans at our campsite downstream.

We visited the Jewish Quarter and marveled at the beauty of the synagogues and the amazing old cemetery. Not being allowed any extra land to bury their dead, the Jews had had to crowd the corpses on top of one another in the ground. The headstones resembled crooked teeth. Inside a nearby building, an

exhibit   of   concentration   camp
artwork by children during the war made us gasp. Powerful and horrible.

Back at the campground, we met some lovely people. Terence found a busload of Russians that kept him very busy for a while as they helped him study their language. On our second day there, we met Pip and Susan, a lively couple of artists from London. Someone had pushed their Range Rover into the Moldau/Vltava while they were registering in the office and they were standing on the rocks above wondering what to do. No one among the East German, Russian and Czech campers seemed eager to say if they had observed anything, much less help the couple pull it out, so Terence knocked on van doors until he found a New Zealand couple who were happy to back their van down the path to the river. The guys tied all available ropes to the Rover's back bumper and with much slipping and bashing against the moss-covered boulders, we managed to slowly guide the heavy thing back up the riverbank to the road. None of us Western degenerates could come up with a good reason why someone would want to push the Rover into the river. On the other hand maybe it really wasn't all that hard to understand...

Later, Pip and Susan and the couple from New Zealand joined us for a night out at the Opera, which cost us each about four dollars for box seats! The opera was "Lucia di Lammermoor," sung in Czech. The singers were not quite as wonderful as the Baroque interior of the Opera House, but we all had a good time and later found a little bar open that served what must be one of the greatest dark beers in the world. For about thirty cents a mug. Terence was ready to get into the export business when the proprietor said they made it in the back room--just to drink on the premises! Terence's disappointment was a pathetic thing to see.

One afternoon on a side street in Prague, a Trabant cut us off, and a young fellow popped out to shake our hands and introduce himself. His name was Ludwig Balaz and he spoke a little English and some German and was intrigued by the motorcycle and was also interested in having us come to the restaurant that night where his father played the lead violin with a gypsy band. Oh oh. We felt we shouldn't refuse because it would be a good way to meet the natives and how expensive could it be if it was a genuine restaurant for Czechs? And as it turned out it wasn't all that expensive...although we began to question our wisdom on the way there as we got lost several times--finally finding it in a very scary part of the city and then had to pound on a dark door to be let in. Inside, it actually was a pretty jolly place compared to what we'd seen in Hungary, and no doubt due in no small part to Ludwig's father, the violinist, who was what a true Gypsy violinist should be--a real entertainer who could make you laugh and cry and clap your hands and he would still stay on pitch...not to mention being able to finish the piece! We thought he was splendid. Ludwig was there as promised, but wasn't much help in deciphering the menu so we wound up with a sort of salty, dry pork chop with canned vegetables on the side. When I think about it, it was probably all they had. I should have been grateful it wasn't cabbage.

Ludwig had a friend with him he introduced as George. Neither of them ate anything but just watched us as we tried to swallow the dry food and stay smiling. His father came and sat with us on a break and told us how he had once many years ago, been invited to play in an orchestra in England but his government wouldn't let him.

There were no campgrounds on the way to Bratislava, our next destination, and we knew we couldn't make it by nightfall. Out of Brno and up into some mountains, we spied a large abandoned-looking racetrack with the sign saying: GRAND PRIX-CSSR. Frantic, as night was closing in, we begged the watchman in pantomime to let us stay the night within his wire fences so we wouldn't be found by the Polizei. He took pity on us and with a shrug waved us in. I made dinner in the parking lot as the icy wind picked up and we piled on the sweaters.

The old fellow wouldn't give us anything resembling a stamp for the border police the next morning so we had to do without and roll on.

The city of Bratislava struck me at first as little more than endless undulating oily cobblestones with deep and jagged potholes that, if you didn't pay constant attention, could throw you off your bike in a microsecond. These weren't the same cobblestones that we had seen in quaint villages in Western Europe, these suckers were carved into squares, and when new and placed closed together on a reasonably flat surface, I could see why they might be fine for automobiles or even horses and carts in countries with lots of rain. But time and heavy traffic and monster neglect had made those little cubes part and sink and in some places disappear altogether so that riding a motorcycle in stop and go traffic and across the constant slippery tram tracks that meandered over every blessed street made the riding experience about as enjoyable as the bridge over the river Loire in a hurricane!

I was so glad when we finally found the municipal campground. And so pissed when we were told it was closed. Of course the book said it was open all year. We drove through the open gates anyway. Let the Polizei descend. What do they expect us to do? Camp in the street? There was a sort of kayaking class going on about fifty yards away on a dirty-looking river, but no one else occupied the field we chose to camp on and feeling brazen and somewhat invincible having gotten this far in a rather hostile land, we set up our big tent and made dinner. Terence announced that we had to find a way to get rid of the rest of our Czech money, so we decided to go to the only show happening in town that night, billed as a concert of the winners of the International Music Competition, who would be playing with the Czech Philharmonic. We locked up the trailer and rode the Gold Wing into town. Waiting for the doors to open, we met a nice Belgian who asked us into the local bar for a glass of wine. Who could refuse?

The concert was delightful and the hall a wonder, with clean and sparkling chandeliers. Bohemian glass at its showiest. Later, our Belgian friend invited us to accompany him and some of his pals to a private Disco Club where they almost didn't let me in because I was wearing jeans, and after looking around at the clientele, I could understand why. The young men and women were all dressed to kill--or at least capture--in threads I hadn't seen since the sixties. Through the clouds of smoke I caught glimpses of beehive hairdos and polyester mini-dresses and enough makeup to rival a drag queen's. After one horrified glance, they ignored me, no doubt considering me harmless enough and as Terence was practicing his German, I was left to wonder how I was going to get the smoke out of our clothes. We were served our drinks. One could order anything one desired as long as it was something that tasted like diet Pepsi and it came warm.

Dragging ourselves away about midnight, we drove through unlighted streets to our dark and deserted campground and discovered that we had been relieved of our stove and lantern! So much for the "Crimeless Society". It made us angry, but of course we knew we were at fault for leaving such treasures unattended. Terence sadly observed that it was truly annoying to realize that the thieves wouldn't be able to use them long without replacement parts, which they would never be able to find in Czechoslovakia.

After a sleepless night we broke camp and pulled the trailer into town for one last look at Bratislava. We found a place to park it on a side street and locked the whole rig together that would take Godzilla to pull apart. Enjoyed the paintings in the Czech National Gallery immensely and then wandered into an exhibit in a sort of Department Store that blew our socks off! It was works by the best of the world's Children's Book Illustrators. About ten room-fulls of the most outstanding imagination and detail and expert rendering I have ever had the pleasure to gaze upon. I came out inspired and resolved to be a better artist, and Terence planned to make it his life's work to collect the best illustrated children's books of every country. He said it would be a great way to learn the languages.

At a filling station, we struck up a conversation with a very nice professor of Psychology at the local university. After hearing of the theft the night before, he became upset and insisted we visit his family for tea that evening. By now, Terence and I knew enough about Czechoslovakia to be aware that the gentleman was putting himself and his loved ones in jeopardy by inviting us to his home, but it seemed that it meant a great deal to him that we should not leave his country with a bad impression, so we accepted.

The evening was another eye opener for us. I was reminded of the tragic young couple in Budapest who couldn't find a way to be together. Again, that feeling of hopelessness and trying to cope, serving a lifetime sentence as a victim of a cruel political hoax--while the rest of the world seems to be wallowing in freedom. Dr. Igor Brezina and his wife and two children lived in a neat but very small apartment near the Comenius University campus. He had studied in London and was desperate to talk in English. His wife could understand enough to follow, but was too shy to try to use the language to speak much. We were asked to please keep our voices low because the neighbors would certainly be curious and there would be rewards for any information at all that might be given the local police as to our unusual visit! Two small children stood in the doorway in nightdress, polite but obviously waiting to see if we might grow horns as they watched. Dr. Brezina poured us wonderful vodka and his wife served sandwiches with much apologizing for the staleness of the bread. Apparently, she had been unable to locate any bread for days. The professor seemed to be in some pain and after a while he confessed that he had had a terrible toothache for weeks but of course it was unthinkable that he should go to one of the "butchers" at the clinics. He said he would just live with it. "Good God!," Terence's look said. Months later, after Czechoslovakia became free, we often thought of the kind couple and hoped the poor guy got his tooth fixed!

At the Austrian border we were commanded to open all compartments in the trailer and bikes, but otherwise the crossing was hassle-free and no one even asked for that stupid over-night-stay stamp we'd sweated over for ten days! We probably could have slept in the fields without a hassle!

October 13th brought us back to the Petzes. We'd brought books for the kids and jars of cabbage (we'd learned to like the stuff!) for Alex and Patsy and everybody seemed glad to have us back. We all went to the Museum of Natural History in Vienna on free Sunday and the kids were thrilled to see the great Dinosaur Exhibit (imported from the USA!) Back in Obersdorf, Alex and Terence begin the tough job of fashioning brakes for the trailer and I knuckled down to catching up on my drawings.

Chapter Twenty-Eight

RIDING DOWN THE BOOT OF ITALY

FINALLY THE TRAILER had brakes and, with the weather darkening, we packed to travel to Italy again. This time to stay the winter and hopefully find jobs. It was November 8, 1989. The Petzes actually seemed sorry to see us go. How to possible repay such kindness and generosity? I had drawn a picture in pen and ink of their home for them, but it seemed so inadequate. I liked to think we enriched each other's lives.

We made it to a forest just outside of Graz that night. The rain was holding off, but a very cold wind was blowing as we set up camp and went to bed. We were astounded to discover it was only 6 p.m.! Time to go south!

In a mountain parking area the next morning, we spoke to four Czechs who were on their way to Rome for the canonization of some female saint who founded some monasteries 900 years ago. I was surprised at all the fuss over some ancient businesswoman, but they made it sound terribly important and also seemed almost hysterically happy about being allowed by their government to make the trip. I began to understand a lot more when one of them cracked that if we planned on going back to the Communist countries, we'd better hurry or there might not be anyone there! As soon as we could, we bought a newspaper whose headlines proclaimed that the iron curtain was at last parting--the Berlin Wall was coming down!! Indescribable excitement everywhere we went. And we were in the West. What could it have been like on the other side? We thought of so many of our new friends over there. Good luck, dear people.

The icy rain began to fall and snow appeared at the side of the road in the mountains. We talked it over and decided to hang tough and take the shortcut over the top, instead of the longer but warmer route through Yugoslavia. Our electric vests and gloves kept us warm as we rode through blowing mists and sleet. At the border high on a mountain top, the Italian guard told Terence he was crazy to be pulling such a rig in those conditions, but Terence was feeling smug. He now had brakes on his trailer! We bought petrol coupons and changed some dollars into lira and soon were eating lunch in Italy--underneath a lovely overpass that kept the rain off us.

We found a small abandoned house off the road that evening to hide behind. The sky was clearing and to the west the clouds were several hues of gold and pink. Ah..Italia. We tried to keep our eyes and noses high as long as possible because too soon we discovered our homestead for the night was a dumping ground for what appeared to be several restaurant's leavings--or maybe just one that had been dumping its garbage there for months. Years? Sure saves on trash collecting costs, I'll bet. There were tons of it around. We were grateful for the cold night air keeping the flies away. Some of the food looked almost fresh. I drew closer. Pasta, bread, salad...Hmmm. I wondered if Terence would know the difference...

Now, I know there is nothing original about falling in love with Venice. I hate being like everybody else in saying it's my favorite city. What can I do about it? Sue me, I'm gonna gush. I'm Venetian Blind!!!! Everything written in the gooiest brochures don't even come close. I had passed through once before as a blushing twenty-one-year-old student, but thanks to a young Venetian named Paolo, I wasn't really aware of my surroundings. Or maybe I just wasn't mature enough to appreciate how, maybe once in a blue moon, time and nature can take something mere humans built and transform it into a thing of the rarest beauty.

As at Mount St. Michel in France, the absence of the automobile no doubt has a lot to do with the magic of Venice. And the sea, of course. The salt air in those places is enough to make your heart soar to start with, and the clarity of line and color bouncing off the ancient walls, forces you to realize how much junk most of us are accustomed to looking through every day--smog and dust and chemicals. And the notorious canals? Hey, we just spent the night in a garbage dump. In comparison, Venice smelled like a bouquet of roses.

We were there three short days, camping on the mainland and riding together on my motorcycle over the long bridge and in as far as we were allowed. Then we'd lock it up and load our cameras on our backs and trek with all the other tourists over the bridges and by the canals to the center of the islands, happily getting lost in the mazes along the way. Terence gamely tried several times to meet with the Maestro at the La Fenice Opera house to see about a viola job, but the man never appeared, so we just left our résumés and gave up. The sun shone each day and the full moon rose the minute the sun set--to turn the sea purple and the Byzantine houses rose-pink. We were so happy in such splendor, we were extremely patient with each other as we dawdled for hours looking at things. While I had to stare into every window and inspect every glass bead in case I ever came back with money some day, Terence just stood quietly by. And I waited patiently and smiled like a saint while he poured over windows of camera equipment and ogled the pretty women. It was as if we were on drugs. We both knew such contentment couldn't last forever.

After two days, we couldn't get lost anymore. Then it was "Hello, piazza, we remember you!," and then it became really hard to leave. We wanted to live there for a year or two and see what Venice looked like in the fog or the snow. Even the rain! (Did I say that?) But we had to move on. As we rode down the eastern seacoast toward Ravenna, thick fog appeared. Something terrible was happening to the clutch on the Gold

Wing, and of course all the stores were closed. As we searched for a garage, we realized that we had been riding past miles and miles of housing developments--very upscale ones--and hadn't seen a soul. They were all empty! Summer homes, we guessed. I couldn't help thinking about all those Eastern Europeans with no place to live. The newspapers were saying that many Western Europeans were pouring into the Eastern Sectors claiming land and houses the communists had taken away when their families had fled the countries. Thousands of people were being turned out of their homes. And November can be cruel in Europe.

We found a sandy road to a beach that we camped on. No one around to bother us, but the freezing wind and blowing sand made us pretty uncomfortable and we were glad to yank the trailer back on the road the next morning. Half a mile down the road, the Gold Wing's clutch went out entirely. While I sat on my bike and wrote in my journal, Terence got out his tools and slaved over the problem for awhile and then he nursed the bike the rest of the way to Ravenna. He left me standing next to the big rig in a parking lot reserved for visitors who wanted to see Theodoric's Tomb, a sixth century structure that didn't look all that interesting which was just as well, because it was closed for the season anyway. While I guarded our goods, he drove the Ascot into town to see if he could locate a garage or a (dream on!) Honda parts store.

Amazingly, he actually did find a Honda parts store and even more astonishing, it was open! He was able to buy what he needed and then came back and fixed the darned thing. However, it took him all day so there was no time to look at that famous city's mosaics which was pretty disappointing. We had no choice but to keep going. The good weather of Venice was a fluke. If we didn't go south, they'd be finding our frozen corpses on some side road--still stuck to the motorcycles.

It was after dark. Somewhere out of Rimini, I got grabbed by a peasant on a bicycle. I had just asked him for some directions to a good place to camp and had made the mistake of saying "no" when he asked me if Terence was my husband. That wasn't the first time in Italy I'd been asked if we were married, then the next question would be in the nature of "Was I available?". After all, what was I doing on my own motorcycle if I supposed myself to be a decent woman? I was beginning to be very glad we hadn't followed a whim to cross into the Islamic countries from Gibraltar. ("Nuke 'em all!" said Terence, later.) I shook the man off and rode ahead with Terence following. Feeling our way in the dark a few miles down the road, we found a deserted barn to hide behind and woke the next morning to a busy freeway about 30 yards away!

We had a phone number for an Esperantist who might be able to put us up for the night in Rimini. Unfortunately, he had some sort of problem with the apartment and couldn't let us stay but was most interested in meeting us, so T. invited him to visit us in our tent in the campground in nearby San Marino. His name was Stefano Focchi and when he arrived, I was just serving a pretty good chicken dinner, so we asked him to join us. The "problem" was that he was about to be married and his fiancé was decorating his apartment and we would have surely upset things and of course we understood. His Esperanto was better than Terence's Italian at the time, so the men chatted away, delighted to have someone to speak the language with, and I, wondering if I'd ever gain enough courage in Esperanto to join in a conversation, busied myself with the dinner things and listened in.

Young Stefano enjoyed himself so much in our freezing tent, he insisted we come to dinner the next night at his apartment and meet his fiancé. Of course that meant that poor Franca, his lovely intended, had to do all the cooking--for a couple of complete strangers from a country she didn't seem very fond of. But after the ice was broken--and Terence's Italian was improving fast enough to use it instead of Esperanto, she warmed to us and we had a wonderful meal of northern and exotic Italian delicacies that we're still remembering in our dreams. May they have many happy years together and multi bambini!

On to Rome where all roads are supposed to lead, but somehow we got terribly lost out of San Marino and it took us hours to find the right one. Finally finding a telephone, as the rain began to soak through my tattered jacket, I called Donna Blair, my sister's good friend, who had a large apartment in the heart of the capital and had kindly agreed to put us up a couple of days while we looked at work prospects. She told me she was sorry, but it wasn't "convenient" to have us that week because she was preparing to have ten people for dinner on Thanksgiving Day! I hung up and cried on Terence's shoulder. We hugged each other miserably there while the rain slowly made its way past our jacket collars and down our backs. It had been three years since we had celebrated Thanksgiving and we were homeless and didn't even have a Salvation Army to take us in for a turkey dinner. I hated her thinking she would be doing us such a big favor by letting us sleep on her floor for a couple of nights. Especially as it was the truth.

Long drives and nights next to not-so abandoned rubble heaps. We were seen, but we were no longer afraid of being discovered. It was always raining and the thought of a nice dry police station had its appeal. We made lousy time because of the unmarked and slippery roads, but what did it matter? We had no real destination except south and we were both pretty depressed, money was low and news was bad from California about the renters again. We had to find a job. But where?

On Sunday, November 19th, we realized we were on the outskirts of Rome. It was getting dark. No campground was listed and the area looked like any big city's suburbs today, new housing tracts sprouting where farms and fields had been. Terence said we'd have to look for some trees to hide behind but I was not thrilled. You could smell the city and feel the pressure of a giant population just around the bend in the road. The people who watched us go by were not peasants anymore. There was street savvy in their eyes.

Between two construction sites was a small hill with a stand of yellow-leafed trees on top. The trail going up was like a creek bed, muddy and full of rocks. Terence stopped and looked up at it. I couldn't believe he was going to try to yank our heavy trailer up that terrain. I sat on my bike in total shock as he gunned the motor of his poor aging machine and hit the trail and slipped and dumped the bike a couple of times and cursed and dragged about one metric ton of gypsy-wagon up that sucker with little more than sheer determination and brute strength. "What a man," I thought. "What a deranged, maniacal, and berserk young man. He's found us a campsite!"

Somewhere during the night, the roar of motorbikes woke us up cruelly from our dreams, and headlights played along our tent walls. What seemed like an angry lynch mob but was probably just a few teenagers, spoke rapidly in dialect that we couldn't understand at all. Terence reached for the hammer under his pillow I hadn't even realized he'd put there and we waited for them to attack. We didn't move. After they'd bellowed and blustered and ridden around us several times like Indians on the warpath, they rode away and on down the hill, and we breathed a heavy sigh of relief. I think Terence spent the night hammer in hand.

We packed up the next morning under a cerulean blue sky framed in the bright yellow leaves of sheltering trees. So beautiful that I began to drop some of the gloomy thoughts I was hauling around about being poor in Rome, and actually look forward to seeing it. We skidded down the slimy path and right into the astonished company of a bunch of construction workers at the bottom of the hill. We'd been listening to their shouting since dawn and were a little nervous about our reception but it turned out to be a delight. I didn't drop my bike in front of the men, to my great relief, and we rode out of the trees and over the slushy leaf-covered path as if we owned it. Jaws dropped and smiles beamed because they hadn't known we were up there and really didn't have time to think. I said "Buon giorno!" to all and they said it back softly--as if to an angel from the sky. Very pleasant.

This was not the way to see Rome. Our funds were so low that we made the very foolish choice of a cheaper campground way out of the city where we were the only campers and where starving cats and dogs took up residence under the trailer and around the tent in hopes of a hand-out that might save their lives. We Americans can't begin to imagine such cruelty. Birthdays and Christmas and whatever, Italian kids get pets. The pets grow out of babyhood and the children lose interest and the cats and dogs and ducks and rabbits are dumped out of the car somewhere far enough away from home that it's a pretty good chance they won't be able to find their way back. Of course no one ever bothers to neuter them and most of them live long enough to give birth a few times so that there are millions of starving and sick little animals in the Mediterranean countries and no one seems to mind. Terence and I could hardy bear it. And this campground was the worst. We learned from talking to the campground managers, that many campers would bring their pets with them on their vacations and then leave them behind when it was time to go home. Raised to get their food from humans, the dogs slowly starved to death waiting for their masters to come home and cats didn't do much better. While Terence rode into the city trying to find a job that week, I was left to deal with the frantic animals and it was scary. I couldn't afford to give them our food, but I also couldn't ignore their suffering. I made a pot full of oatmeal each day and both dogs and cats ate it so fast it had to have made them sick. I knew when we left they'd just be hungry again, but what could I do? It made me feel better to see the poor things get some-thing in their little bellies. The whole thing made me a nervous wreck. And Terence kept coming back in the evening with no job and no answers. He began to have a terrible headache that wouldn't go away, and I knew it was just nerves. We could barely come up with something nice to say to each other. I rode in with him a couple of days to get away from the animals, but the ceaseless rain and horrible traffic and smog in the city and then the constant rejections and dead ends for every endeavor wore us both down to our lowest common denominators and for the first time I seriously considered quitting. We treated ourselves to a piece of greasy pizza for lunch and discussed it. Terence didn't try to stop me with the old argument about how hard we'd worked to have this trip and all the great things we'd done together and would do in the future. Instead he wearily presented the alternative. He would stay. He wanted to see it through even if I didn't. (Ouch!) We could try to sell my motorcycle to buy me a ticket home and then I could deal with the delinquent renters on my own. Somehow he would manage, maybe pick up another person to join him and they'd somehow find a way up to Scandinavia and down to Greece and Turkey and across Russia, etc., etc. My mind was made up to stay before I finished my pizza.

We bought a small chicken and called it "turkey" on Thanksgiving. I had drawn T. a special card and he had splurged on a bottle of rum which cheered us up considerably, although it didn't do much for his headache. The next day we gave up on Rome. The cats had taken to scratching the walls of the tent and following us in a meowing frenzy every time we walked across the grass to the restrooms. We just wanted to get out of there. We packed up and fled.

Somewhere near Naples as dawn was breaking, we were asleep in a field when our tent was shaken and an angry voice shouted at us in yet another Italian dialect we couldn't understand. We peeked out and saw a very old man who made himself understood that we were in his field and as payment to him we would have to stop by the farmhouse down the road and buy his family's goat cheese. Si, signore, you bet. We drank a quick cup of coffee and rode to the farmhouse. The whole familia solemnly came out to stare as the old man waved us into the barn. It was very dark in there but I could tell there were several men standing around watching. Were we going to be shot for sleeping in their field? The odor was over-poweringly of goat and I remember thinking it was not the classiest place to die. A small piece of cheese was handed each of us and as our eyes became accustomed to the murky interior, I noticed the expectant and eager looks on the men and the rest of the family crowding the door of the barn. Terence and I both realized at the same time what was called for. We chewed thoughtfully and then looked at each other. It was the most fabulous cheese I have ever let cross my lips. We began to smile and nod. Then everybody began to smile and nod. After much laughter and exclamations of benissimo and bellissimo and delicioso, we ran out of superlatives and took out our wallet. We bought a lot. Fortunately, it was cheap out there on the farm, but we would have happily spent the gas money to buy the wonderful stuff. Everyone shook our hands and hugged us and waved bye-bye and as we rode south, I thought about how glad I was that I hadn't gone home.

We rode hard and fast that morning. While in Rome, Terence had been told about a Taekwon Do tournament in a village named Vincitalia near Naples. He planned to be one of the referees and we hoped someone he met there would let us camp on their property because the price of the campgrounds in Naples and environs was astronomically high. We had gotten lost again and were late, so pulling up in front of the gymnasium, T. leaped off his bike and changed into his Taekwon Do uniform right in the street--in front of an amused passel of onlookers--and then ran into the gym leaving me behind to guard the rig. Stories of what could happen to one's unattended vehicle in this part of the country kept me rooted there for over an hour and then it occurred to me that this tournament could go on all day and I couldn't possible pull that trailer into a more secure place all by myself, so what the hell, I thought and went into the gym to watch the show.

Terence was refereeing the least popular group: female children. As I watched, two little girls, about seven years old, struggled to kick each other in the head, trying desperately not to cry. Mothers in fur coats and fathers standing on folding chairs were screaming encouragement to their terrified daughters--as well as not so nice things every time Terence made a call. I had to leave. Walking back to the bikes, several young children asked me to please write my name on their outstretched palms. Bizarre, but why not? As I wrote, and the children shrieked with the tickling, I found myself wishing I had a pen with indelible ink. Oh, the conceit! With my fans watching, I took a beer out of our little cooler next to the trailer's brakes and stuck it in my saddle-bag and with much waving and cheering from the throng in the street, I rode my bike out of the village to a place where I could get some privacy.

I had climbed over a stone wall into what looked like a persimmon grove. With my back against the wall and the afternoon sun warming my jeans, I was extremely contented. The beer helped. I dozed a bit and looked through the drying leaves of the fruit trees at a very peculiar-looking mountain rising above the orchard. I had passed a snack-bar by the road named "Vesuvio". Could it be? Should I check one of the plowed furrows nearby for ash? If I dug a bit, would I find a piece of mosaic floor? A coin, at least? What an imagination I have, I thought boozily.

I rode back to the village around 4:30 to find Terence looking pale and not a little annoyed. It seemed he had worked all day without a break and was offered just a tiny piece of a sort of Italian quiche someone had brought for the judges. He had come right out and asked if anyone had a space for us for the night, but no one had offered. In fact, he said, there was a conspicuous absence of interest in us by the other Taekwon Do people all around. He was hurt and disappointed and very hungry. Not wanting to give the street crowd the satisfaction of watching him wolf down some food out of our fridge, he just slammed on his helmet and snapped, "Let's get out of here!".

The road out of the village climbed dramatically once we located the correct one to Pompeii. It didn't take me too long to realize we were heading up my mountain--the one between the persimmon leaves--and it was Vesuvius!! My excitement cooled a little as darkness fell and our road snaked slowly up through the most depressing villages. There was no greenery of any kind; no trees, no gardens--just mud and mud houses and muddy, staring children, and all lit by that horrible sodium street lamp so popular in Europe, its sickly pink light turning everything into one queer hue so that you find it difficult to distinguish between objects like people, cars and buildings. I would much rather it be completely dark, so that my headlight could give me clearer information. The awful things must be lots cheaper to use than regular light bulbs or people would surely object! For the distance, that damn road was worse than anything we'd experienced in Portugal. As I swerved to avoid long black mud slides in the street, I kept thinking about Terence's crack earlier about "What this place needs is a good volcanic eruption!". The stuff was slimy and made ugly sucking sounds when my tires rolled through it. Terence insisted it was just asphalt left by street workers. It looked like lava to me. I amused myself on the rough trail by singing truly silly songs in my helmet: "Lava, when I'm near you and I hear you call my name...Lava, in my ear you breath a flame!" giggle. And of course the immortal: "Lava, come back to me!"

Things didn't improve much coming off the volcano, either. Still the same awful lights, and the traffic had picked up and everyone seemed to be short-tempered. Signs were all but impossible to see through that orange and black haze and many of them made no sense at all. When we finally located the campgrounds near the ancient city of Pompeii, two out of three were closed and the last looked like a front for a local drug-dealing organization. We talked it over. We could drive on into the night and get out of the city but I wanted to see a bit of Naples. Something about its truly terrible reputation intrigued me. Terence too. We rode into the sleazy campground and elbowed past the men surrounding the manager's desk and registered.

It was very cold. Terence warmed up some red wine and we had a mug of it before I made dinner. Ahh. He stretched out in his little camp chair and put his head back and began to relax. I had just handed him a hamburger when a mangy dog appeared, looking hungry. Oh, not again. T. put his dinner plate on the table and went over to the manager to complain. The manager said the dog wasn't his, so there was nothing he could do about it. The fellows around the desk mumbled behind their smiles something about the Americani that made the young manager laugh. Terence walked back to me with a dark look. Before he could pick up his hamburger again, another dog leaped out of the bushes near us and trying to get it, knocked the plate to the ground. I quickly dove for it and picked it up off the grass before the dog reached it as Terence blew up. He picked up the large animal and stomped up to the manager again and dropped the dog onto the man's desk. As he turned away, the guy threw something hard at Terence and the fight began. I don't know what happened before I got over there but as I walked up, Terence was shouting obscenities in several languages and he was being circled by the man's friends who were slowly picking up rakes, shovels and whatever else they felt might inflict injury. Terence disagrees with me to this day, but I can't help feeling that after such a frustrating day at the gym and all the other bad things that had been happening to him, he was dying for a fight. He knew he would probably prevail one on one, even if he had to do it ten times over, but the Italians weren't about to take that chance. I found myself wondering what good it is to have a black belt in the Martial Arts when the mob has never heard of the rules of the sport and all they want to do is kill you? Someone threw a shopping cart but Terence saw it coming and moved out of the way in time. Blows were exchanged, a back-hand from Terence broke the manager's glasses but the Italians were connecting too, and I was frantically looking for something to hit one of them over the head with, when a plain-clothes policemen appeared--he may have been one of the drug dealers at the desk--and ordered everyone to stop fighting. He went to the kiosk to telephone the police as the other men all talked to him at once in Napolitanese of course, and when the squad car arrived, they arrested Terence! I made several gestures I figured Anna Magnani would be proud of, and they told me they were only taking him down to the station for a statement. "Oh that'll be swell," I thought. "Meanwhile, I'll be left alone with at least two starving dogs and a bunch of Neapolitan street fighting drug dealers who don't speak English!" I looked around. There was a German camper down the path and I know they had been watching the excitement from behind their van's curtains. I could run and pound on their door if things got hairy. After the police car drove off, the men all turned away without so much as a glance at me and resumed whatever they were dealing before Terence tossed the dog. Apparently, I wasn't interesting enough to even scare. I sat on my motorcycle and ate my hamburger.

The police brought him back about two hours later. They announced to the manager and his pals that we were to be allowed to stay the night free, and we could have our passports back immediately! He may not have liked it, but the manager complied and Terence came back to our site and told me the rest. Apparently, they had been ready to lock him up for the night on what the men had told them. But Terence spoke enough Italian (heavily laced with French and Esperanto, he told me) to get his side heard, and they changed their minds. Learn those languages, students! I expected to remain awake all night listening for approaching thugs, but my fatigue got the better of me and I slept like a baby.

On the freeway the next morning, T. had forgotten to put up his bike's kick-stand and I must have been following too close, because as he started to turn out to a lay-by to take a picture of the last of Naples, he wobbled and came to a fast stop in front of me and I plowed into the back of the trailer and fell off my bike and sprawled into the highway. If it had been rush hour, I wouldn't be here to write about it. Amazingly, no injuries and nothing that couldn't be fixed on the bike. Saints be praised.

After another very cold night spent camped under a train trestle, we found ourselves in Reggio di Calabria, where we bought some groceries as we waited for the ferry to Sicily. We could see Mt. Etna across the water-- spewing and snowy and absolutely magnificent. Let it rain in Rome, we were going to winter in the citrus groves of sunny Sicilia!

Chapter Twenty-Nine

SICILY, OUR WINTER HOME

THE PORT CITY of Messina was not a pretty place. After enduring far too many occupations and earthquakes, it resembled an old woman who had seen it all, done it all and no longer bothered to put on her make-up for the uninvited guest. We found the Tourist Information Office and picked up some good maps and brochures, and then took the northern route heading for Palermo and a job. By the looks of the several men standing and sitting idly about the streets on that Tuesday afternoon, we were fairly certain that if there were any jobs to be had, they would be in the capital. We rode through several coastal towns that all seemed to look alike. No gardens, no trees. Everything was made of concrete blocks badly stacked and with the cement oozing out of all the cracks except where they had not bothered to even use cement between the blocks! Strangely, even the wealthier-looking homes had roofless upper stories or just unfinished rooms that looked like the construction workers had left long ago. Like Messina, earthquakes and perhaps invaders' artillery had defaced and torn down the walls so often, the inhabitants had given up caring how things looked and so patched and plugged up the holes only if it could be done with a minimum of effort and materials. Again, that feeling of the poverty of unemployment which did not bode well with our plans to stay on the road. Horror stories of Italy's deprived south that we'd heard in the better-off north began to surface in my mind.

Using our new tourist map, we found a campground--obviously for the rich foreigner--called Riva Smerald near Melazzo. It was placed on a euca-lyptus-covered slope above the Tyrrhenian Sea and was very beautiful indeed but the manager wanted ten dollars a night. Perhaps we were supposed to haggle, but neither Terence nor I had a taste for it. Anyway, how could we pretend we'd go somewhere else when we all knew there wasn't anywhere else. We paid for three nights so we could rest and plot and plan for what were going to do when we got to Palermo. Again, we were the only campers and were immediately adopted by a couple of cats. At least this time, the cats weren't starving--they may have even had quasi owners who fed them from time to time, so they were actually nice to have around. The manager, however, was another story. Obviously lonely with no one to talk to during the off-season, and entranced by our "exotic" mode of travel, he rarely left us alone and often amused himself watching Terence work on the bikes and me prepare our meals and didn't even leave when we ate. He did say no to my invitation to join us at the table, thank God, but Terence liked having him around so that he could practice his Italian and I had to admit that Terence's fluency at this point was more important than our privacy. I was still floundering with the language, picking up a word here and there but hardly in any shape to speak in it, while my companion was beginning to show signs of a pretty good command. I was so envious I wanted to poison his pasta.

By the time we had packed up on Friday, December first, the fine weather we'd been enjoying at Riva Smerald turned cold and gray. After attempting to follow the Tourist Book about cheap hotels, and getting turned away in every village on the way to Palermo by vastly augmented prices and stern looks, we realized the Sicilian country folk were simply afraid of us and wanted us out of town by sundown. Our knowledge of Sicily was sadly lacking. We had thought Americans were their friends and couldn't understand the hostility. The truth was, and we didn't find this out for weeks, that Americans are liked in Sicily. A lot, in fact. But Germans aren't. Something about the Occupation during WWII, no doubt. And until they actually saw our passports, each and every Sicilian was positive we were "Tedeschi," their word for Germans. After all, whoever saw an American couple ride motorcycles all over Sicily? Old motorcycles, even. And our pulling a trailer that resembled a Panzer tank didn't help either.

Dead tired and discouraged, we huddled over our campfire on a deserted beach somewhere about a hundred miles east of Palermo. The wind was cutting and, trying to blot out the cold, the fear and the distant sounds of the highway, we drank far too much of the cheap local red wine. It rained not hard, but steadily during the night and being a couple of stupid drunks, we'd forgotten to put the tarp over the trailer tent and so woke early the next morning sopping wet and I with a massive hangover. Terence announced that what I needed was a long motorcycle ride and as I was aware that I had no choice, I forced myself to suit up. We were illegally camping anyway, and who knew what Sicilians did to you if they caught you on their beach without a permit?

The long road to Palermo wound through village after sad little village along the coast. I was green-faced and miserable and every time we stopped to ask directions, I concentrated on not embarrassing myself in front of all those men by throwing up on their shoes. Just outside the city as we were filling up at a gas station and surrounded as usual by curious males, I decided to pantomime why I looked so sick and they loved it. They all understood (It was probably the same wine they drank), and everybody laughed and nodded and I began to feel much better. I should have done that bit from the start.

Entering Palermo, the cacophony was almost painful. The Italian fascination with their automobile horns is nothing new, and it seems the farther south one travels in Italy, the less time between blasts. As we tried to stay on the road in the rush hour congestion, two young men in a car shouted out their windows and waved us to halt. Terence yanked the rig over to the sidewalk and I pulled up behind him as the fellows parked their car partially upon the sidewalk and ran over to us jumping up and down. Never in all our days of entertaining the masses had we had quite such an appreciative reaction. They walked around the trailer and slapped their foreheads and laughed and hugged each other. We had met Salvatore Genduso and Giovanni Belli. They had noticed our USA plates (thereby ruling out German as our probable country of origin), and were absolutely astounded that two Americans--one perhaps even female!--could be roaming this far south. And on such dirty, old motorcycles! Que fantastica! They offered to show us the way to the Tourist Info Center and wanted to be our friends for life. (They are.)

T. and I discovered that rooms were as hard to find in Palermo as anywhere else, but thanks to Salvatore (Salvo) and Giovanni, we were able to stay with a family for two nights while we looked for something better.

The next day was a sunny Sunday. Our two enthusiastic friends drove to our pension to ask us to come to a party somewhere west of the city. They had an attractive young lady with them who said she worked as a policewoman in Palermo. That would be some job, I thought. Terence and I jumped onto my bike thinking our destination was probably just down the road, and were led out of town and practically to the other end of Sicily! The car ahead of us stopped twice in various villages along the way and told us to wait while they looked for food for the party. We sat there in the heat and dust for so long we thought they'd forgotten us. But no, they finally found what they were looking for, I guess, because finally they led us at last into a driveway of a very pretty cottage by the sea that would be gorgeous when it was completed. (Later, we learned that few homes of any level in Sicily are completed. The difference between taxes on a finished home and one under construction are so vast in Italy that practically everyone in the south has "work in progress." That explains all the concrete-block third floors with no roof that we kept seeing on the way to Palermo.) We think the place belonged to Giovanni's parents.

He went out into the backyard to cook some sausages on the grill while Matilda, our policewoman, boiled some pasta and heated up some sauce and by three o'clock we were finally allowed to eat and it tasted wonderful. Three other young men arrived, wearing long black coats and looking a little sinister. However, it didn't take long for us to like them and one of them, John Franco, spoke English pretty well, so I was able to chat too and he translated for the others and it was so nice for me to know that the others could see I was perhaps not a total dunce. After the meal was cleaned up, we all went in the two cars for a drive. They all seemed eager to show us their island and we were thrilled. To my relief, I was put in the car with John Franco. Terence, of course, had been fluent in Italian for hours and hated to listen to me speaking in English so he got in the other. The Italians drove us around that part of the coast. While Giovanni and Salvo and Matilda took us down to the shore to look at the tide pools, the other fellows stayed behind on the cliff above, lighting up cigarettes and letting the wind whip their black longcoats around their legs, looking like Sicilian Marlboro men. They shouted things down to us and our friends shouted back, and the lilt and cadence of the beautiful language seemed to turn our little escapade into grand opera. I decided I would try a little harder to learn to speak Italian. Peering into the seaweedy little pools, I was surprised to see how very much the marine life was like that of Santa Barbara. The smell of the salty sea was delicious. I felt right at home.

We came to a small village, and as we pulled up at the curb, a marching band of some sort was slowly appearing around the corner about three blocks away. I was ecstatic and began to run towards it when John Franco grabbed my arm and told me it was a funeral procession! There were about thirty or forty men in the slowly walking band; all dressed in black uniforms and with white hats that looked a lot like my father's officer's hat in the Navy. The tune was doleful but quite loud being mostly brass, and it reminded me a lot of the Black funerals of New Orleans. Very slow, with great feeling and timpani: "Boom--step...boom--step." The horse-drawn hearse had glass sides so the flower-covered casket was visible inside. Small electric "candles" flickered around the base of the windows and a long parade of mourners all in black walked behind with heads bowed. The women wore big black scarves over their heads that partially covered their faces. The whole town must have been in that procession because the streets were deserted except for our little group. John Franco disliked the affair. He said it was "dishonest". I felt I didn't know him well enough to probe but I didn't quite understand what he meant. The people had seemed sincere in their grief as they passed. Was the deceased Mafioso? Perhaps the young man was simply like many college kids today--embarrassed by the old ways. There was no way at that point I could get the information I required to make sense of his anger, so I let it go.

We climbed back into the cars for a bumpy ride up a rough trail to fill the several water containers somebody had put in the trunks. There was a trickle of spring water coming out of a crack in the rocks there in the tree-less mountains. We joined a long line of other cars doing the same. The boys patiently leaned back in the seats and lit up--obviously they did this a lot. We learned that afternoon that Sicily has a tremendous water shortage. We had gotten an inkling of it back in Palermo at our rented room. The landlord had explained several rules about water usage--only part of which I understood, and handed us a bottle of water for our drinking allotment, which made me immediately thirsty. Several huge cisterns were placed around the "common room" in case of a shortage. I thought about Sicily being surrounded by water. Was desalination out of the question? What about all that snow on Mt. Etna? No wonder the economy was in such a bad way. No water, no grazing land, no farms, no orchards. And the trees had been cut long ago and never replaced. And the population keeps growing.

The next day we moved out of the "Condominio" at the Palazzo Briuccia and while I guarded the rig again, Terence followed up on each lead for a more permanent place to spend the winter. He thought he had found one and we pulled the trailer into the noisy traffic and discovered too late that we would not be allowed to park it in the private courtyard of the apartment. Terence tried to be his most charming, but the signora was horrified at the sight of our outfit and slammed the door in his face. Now we were in trouble. Night was approaching and we had nowhere to go. The book said there was a camping spot about thirty miles out of town and we headed for it. The city traffic was our worst nightmare, narrow streets, sodium lights coming on and Italian Christmas shoppers at rush hour! After going around in circles a while, Terence stopped a couple of bikers and asked them if they knew how to get to the campground. Fortune smiled. They offered to lead us out of the city and then, enjoying themselves, took us all the way to the campground itself.

We stayed at the Ulivi Campground in Sferrocavallo for about two weeks while we looked for a small apartment in the city. We even tried the tiny fishing village of Sferrocavallo itself, but because the only foreigners the villagers ever saw were rich tourists, the few willing landlords demanded summer prices and it was simply beyond our budget. We sadly had to say no to them. That was O.K. with the locals. They really didn't want to rent to Germans anyway. "Aufwedersen!," they said as they waved us away.

We really liked the Ulivi. I believe only two other campers in vans popped in for one night each during our stay, one from Great Britain and one Dutch. Our young Arab-looking manager was a delight. He showed no concern about the water shortage when I needed to wash clothes and things, and for part of the day there was even hot water! Such luxury. But it was December and becoming very cold and damp at night, and T. and I yearned for a bit of privacy and a roof over our heads. We experienced some frightening electric and wind storms there which turned the roads to Palermo to soupy mud.

Through Salvo and Giovanni, we met other wonderful young people...mostly university students. Around the second week in December, we were invited to dinner at the apartment of two young ladies named Jennie and Amelia. The small apartment was packed and the food was definitely college fare but we had a great time. Jennie brought out a very tired and bent Christmas tree and a shoe-box of ornaments and we all sang and laughed and decorated the poor thing. It all felt so familiar it was hard to believe we were so far from home. Terence played his viola and I sang a couple songs while he accompanied me on the guitar. They loved us. We loved them.

It was December 15th before we found a home. Giovanni had met three

University students who were seeking another roommate for their three-bedroom apartment in a low-income housing project. I've no doubt he had a great deal of persuading to do, especially in that one of the Americans was a woman old enough to be their mother, but they needed the money and were told it would only be for a couple of months, so they said O.K. The place cost us about $150 a month, plus some utilities. The apartment was on the third floor of a huge vertical granite slab of a building surrounded by other identical slabs. Every flat was allotted three and a half windows and two small balconies which looked out upon everyone else's three and a half windows and two balconies. Looking up, you could see a patch of sky from where, at certain times of the day, a long sunbeam would reach down and shine on your balcony but you had to be quick to look or you'd miss it. Directly across from our balcony was its twin where a woman of indeterminate age could be seen much of the day leaning over her railing to shout at whomever she could catch coming onto their balconies. She always wore a thick blue robe and on really cold days had red jogging pants on underneath. Being idiots and trying to be friendly neighbors, we cheerily called back to her the first few days, filling her in on who we were and what we were about. She was thrilled and gushed about how happy she was to have us as neighbors. Giuseppe tried to warn us about her, but it was too late. Rain or shine, there she stood, watching hopefully in case one of us stepped out for a breath of air. "Americaniii!," she'd sing out, morning to evening. "Cheriiii!," when I'd step out to hang up our wash on the line. Poor thing. So lonely. Once I peeked through Giuseppe's Venetian blinds to watch her as she trolled over her balcony to find someone to talk to. How did she provide for herself, I wondered. Perhaps she was someone's middle-aged daughter no one had wanted to marry so they had set her up in her own little apartment--maybe with the door locked to keep her from bothering folks on the street.

The parking area for our building was a cruel joke. Cars occupied every inch of space; with most people showing unlimited imagination as they searched for different ways to fit their cars into spaces either too small or not meant for automobiles in the first place. We were not daunted. Our roommates, Giuseppe, Salvuccio and Franco were very friendly, the days were sunny again and people's wash-lines flapped cheerily in the breeze on their balconies. We had a big room all to ourselves and Terence immediately began to study while I caught up on the paperwork I'd put off for much too long. We could hear the big city sounds wafting up from Palermo's clogged streets and for some reason, it was soothing in a way. A very popular car horn played the first twelve notes of the music from the movie, "The Godfather", which we thought terribly cute. Especially at night between ambulance sirens.

We tried to find work in the city but after a while we had to give up. There wasn't even enough work for the Sicilians, how could we expect to be hired without even speaking Italian properly? Perhaps we would have to return home without finishing the trip. I tried not to think about it. I began gathering material for an article about our journey for a motorcycle magazine named IN MOTO that had shown some interest, and doing more drawings from the photos I had taken. Terence found a local Camera Club that was happy to let him exhibit his photographs on their club walls and also loan him the use of a darkroom. We met more nice people and we were asked to parties and Terence would bring the guitar and I would sing and our Italian improved. The two bikers who had escorted us to our campground became good friends. One of them allowed us to store the huge trailer on his family patio which was a tremendous relief because we had heard so many horror stories about how everything was stolen from you if you turned your back in Palermo. We shopped for groceries down-town in the street markets where the prices were much cheaper than the mini-markets in our own neighborhood, but we bought bread just like everybody else, from our corner store--fresh and warm and heavenly fragrant--clutching it to our bodies to feel the warmth through our jackets and yanking pieces off the ends to munch on the walk home. A wonderful habit I miss nowadays.

Sometimes, on our walk home, we passed by an open window at waist-level where a little old lady with wispy white hair would sit peering out. We were used to old women watching out their windows at the passer-bys but they were invariably swathed in black, and usually with an expression to match. This sweet old dear not only had a smile for every-one, but was usually dressed in a bright orange shawl or red and yellow sweaters and she was just a ray of sunshine in that decrepit old neighbor-hood. One day as we turned the corner onto her block, we saw an open door and a long coffin lying on chairs inside the tiny room. Candles were placed around it and mourners of all ages were filing past. I clutched Terence's arm and said, "Oh honey! It's our little old lady!" We felt terrible as we walked on, but just a few windows past, there was our bella donna at her place--resplendent in her brightest colors and smiling and appar-ently completely oblivious to the funeral next door.

One evening Terence was practicing his viola in our room when he noticed he was having trouble hearing out of his right ear. I peered inside it for whatever might be blocking the passage but I didn't see anything. The next morning he was completely deaf on that side. What to do? We found our papers on IAMAT, our international traveler's insurance he had used for his allergy shots in Scotland and France. The little booklet listed a clinic in Palermo where we supposedly would find an IAMAT doctor, but we weren't overly optimistic. At first, our worst expectations materialized as we pulled up to the grim buildings of the Clinico Publico. But although it took much too long, people were helpful all along the way and we were propelled by gentle hands on our elbows down this hall and that and out this door to across the courtyard and up the stairs until we found ourselves in a small room off the hall in one of the buildings. It had several men and women in not-very-clean uniforms bustling about, and what must have been patients--leaning back in reclining dentist-type chairs. I was waved out after Terence was told to sit in one of the chairs and as I stood nervously in the hall, I wondered what I would do if something went terribly wrong and it would be up to me to get us out of there.

I was trying to translate a colorful poster on the wall when Terence walked out of the room with a big smile on his face. He told me he had watched a nurse hand a doctor a huge syringe. Thinking it was for the woman in the next chair, he was feeling sorry for her when the doctor turned around and jabbed it into his ear and pushed in the plunger; forcing in a great shot of warm water that expelled a big hunk of dirt and wax that must have been accumulating for months! Terence said he felt his hearing come back immediately. We both stammered our thanks to the people in uniforms but they were too busy to talk to us about what we were supposed to do next, like pay for the service, and after a bit, we realized we weren't expected to! We obviously were not in the USA.

One sunny December morning, we both got on the Ascot and went up the coast to the seaside village of Mondello. It seemed deserted, obviously another summer spa. We rode past the usual mixture of very wealthy villas (shut up for the season) and tacky tourist hotels and souvenir shops. We ate our picnic lunch on the nice clean sand of the beach and remarked how odd that the Sicilians didn't seem to be enjoying their playground now that the hordes of tourists had left. Maybe they were all in Palermo doing their last-minute Christmas shopping. I picked up a large pine cone to take home to our little concrete block flat and also some tiny shells to glue on as ornaments. It looked pretty good and I thought it made the room jolly, although Terence really didn't care. Holidays could slip by him unnoticed completely if other people like me wouldn't pester him about them. We were raised differently. It was just as well. We had no money to spend on presents or decorations anyway. I was determined not to care, either. But I did need to call my children, and although finding a phone I could use and getting through to them was traumatic, we managed to speak with both Meredith and Lucas for a few minutes each and I felt worlds better.

Christmas day we rode my bike again up the nearby mountain to Monreale to see its beautiful medieval church and watch the locals celebrate the holiday. It was a warm, sunny, day so much like home, and the bougainvillea and oleander bushes were in full bloom. We strolled around the little mountain village and enjoyed listening to the happy families at their Christmas dinners. The delicious smells from the open windows made our stomachs growl, and yet Terence and I were quite content. We were having a marvelous experience and we had each other to share it with. We felt fortunate indeed.

The interior of the great church at Monreale holds what some guidebooks claim to be some of the most extensive and impressive Christian medieval mosaics in the world. The "apex" of Sicilian Norman Art. We walked around and around the huge interior with our heads thrown back and our eyes wide until we got dizzy. As we were between Services, and everybody--including the priests--were at a table somewhere, no one bothered us, and we indulged in our own private feast--one for the eyes and senses--never to be forgotten.

Our roommate, Giuseppe, had a kitten. As the young man was often out, the tiny animal adopted us, of course. I fell in love. "Pacchi" was a silky black, short-haired, yellow-eyed bundle of delight and I hated going anywhere because it meant we would have to leave her at home. She was probably about two months old and teething, which meant her little needle-teeth were constantly around something--like pens and corks and an arsenal of toys we tried to keep her busy with so she'd stay off my drawings or the typewriter while T. was doing his homework. She loved rolling film canisters and attacking and then "killing" my clean-up sponges. God, she was cute. One minute she'd be leaping out of nowhere upon us in a frenzy to play, the next, she'd be curled up in my lap looking like a piece of spiraled licorice; her huge triangular ears slightly twitching to pick up the last of the interesting sounds before she fell sound asleep. We began to make plans to kidnap her for when we would have to leave Palermo.

Our flatmates were all engineering students. Very easy to live with because they were super busy--going to their classes at the university and studying and watching soccer (football to them). Our meal times were completely different, and after we all got used to the idea that the other guy sure had crazy eating habits, we forgot all about it. The boys got up around 7:30 a.m. and one of them made coffee. That's espresso coffee, the super strong steamed stuff that's poured into tiny cups and drunk fast on the way out the door. Around 8 o'clock (Ah, the luxury of not having to get on the road!), I went into the kitchen to prepare cereal or eggs for Terence and myself--with lots of fresh bread and mugs of our "Cowboy coffee" mixed with milk. Around noon, the boys would stream in, famished, and then they'd always cook spaghetti, using some of the sauce either Salvuccio or Franco brought from home that their mothers had made for them. I don't know why Giuseppe didn't get sauce from home. My Italian still wasn't good enough to ask him properly and they spoke no English. They would usually eat so much of the pasta it made them sleepy and instead of going to their afternoon classes, they'd take a long nap. That's when I'd slip into the kitchen and make some soup or a sandwich. The boys couldn't believe we could live on a bowl of soup for the midday meal! In the evening while they were preparing to go out to meet friends, I would begin our dinner, which would often resemble what they had had for lunch. They would shake their heads in disbelief at what they felt I had all wrong. And I would have loved to be able to tell them what I thought of their going to classes with only a shot of caffeine each morning! It was just as well that we didn't speak each other's language. We all just smiled at one another and cooled it.

Our new friends, Jenny and entourage, dropped by on New Years Eve as we were quietly reading in our big room, and insisted we join them for a celebration somewhere downtown. We grabbed our jackets and followed their car on the Gold Wing. First it was a party at Maurilio's, then a sort of mob gathering at the University which, at the time, was being "occupied" by the students in protest of fee hikes and bad politics. We reveled and roared the New Year in with our pals and when we were sure they wouldn't miss us, we went home. The city was noisy for hours after midnight with gunfire and firecrackers, and we were not surprised when the next day we read in the local paper about several people being injured. Of course that was nothing new in Palermo. Often somebody was being murdered and usually by the Mafiosi. And all in the family. It seemed that everyone we met had boys who were in the police or the priesthood or the

Mafia. Many times all three. Many of the young women had to leave Sicily for the north of Italy to find work as maids or factory workers. Or worse. But Sicily is a proud island. As we explored her many museums and ancient sites, we were amazed at the wealth of history and art that had been unearthed and was still lying about for anyone to study. Just east of Palermo was a hill called Solunto, studded with early Roman remains. You could still make out most of the town. Masonry and foundations still squared off the homes and streets and many fine mosaic floors were left-- some with beautiful designs. Walls with peeling paint still displayed murals in the ancient folks's living rooms! And all unprotected against the elements. We realized that if the place still had roofs, somebody would probably be living in them!

One morning we took a field trip to Piana degli Albanese, about 45 minutes due south. As we rose above the valley sweeping away from Palermo, the view was gorgeous. We could see our city squatting next to the coastline, and then up the other side of the valley, the spires of the church of Monreale. The wind was fierce but the sun made the giant white rocks sparkle around us as we rode past. Tiny dark blue dwarf irises peeped from cracks in the stone and here and there a small grove of very hardy almond trees were just beginning to blossom into baby girl pink.

The "Plain of the Albanians" was touted in the guidebooks as a charming little village where Italians of Albanian descent kept the traditions of their forefathers alive, etc. Although the local sign-posts were in the two languages, and the small church looked to be sort of Byzantine-Greek, nothing else much smacked of any other culture than Italian and certainly no one had gotten the word yet that if they had been a little more enterprising, they could have wrested a few lire from the odd eager tourist who had made the long trek to see an Albanian in native dress or taste an Albanian dish in a restaurant. The place obviously could use the business. Men of all ages stood around with nothing to do but stare. I wanted to say Carve something, for God's sake!

We bought bread in a place where a very old woman dressed in black sat in a shaft of light from the high window, grating a hard block of cheese--her hand wrapped around the large ball like a claw. She was bent and dry and there were large growths on her face but in that bright spotlight her white hair looked like new snow. Neither Terence nor I had the guts to ask if we could take her picture. Somehow we felt it would be disrespectful.

Chapter Thirty

AGRIGENTO, CATACOMBES AND THE SEARCH FOR A LIBRARY

TERENCE HAD MET Salvatore Veneziano at a photo club meeting and the charming young man asked us to a weekend at his parent's place near Agrigento, a historical city on the south shore of Sicily. Friday evening we piled into one of two cars going on the trip with Pippo, one of Salvatore's many friends, driving. He and his girlfriend, Anna, immediately lit up and smoked the entire two hours it took to get there. Terence and I hung out the windows and seriously wondered if it was worth it. As soon as we arrived at the house we were introduced to several more friends--all with cigarettes in their hands. Oh well. We were shown a bed to spend the night in and the next morning we were told our host was going to sleep late, so we decided to explore the little fishing village of Siculiana Marina where the Veneziano house stood. The village was almost deserted now because, as one of the men mending a net told us, there was no more fish to catch in that area. The only people who still came around were the weekenders who had money from somewhere else and who had built their nice homes next to or on top of the rubble that had once been the fishermen's homes. The tiny old church was roofless and crumbling and there was no store or place to buy bread so we walked back to Sal's place and waited for him to get up. Around noon he appeared and drunk his little cup of espresso. Then he ordered us all into cars because he knew the Americani would like to see the Greek temple ruins at Agrigento. At last! Terence and I grabbed our cameras and hopped into Pippo's car with some other people and we all drove the five or so miles to the famous site.

It was an astounding place. The Sicilians boast that it rivals the Parthenon in Greece and who am I to disagree? The best part is that most of the world's tourists don't know about it yet! Two roofless but otherwise intact temples and some smaller columned ruins lie on a crest of a hill that one can see from miles away. The modern town of Agrigento sits on a nearby valley, discreetly going about its business and far enough away that the visitor to the temples can feel himself yanked back in time to that amazing civilization of so long ago. The temples glowed golden in the midday sun. Apple trees smothered in white blossoms bordered the steps and paths leading down to a dark blue sea. Terence and I were transfixed. We were just starting to set up the tripod when Signore Veneziano shouted up to us it was time to go into the city and eat lunch! We gasped and begged to be left at the site while the Italians ate their long midday meal but they wouldn't hear of it. Salvatore was used to getting his way. We were told, in effect, that we should stop our silly ogling and get on with the important things in life, for the love of the Madonna. We both understood the Italian perfectly. Sick at heart, knowing that the light would be gone by the time they brought us back--if they would bring us back--we hung our heads and got back into the cars.

Lunch was a painful experience for us in more ways than one. A lot of money for mediocre food. We knew there was no way the Italians could understand our budget restrictions and we certainly weren't going to allow them to pay for us, so we bit the bullet and ordered the cheapest things on the menu and tried desperately to be patient while the group chatted in a dialect we couldn't understand and the sun sank ever lower over our precious Greek temples.

Three hours later, they drove us crazy Americans back "to get our photographs," as if any other reason for wanting to be at the site was unthinkable. Terence and I were aware that had we been alone, we would have happily spent a few hours just sitting on the ancient stones and gazing out to sea, letting the ghosts come and feeling a part of another time... We snapped a few shots before the sun disappeared over the horizon, but the magic was gone.

On the drive back, past the haunted fishermen's cottages of Siculiana Marina, we spotted a group of policemen and patrol cars and found out that a car belonging to a couple of murderers recently making headlines in

Sicily was found ditched at that very spot! Our weekend party was unimpressed. After all, this was Sicily. What was so new about murder?

That night, Saturday, a new group of friends arrived--among them an old man whom no one seemed to notice. I felt sorry for him and to the amusement of all, introduced myself in my best pidgin Italian. He lit up like a Christmas tree and insisted I follow him into the night to see his house. "Why not?," I asked myself. "It'd be a good way to get out of the smoke!" As it turned out, he owned the much larger villa next door. He was a retired doctor from Naples and had lost his wife three years ago. If my Italian had been a little better, I'm sure we would have had a very interesting conversation, but just as I was running out of Italian phrases and vocabulary, Terence and all the others poured in looking for me, and the party started all over again in the good doctor's villa. Salvatore had brought over a slide projector and he and Terence showed some slides they had brought from Palermo. Being a member of the Camera Club, Sal had some great stuff, and Terence was no slouch either.

The next morning, we didn't bother arising early, having learned our lesson the day before. Still, around 11, we got so hungry we prowled around the kitchen and ate some bread and cookies left over from the night before. Around 2 in the afternoon, our host got up and drank his espresso and called one and all to gather last night's leftover pasta and bread and cookies and to go with him to feed the town's cats! Pied Piper-like, the young man trotted down the lane calling "Gati, Ga-ti!" and Terence and I had a nasty case of deja-vu and tried not to think about the campground in Rome.

Dozens of starving cats came from all directions at once, clawing and snatching whatever they could win from the pitiful amount on the plates. Sal said he was disappointed because at Christmas-time there were "lots more". Such a jolly excursion. I hadn't had such fun since I watched the seven-year-old girls flailing at each other at the Taekwon Do tournament in Vincitalia. In my naïveté, I attempted to explain to Salvatore that people get cats and dogs neutered in the United States, so the poor puppies and kittens won't be roaming the streets hungry and sick and unwanted. He said he thought that was a dreadful thing to do. Barbaric, even.

On the way back to Palermo that afternoon, we were told we must see the Castello Incantro. It turned out to be a fine example of Nâif art, Sicilian-style. The story was that sometime in the early part of this century, a young man had gone to America to study, and fell hopelessly in love with a woman. She dropped him for someone else and it not only broke his heart, but something gave way inside his mind as well, and he came back to his little village incapable of doing anything else but carving an image of a man's face on all the rocks that he could find on his family property. After he ran out of rocks, he carved the same image on the trees and then began to dig into the earth to form caves and grottos--full of the same visage--row after row of them lining the walls and ceiling. We couldn't learn if the face was of anyone in particular and in truth, the man had so little sculpting talent that it was simply a child's version of a face. The true Nâif artist. I, for one, would have loved a few more details about the man, but they were not forthcoming and we had to settle for the sheer amusement of seeing all those silly faces dotting the landscape. I was glad to see Terence and Salvatore taking arty shots with their cameras and flash equipment, which incidentally came out beautifully and makes for quite a show.

Wishing to know more about Sicily--especially her history, Terence and I ventured out one day in Palermo to find a library that might have some history books in English. Of course there were book stores that sold books on the subject, but the prices were double what we would have paid at home and way beyond our budget. Usually a city as large as Palermo would have separate British and American libraries--often stocked and run by ex-patriots. After some exhaustive sleuthing, we discovered there had been an American library once, but now what was left of the books were in such and such a bank and it would be OK to go and ask them if we could see the books. We found the bank and they were very polite when we explained that we simply wanted to know more about their beautiful country. (By this time, Terence's Italian was pretty good). A guard showed us to a guide who talked to somebody behind a barred window who took a while but found one book on the history of Sicily written in English that we would be allowed to look at at a nearby table while the guard watched! We felt that was a little much, but in that they had gone to such trouble, we sat down and shared skimming through it and then thanked them profusely for the privilege. It had been written in 1853!

We decided to try the University Library which was also the only library the whole city of Palermo had to use! Hard to believe. We were met at the door by a policeman who asked for our passports. They were then handed to someone at a nearby desk who copied down our names and numbers. Then we were told to go into an office to explain what we wanted. The lady in the office was not very friendly. She told us we would have to give her the exact title of the book desired and have a signed note from our teacher at the University! Terence tried to explain. Out of the goodness of her heart, she allowed us to look at the books on the shelf, but when I took one down, the policeman ran up to me and shouted at me to put it back. Apparently, we were only supposed to look at the spine titles! Without knowing exactly what book we wished to peruse before even knowing what was on the shelf, we would not be allowed to even turn a page! It was a very good lesson on appreciating what we had at home.

One day we went with Salvatore and Giovanni to the famous Palermo catacombs that we had read about in our guide book. I believe I can safely say there is nothing quite like it in the USA! For a small entrance fee, a silent monk let us in the gate and we all proceeded down the stairs to a series of long rooms, lit here and there by naked light bulbs dangling from the ceiling. Tethered by wires against the white stuccoed walls were hundreds of human bodies, dressed in their very best clothes and thanks to the wires, all standing jauntily about in various attitudes of slump. These were no peasants. For hundreds of years, only the high and the mighty were placed here and their families had no doubt paid a princely sum for the privilege. Although there was no jewelry left, the fabrics were velvets and brocades and with much intricate stitchery. Amazingly, except for a thick layer of dust, the clothes were largely intact after all those years. Alas, not so the bodies underneath. Even though the air in Palermo is very dry, there was enough mold on those corpses to have changed all the original features on the faces to something only a group of hard-core horror buffs could appreciate. Still, we didn't actually find them scary...probably because most of them were so far removed from anything human. The flesh had shrunk and slid and they rather resembled large dolls with rotten apple-heads. At one time the eye-sockets had held marbles placed there by the morticians, but no longer. Apparently American soldiers had stolen them during the occupation of Sicily in WWII to take home as souvenirs. Embarrassing.

Chapter Thirty-One

OUR GRAND OPERA AUDITION

MID-FEBRUARY WAS Carnevale week in Italy. We may have missed the Mardi Gras in New Orleans, but we certainly made up for it in Italy. First we went to the parks in Palermo and shot roll after roll of pictures of too-adorable children in their costumes. Then we went to Venice and found ourselves smack dab in the middle of the final madness of the festival and if I should be asked (and I am, all the time), what my favorite experience was in all five years of Europe, well it is simply no contest. Let me explain.

In his search for a job, Terence left all sorts of résumés; even one for me I hadn't known about. In applying for a viola job at Le Fenice Opera House in Venice, he had included one of my singing résumés for the heck of it, and the Fenice sent me a telegram to come and audition for the next season's opera chorus! At first we had a good laugh and rather wished we were close enough to go audition just for fun, and then we began thinking seriously about it. What an opportunity it would be. How tough could it be to get into the chorus? So what if it was 900 miles away, we'd LOVE to have an excuse to live in Venice. And get paid for it? It was an opportunity too good to pass up.

But the excursion would be expensive. If I didn't get the job, we would definitely have to return to California and work a while there before returning to complete the trip, and we both knew how hard it would be to come back once we'd gone home. We had just one other possibility for work in Europe. We were getting letters from our friend Dirk Kraaij, in

Holland, who was telling us that there was plenty of work for Terence rebuilding people's roofs that had blown off during the terrible hurricane that had occurred during December. Holland seemed a long way away, but it might be the only way. We decided to take the long trip up the Italian boot to Venice!

First we went to the local Music Academy in Palermo, and thanks to a truly disgusting display of charm and flattery on Terence's part, aimed at the elderly lady at the gate, we were allowed to select and even xerox some music to sing for the audition. In a weak moment, I suggested to Terence that he ought to learn something to sing too--after all, it was only for the chorus, right? He thought it a fine idea. The man had no fear.

Our friends gave us names of relatives we could stay with on the long journey and the plan was to ride up there on my bike and then leave it somewhere safe and hitch-hike home to Palermo, thereby saving money on gasoline on the final trip north again. Terence told me to leave the particulars to him. He didn't want me to get nervous and realize what an insane idea it was. I decided to concentrate on learning my music. It was going to be tough learning it without a piano. I had chosen "Musetta's Waltz" from Puccini's "La Bohéme," and Terence tackled the bass solo from Mozart's "Magic Flute," which he planned to sing in German. We took turns practicing in the various rooms of the small apartment when the guys were at school and both of us became very excited and were sure we were going to WOW 'em at the Fenice.

On February 20th, 1990, three years from the day we had left Santa Barbara, we rode out of Palermo to cut south across the island, and ran out of gas trying to find an open filling station. Gloom. Not a good sign. We unloaded my poor bike of much of the heavy stuff and while I stood next to the bundles by the side of the road, Terence pushed the bike all the way to the next village. Hours later, we were once more on our way, though we had lost precious time. We could see Mt. Etna puffing away far to our left, and passing dry little villages along the way, we'd wonder again...just what did those people do for a living. No fields, no industry. Just rocks and dust.

We rode through the city of Catania on the east coast. It seemed to sit on lava-- from Mt. Etna's earlier eruptions, no doubt. Houses were made from it; their walls turning black through the whitewash as the lava seeped through. Great hunks of the stuff jutted up here and there--in gardens, by driveways--even between buildings. It seemed as if people found it too difficult to move and take away. The black dust was everywhere, reminding me of the slippery climb over Vesuvius we had had last November, and I remarked to Terence in front of me how hard it must be to keep things clean there. "How about lungs!" he shouted back.

On we rode--past touristy Taormina and then into the harbor town of Messina and down to the ferry. While dozens of cars and trucks cooled their heels for perhaps hours--waiting to get on a ferry, Terence maneuvered us around the poor souls and up to the front. One of the nice things about being on a motorcycle! As soon as we were on and the ramp was up, I yanked out our lunch and, sharing a bottle of beer, we celebrated our third anniversary on the road. Three years had gone by so fast!

The ferry docked in Reggio Calabria and we rode hard to Cosenza up the west coast. We were there by about 7:30 and looked up one of Sal Veneziano's friends, who was expecting us, and she showed us the way around the dark streets to an apartment that belonged to her brother who was out of town. She left us at the door and waved goodbye and after looking around a bit at the very neat and clean surroundings, I pulled out a large pot from the kitchen cabinet and made us some pasta. We slept in our sleeping bags on the bed and the next morning, after writing a note of thanks, we took off again.

A long day's drive up into some mountains and again the romantic-looking villages on the peaks--some with castles still standing. It was too bad to realize that my happy innocence was gone about those places. As charming as they seemed from a distance, I knew closer inspection would reveal TV antennas sprouting like weeds from every tiled roof. Women dressed in shabby black standing and sitting in doorways staring at starving dogs in the street. And the men, young and old, with nothing to do but hang around the local bar puffing on cigarettes.

That evening we made it to Donna Blair's in Rome. She was my sister's friend whom we had missed in November due to our ill timing of riding through around Thanksgiving. She wasn't home when we arrived, but we had instructions to knock on a neighbor's door who let us into her apartment. We took life-giving showers and I went into the kitchen and made us some dinner from things we'd bought in Cosenza. Still no Donna. We were very tired from sitting on that uncomfortable motorcycle for all those miles, so after I washed out a couple of things for us, we fell into bed and were just falling asleep when we heard her key in the door. She wanted to chat so we got up again and opened up a bottle of wine we'd brought and talked until the wee hours; not a very smart move, actually, but we thought it was important to get to know each other and as she had seen my sister and brother-in-law recently, I wanted to hear all about their time together.

The next morning Terence had a nasty hangover from drinking our cheap wine and too much of Donna's brandy the night before, but he didn't mention it until we had ridden awhile, and I had to marvel at his restraint. We arrived in Florence that afternoon and looked up a young Gold Winger whom we had met at the Italian GW Treffen in September. Alex Levy's family owned a coffee shop very close to the Duomo--right in the heart of Florence! Alex had sent us a Christmas card and told us to stop by whenever we were coming through, but he seemed pretty surprised that we'd taken him up on it and confessed that he'd forgotten what we looked like! Still, he offered us a cappuccino and two sugar doughnuts that I thought must have been made in heaven, they were so delicious. Terence was dying for a beer but for once was too polite to ask, thank God. Alex walked us out to the motorcycle and as we were saying goodbye, Terence noticed he had left his good shoes in Donna's apt. in Rome! A calamity. He had on his heavy, clunky rain boots which he could have lived with, but no way could he audition at the Fenice Opera house with those things on his feet. With a mounting sense of horror, we knew that there was no way out of it. We would have to spend some precious coin on a new pair! Alex was sympathetic and insisted we follow him down the cobbled lanes of Florence to a "cheaper" shoe store he knew about, but of course to us, the prices for the simplest shoes in Italy were astronomical and we stumbled along after him with long faces. I am ashamed to admit that the thought crossed my mind that the shoe store owner might be a friend that Alex was doing a favor for by bringing in a couple of "rich" American tourists. A pox on my evil skepticism! After Terence had selected a pair, we walked up to the cash-register to be told that they were already "paid for." We were speechless. An hour ago, Alex Levy couldn't remember who we were. Viva Italiani!

Salvatore Veneziano and I may have had our differences over neutering animals, but there's no doubt he saved us from having to sleep in the road on the way to Venice that cold February. Still another friend of his welcomed us with open arms after we had tried to find other accommodations in Bologna and had all but given up. Her name was Litizia Moretti and she was beautiful. Her small apartment showed such taste and flair, it was no surprise to discover she was a professional designer and although she really had no time to entertain two bedraggled bikers from America, she told us to consider the place ours and help ourselves to rice she had left on the stove for us and then blew us a kiss as she swept out the door on a date, looking like a movie star. We liked her immensely and wished we could stay a week and get to know her better. We were so hungry we took her up on the rice offer and licked the platter clean!

Somewhere in the Veneto, several miles north of Venice, lived a lady doctor from Sicily named Mariangela Campolo. We had been given a letter of introduction by another friend in Palermo and the good woman had stood in front of her door, reading it over and over. She gave a big sigh and explained that at the moment, she had several members of her family living in her home and there was simply no room for us. However, if we were really desperate, we could sleep for the night on the floor of the room she used as her office, and although there would be no toilet facilities, there was a small sink in the room where we could get a drink of water. The office had a marble floor. The Hilton it wasn't. At least nobody bothered us after we closed the door and spread out our sleeping bags. We placed what soft belongings we had under the bags and then scrounged around our stuff for something to eat. I remember I found some cookies, and that may have been all we had for dinner. As soon as it got dark enough, we sneaked out to find a place to relieve ourselves. Several large dogs barked and told everybody we were out there. How humiliating. I just hoped the blasted mutts would be blamed for the mess.

Chapter Thirty-Two

HOW NOT TO PREPARE FOR AN AUDITION

THERE WAS A TIME, not really all that long ago, when I looked forward to singing auditions. I was younger and prettier and rested. I prepared carefully and often with a vocal coach. I got my hair done in plenty of time and made sure the clothes fit the occasion. I kept away from situations that might upset me and asked friends not to call on the day of the audition. I needed to concentrate on my performance. I was fanatical about my diet the day before and avoided breathing the unpure air of the street or god forbid, secondhand smoke. I did not check my horoscope, although I had plenty of other singer-friends that did. I did well when the time came and often got the part. Somehow, I felt, this experience would be different.

At 6:30 a.m. on the day of our Great Italian Opera Audition, I woke from a fitful sleep on my marble slab with stabbing pain in my neck and back. It hardly surprised me. Somewhere way back in Sicily we had hit a terrible bump and rather than flying off the back of the bike, I hung on to Terence and absorbed it along my spine and wondered if it would show up later. Then, incredibly, in Donna's apartment in Rome, I had tripped over a rolled-up rug and fell on my knees onto her marble floor and felt the crack all the way up my spine again, further damaging things and certainly a lousy way to prepare for a relaxed performance. There was nothing to do but try to ignore it.

The morning was icy cold. We rolled up the bags and with some warm water coming out of the tap at the sink, I made us some instant coffee from packets we had in the tank bag. We put on our best clothes over long underwear and jeans against the cold. After the bike was packed, I put on my thick riding gloves and heavy face-helmet which made my neck hurt and I prayed the ride to Venice would be short. It wasn't.

Our appointment was for 9 a.m. and we had given ourselves two hours to be sure we would be on time. It was pea-soup fog. I was grateful that Terence was doing the driving. Still, unable to see the street signs in the murk, we took a few wrong roads and he couldn't see the holes in the road until we were upon them and my back and neck screamed at every bump. It was much farther than we thought. The freezing wind whistled into my helmet. I tried to relax. I could tell T. was (finally) getting nervous about performing, and so was going over and over his song as we barreled through the fog. It made me irritable and angry at myself for ever suggesting that he tryout. He wasn't a singer, he was a violist, for Pete's sake. How dare he bother me when I needed peace and quiet to study my own part! I felt the panic rise. I began to vocalize in my helmet. Do-Re-Mi-Fa-So--Oh my God what am I doing thinking I can sing after four days of bouncing on my spine breathing dust and pollution, getting little rest and not eating properly? What am I trying to prove? And my hair's dirty! EEEK! Get a grip on yourself, Gail. It's only the chorus. They would be so lucky to get me in their nice little chorus. Look--I can read music pretty well...I can be a team player! I can look older with lots of makeup. All right, with lots of makeup I could look younger, too. And I could live in Venice..Alll Right!!

We pulled up to the end of the road where all motorized vehicles must stop before one enters Venice. Taking a water taxi or vaporetto would be too expensive, so locking the bike and helmets, we clasped hands and ran for the Theater. It would be a good thirty-minute dash, but we knew the way by heart thanks to the dozens of times we went to the Opera offices in November to try to find the Conductor about a job for Terence in the orchestra.

We made it just in time, disheveled and sweaty. We were asked to wait in the hall with the other contestants. I told Terence we had to find a place where we could take off our extra clothing and try to vocalize a little. We were beginning to hear other people singing scales and warming up behind closed doors on several floors. Terence pushed me into a musty broom closet an pulled the door behind us. While he went through his song, I took off my jeans and long underwear and yanked on my pantyhose. Then he went into the hall and guarded our door while I hurriedly sang through mine. I was not in top form.

It didn't take us long to realize the other singers were amazingly good. And not one over twenty-five. What was going on here? A stern-looking woman with a list in her hand explained that they would take the singers first who came from the greatest distance away. Guess who?

I gulped. One of the best advantages a singer can have is getting a chance to hear the competition and there went that advantage for me. I walked to the door with Terence who would be my interpreter in case no one spoke English and I didn't understand the Italian. Not you, signore, they said to him and pushed him out the door. He looked helplessly over his shoulder at me as I watched him go. My knees began to give way. I was shown where to stand in front of a long table where about 10 judges sat with expressions of some nameless pain. No one spoke English and I was so nervous I didn't understand the Italian the head person spoke to me. From long force of habit, I walked over to the accompanist and handed him the music and turned to the judges at the table. The pianist said something I couldn't understand which in hindsight, must have been questioning me as to how fast I wanted it, because when I didn't answer, he threw up his hands and angrily began the introduction--too fast and too loud but I was too frozen by then to do anything about it.

How did I do? Lord only knows. I muffed some words, but nothing serious. My voice was O.K. but I had been better in the past. Lots better. I had broken my own rules for getting in the right frame of mind and being well-prepared both mentally and physically but hey, I did the best I could do under the circumstances, I felt, and decided to forgive myself. I probably should have sung "Summertime," I thought. Oh well. Too late.

Terence's turn was next and they didn't let him get far. Cruel. Neither of us got a chance to sing solfeggios or scales. He told me later that when he first came in, one of the women judges was saying that I had sounded good but a little too mature. Italian choruses shouldn't include mature voices? We were perplexed. Obviously, both of us were out of our league. Things were being lost in the translation. I wondered if the audition really was for the chorus! Months later and after some research, we found out that, unlike the U.S., where young opera singer-hopefuls wouldn't be caught dead in a chorus--afraid that their reputation as a soloist might be sullied, in Europe, that's part of their training. Everybody starts that way. Thus the big voices and the young ages of the kids in the hall. Just as well we didn't figure it out too soon!

We went into the empty dressing rooms of the big theater and took photographs of ourselves in the mirrors for fun and began to relax. "Do you realize what's going on outside at this very moment?," Terence asked. "CARNEVALE!!," we both shouted at once and dashed for the door. The rest of the day we spent resting from our ordeal--visiting old haunts and favorite places, and taking rolls and rolls of film of the splendid costumes that whooshed by us in the narrow alleyways. We sat on the quay and shared a baguette and a beer and watched the shiny black gondolas bob up and down at their moorings near the plaza San Marco. The sun shone thinly and by early afternoon it was getting cold so we walked back through the labyrinthine passages to our bike and I slipped my jeans back on under my dress and we rode slowly through the little villages on the way back to Dr. Campolo's house, enjoying the celebrations and parades along the way. The good doctor was kind enough to allow us to sleep on her floor for two more nights so we could spend one more whole day in our beloved Venezia.

Chapter Thirty-Three

LA SERENISSIMA

TERENCE and I had said to each other in November that we would never want to be in Venice during the carnival because the crush of too many tourists would probably spoil everything. Three years ago, when we had arrived in New Orleans the day after the Mardi Gras celebration, there were still so many revelers in the streets you could barely breathe. It was hot and sticky, and debris from the parades the day before lined the streets and sidewalks and horrible, dissonant "music" blasted forth from every doorway. I for one, didn't want to see my favorite European city trashed and abused like that from the mass of humanity swarming like picnic ants over the fragile islands in the Adriatic. Yet, to our surprise, we found that except for the nature of the celebration--the last gasp of hedonism before Lent, as it were--the two cities had very little else in common. No doubt weather played a part. February in northern Italy is cold and damp. The thick fog that lasted all day served to shut out not only the sights, but the sounds as well. We would be listening to our echoing footsteps down a narrow passageway one second and then out of nowhere the sound of laughter, as great costumed creatures would emerge from the fog behind us, sweep by and disappear around a corner leaving an eerie silence as we stood, mouths agape and senses twirling.

We splurged and bought tickets, to be taken by vaporetto to the island of Murano to tour the glass factories. I had high expectations about seeing the birth-place of the shimmering beads I lusted for, and chandeliers I'd admired in pictures for so long. Sadly, the first museum, the old one, gave a shabby little "off-season" tour. Of course everybody who normally ran the place would be at the Carnevale. The sole guide was short-tempered and bored and the exhibits shoddy. It seemed as if all the really good Venetian glass was elsewhere. The few of us that had bothered to come out to the island in the fog were bundled up to our noses trying to keep warm and the rooms of the tour were unheated and depressing. But our tickets were also good for seeing the "Modern" museum, and after a few fits and starts in locating the place, we were ushered into warm rooms with some really exciting exhibits of what's happening in contemporary glass. Certainly well worth the ticket price.

Afterward, we walked the tiny streets of the island looking for interesting architecture or more Venetian-looking scenes, but there was little to suggest anything at all of the splendor of the main isle. We might as well have been in Sicily for the dismal scenery we saw on Murano. We boarded our return boat and pushed off. Landing once more upon the big island, we found our way to the Miracoli church and the big Colleone statue that prances just outside. I was thrilled to see the statue, having studied it many years ago in college, and the interior of the massive church took our breath away. So many treasures in Venice...we needed more time. We shamelessly warmed our frozen hands over the votive candles and debated whether we had the stamina to stay for the 5:00 concert that was to be offered that day. Not if we wanted to see more of the Carnevale, we reckoned. Out of the church and into the fog again. Not being able to get our bearings in the mist, we became happily lost. All the cozy little canals looked the same and when we found a wide one, we couldn't tell north from south and we didn't care. When we got tired of playing in the side streets--taking pictures of beautiful peeling walls and renaissance windows and cats on crumbling balconies, we waited for a group of revelers to appear and then we followed them to where the action was-- always the Piazza San Marco.

There, the fog had parted to reveal the celebration at its most flamboyant. It was packed with people, all right, but everybody seemed to be having so much fun that all we wanted to do was join them and be swept along among the colorful merry-makers. And what a show! This had to be the Mecca for everyone in Europe to appear and be seen in costume. There were outfits that must have broken the bank to make, not to mention the time it must have taken to sew them. It was really overwhelming. Silk and velvet, gold and silver, feathers and jewels. The best ones were worn by people who constantly posed for the cameras, as if they had waited all their lives for this moment to shine and be immortalized. Everybody was taking pictures of each other. One of the funniest sights was a man dressed as Mozart down on one knee taking a picture of a couple dressed as the sun and the moon who were at the time taking a picture of a woman all in crimson feathers..and she was shooting at the kneeling Mozart! Full circle filming!

Chapter Thirty-Four

THE LONG ROAD HOME

On Monday, February 26th, we rose early, thanked our hostess with hugs and kisses and slid into the fog for Bologna. We had forgotten to pick up some camera equipment for Sal V. at Letitia's that Terence had promised we'd bring back to him. She wasn't home so we rode around that ancient city looking at some splendid renaissance architecture and museums and were delighted to find the restoration of the famous Neptune fountain was open to the public for a small fee. We also discovered, thanks to our bible, the Rough Guide to Italy, a most unusual collection housed in the University of Bologna's Medical school. Sometime in the early eighteenth century, two artists, Anna Morandi Mazzolini and Ercole Lelli, for study purposes only, no doubt, fashioned out of colored wax the most realistic human parts imagineable. Mostly without skin--muscles and organs and everything else--unadorned and looking so fresh in their glass cases you would swear they could use them for transplants. A really fascinating exhibit.

Letitia still wasn't home, so, frantic for a place to spend the night, we called the local Esperanto society director, Sr. Mario Amadei. He answered the phone in Esperanto and Terence racked his brain for the right words, doing a quick little dance from English to Italian to Esperanto. Sr. Amadei was terribly sorry he had no place for us to stay but wanted to meet us. So we three had a nice cup of coffee in a local cafe and a lovely chat and then T. and I went back to Letitia's and to our immense relief she was home, and although she had several gentlemen callers in her living room, she pretended to be happy to see us. There was lots of leftover spaghetti and wine and once more we were offered the narrow bed in the spare room and after a hot shower, we fell gratefully upon it and slept like babies. She could have had a rock concert in that living room and it wouldn't have disturbed us, it was our first bed in three days!

Letitia was gone when we awoke so we made some coffee in her cozily cluttered kitchen and wrote her a note of thanks--begging that wonderful lady to try to get to Santa Barbara some day so we could show her some real gratitude. We discussed our next move. The part Terence hadn't wanted me to think about while I concentrated on the audition was about to happen. It became fairly obvious that Terence hadn't wanted to think much about it either because he hadn't really decided exactly where we would be stashing my motorcycle, nor how we were going to get home without it. Neither of us actually wanted to hitchhike, but it seemed there was no other way. We rode back to Florence and Alex Levy. He didn't have anyplace to keep the Ascot himself, but he telephoned several bikers he knew--between serving customers in the Deli--and found a fellow named Andrea whose family had a big backyard where they thought it could be stored a couple of months. Saved again! While we waited for Andrea to appear and lead us to his home, Terence and I leisurely toured the incredible Duomo and Baptistery in the Piazza S. Giovanne. From the sublime to the ridiculous, an hour later we were bumping on terrible roads behind Andrea, choking on the dirt and sand a fierce wind was blowing into our helmets. I tried not to worry but who was this guy taking my motorcycle for months? Would his family have a fit with the Ascot sitting in their garden? Was there no other way but to leave it behind?

We pulled into a driveway in an old section of the Florentine suburbs. The wind was mean and everything seemed covered with dirt from the street. Fortunately, Andrea's family didn't seem to mind the inconvenience and even asked us in for a cup of coffee after we had tucked in my bike for its long winter's sleep.

It felt pretty strange standing by the autostrada with my thumb out to the wind. Andrea had driven us to a place where trucks had to stop--to give us a better chance of getting a ride. Every part of me wanted to turn around and quit. Thinking we'd do better standing apart from each other, Terence was several feet away from me and when the first truck stopped to pick me up, the driver motioned me in and I explained that there was two of us whereupon he shut his door and drove away with a word not meant to be a compliment to women. Nobody stopped for Terence. It began to rain. I stood there in the darkness between trucks going by with my hair and clothes whipping and dripping and shook my head. I thought about the envy other women had expressed when they heard about my trip. Many of them had said the same thing. "I'd give anything to be doing what you're doing!" I had to laugh.

About an hour later, a French trucker stopped to give us a lift. When he heard Terence speak French he was delighted to have the both of us aboard. He said it would help keep him awake. We were very happy to crawl into the cabin with him. I curled up on the funny little bed behind the seat and tried to get some sleep while Terence babbled away with our driver. I was just falling asleep when the guy pulled off at a restaurant and announced that by law he had to stop for an hour and take a nap, but if we were still around when it was time to go again, we could get back in. We thanked him and hauled our heavy loads back to the freeway and had just held up our make-shift sign when a big rig stopped and an Italian driver opened his door for us. He too said he needed to stay awake and so we could ride with him and off we went again.

Two hours later, somewhere south of Rome, that driver needed to pull off the road and rest, so back we went to the road to try again. In about ten minutes, we were repeating the act with another Italian trucker with an English-built rig that had the steering wheel on the right side. The cab was very noisy and smelly and I was stuck in the middle--perched on a kind of plastic tool box because there were only two seats. I was pretty uncomfortable, but there was nothing to be done for it. Even though he had said he wanted us to help keep him awake, he didn't seem to have much to say and after a while Terence gave up and we rode through the windy night in silence.

Around four o'clock in the morning, our driver said that because he'd been driving all the way from Paris without much sleep, he'd have to take a short nap. He pulled off at a small truck lay-by that had a snack bar--closed for the night. He told us we could stay in the front seats while he stretched out behind them and pulled a little curtain. In that he had told us he was going to all the way to Sicily, we decided it was probably best to remain where we were than look for another ride at four in the morning! We heard him snoring softly. We munched some cheese and shared an apple and dozed. The sun came up. We discussed waking him but in the end figured it was not our business and instead let him sleep.

About 7 a.m., he woke up cursing and waving his hands around in despair because he'd overslept! Leaping into the drivers seat and turning on the huge engine, he tore out into the fast lane which soon turned into a steep downhill grade. A great blasting of brakes accompanied groans and pleas to the Madonna for help and salvation as he alternated between grasping the wheel as if it were a lifesaver, and lifting his hands to wave in agitation and appeal to the saints to spare him the awful consequences of the late hour. We guessed he was Sicilian.

I was hurting from my plastic perch and asked if it would be all right if I laid down behind the seats. "Si, si," he snapped. I wished he'd told us to wake him earlier so he wouldn't be so angry and drive the old truck like a madman. Actually, I was too tired to care much. I slept on and off as we careened down the mountains. Later, after I woke up and got back on my tool box in front, the southern Italian sun came out in full force, making up for all the rain and fog of the north. Soon we were baking. T. and I took off as many clothes as was decent but it was still terribly hot. The madman at the wheel wouldn't let us open the window because it made his big poly-ester poster of Samantha Fox flap on everybody's head and he was concerned it might tear. It occurred to us that he would rather we all died of heat prostration than take the thing down! So we sweltered and he smoked one cigarette after another and that and the smell of old lunches and sweat and dirt made me a little sick but we were at least on the road to home.

After a while he had calmed down and was enjoying himself hugely yakking into his C.B. in a dialect he knew we couldn't follow. Apparently he was in his "home range" and most of the trucks sharing the road were buddies from Sicily. I was glad to see him happy even though I could tell he was telling them about us in perhaps less than flattering terms. I caught a word here and there I wish I hadn't.

He stopped at a snack shop and bought himself a sort of pizza/sand-wich thing and offered us a bite. We declined even though we were both very hungry, because we were sure he was too, and it was probably his main meal of the day. Down the road a couple of miles, he stopped eating it about half way through and proceeded to throw the sandwich, paper bag and all, out the window! T. and I looked at each other. We wanted to kill something.

Each cigarette butt went out that window too, still lit, and while I watched, horrified, in the driver's right rear-view mirror, the burning brand would hop to the side of the road among the trash and brush to die. That explained all the burned places by the side of the road in Italy! By the time we rolled up to the ferry, all three of us were wilted and frazzled and we parted ways without a whole lot of feeling. The tickets for passage to get across the straits to Messina were twenty cents each! That had to be one of the few bargains left in Europe. The sea air and breeze sure felt good after that furnace of a truck ride! We noticed our driver stayed in his truck with the windows rolled up for the whole ferry crossing!

We tried hitching for a while on the road leading out of Messina, but no one gave us so much as a glance. It was late afternoon and Terence walked back to the train station and bought tickets for Palermo. He'd decided we'd saved enough money for one day and I was in no mood to argue. It was about twelve bucks each, but a nice long ride and clean enough seats so we curled up and slept as there was nothing to see out the windows because of the dark night, anyway.

After the train stopped in Palermo, we grabbed a bus at the station that took us to the center of town and then had to board another bus. It took us awhile to notice that nobody else was bothering to pay the fare. The supposed process for payment is to buy a ticket for 700 lira and then get it stamped but no one bothered and the drivers didn't seem to care either. The second bus driver was not happy to see us. We were the only people who boarded at that late hour and I think he was planning to skip his midnight run and instead have a smoke with his buddies at the station. But he swung heavily into the seat and with a sigh, took off into the night-- zipping through the dark streets as fast as the old bus could handle it and only made a complete stop when he saw a group of soccer players in front of us, waving their hands wildly for a ride. He couldn't kill his nation's "fut-ball" hopefuls, for the love of the Madonna. They boarded without money changing hands.

Chapter Thirty-Five

OUT OF SICILY AND UP THE BOOT

THE DAY finally came when we had to leave Palermo. I have to confess that the worst part was leaving that wonderful cat. Franco and Salvucio told Giuseppe he ought to give her to us. His eyes grew wide. "Mia figlia?!!" he said. There was no way we could have taken his "daughter" anyway, of course. But oh, we just might have tried...

At last we were packed--and hugged and kissed by so many great new friends, and the photographs taken and the gifts pressed upon us and it was like trying to pull away from quicksand, the love and kindness of those people was so extreme. Dizzy from the effort, we pulled heavily away and onto the highway and I was battling a giant lump in my throat when I noticed the day had turned dark and big black clouds were gathering on the very horizon we were heading for. A few more miles down the road and it began to rain. We simply couldn't believe how often that happened to us. Fine days when we had shelter, but once we were on the road for a long ride....it seemed like a pattern. Or a mighty cruel joke. A joke of the All Mighty. We pulled over, grumbling into our face-helmets. Yanking on my rain gear, I noticed the lump in my throat had turned into an odd sort of sore throat. Oh great, what else?

We rode into Trapani, the closest port in Sicily to northern Africa. Snack shops offered cous-cous instead of pizza and french fries, and several of the women had their heads covered. Men and boys in baggy pants and dirty clothes streamed out of the bars and clustered around me and my bike to stare while Terence was in the Information Office, and they weren't very friendly. They seemed to keep coming from every direction, and I was awfully glad when Terence returned, elbowing his way through them to the Gold Wing. Immediately the mood changed. Everyone seemed to relax and gap-toothed grins appeared. I bet even German bikers didn't get this far out very often. Not much for tourists to see and what there is sniffs of unrelenting poverty.

As it grew dark, we pulled off a mountain trail we were following to Erice, our next destination. We were dangerously low on gasoline and were wondering if we might have to turn back, but because it was so late, we elected to camp by the side of the road for the night and put off the decision to morning.

We rode by first light up the side of the mountain to Erice, at the top. There was no filling station there, but we really didn't expect one because this was supposedly a "unspoiled" quaint old village and surely nothing spoils quaint like a gas station! We walked around the lumpy cobbled streets and took pictures of some walls and facades that really did look medieval, and after a couple of hours of soaking up the scenery, we boarded the bikes again and coasted down the mountain looking for petrol. The heavens opened again and we were thoroughly soaked when we pulled into a station where we sought a bit of shelter under a piece of roof and ate our lunch while we waited out the Sicilian's mid-day three-hour recess before we could fill up our tanks. We were quite used to the inconvenience of business closures by now, yet being used it doesn't mean we liked it any better. It would always seem to us a strange way to run a business. My throat was feeling worse.

Checking our "Rough Guide," we saw that we ought to stop in Marsala and visit the museums there, and so as soon as the first one opened for the afternoon tour, we ambled through and saw some fairly interesting diggings from the area of ancient peoples and a partial reconstruction of a Punic warship. Riding into the center of town to the other museum in Marsala, we could see there would be no place to park the motorcycles and trailer, so we decided to chance it for a few minutes and park illegally in the only street wide enough for cars to make it around us, while we ran into the museo Arazzi to see some famous tapestries. The curator there seemed surprised to see us and a tad embarrassed to take our money, and with great formality walked us through the gloomy rooms where the great tapestries hung dusty and all-but forgotten in the dark. At each doorway the old gentleman, who himself resembled something out of the Palermo catacombs, would flip a light switch and in a crackling dry voice, narrate the stories of the massive weavings while we craned our necks to take in the intricate details. He would then turn out the lights--often before we had finished looking--and hustle us on to the next room to repeat his peculiar little performance.

The work was certainly gorgeous and we were very glad the guide book had insisted we come. Made in Belgium in the 16th century, the theme was the "Capture of Jerusalem"--all about manly heroes in helmets and sandals and fainting voluptuous young women holding infants, and lots of bloodshed and one or two Wise Old Men trying to help. I was piqued again to note the total absence of middle-aged women. They were probably the first to be put to the sword on fighting days. Maybe I was being too sensitive. After all, there weren't any teenagers around either.

After our whirlwind tour past the tapestries, the old fellow motioned for us to follow him down the street to visit someone he thought we should meet. As we walked behind the elderly curator, we saw with horror three cops standing by our illegally parked trailer! "We're busted!," Terence whispered out the side of his mouth, "Pretend they're not ours!," and we looked straight ahead as if we had an important appointment to get to. People came out of the stores and leaned from windows to watch us American lawbreakers being led down Main Street, and I wondered what a night in a Marsala jail would be like...or what Terence was going to come up with to get us away from paying a hefty fine.

We were ushered into the office of Signore Angelo Vita, Cavaliere al merito della Republica, a handsome white-haired gentleman who formally introduced his secretary, Antoinella, and pushed us into two rather plush chairs in front of a video screen that immediately begin to spout the greater points of interest of the Marsala region. We were in a Tourist Office! We were handed two small paper cups of sherry--not Marsala, we are told, but equally interesting, says Sr. Vita. From the island of Canteleria, just off the coast, where he hopes we will want to visit. (Sure.) We were cosseted and cuddled for a charming half-hour and I was trying to live up to the rich American image these guys must have had of us and hoping for another swig of the off-shore island's finest to soothe my poor sore throat, when Sr. Vita informed us that we really ought to be out of town by sunset (tramonto). It was his sad duty to inform us that the stories of the "bandits" in Sicily were, alas, all too true in these parts, and that's why he ordered the police to guard our rig for the last two hours! That's what the cops were doing--guarding our rig! We cracked up. Who was this guy who had the only secretary in western Sicily and could order the local Polizia to guard a couple of filthy motorcycles? Who cared? No fine. No jail time! We just needed to be out of town by sunset. No problema!

We bumped along the coast for awhile heading for a spit of land near Selinunte that our guide-book said was free to budget-wise campers. It was now dark and the road took us past the busy bars in the village where dozens of men (probably every man in town) were standing around waiting for the dinner that they could go home for and eat quickly so then they could come back and stand around some more in the bars. They were delighted to see us go by, thereby giving them something new to talk to each other about, and they lined the streets waiting for us to come back which they knew we'd do, because the "free" campground was now closed and we had no choice. After we made our way past the "No Entry" sign and were desperately trying to find a spot hidden from view, we were unnerved to see a car drive up and a window roll down and a man yell for us to come talk to him. We walked over and discovered he was the owner of the local campground, no surprise. Although we knew it was probably he who put up the sign and the place probably was O.K. to camp on, we also had to face the fact that at least half the town knew where we were for the night and everybody was curious. Not to mention the dreaded "Banditi." We agreed to follow him to his campground. Terence struck a deal for 10000 lire, which wasn't too bad, and as it happened, it was a good thing we let the guy have our business. My sore throat turned into the flu, and we had to stay two days while I recovered.

The day after we arrived was Sunday and sun-splashed. On his way to the restrooms, Terence discovered our campground was right across the street from a couple of splendid Greek temples in a field of yellow daisies and here I was--too sick to get up! The manager watched his only campers from his window. After a while he came to talk to Terence about what was wrong with the "Signora." Terence tried to explain I'd be fine in a couple of days, but I think the poor man thought I had the plague by the way I looked. (How I would have loved some privacy.) He told Terence where we could find a doctor in town and then later, walked over with a plate of roasted (actually burned beyond recognition) artichokes and two little pastries from a big Sunday dinner he'd just had with his family in town. I was touched by his kindness.

Later, in the afternoon, I felt a little better (it had to be the pastries), and accompanied Terence across the street to catch the magic light of a setting sun on the biggest temple. It was indeed something to see. The fabulous structure with its massive columns and an ambiance of the ancients now being washed in rose-gold light against a pollution-free azure sky--eat your heart out, Athens! Adding to the already unbeatable color scheme were the daisy-type flowers. Each were on stalks taller than I, and swirling around the old stone temples like some golden tide. We could understand how easy it must have been to worship there.

I felt much better in the morning, so we packed up and paid the nice manager and rode on over to the other famous Selinunte site where there was not as spectacular a scene perhaps, but much more in the way of acreage--a whole 6th century Roman town excavated near the ruined temples. Thieves of all stripes had denuded the place--one type of thief taking everything away to museums. We had seen much of the exquisite stone carvings and mosaic artistry in the Museum of History in Palermo. Now, on the original site, very little remained to speak of the incredible civilization that once existed there. Pictures and drawings in Palermo had shown us how the city had once looked. Even the wealthiest Sicilian today rarely had homes as fine in line and stonework as the ancients. Today's cheap and hastily constructed houses--with rusting ironwork bleeding from the concrete, would probably have moved the 6th century builders to tears.

Drove all afternoon and pulled into Sal Veneziano's summer place at Seculiano Marina. Sal wasn't there, we didn't expect him to be, but we talked to a few of the locals so that they knew we were friends of the Veneziano family. Then, leaving my motorcycle and the heavy trailer in Sal's driveway, we took the Gold Wing to the temple at Agrigento to enjoy the sacred spot at our leisure without the well-meaning pressure of our Sicilian friends. We got some great shots this time, slowly strolling around the grounds in thought and serious contemplation as we had so badly wanted to before. It felt wonderful. Then we rode the bike into the city of Agrigento across the narrow valley. Some sort of celebration was going on with strings of colored bulbs criss-crossing the streets and people carrying heavy religious floats and everywhere--hordes of humanity. We couldn't even get the Wing through the throng and so gave up after a while and made our way out of the city. Looking back after a bit, the old city looked beautiful as it sat on the crest of the opposite valley, sparkling in the clear night and with the dark band of the temple valley beneath.

A very restful night spent in the Veneziano driveway. No barking dogs nor auto horns. Just the slap of the surf across the street, a cool breeze and peace...

Several small and dry villages later, we rolled east into Modica and thought it delightful. Built up the sides of a rather steep grotto, the town had retained much of its architecture from the Baroque period, and the Portuguese influence was everywhere. We were especially taken with the many 16th century balcony support carvings. Another welcome serendipity was the discovery of fresh milk--always hard to find in Sicily. With little water, no fodder, no cows, no milk. We had missed it sorely.

Wednesday, March 21, the first day of Spring. We rose from some farmer's field or other to face the beautiful day at 6:30 a.m. The sun was just coming up and it wasn't cold. We ate a quick breakfast and were in the saddle by a little after seven to "pile the miles," as Terence was fond of saying. Still, we had to stop for Noto, a small but intriguing town our "Rough Guides" told us to not miss. After the 1693 earthquake leveled the existing settlement, a hot shot city planner named Giovanni Landolina was called in, and he laid out the inner city while another expert "adorned" it. A stupendous Baroque plan and great for walking. Unfortunately, yet another town built without the automobile in mind. Blemishing the beautiful marble expanses, the inhabitants of Noto parked their ugly little cars on sidewalks and courtyards giving the impression of so many beached whales. We pulled our own unattractive contributions to pollution up to the huge arch marking the center of the city, and got off them and walked around. The Tourist Office was very pleasant and obviously used to tourists, but as usual there were no toilets for ladies anywhere. I was forced to beg at a girl's school for relief. Criminal. Later, a nice guy in overalls took it upon himself to show us around one of the churches. There were lot of paintings from the Caravaggio school and one he swore was a genuine Valesquez--unguarded and hanging in the dim light of one of the side chapels. A very impressive tour.

Bumping along the outskirts of Siracusa, I was stricken by how much like Portugal the architecture looked. It was hard to believe the tiny country we had traveled through a year ago had at one time been colonizing like honey bees over much of the known world.

The kind gentleman at the Tourist Information office in Siracusa told us that the opera performance was free that night to any tourist staying in the local hotels. We thought, "Why not the local campground?," and raced back to ask our Patrone if she'd give us a receipt to use as vouchers. First she said yes, then she disappeared and our time ran out for waiting so we dressed up and grabbed Rolf, a new motorcycling friend from East Germany and the three of us zoomed back to the city to the Opera house.

Without proof from a hotel, Terence had to do some pretty fancy convincing at the box office to get us in free of charge. But while Rolf and I chewed our nails behind him, Mr. Charm prevailed once again and we were given wonderful seats about six rows from the front.

There were no posters or programs but just before it started, the word got around that the company was Romanian. Terence was ecstatic. A language he hadn't learned yet!

Rolf, our young ex-Communist, had never been to an opera before--he hadn't even heard a recording of one. Having just been allowed through the gates to freedom, he was eager to learn, but a little nervous about how to act. Everyone around us was in furs and dark suits and gowns and there we were, in jeans with helmets in our laps. I told him not to worry. "They may be looking at us now, Rolf," I said, "But they're Italians. Once the music begins, all else will be forgotten!"

Luckily, the performance was Puccini's "La Tosca," one of our favorites and one that's very easy on a beginning opera-goer's ear. I explained the plot to him and as the melodies poured over us I could see he was loving it. The soprano was a bit over the hill and the whole cast was definitely of the Silent-movie school of acting, but the tenor was fine and the music glorious and the three of us were enjoying it tremendously when something unheard of happened. I had just whispered to Rolf about how important the "Vissi d'arte" solo was in the opera and how, if a soprano didn't do it perfectly, Italians were known to throw tomatoes and worse, when to my horror, I realized our Romanian prima donna was rushing the solo terribly and even cut short some important high notes in the song! We looked around. The faces were stony but no one jeered. Then they all started to clap. Apparently, the crowd was a good-hearted bunch and willing to forgive the Romanians anything. After all, this was the poor singers's first taste of freedom--maybe their first performance out of their country in how many years? Forty? Fifty? Also, this was not La Scala, where the audience was far more snobbish. Another reason to like Sicily!

The intermission between the second and third act drug on and on. It had been almost forty minutes. Rolf was glad to escape outside and have a cigarette. Terence had gone backstage to talk to the orchestra members and was waving me over to join him. The black-clad musicians were gathered around him and the languages were flying. Several of them spoke French and they were thrilled to be talking to Americans. Terence whispered to me that he had just discovered that one of the violins was made out of plywood and painted black to cover the cheap grain. As a string-player himself, he was really shaken by his discovery. The Romanians spoke freely about finally getting rid of their terrible dictator, Ceausescu, and several black jokes were bandied about concerning the dictator's execution but I missed the meaning of most of them. Then someone mentioned that the soprano had the flu and was too sick to continue and the mystery of the shortened high notes was solved.

After a bit, her understudy, who had been singing in the chorus, had shoved her formidable bulk into the Diva's costume and the third act began. The tenor sang the popular solo "E luce van le stelle" so well that the relieved audience went wild--standing and shouting "Bis!" (encore) and stopping the show with their applauding. Terence was blubbering--it's his favorite solo in opera--and we were all elated when the tired but game tenor signaled to the conductor that he was willing to repeat it. (The musicians had told us of a grueling schedule the week previous.) Incredibly, it was almost better than the first time and the house rang again with applause. When the understudy for Tosca came on the mood was warm and welcoming and the young woman must have felt it and so did a very good job of the last act.

Rolf declared himself totally converted to Opera, and T. and I were very happy at how it all came out. In the street next to the motorcycle, I pulled on my jeans over my dress to the amusement of the folks coming out of the theater, and climbed on the Gold Wing behind Terence--feeling absolutely drugged by the experience. On the ride home, T. mulled over about how he could get some real instruments to his new friends in Romania.

We spent two more days enjoying that ancient harbor city and the various digs and antiquities around it. There was so much to see and most of it free. Being March, we had the place pretty much to ourselves as tourists, and the weather was warm and the sea sparkled and life was glorious.

On Saturday, March 24, we waved good-bye to Rolf and pulled away from the charms of Siracusa, and headed inland up a mountain to visit the remains of the Castello Eurialo, which proved somewhat disappointing, and then kept climbing up and up until we found the famous Pantalica Necropolis. There was no one else about, and it was a fine afternoon. We parked the rig on the gravel siding area obviously meant for tourists, and walked over to look at the scene below us. Stretched out before us was a deep series of grottos where over 1200 grave-caves had been dug by people in the 12th to 13th centuries--B.C. There were some trails going down to the river below and we took one, carrying our water jugs and cameras and inspecting the many rectangular holes in the rocky cliffs. The silence was eerie but of course perfect for the setting. We were so grateful to be alone on the trail. Somehow, being in the midst of a gaggle of other visitors talking and laughing as we snaked our way down past the tombs would have seemed disrespectful. Most of the cave-tombs had been broken into, not surprisingly. Still, there were quite a few still sealed. The grave robbers probably gave up on finding much of value. This was after all, a final resting place for the common people, not for Royals. I thought about the Palermo aristocrats wired to the walls back at the catacombs. All that money spent so that people who never knew them could walk by and stare at their decaying corpses. And here, under a beautiful blue sky, the common folk lay in their own private little bedrooms near where the river gurgled and the birds chirped.

We filled our water jugs down at the river and lazed around on the grassy banks. Terence took his time shooting pictures of the tombs all around us and the bees buzzed, and as the sun slid behind the rocky cliffs, great purple shadows began to blot out the afternoon light and we gathered our stuff together and took the long steep hike back to our bikes. There being no one else around, and our map showing nothing resembling a campground in any direction in this part of Sicily, we just pulled our camp chairs and table off the back of the trailer and opened its lid and made ourselves at home. It was a windy night. As we lay on our pillows, we did our best to imagine ghostly moans and howls coming from the grotto below us, but I guess it was just too long a time since the 12th century B.C. Every last spirit must have departed for good, so we simply turned over and slept the sleep of the dead by ourselves.

The next night's lodging was not nearly so inviting. We had traveled over the plains of Catania until we found an abandoned farmhouse off the road about thirty yards that was sitting in mud from the recent rains and with quite a lot of rubbish. The smell was off-putting, to say the least, but we had no choice. There were no campgrounds here in eastern Sicily and no trees to hide behind. We were just grateful we didn't have to share the ruin with a local goat-herd and his flock.

Terence pulled the trailer into the attached barn area and I set up the table and chairs in the house in what might have been a dining room at one time. The rooms were very small, and nothing was left of the windows but big gaping holes. The wall plaster was pealing off in great chunks and as before, there was much evidence of recent shady goings-on in each of the rooms, something T. and I had become accustomed to by this time. As long as it wasn't dangerous like a syringe or crawling, I could just kick away the offending articles and proceed with dinner preparations.

The higher we rode up the slopes of Mt. Etna, the colder the wind became. We were wearing our electric vests and gloves and lots of layers, but we could still feel the icy wind slicing through. Still, the long zig-zag ride up the lava-covered mountain was a tremendous thrill. We pulled our heavy rig as far as we were allowed, and then the signs barred the road and we had to turn around. We pulled into a parking lot for tourist buses and got off the bikes to munch some lunch. The Catania valley could be viewed from our lofty perch but it was a dark gray, gloomy day. The wind was fierce but seemed to lighten once we were on the road that wound around the north side of Etna. We saw some truly phantasmagorical evidence of the mountain's wrath as we passed by deserted homes, walls and trees partially covered by lava and ash. One rather large once-pretty home was now blackened from fire, and lava covered its garden. Fruit trees stuck out in strange angles from the black earth but were all in spring bloom! What a sight. The soft white and pink petals against all that evil-looking blackness. As we looked for shelter for the night, we could hear the volcano grumble above us. We found a spot on top of a hill not too far away from the mountain. When the clouds lifted, we could see a plume of smoke from the old volcano's peak rolling away in the wind.

The crossing back to the mainland of Italy the next day was a piece of cake; we had become old hands at taking the ferry at Messina. We rolled off the ferry ramp at Reggio Calabria and rode up the toe of the boot to the same train trestle we had camped under when we had first traveled south on our way to Sicily--five months earlier.

Waking to a hard rain, we packed up as well as we could under the tarp and then yanked it off and shook it and threw it--folded and wet-- between the mattress and the trailer bed. We rode through the storm for several hours to Naples, and checked in to a campground next door to where, in November, we had experienced the uh..unpleasantness concerning the dog, the manager, and the local Polizei. We tried to keep a very low profile. After getting settled and unhitching the trailer from the Gold Wing, we rode out and looked around a bit--the museums in Naples and the local scenery. We'd heard so much about how "rough" the city was...how crowded and dirty...so much poverty, etc. ,etc. For some reason, except for the pouring rain, both Terence and I liked what we saw a lot. The people seemed tough in the streets, sure, but they also exuded a friendliness we had missed in other places like Rome and even Palermo. A sort of "I'd like to take your stuff, but if you're going to keep watching it, forget it and let's be friends" kind of attitude that appeared totally non-threatening.

Bureaucrats, however, are the same everywhere. We had sloshed our way up a couple of flights of stairs at the bank to cash a check with our American Express credit card and after much sitting and waiting, we were told that our card could not be honored due to some problem with the company in the States. We were stunned. What the hell was going on? We knew we had paid our exorbitant membership fee and had never had a problem before. The embarrassed young clerk told us he was unable to inform us as to the nature of the problem and we would have to check with the larger office when we got to Rome, but he was happy to be able to tell us that he would not have to confiscate our cards, at least. Thanks a lot.

Feeling very foolish in our dripping and tattered rain gear, we clomped back down the stairs in misery. Luckily, we were able to get some lira with our VISA card at a nearby bank, but it was irritating to know that we were being charged a healthy fee for the privilege and we certainly couldn't do that very often.

We returned to a campground sloppy with mud from all the rain. I went into the washroom to take a shower and discovered the water was turned off during certain hours of the day because of a nasty drought they'd had during the winter. Again I was stricken with the thought of how odd it was that it never seemed to rain when we were in a nice dry apartment, but once we'd get on the road again, down it would come! Anyway, I wrapped my damp towel around my freezing form and--all pride and dignity gone by this time-- yelled for Terence. He walked over to the manager to get the water turned on and while I waited, standing in the odoriferous bathrooms (the toilets hadn't been flushed for days either, no doubt to save water), I had visions of perhaps another Neapolitan street fight like the one next door in November. But Terence managed to move mountains again--even volcanic ones--and before the Vesuvians got a chance to erupt, he'd convinced them that the tacky sign out front did say the price included hot showers, and they must have agreed, because suddenly, with much clanking and rust coming out of the pipes, I got my hot water and stepped in to take my shower. Ah, but the management got the last laugh because now there was no cold water to mix it with! I had three choices. I could waddle out and scream for Terence to go back to the manager, I could give up and stay dirty and seethe, or I could try to take a shower and wash my hair in boiling water. After a week on the road, I chose to scald myself and get clean.

Two days later, we rolled into Terracina, a small town some miles north of Naples, looking for a fellow Terence had met at the Taekwon Do tournament in Vincitalia the year before. The young man wasn't at the martial arts studio, but someone kind let us use the phone and Terence was able to make contact with Dario who rushed over to greet us and give us a name of a friend of his who would let us stay a couple of nights for free.

The friend's name was Walter and he owned the local campground! It was closed for the season, but as a favor to Dario, he allowed us to roll in and camp for two days. While Terence worked out at the studio with the guys, I managed to dry some sheets and stuff back at the camp by throwing them over a line every time the sun came out and grabbing them back in when the rain fell. It kept me busy.

The day we were to leave Terracina was a Sunday and Dario had invited us to the family dinner. His mother had put on a gargantuan spread, not just for us but for about ten other assorted family members and friends invited to "Meet the Americani." No one spoke English but I understood most of the conversation directed at us. It consisted of the usual questions about our trip and the motorcycles and the size (and illegality) of the trailer, etc. Terence loved answering everyone so he could show off his Italian and I sat there eating and smiling like a blushing newlywed. I certainly didn't mind being allowed to concentrate on the food. It was a dream feast. Antipasti consisted of freshly made mozzarella mini-balls, tender and singing with flavor, plus fat olives and tiny anchovies. A huge plate of spaghetti with shellfish in a tomato sauce was placed before each of us and after that, a platter handed 'round of some other treasures of the sea, including some small lobster-looking things. I would have called them crawdads at home. Succulent slices of a white fleshed fish were next and then great platters of artichokes in olive oil, small and very tender. A large dish of steamed peas with ham was not to be ignored before the enormous plate of sliced beef appeared, sending Terence and me to Hog Heaven because it had been a while since we had eaten meat and we had sorely missed it.

When the massive green salad showed up, I excused myself from the table to go to the bathroom--hoping to avoid being served any because I was full for one thing, and positive there would be some divine dessert at the end that I wouldn't want to miss. Oh, I know how good salad is for me and I was naughty to skip it but hey, they served it at the end of the meal, how was I supposed to know it was coming when I was filling up on all that meat? And dessert was as good as I'd guessed it would be. A lovely assortment of pastries, then coffee and liqueurs. We were purring. When we gathered ourselves to go, Dario's mama gave us a foil-wrapped package of leftovers to take with us. A saint.

Over the hills and through the rain, to Donna Blair's house we go again...This time in Rome we got to know my sister's good friend a lot better and even though she was being very generous to let us stay with her for three days, I believe she enjoyed our company. I decided she missed some good old American conversation!

While taking in some of the Roman wonders, we remembered to go to the American Express office and inquire as to the reason for our great embarrassment in Naples. Fortunately, the gentleman in Rome was able to contact someone in the United States office and we were told that we were refused service because their computer lacked a telephone number where we could be reached! Without a phone number, how could we be trusted to pay our bill? We reacted to the news appropriately, I think. We let him know we were, in reality, a very wealthy couple who had nothing better to do than float around the world while other people had to slave away in offices, and in our eccentricity, we particularly enjoyed fooling underlings by wearing tattered clothing and riding dirty old motorcycles, and as we had presumed our business manager's phone number was on file, we really didn't see why we should have been inconvenienced in the first place and could he please take care of it? He could.

Giovanni di Nuzzo was a young journalist-biker whom we had met at the Gold Wing Treffen in Castigliano del Lago. He had asked us to ring him up when we arrived in Rome. He spoke English and expressed an interest in having us write our story to date. He even thought his magazine, IN MOTO, would be interested in my ink drawings! Terence and I got to work. We thanked Donna for her kind hospitality and stayed two rather intense days at Giovanni's apartment while I gathered together what I thought might be of interest and wrote our first rough draft and Terence started translating it into Italian. We couldn't finish it in Rome, however, because we needed to get on the road if we were going to get a job in Holland roofing and picking tulips. So we promised Giovanni we'd send it to him when it was finished. Actually, it took us until Germany to finish it, but good as his word, Giovanni got it published for us with few changes and although the money was good, it was the thrill of actually being in print that was the real shot in the arm, and gave us heart to attempt to finish our marathon journey.

It was Saturday, April 7th, and Terence was not in a good mood. The constant rain was getting him down. He was way behind in his Law homework and there seemed no place for us to keep dry while he studied. I knew we were passing some truly spectacular countryside under all that mist on the way to Sienna, but neither of us cared to drag out the cameras in such weather. It was beginning to get dark and our maps showed no campgrounds in sight. In Prague, Pip and Susan had told us of a marvelous monastery that allowed travelers to camp free on their grounds but we had no address. People we met on the outskirts of Siena had never heard of such a place. Desperate, we headed for the nearest monastery on our map, the Lucetto Hermitage, located way up into the forested hills after miles of muddy road. It was dark when we reached it. Terence pounded on the door of the crumbling old building but no one answered. There was a small grass parking lot in front and we curled up the rig in the corner, trying to look inconspicuous. As we munched some leftovers out of the little fridge, we decided the monks had probably taken a vow of silence or something and were not about to race out into the cold drizzle to shoo us off their property. We slept well.

Terence tried again the next morning to rouse someone and ask permission to leave the trailer there while we rode the Wing into town for the day. Still, no one appeared. The only sound to be heard was our own voices and the sighing of the pines. We decided to chance it and so locked up trailer and rode the big bike unencumbered down the mountain and up to Siena.

The cathedral at Siena was a marvel. Huge and cavernous yet so full of people it appeared quite cozy. An Easter week service was in full swing down by the altar, but sightseers were allowed to pass freely inside and walk around, only a small sign asking for quiet. At one point the organ boomed out a Bach Toccata and as it bounced off the great walls and vibrated through the incense, we couldn't help but feel a part of the worship service. Our senses were pleasantly jarred by the sounds, sights and smells and after a week of gray days and lonely campsites, it was fun to find ourselves in the swirl of the masses for a bit. Several languages echoed around us as we studied the colorful mosaics on the floor and the murals above, and we realized we were getting just a taste again of what high-tourist season was like. We had been very spoiled in Sicily!

After a couple of hours, however, walking around the medieval part of the city, shoulder to shoulder with chattering strangers doing the same, we lost some of the delight taken earlier in being one with the crowd and decided to get back on the bike and check out another monastery a few miles out of town called the Mt. of Olives. This place turned out to be a "going concern." Another site mobbed by tourists--could we all have been reading the same brochures? We were asked to buy tickets to visit the grounds and inner courtyard and every few feet some emaciated young monk was offering tiny olive branches for lira and Terence and I began to yearn for our quiet little hermitage. Again the weather wouldn't cooperate as we rolled around the hills of Tuscany eager to take pictures. I'd just have to buy a few postcards instead.

The invisible brethren at Ermeto Lucetto hadn't touched our rig and once again, in their spiritual generosity and kindness, allowed us to spend that night in their parking lot. The perfect (g)hosts.

The first campground we came to in Florence was expensive and drab. We rode across town to another. It too was expensive but had a great view from its hillside site. We could see the Duomo and all sorts of stuff and the showers were long and hot. Oh joy!

We went to pick up my bike from Andrea's garden the next day. It had been sitting there since February, so of course the battery was totally dead. Terence tried everything he could think of to revive it but even he had to admit defeat and we had to go into the city to buy another battery for it. I began to sink into another of my famous "money worries" depression. Later, we called Canon to find out what happened to Terence's typewriter they were to fix and have here for us by the time we arrived in Florence, and we were told it had been sent to Rome! The phone call took so long at about six bucks a minute I was tearing my hair. Then we had to call Rochelle, my business manager, who told us she had sent all our important mail to Palermo! Also my taxes were still floating around somewhere waiting for my signature...I was developing a sick headache.

Our moods didn't improve the next day when we had to stand for 45 minutes in a long line to see the paintings in the Uffizi, pay an exorbitant five dollars each to get in, and then were told several of the best rooms were closed because of lack of staff! Meanwhile, several of the "staff" were standing around on breaks, talking and smoking--smoking!-among several of the most valuable paintings in the world! I was astounded. How could they allow such a thing? Still, there were works there to calm the soul and I emerged in much better spirits than when I'd gone in.

The next stop after Florence was Pisa and once again, mobbed with tourists. Who could blame them? It was everything we'd heard about and more. Even with gray skies, we couldn't take a bad picture. The great white marble against the dark clouds...wow! Terence went nuts with his infrared film and I had a pretty great time myself--taking all sorts of arty shots and drinking in the magic of that immense leaning wedding cake in the sky! Even without the tower, the church and basilica were a dramatic sight to behold--all those years, powerful and solid on the flat plane. The architecture and construction--certainly a tribute to the best things in man.

The Gold Wing's battery was dying again so we knew we'd have to find a camp before dark because Terence couldn't chance switching on his headlight. We reluctantly pulled away from that wonderful place and headed over the hills toward Lucca. The clouds began to look mean and the cold wind picked up. Soon Terence would have to turn on the headlight, which would probably blow out what was left of his electrical system. After a few false starts asking some local farm hands if we could park on the land, and getting negative responses, we found a soft-hearted lady who peeked around her front door after Terence knocked and said we could stay on the shoulder of the road next to her vineyard. When we went to thank her the next morning, she told us that she was used to having people on motorcycles camp in her vineyard on their way to Pisa-- mostly German, she said. It was rare, she added, for anyone to ask permission and even rarer to thank her. It was nice to think we might have polished the old American image a bit.

Lucca was a special treasure because the sun actually came out to show the beautiful old town in all its glory! We parked the rig and Gold Wing outside of the massive wall that surrounds the old part, and rode my bike through the narrow alleyways and to the dusty squares where the handsome churches had stood for centuries, their shadows cooling the streets below and their enormous dark interiors providing a haven for the faithful as well as the just curious, like us.

We visited Puccini's birthplace, being good little opera fans, and saw his piano and a few of his other things scattered around the tiny apartments, and then, walking down a long crowded street, we came upon a great Renaissance tower with a large oak tree growing out of the top! Its roots must have been using the soft old brick of the walls for soil. It was a very bizarre sight.

Eating our lunch just a few miles north of Lucca, we lolled on a leaf-covered riverbank and watched the puffy clouds trying to look fierce. But it was the sun's hour for once and we felt warm and drowsy and happy again. Between some fluttering poplars on the opposite bank, we could see the spires of an ancient church turning gold and copper in the sun and watching it all from under our sleepy eye lids, we both realized it was just another example of why we were making this crazy trip.

We piled on the miles. Somewhere along the way I braved a recalcitrant telephone to call Meredith in California to wish her a happy birthday. Talking to her put a lump in my throat and made me miserable with guilt. I could tell myself--all I wanted to, that my daughter didn't need me around, but I knew it had just been too long. Who'd have thought this wild man would really see this thing to the end? And where would the "end" be? Better not to think about it.

The shadows grew long and Terence came to a stop ahead of me. We were in the mountains again and he was pointing to a narrow wooden slat suspension bridge over a river. "It looks like we wouldn't be seen over there," he indicated with a lift of his chin. I looked down and followed his gaze. There was a little sandy inlet by the river--half hidden by some small fir trees. "But we'd have to ride over that slat bridge," I said, not liking the idea at all. "Follow me!," said my intrepid leader. "If I can make it, you can!" And he wrenched the handle-bars of the big bike to the right, and sped over the rocky path at the side of the road, and with both feet treading the slats to hold his machine upright, he clattered and slid and pulled the 1200 lb. trailer behind him over that river while I was left in the street holding my breath and wondering how anyone could be possessed with such foolhardy courage without massive doses of a very strong drug.

He made it though, and as he barreled down the embankment on the other side in a huge cloud of dust, I shouted "O.K., Here goes!," and put my mind on the shelf to be retrieved later. "If he can do it with all that weight, I can with this little bitty bike! And although the bridge creaked ominously and several of the wood slates popped up as my bike hit them and I could see, between the thin slats, the river rushing over great boulders below, the ride over really wasn't all that bad and I wished I had been braver. Terence had found a secluded spot behind some tall bushes and I congratulated him on his discovery. Some one had camped nearby earlier-- in fact it must have been a very popular spot on warmer days, because there was trash everywhere and for some reason I didn't feel comfortable settling in and cooking dinner until I'd picked up the paper stuff and burned it on the previous guy's campfire and buried the unburnables. Then I felt better and even decided to forgive myself for being such a wimp about the bridge.

Foolishly consuming a couple of cups of some cheap white wine with some really questionable leftovers the night before, I felt too sick to travel the next morning. I liked our secluded home by the river and it looked like it was going to rain again, so staying in a toasty bed all morning until I felt better sounded like a great idea. Not to old El Push-on Geoghegan, however. Stoically, he made himself breakfast (I couldn't look at food), and packed up around me. I think it was when he began preparing to close the trailer top with me inside that I got the hint and groaning, rolled out and put on my boots with much grumbling. He knew I was too sick to slug him.

I was ordered to take pictures of him riding the rig across the suspension bridge (Aha! So he did think it was scary!) and then, as he rode up the slippery embankment on the other side, the big bike's engine failed and it slid out of control on the rocks and flipped over onto the narrow mountain road--smack in front of any oncoming traffic that might be coming around the curve. I yelped and threw the camera into my tank-bag and jumped on the motorcycle and tore up the slope and over that damn bridge over to where he was frantically trying to right the Wing. Because the trailer was still over the side of the road and starting to pull the whole thing down the cliff to the river, Terence couldn't get the motorcycle up over the rocks by himself, a fact he was not prepared to face as usual. I left my bike on the end of the bridge and ran up the bank to the fallen Wing. With all the strength we could muster--and spurred on no doubt by the terror of knowing a car might be roaring around that curve any moment, we managed to get the thing up. I pushed hard between the trailer and the top-box of the Wing as Terence gunned it up the slope, then he rode it free at last and on down the road and I ran back to the Ascot and bounced over the rocks to follow him.

The rain was coming down in sheets. I hated it. I was feeling nauseous and wanted my mama. My helmet face shield was so scratched I could barely see and looking through that plus the also- scratched plastic windshield on the bike, now covered with giant splats of water and mud, added up to a very dangerous situation in my opinion. "Gee," I thought... "I wonder why there are so many motorcycle accidents in bad weather? Duh. I don't suppose it's kosher to put windshield wipers on the damn things. That would just be so un-macho!" I tried lifting my face shield to squint through the rain but the needle-like drops in the wind felt like bullets in my eyes. I stood up out of my seat to look over the fairing shield. Freezing rivulets of rain-water found their way into my underwear and down my legs. "Oh whoopee! Are we having fun yet!" I sat down in a pool of ice water and thought again about all those ladies who give "anything" to be in my place. "Hey girls!," I shouted inside my helmet, "Wanna trade NOW? Huh? Huh?!"

Just outside of Genoa we entered a tunnel. Usually uncomfortably claustrophobic in such places, I found great relief in escaping the storm and being able to lift up my face plate and see better. It was one of those tunnels that had a concrete wall between the two directions in traffic. Every so often there's a walk-through space in the wall for maintenance and emergencies. Glancing through the spaces as we sped along, I noticed that there was a huge traffic jam on the other side and thanked the Gods I was spared the experience of being stuck in the middle of an airless tunnel on a motorcycle. I shivered at the thought. When we emerged, we heard the sirens and then saw the ambulances trying to get through the morning rush-hour traffic to the accident in the tunnel. There was absolutely no path for them to take to make any progress. No turnouts, no wide shoulders. Nothing. Brilliant planning. The victims could be in there for days. At least they were out of the rain, I thought morosely.

After a couple of hours in downtown Genoa looking for Tourist Information Offices, etc., we found the municipal campground at the north end of the city and signed the register and put up the trailer and the tarp over it and I heated up a meal and although soaked to the skin and steaming we were both very glad to be alive and through bad times once again. Hot food put us both in much better spirits and we looked forward to seeing the famous city in the morning.

Unfortunately, it was Easter Sunday the next morning, so nothing but churches were open and they of course, were crammed with the faithful and the not so faithful who only made it to church on Christmas and Easter. Just like home. In any case, it was not a proper destination for the likes of us at this time, so checking our beloved guide book, we decided to go see the most "happenin'" place left which turned out to be the (justifiably) famous cemetery near the old part of the city.

We truly loved the place. Fantastic tombs and marble carvings that would do any museum proud. Nobility and the very wealthy had outdone themselves for centuries competing with the Joneses (the Gionneses?) in various tributes to their dead. We took gobs of pictures and were grateful for the weather holding itself back for awhile. Later, we ate our boring tuna sandwiches down at the port in a freezing wind. I had become so sick of tuna. Terence said he could eat it forever. I thought he was nuts, but looking on the bright side, it was nice to know he'd be happy with whatever I threw in his plate and that's the kind of insanity I like in a man!

Monday was also a holiday so it didn't look like we were going to see anything of Genoa after all. But the day dawned warm and dry and so with joy in our hearts and breakfast in our bellies, we packed up and rode back to the autostrada for the trip to Turino. Tunnel after tunnel shut out the sunny morning. No wonder the autostrada cost so much to build with all those mountains to dig through. The long dark caverns leaked and dripped and were as cold as tombs. At our lunch rest stop, Terence admitted he was not a happy camper driving into the horrible black things with no headlight thanks to the bike's electrical problems, and suggested we head into the hills and off the autostrada. It turned out to be a good move. Largely due to the break in the weather. Everything looked wonderful. Spring had returned. Pale-colored cows chewed on new grass in front of white-washed walls shoring up old tiled roofs and chimney pots. I took deep breaths and sang over the roar of my machine.

At a place the sign called Santuario, near Mondovi on our maps, we stopped to stare at an amazing sort of temple--a brick round structure with four square towers. Built probably over such a long span of time that tastes and architects changed many times--not an unusual occurrence in Europe. Out of the huge, many-styled wonder, came a stream of Easter pilgrims eager to look at our rig and ask us questions. It was a pleasant half hour for all of us before we started the engines and waving to the throng, rode out of town.

Trying to find a place to camp that afternoon, we turned off the main road and up to a barn to ask permission to spend the night nearby, but the entire family and assorted domestic animals ran out of the buildings to order us off their property. I think we scared them. Farther on down the road we found a couple as sweet as the others were hostile and they told us we would be welcome to camp in the cornfield right next to their little farmhouse, so Terence dragged the trailer over the furrows and I followed on my bike. The folks over the wall waved once and then disappeared, probably too shy to come over and chat but that was fine with us. We ate dinner and turned in early and would have had a good night's sleep except for the incessant ringing of bells down the lane coming from a tiny old church that must have been reluctant to say goodbye to Easter. We dragged ourselves out of bed the next morning with freezing noses and fingers and hurriedly made coffee so we'd have a nice warm mug to hang onto. While we sipped the steaming brew, we looked around and saw ourselves encircled by snow-capped mountains. It was cold, but oh, how magnificent the panorama! After leaving a note of thanks on our farmer-host's door, we rolled on to Turin.

We had met the Walter Quaggias in a campground in Scotland in the first year of our trip. They had warmly invited us to their home if we ever made it to Italy and were now in for a big surprise, for three years later here we were. Dr. Quaggia was a dentist in Turin and as pleasant as could be when we visited his office. He had to work for the rest of the day but insisted we come to his home for dinner. So Terence and I saw what we could of Turin while Dr. Quaggia drilled teeth, then that evening we all drove out to the pretty Turino suburb where they lived. It was a much longer ride than we had planned on and I hadn't bothered to change to my rain gear and rubber boots which I soon regretted because it poured just after we got on the highway and by the time we rolled into the Quaggia's garage, we looked like a couple of drowning victims, and had the embarrassment of having to lift the top of the trailer in front of our impeccable hosts, and forage around in the mess of many muddy days, for dry if not very clean clothes. The expression on our new friends was one of shocked disbelief as they showed us the way into their immaculate living room. There were no children and both of them had jobs so they were definitely into the "Good Life" and their home reflected it. Persian rugs adorned the floors and some very nice paintings glowing with little frame lamps hung on the walls. Everything was scrupulously clean. We left our soggy shoes at the door. We had bought a wine--a step or two above what we usually drank, and Signora Q whisked it away with a smile, saying it needed to "warm up." After Valter poured us a glass from a bottle they must have had warming up before we got there, he proudly showed us his wine cellar. I had the thought that his wife was probably upstairs in the kitchen pouring our poor offering down the sink, rinsing the bottle and refilling it with one of theirs. Hey, that was just fine with me. I don't get sick on the expensive stuff.

Dinner was again the superb feast we had come to expect in Italian homes. Very nice salami sliced paper thin for the antipasto, then orecchi pasta, then sliced tender pot-roast and steamed greens and a sensational dessert with pears and a warm fruit sauce. I wanted to put them both in my will. We talked awhile after dinner and then they showed us the guest room and told us they would both be gone the next morning to work but that we could sleep as late as we please and the morning-duty maid would let us out whenever we wanted to leave. I think I remember there was coffee waiting for us when we arose around 7:30 and indeed, our hosts had gone. I really hoped I'd get a chance to repay their kindness and generosity in California some day.

Another invitation to visit. This one in Novara, outside of Milano at the home of a delightful couple we had met at the Gold Wing Treffens. Lucky for us, Maurizio Oldani and his fiancee Nunzia were perishing to go to the United States someday and thought we were Gods. Maurizio insisted we stay in his flat as long as we liked while he moved in with Nunzia's family who lived in the same building. It was obvious that the two were going to be married soon because everything Maurizio had in his apartment looked like a wedding gift--new and unused and we realized it was terribly generous of them to let us mess up the place as it were.

While the young people had to go to work, Terence and I rode into Milano and did some chores and checked out the great cathedral. We loved all the gothic trappings on the outside--all spires and filials with tasteful later additions of sculpture in the 500 years or so it took to complete. The inside was dark and cavernous, the zillions of prayer candles doing little to dispel the gloom. We thought the wooden statue of St. Bartelomeo first rate. He strides purposefully on his pedestal wearing his flayed skin over his shoulder like a cloak and with the skin from his head dangling down his back like the glass-eyed foxes women used to wear in the forties. A splendid study in anatomy if slightly macabre. Then we looked in on a few of the free museums and were under-impressed. They seemed to be full of quite a lot of minor works plus a few sketches and unfinished things by major names. We became convinced most of them had been fished out of the artists trash cans at some point and probably should have been left where they found them.

We introduced ourselves to the Esperanto people in town. A sad experience, actually. Italy's "Head Office" was nothing more than a couple of rooms stacked to the ceiling with books in Esperanto and seemed to be run by one very grumpy old woman and her "Igor" type servant, who really didn't want to let us in at first and then hung around looking embarrassed as we tried to tell the elderly librarian how we hoped to "spread the word" about Esperanto, etc. Both of them looked at us as if we'd lost our minds and seemed irritated that we had bothered them in their dusty lair. Walking back to the bikes later, Terence remarked about how the International language was doomed if the people who guarded the flame found youth and enthusiasm disruptive to their daily rituals in their ivory towers.

When we had driven back that afternoon to Maurizio's electric gate at the apartment building, we discovered we had lost the key-ring we had been given that morning. I think, except for the accident in Spain, we had had no worse moment in the entire trip. Maurizio had entrusted us with around 10 to 15 keys on a large ring. Replacing them would surely cost us over a hundred dollars in Italy--provided they could be replaced. We both wanted to die. Finally facing the music and calling Maurizio from a pay phone, we found out that a neighbor had found them and returned them to him! Perhaps there was a God.

That night Maurizio and Nunzia took us to another Gold-Winger's house in Bergamo for dinner. Adelmo and Grazia Zanardi treated us like long-lost friends even though we had never met, and dinner was a sumptuous repast of thinly sliced beef for an appetizer, then polenta under a white mushroom sauce and then last, as usual in Italy, a monstrous green salad. Dessert was cheeses and little sweets with a very bitter liqueur called Amaro. We found ourselves in another spotless house, with an apartment on the floor below for mama. In the garage, Adelmo's 1500 Gold Wing looked like it just came off the showroom floor, even though he'd just come back from a rainy week-end in Belgium. Both he and Maurizio obviously got great pleasure from shining and modifying their Wings. It must have made them ill to note the present condition of ours.

The next day was Saturday, and while Terence slaved on translating our article for the motorcycle magazine, Maurizio invited me to take a ride seated behind him on the back of his prized possession. The weather was windy but dry and although another motorcycle ride was not exactly high on my list of things I wanted to do at that particular point in time, I saw no way to get out of it without hurting his feelings, so I put on my helmet and waved to Terence, and we took off into the ether. It soon became apparent to me that he was trying to scare the shit out of this old lady or maybe he just wanted to show how fast he could go, because he drove that fine machine a good 95 miles an hour and on back roads--passing cars at the last second--as if they were parked! I hung onto the side-bars and prepared for death--damned if I'd give him the satisfaction of begging him to slow down. I told myself maybe even if he didn't care about his or my life, he surely wouldn't want to dent his beloved motorcycle, would he? Unfortunately, I remembered a newspaper article we'd read the day before--about a young man who had just lost his parents in an auto crash and whose rich aunt, trying to help him "forget," gave him a new Testarossa sports car in which, a few days later, he died and also killed his best friend. (I think in

Italy, they ought to call those cars Tes-tos-terossa...) Anyway, there we were, whipping around mountain passes when suddenly I saw big black clouds overhead and thinking hopefully that he might want to turn around and go home because neither of us was dressed for rain, I yelled up to the pilot that I thought it was going to get very wet (or whatever it was I said in bad Italian). He disagreed cheerily and went faster and I gave up. A couple of minutes later the rain came down. And then hail. And still he drove like a madman. (A bat out of hail?). Soon we were flying past drifts of the white stuff at the side of the road and sitting in ice water, my favorite pastime. What fun! I thought about Terence back in Milan, typing away happily while his old lady was getting herself killed in the scenic Dolomites. The hail turned to rain again. A lake began to appear between the trees some miles away. "Lago Maggiore!" Maurizio shouted back and I began to hope I might live long enough to see the famous spot up close.

We were now sloshing past some pretty expensive-looking villas that I could barely make out through the downpour--standing dark and quiet behind their iron gates. They seemed empty. Maurizio, in true Italian form, was prudently sounding his huge chrome truck-type monster horn that he'd attached to the side of the Wing to warn anyone around the corner that he was coming fast and not stopping for anything so they had better get out of the way. I tried not to listen for the sound of horns coming from the other direction. I just sat in my ice water, concentrating on the posh architecture whizzing past. Incredibly, the oncoming traffic missed us, although not by much.

Some guardian angel I hadn't known about must have been along for the ride that day because we slid into the little touristy village by Lake Maggiore soaked but unscathed. Maurizio, exhibiting a magnanimous understanding of women, allowed me to peer at the jewelry and other touristy eye-grabbers in the expensive windows for a few minutes while we waited out the storm under the shops's overhangs, but he soon grew impatient and said "Andiamo!" and started the engine. I crawled up behind him and prepared for another wild ride but for some reason his mood had changed and we rode home just like normal racing bikers on drugs.

Next day was Sunday and Terence and I wanted to visit the castle museum in Milan. Maurizio and Nunzia and two other friends, Paolo and Didi came along, although we had the feeling they really would prefer a fast motorcycle trip out of town. They had never visited the museum in the castle and I hoped they weren't too bored. Terence and I enjoyed it immensely, especially in that it contained a large collection of wonderful old musical instruments. I had been trying not to think about the fact that I was in the city of one of the most important Opera Houses in all of Europe and wouldn't be going to an opera. Ah, but once you've heard "La Tosca" performed by the Romanian National Opera Company, you've heard it all...

On the way back to Novara, we stopped by Maurizio's uncle's Pasticciria where we all were fed fabulous tiny pastries by his darling aunt and uncle, who had emerged from the warm back kitchen all welcome and smiles and smelling of baking. Benisissimo! I was in sugar heaven. As the six of us sat at a little table and chattered away--our mouths full of cake and frosting and almond paste, I suddenly realized I was talking with them--in Italian! I stopped for a minute and looked around. Nobody seemed to notice. It had taken me six months to get comfortable in the language and tomorrow we were leaving Italy! What a shame. If I had known I could do it, I wondered, would I have studied harder? Too late now. Maybe someday I could come back and try again. Maybe Venice... I slipped back into the conversation and relaxed.

Bleak and rainy outside, we packed up the next morning and moved out. We passed through several small northern Italian villages and had no problem at all crossing the border near Lake Como. The smell of money and well-tended flowers began to show around the freshly painted homes and businesses. We knew we were in Switzerland.

Couldn't find a wild place to camp that afternoon, so there was nothing to do but bite the bullet and pay the high price of being legal campers. We woke to mountains all around us sprinkled with snow. The Swiss flag snapped smartly on a pole by the entrance and we could hear a rushing river somewhere nearby. There were no other campers and the clipped grass was spongy as we walked on it to the restroom. The season for campers here must be very short, indeed.

As we neared the tunnel for the famous Gottard Pass, I began to feel sick. The year before, we had had he heady experience of climbing the huge mountain with the police car on our tail, I remembered. This time there was no question about taking the only other route when heavy snow covered the pass above. The tunnel was 17 kilometers long and I had been trying to prepare myself for the experience for days. I wasn't going to give in to my claustrophobia. Anyway, what choice did I have? Nobody could ride my bike through it for me. And knowing the Swiss as I felt I did, there were probably nice clean turn-outs every mile or so and flower-boxes on specially provided ledges along the way.

Wrong. We were greeted by a blast of warm air at the entrance. Then, the road seemed to descend, to my fevered brain, as if into Hell. Horrible little sodium lights glimmered on the walls, turning the air orange-pink and sickly, and the air, hot now, was full of noxious fumes. People in automobiles could roll their windows up, but for us, Hell was what it was. I felt my panic rise. The car behind me was terribly close and I soon became aware that there were no turnouts--just like the awful tunnel outside of Genoa. The bloody lights were spaced evenly and began to make me dizzy with their hypnotic repetition. I was going to faint. Poor Terence would have to stop his rig and come back to pull me from under the bumper of the tailgater that had rolled over me after I fell off the bike. I simply had to get my mind onto something else and hope I could stay conscious until we could get out of that dark pit.

I started to sing. Bellowing lustily over the noise of the engines, I tried to remember all the words to the big three patriotic American songs we used to sing in Elementary School. "Oh, Say Can You See?," "My Country, 'Tis of Thee," and "Oh Beautiful For Spacious Skies" were the first lines. I got stuck a couple of times forgetting the words, and I really believe that the effort to try to remember saved my life in that blasted pit. I also spent quite a lot of time dissecting the "true" meaning of each song. Our national anthem was the most complex. Talk about sentence fragments...or was it split infinitives? I remember giggling over Whose bright stripes and bright stars? The Perilous Knight's? My world had become Looney Tunes when the end of the tunnel appeared and I felt the icy wind through my jacket, I felt as if I were waking from a long dream. It must have been the fumes in there. Another couple of minutes and I might have been brain dead.

Remember that scene in the movie "Dorothy and the Wizard of Oz," when her little wooden farmhouse finally falls out of the terrifying twister and the film goes from black and white to color? Dorothy, with Toto in her arms, slowly walks out of the broken house into this phantasmagorical rainbow world that only Hollywood could have dreamed up and I'll never forget the goosebumps on my little arms in that theater when I saw it. Well, coming out of that tunnel and into the wonder of Lake Lucerne was about as close to an Oz experience as I'll ever get. From the fires of Hell to Heaven's Gates. Color was exploding from every window box, and every neat little garden held its quota of tulips and daffodils. Between villages on the mountain passes, elderly Munchkins in dayglow highway maintenance uniforms were on their knees planting bulbs and as we rounded a bend, each vista looked like a travel poster. Spring seemed to have chosen Lake Lucerne for its kickoff party.

I wanted desperately to stop and absorb things, but there were still no turnoffs and we were lucky to have as much road as we got--cut away from what appeared to be sheer rock against the mountain. We finally parked the rig in a Bus Stop and ignored the disapproving looks of the People Whose Business it Was to Be There. We ate our lunch, and over bread and cheese we commiserated about the long scary ride under the mountain. We were both very glad it was over.

We spent three days with Fabio and Leonora in Brugg. They were very kind to let us wash our clothes and stay out of the rain for awhile--especially in that they barely knew us. Our friend Lukas, who used to room with Fabio, had now moved to Baden, and one evening we went to visit him. We brought dinner. He supplied strawberries and wine, bless him. After a cozy repast in his adorable attic apartment, we all took a walk around the little lakeside village and had a coffee in a Swiss pub.

Chapter Thirty-Six

THE ROMANTIK STRASSE

APRIL 27TH WAS a Bad day on the road. Traffic jams on the "Romantik Strasse" I'd renamed the "Traumatic Stresse." Terence stopped at one point to pour our water from our large container into the radiator of a guy's car that had stalled from being overheated. My wrist was hurting from the constant gear changing so to get relief and cool the bike's engine, I decided to pull out of the bumper to bumper line, and ride on the bicycle/pedestrian lane for awhile, even though I knew it was a no-no. Nobody else was in it. I thought I'd travel awhile in unobstructed luxury and then sit a spell and wait for Terence to catch up pulling the rig. Of course a Polizei car had to appear from the opposite direction just as I hopped the curb to get into the unoccupied lane. I slipped back into the jam quickly and later Terence thought it his mission in life to tell me the cop looked furious and had shaken his fist at me, etc. I was scared but didn't want to show it. It had taken a lot of nerve for me to pass cars on the right in the first place and the whole idea of me getting "busted" for such a little thing when Terence is constantly breaking the local laws and nobody minds, was beginning to make me very angry. I decided he was just jealous because with the giant trailer on his back, he couldn't do it himself. That and the damn rain and not knowing where we would be camping was taking its toll on our nerves.

But that evening, Terence found us another cozy forest camping spot, so I decided to forgive him and then the morning dawned warm and clear and my mood lightened further. The sun shone between the fragrant pines and the nasty road was far away. We packed up and went to visit our buddies, Thomas and Evelyn in Windach after a quick camera-shoot in nearby Landsberg.

Once again our German friends took such good care of us it was difficult to get away. Thomas took Evelyn on a long ride around their village on my Ascot and when they came back he had a glint in his eye I'd seen on males all over Europe when they alighted from one of our bikes. It was still hard for me to believe that my little motorcycle could inspire envy in grown men. I was still stinging from the nasty comments made by the guys at the local bike shop in California when Terence told them I would be riding it around the world. "On that piece of shit!?" they'd laughed.

Spring was everywhere and Germany was glowing. Every village had its May pole, that glorious pagan hymn to love and the renewal of life. The proud striped trunk-poles of great pine trees stood in the center of the square, so tall Terence and I could see the ribbons and garlands flapping in the breeze from far out of town. Each town had their master crafts depicted in carved wood and sprouting from the pole like branches. Thomas told us it was great sport in Bavaria, for the young men to steal a rival village's May pole. Then the men from the violated village would have to find it and try to get it back. Sometimes it took them all year and with several bribes and so on before it was returned. The fun had been going on for centuries.

We found a rather dark and spooky wood to stay the night in after leaving Thomas and Evelyn. No lights for miles around and very few cars on the road we had left. The silence and strange lack of wind made for a restless night and we were glad when the morning came, although the trailer got stuck in the muddy ruts on the soft forest road and we came close to giving up trying to get out. The darn job took over an hour and as we climbed hot and sticky onto the bikes, I tried not to think about when I might get my next bath.

May 4th, my birthday again. Didn't I just have one of the damn things? Don't need to worry about Terence noticing, that's for sure, so I might as well not think about it...

Lemon yellow mustard fields fly by. The villages begin to get cutesie on this famous tourist trail. Freshly painted hearts and flowers on half-timbers and doorways begins to make homes look oddly like restaurants, restaurants like restrooms. Still, all that shmaltz was what we too had come to see, I had to admit, and T. and I took the obligatory pictures. After slicing the cheese for lunch on the trailer top somewhere, I forgot to pick up my faithful Swiss Army knife and after a few miles down the road I realized what I'd done and cursed myself. Terence insisted we turn around and look by the side of the road for it but it was a futile exercise, of course. I was going to miss it.

We mingled with lots of other tourists at each Adorable Site. The walled city of Dinkelsbühl was one of the more interesting, with a big Baroque church set among great leaning half-timbered shops and houses. Inside the church, in one of the dark chapels with bars for the door, enclosed in a thick glass coffin, was the withered remains of a man in the last throes of some kind of painful agony, dressed in bishops raiment--all bejeweled and gold threads--and writhing forever under the glass and behind bars. We watched in wonder as a housefrau type knelt in front of the thing and prayed. Other people were doing the same in front of the other bleeding and tortured Tussaud-like images hanging from the walls around the church. The dust of centuries lay heavy on the wings and upturned faces of the holiest. Would it be sacrilege to clean them once in a while?

Wemding. Oettingen. Harburg. Nordlingen. All very pretty villages. Watched a wedding party come out of a church somewhere while a lively oom-pah brass band played in the parking lot to the happy couple.

Stopping in Schllingsfürst for gas, we met a friendly American ex-military man who had settled there with his wife and daughter. He took us home and to lunch and they, being very sensitive to our needs (or was it to theirs!) let us take a shower which simply turned the world around for me. How long had it been? We all got along famously and it sure was good to hear the language again and really relax with like minds. They had a lovely home, but little money. Donna Bond taught school and Jerry was an artist. Still, they loved the life they had carved out for themselves in Germany and their little girl was adorably bilingual and definitely showed the best of two worlds. We hated to leave them that evening knowing we might never see them again. That same problem kept happening on our journey...

Rothenburg ob der Tauber is a rather large city but the old center is lovingly restored with an eye to the real thing. We walked a bit on the castle ramparts that circle the old town and then rode my bike into the center to check out the galleries and touristy shops. Everything closed because it was a weekend--a very strange practice to an American, but it does tend to keep the money in the pocket, and for us that was a good thing.

We drove through a few more dah-ling bergs and as the light began to fade, we turned off the highway to find a place for the night. First attempt down a wandering path was no good because soon a sign proclaimed that it was an important bird refuge and that would be an even more strict no-no than simply trespassing. Terence had to unhitch the trailer because the little dirt road we'd been following had grown narrower and narrower until there was no way he could turn the big rig around.

Next we tried a farmer's trail up a newly plowed hill and with no other choice as dark closed in, we curled up the rig on a small tractor turnout at the top, and hoped no one would notice. A fragrant mustard field sloped from us down to a small group of houses below and we could hear the faint sounds of dinner preparations and the settling in for the night. A man walking his dog eyed us suspiciously as they went past, but he didn't seem to care all that much and as the moon rose and we huddled over our dinner, it was really quite pleasant to be perched on that hill. The soft wind was fresh and smelled of warmer days to come.

As Sunday church bells pealed, we tumbled out of our little trailer-tent to discover a bright blue sky and golden rising sun. Lots more people were out walking their dogs up our hill but they waved and smiled and didn't seem to mind us sipping coffee in their mustard field and we felt very comfortable indeed.

What a difference to be warm. It took a lot of self-discipline to move ourselves to pack and climb aboard the motorcycles and ride off that pretty yellow hill. Yet the ride in the glorious morning was an equal treat. We tied our steeds outside of Wertheim, one of the most famous of the "Romantik" villages, and along with several groups of cheery German tourists, proceeded to climb the long hill through the charming, storybook town and up to the castle at the top. Again, the shops were all closed and all we could do was peer in and wish we could see more. The big church at the bottom of the hill had some interesting seventeenth-century tombs. Sculpted figures of the noble deceased fascinated us. Especially the men in military garb with their larger-than-life cod-pieces. Perhaps one way to put fear in the hearts of the enemy!

We covered many more miles. The Gold Wing was fading fast. More and more, we had to hook up the aging machine to mine with the jumper cables to keep his battery alive. I stood in the weeds in the hot sun wishing I were somewhere else. So did Terence, no doubt.

That evening we found ourselves in the forest parkland known as the Ammer Wald. After scanning each side road for a hidden spot we could call our own for the night, Terence borrowed my bike and took off over a hill to follow a sign that said "Jugensportsplatz." (Youth playing field). He roared back down after a while to tell me that some guy had told him that it would probably be all right if we camped for the night up there because as soon as the kids went home, we'd be alone with nobody to bother us. Sounded good, so we "jumpered" the Wing again and it limped up the hill pulling the trailer, with me following behind and praying the dying machine could handle the strain for just one more job. It made it over the top, and then it was an easy ride down a path and onto a large grassy playing field where there were a bunch of boys playing soccer. The game came to a halt as we approached, and we were immediately surrounded by people who seemed to be speaking something other than German, but I didn't know what it was. Dark eyes were staring all around and from under a stand of trees at the bottom of the field a great group of women and girls in kerchiefs and long flowing dresses advanced upon us, laughing and calling and welcoming us as if we'd landed from heaven above. Turkish! Our first friends of the Turkish persuasion! And how nice everybody was! We were handed little cups of coffee by the women and I was so excited. My first real cup of Turkish coffee! I took a sip and to my horror discovered it was instant coffee laced with (gasp) canned milk! Oh well... A couple of the women spoke some English and I was busy telling them about us and it was being translated to much gasping and giggles and when I looked over the covered heads and noticed Terence doing the same thing, after being led away by the men and boys to form a separate group. Islam lives.

After a while they all piled into their cars and waved goodbye and we were left to the silence of the Wald and in the light of an almost full moon. Terence said he woke during the night to hear a car drive around near us but I hadn't heard anything and slept soundly.

The next day we coaxed the Wing to the Metzler factory where Herr Ludwig S. gave us a couple of new tires and then we drove to some other factory where Terence sweet-talked them into selling him a great watch for twenty-eight dollars! And they said it couldn't be done...

With waning patience but incredible skill, Terence managed to pull the near-dead rig the rest of the way to Norbert and Burga's in Mainz. We sure were glad to see them. We stayed three days. I washed clothes and repaired things and Terence worked on the bike and got film developed and sent to our sponsors. We finished the article for the Italian motorcycle magazine and sent it off and even though the Gold Wing was not much healthier than when we rolled in, Terence felt we could make it to Holland.

Not surprisingly, the sky was black and menacing when we got back on the bikes after hugging our friends goodbye in Mainz. Pulling into a parkplatz off the Autobahn, we pulled on our seedy rain gear and as we bit into our bread and cheese for lunch, the first big drops began to fall. We sat under our leaky umbrella and shared a beer and a pickle and watched the German drivers disappear into a little coffee shop at the end of the parking lot to wait out the storm. As the rain became a cloudburst, I knew we were both wishing we could join them in there, but with coffee going at DM2.50 a cup, it was not to be considered.

All that water pouring onto the Gold Wing was taking its toll. Even constant juice from my bike's battery barely gave it life. We crawled through the rain to Cologne, and Terence took out his Gold Wing address book. Unfortunately, although he lost several coins down the throat of the evil telephone machines, we were unable to rouse anyone to let us stay the night or even to get the motorcycle out of the rain. He gave up. I was hungry and irritable and it was getting darker. We yanked the rig onto the Autobahn again and headed away from Köln to hunt for a wooded shelter.

No luck. The Gold Wing was acting like a wounded animal and I noticed from the back that the trailer seemed to be listing to the side as if something was broken again. Cursing, Terence pulled into a wide driveway which seemed to be sort of a train yard and factory parking area. Signs everywhere said VERBOTEN something something...leading me to believe we'd be at least shot for trespassing. The rain fell around us making lakes of the oily puddles and not exactly lifting our spirits.

I was commanded to find some wooden blocks to stick under the trailer to jack it up for the master's inspection. It wasn't a difficult chore. The place was riddled with trash heaps of the trainyard kind and I soon came back with exactly what he needed. The trailer had simply been groaning under all that unnatural weight and T. was able to jam some pieces of wood in the coils of the springs and tie them on and hope that they'd hold to Holland.

Except for an occasional truck lumbering past during the night, we were left alone in our oily little campsite and early the next morning we slipped out and onto the autobahn to head north. We stopped by the AGFA film factory to try to get another sponsor interested in our journey but no one was interested and it was pretty obvious to me that people in the front office were put off by our unkempt appearance and perhaps just a tad annoyed that we had no appointment with the bigwig we were trying to see. Nothing like that ever bothered my companion, however, who cajoled and conversed in beginner's German and clomped around their immaculate offices with his huge mud-caked motorcycle boots to the consternation of the secretaries. It looked like a new record for jaws dropped. I stood at his side, rather painfully aware of what they must have been thinking. Ah, but shyness and sensitivity doesn't win sponsorships. I had to hand it to Terence for guts. We left one of Terence's best photos on the desk of the top executive and rode on to Holland. We were going on a wing and a prayer now, with worries about the renters at home and the bikes falling apart. Everything seemed to hinge on getting a job with Dirk Kraaij.

We were on a bridge (again!) just north of Amsterdam when the blessed trailer lost its piece of wood out of the spring thing and began to lean dangerously to the right. I signaled Terence to stop immediately and he was able to pull over to the far right and practically out of the flow of traffic. It was rush hour, everybody was going home from work, but thank god, the drivers were Dutch and polite and understanding. Terence lay on his back under the trailer while I waved people around and talk about miracles, who should appear but Dirk Kraaij himself, all dusty from a tough day on a roof and driving his tool truck and looking like a sooty saint or at least an angel to two biker bums in trouble!

With his help we were able to make it off the bridge and all the way to his home in Wormerveer largely intact, and after we rolled and pushed the dead Wing into his garage and the broken trailer into the garden and my poor old bike next to it, we all collapsed into his living room laughing and clanking beer bottles in celebration. Terence and I felt we had crossed the River Styx.

Chapter Thirty-Seven

A CHANGE OF PLANS

BUT THEN THE BLOW FELL. Dirk was terribly sorry, but things had changed drastically in the job market in the Netherlands. No longer were employers allowed to hire non-Europeans. Not to repair roofs, not even to plant tulip bulbs. Nothing. Bosses who were caught hiring black-market help or paying under the table were being given horrendous fines and even jail time! The Dutch government wasn't alone in cracking down. We'd come up against it all over Europe of course since the European Community began flexing its muscles. I had since learned that I couldn't have been hired to sing in the chorus in Venice either for the same reason, but nobody had mentioned that at the time... And yet Dirk had told us by letter and phone earlier that Holland still had plenty of work for good workers like Terence. This was a new development. Dirk's hands were tied. We were stunned and sick at heart with disappointment. Opening letters from home, we saw that Terence's Law School wanted more money and was threatening Terence with expulsion from not getting such and such a form back. It seemed like every letter had bad news.

It was the weekend. Dirk had all sorts of things planned for us. Pasting a smile on our faces, we threw ourselves into the fun and met Bor and his son Richard, and Lody and Kip, and cousins Kor and Ans. All of them owned Gold Wings! Going for a grand ride, we were shown a nice slice of the Netherlands that couldn't help but make us feel better. Dirk put me on the back of his wonderful yellow motorcycle (that he swore he loved better than women!) and we flew past electric green pastures dotted with cows and sheep, and soggy marshes full of many-colored ducks, and real live windmills that creaked in the wind, and the warm sun peeked out now and then to turn the flat, watery land to gold. Terence was following us on a borrowed Wing, and he told me later that we were doing better than 100 miles an hour out there! It was hard to believe. I thought about Maurizio in Italy. The difference had to be the roads. And dodging other Italians on mountain passes was quite another thing, too, than passing the occasional bicyclist on long flat hauls where one could see for miles. I hoped Maurizio would get a chance to ride these roads some day. Of course, the odd farm animal crossing the road wouldn't have a chance.

Dirk took us to the little village where he was born and it was perfect. Brick walls and wooden houses, painted dark green with white trim, looked cozy and friendly. Laura Ashley-style gardens full of as many blooming things as they could hold and bursting over and through the slats of their freshly painted picket fences. Canals and brooks criss-crossed everybody's yards, and bicycles and small rowboats seemed to be the only methods of transportation needed there. Birds sang in the garden trees and plump cats lazed in doorways. Lace curtains adorned the small windows and I must say I was enchanted. Back at Dirk's house in the larger town of Wormerveer, his beautiful daughter Sylvia had made dinner, and it was easy for us to put our troubles on a back burner for awhile.

The next day Lou Kip, a good friend of Dirk, took us on several local canals and into the countryside in his small boat. We were fortunate to have a lovely sunny day to admire his green land and handsome windmills and farms at the water's edge. He generously bought us lunch at a charming cafe in one of the canalside villages and it was a beautiful experience.

But Monday comes. Dirk was off to work and Sylvia to school and Terence and I were at last with our problem to face. All our mail had caught up with us and it looked like there was real trouble at home. With no prospect of a job for either of us, the motorcycles broken and needing expensive repairs, and the latest news of my renters squatting for free in my little house in Santa Barbara, there was only one thing we could do. We were going home.

First the confusion and shock. Then, as we slowly began to accept the idea, we started to allow ourselves heretofore forbidden thoughts of the positives of returning to California for awhile. Seeing my family was one. It had been three years. Being at my son's graduation from college was another. Steak. Salsa. Chocolate chip cookies. Libraries! The list began to grow.

Fortunately, Dirk had plenty of space in attic and basement and could also keep the rig for us until such time as we could get back.

Chapter Thirty-Eight

A RIDE TO BERLIN WITH THE FLYING DUTCHMEN

WHILE WE PACKED AND PLANNED, Dirk told us that he and some pals were riding to Berlin to visit friends and help a guy repair his roof in the Eastern sector. We were invited to go along. The notorious Wall had only been down for a couple of months and T. and I didn't want to miss the celebrations, so we hopped on our old Gold Wing that had been repaired well enough to make the trip, and dashed across Germany behind our pals at speeds the autobahn is famous for. Some of Dirk's friends in West Berlin took us all in for the night and then rising early, we all rode past the ex-Checkpoint Charlie with no formalities, which made the Dutchmen gasp because they remembered how it used to be.

The countryside of East Germany looked a lot like our first impressions of Hungary. Collective fields stretching endlessly between small clusters of homes. Everything the color of dried lake beds. Here and there an industrial site with drab housing next to factories, and the rustiest, saddest-looking equipment you could imagine lying around in the big yards. Old WWII train cars used as offices. Dust and dirt and pollution you could chew. Terence's allergies were kicking up and I was wondering if he could hold on until we got back to the States.

Everyone was riding a bicycle except on the main highway where the little bitty cars called Ladas and Trabants puffed and putted and looked like bathtub toys. The men driving them had hardened jaws and wouldn't meet our eyes as we roared by on our magnificent machines. It must have been awful for them. But they should take heart. Times were changing. People standing on overpasses above the highway were waving and shouting and giving "victory" signs, and it made my skin tingle.

We found the home of Dirk's friends, Dr. Hannelore and Jochen Heidemann, and had tea with them before leaving Dirk to work on the roof all weekend with Jochen. For some reason he didn't want any help so after making a date with Hannelore to visit more of East Berlin with her the next day, we left.

Back in West Berlin, our host, Herr Scheafer, found a doctor who could give Terence a shot for his allergies which were now beginning to impair his reason. Then the good fellow drove us around his city and up to the Wall, which, as good American tourists, we wanted to see more than anything else. It was a thrill. Even after several months, people were still close to hysteria at the sight. Lots of the wall still stood, and people were handing over hammers to others for them to knock their own hole in the wall and collect pieces to show the folks back home. We took our turn when it came, and looking through one of the larger holes, I saw young East Berlin border guards smiling and looking a little foolish as if they were wondering what exactly they were supposed to do on the beat nowadays.

The next day Terence was feeling much better. We rode back into East Berlin with Lody to meet with Hanne, who wanted to show us the sights. We westerners were surprised that the old city wasn't as bad looking as we had been led to believe, but Hanne said it had changed fast after the wall was opened. Leading us up to the tower of the church of the French Huguenots, she told us that the fantastic view from there was the only way the people could look across to West Germany before November 9th. We walked by the handsome Opera house and the Concert Hall. "Only the wealthy were able to hear the music inside," she said.

She took us to a cafe nearby where the small tables crowded outside under a dark overhang. We sat at what looked like the cleanest of a grimy lot and waited a long time for a waiter. When he came he was surly and seemed annoyed when we told him there was no milk in the pitcher on the table. We all needed it and although we tried taking other pitchers from empty tables around us, they were empty too and very dirty. The little paper squares that were for sugar had also been emptied by previous customers but not thrown away. They sat in their little white bowl looking strange as if waiting for someone to somehow fill them up again. The waiter told us there was no coffee...only "mokka" which was supposed to be richer (and therefore, of course, more expensive). Hanne tasted hers and said it was just coffee after all. We all knew by now that complaining would get us nowhere so we drank the cold stuff and felt very sorry for Hanne who insisted on paying and as the prices were inflated especially for tourists, it must have galled her.

Hanne was a surgeon. Her practice consisted mostly of Pediatric and Geriatric patients, she told us. She and her husband had decided to spend their precious savings on home improvements and a new car because they knew their money would most likely be worthless when the West German marks poured in. It took courage to make such a decision. Many of their neighbors preferred to wait and see. Those were very confusing times.

Back in Wormerveer, I finished a large drawing I had started for our hosts. Dirk and Sylvia lived in a sturdy old 19th century house that was a joy to draw. I took pains with it and even added watercolor for more interest. It was the least I could do for all their hospitality. Terence spent whole days in Dirk's garage working on the Gold Wing. When Dirk came home from work, we all had dinner Sylvia or I had prepared and then the men would go back out to the cold garage and work for hours on the motorcycles. I noticed they seemed to be having a wonderful time. It never ceased to mystify me how squatting in a freezing garage and tightening things and unscrewing others and meeting frustration after frustration with badly written books on repair-- and getting filthy and breathing noxious fumes and having to listen to mindless noise called popular or rock music or whatever, could be fun. And yet T. and I had so much else in common. Dirk had taught his daughter Sylvia to ride her own Gold Wing. She even passed the very difficult Dutch driving test for her motorcycle license. (A test, I suspected, I would not be able to pass. I still don't know how I passed the easy one in California...) Still, although she could ride like a man--even seemed to enjoy it, I never saw her out in that garage tinkering with the ol' transmission. Nope. It was daddy who kept his little girl's motorcycle in perfect condition. All she had to worry about was what to wear when it was time to go someplace. It had to be a boy-girl thing.

Chapter *Thirty-Nine*

ONE LAST TREFFEN FOR THE ROAD

TERENCE WAS in no hurry to go home, but I began to feel we had outstayed our welcome. Sylvia and I got along fine but it had been two weeks, for Pete's sake. Then I was told that we were going to the Dutch Gold Wing Treffen that weekend and that was that. Terence was convinced that if we made friends among the Scandinavians who would be there, we'd have a place or two to stay when we came back and went up there the next year. I couldn't argue with that, although I was certainly curious as to where we were going to come up with enough money to make that trip to Scandinavia.

The Dutch Gold Wing Treffen was in the south of the country. The ride down there was hot and smoggy. It was the first of June and with everything blooming, Terence's allergies gave him no peace. We were grateful for the cortisone shot in Berlin or he would have been in real trouble. The communal camping spot for the bikers was a huge grass field that had just been mowed. Terrible for Terence. He decided to drink a lot and try not to think about it. We set up camp and walked around and saw some folks we had seen at other Treffens, and then I concocted a pretty awful dinner of macaroni with some sort of nameless meat I'd found for not too much money at a store where I couldn't speak the language. Terence as usual, thought the meal was fine, but I hated it and it put me in a foul mood. I rather half-heartedly attempted to "party" with the gang in the main tent and then gave up when the loud music and thick smoke became too much.

I left Terence to look for some Scandinavians on his own and went back to our tent to sleep.

Around one a.m., he tumbled in and was no sooner in bed then the rain started. It rained all night but stopped by morning and I hung things out on bungee cords to dry. The Saturday tour was a long ride through the Dutch countryside including a stop at the local Nature Preserve. T. and I shared a beer we'd brought while other Wingers bought coffee at a snack stand and the Europeans were shocked that Terence was breaking the law. Apparently, they took their "Don't drink and drive" very seriously and we certainly agreed it was a good idea. Lots better to get killed riding fast with no speed limits! We all rode home in heavy rain Sunday night. Sylvia was on her own bike and I thought she handled the heavy machine like a pro. Dirk must have been a good teacher.

Dirk took us to the Wormerveer train station in his roofer's van. The four giant boxes Terence said we had to get home truly seemed beyond our endurance but Terence told me not to worry about it. He would handle them all himself if he had to and I knew he would.

First stop Amsterdam, and a long walk to the right train track. Terence hauled the horrible boxes one by one while I guarded them at the other end. It was going to be a long day. The fast train whisked through Holland and into Belgium, where we had to change trains in Brussels for Luxembourg. This time we paid a porter with a cart about three dollars to get the boxes on the train for us and it was worth every penny. In Luxembourg, we grabbed a bus for the airport and after arriving there and pulling the damn boxes up to the counter while people gaped, I was sure they were going to tell us they wouldn't take them. But Terence had done his homework and they just made the legal limit for weight. We were free and unencumbered, and as we boarded the flight for Iceland, we began to feel excited and happy for the first time. We were going home!

The food in flight was scrumptious, and before we knew it we were flying low over the strange orange and black and treeless earth of Iceland. The "Duty Free" shop had such high prices we were shocked, and again I wondered about how we could afford to travel in Scandinavia. Soon we were aloft and fed again, and after a snooze or two we were touching down in Baltimore, Maryland.

The USA! Whoopee. I laughed at the intercom broadcasts--all the announcers were so friendly! And in the ladies' room while I was washing my hands, some woman actually started talking to me about something silly and absolutely wonderful. I loved it. A perfect stranger!

Then we were back on another plane heading west. We had lost all track of time and Terence was so tired he fell asleep with his head in my lap and I nodded over him and suddenly we were sliding through the night with the sparkling lights of crazy Las Vegas appearing out of the desert on our right. I sat like a zombie in the waiting area, waiting for the plane to LAX while Terence played a few slot machines.

Boarding again, stewardesses who looked like cheerleaders were showing special courtesy for "folks with children, children traveling alone and people who may have some reason to get "special treatment" How long had it been since I'd seen that done? And how very right it all seemed. Free drinks, free peanuts, free California lemon slice in my Bloody Mary. I was home!

Chapter Forty

NOW THEN, WHERE WERE WE?

THIS BOOK IS NOT about the trials and tribulations of that rough year back home. We worked hard and saved our money. We dealt with some nasty problems concerning the house. We found new renters and put my daughter Meredith in charge, and then in May of 1991, in New York, we boarded the cheapest flight we could find which turned out to be Pakistani Air.

No booze, darn it, and a lengthy prayer to Allah over the loud-speaker that sounded too close--to our infidel ears--to belly-dancer music to put us in much of a mood for prayer. The lovely stewardesses in sort of saris served the men first--I thought it was funny but Terence didn't. I just didn't want to think about it. At least there was food. Even some meat in the stroganoff, though so tough it might have been Islam's way of turning non-believers into vegetarians. A very calm flight and the next morning we were served croissants with an orange juice substitute but very good coffee. I was a little disappointed the night had passed with absolutely no one throwing his prayer rug into the aisle and bowing east.

Dirk picked us up at the Schipol airport--with his van, fortunately, because this time Terence had six boxes nobody could lift, full of parts for the motorcycles and more law books and presents for the gang, etc.

While the men toiled in the garage putting the motorcycles together (when they weren't taking them apart), I took long walks around Wormerveer and as far as Zaanstad, where the storybook houses huddled together and begged me to take their pictures. The days were stormy and dark--Dirk told us it had been that way for six weeks and I wondered how he could possibly stand being a roofer under such conditions. A man of iron. One day we all took a ride out to the oceanside and I realized where all those Dutch paintings of black seas and dramatic clouds came from. People were strolling on the sand as if it were Malibu on a summer's day but with weather like that, Californians would have headed for the hills in fright! We got off the bikes and scrambled down some weedy dunes to walk along the shore. All over the beach was the strangest brown scum. It had apparently bubbled out of the sea and was lying in great spongy heaps like something out of a science fiction movie. People were kicking it and laughing as pieces of it flew up and wiggled into the wind. One man threw a stick into a big lake of it, sending his dog to fetch the thing right in the middle of the creepy mass. I bet that dog glowed in the dark later. No one seemed to mind the pollution. Far too cold to go swimming anyway. Later, at Dirk's house, out of our second story bedroom window, I watched as the wind bent the trees over, and marveled that the birds could fly in such a storm. Black crows seemed to have been thrown out of an airplane as they tumbled around high in the sky--feathers all askew and slamming into the tops of trees. Welcome to summer in Holland!

The only thing keeping us from getting back on the trail now was insurance for the rig which once had been a piece of cake to get in Europe but this time around was proving to be more difficult than balancing the National Budget. It was Thursday, June 13th. In a mad attempt to find someone to give us insurance so we could get out of Holland, Terence and I rode the Wing clear across Amsterdam looking for an outfit that promised the cheapest rate. The directions were vague and we got lost over and over in the city. Terence's mood was not to be trifled with by the time we found the little hole-in-the-wall, and then the man and his business turned out to be a joke. For some reason I've forgotten now, he sent us to a bank around the corner that turned out to be closed. Then when we went back to his office he was hiding from us and wouldn't let us in! Finally, seeing we weren't about to go away, he let us in to tell us that his best rate he could get for us was higher than we had found in the States! By the time we left--empty handed--Terence was furious. The wind was much worse on the freeway out of the city and I had a bad headache from nerves wondering if we would ever get the rig back on the road. I was holding on to my helmet which the wind was attempting to rip from my head when a particularly nasty gust tore off my sunglasses and tossed into the oncoming traffic. I screamed to Terence to stop even though I knew there was nothing we could do. He pulled the bike over to the shoulder and would have liked nothing better than to have killed me at that moment. I tried to slide off. "STAY ON THE MOTORCYCLE!" he yelled, and like the crazed madman he was, dodged the cars on the freeway to where my poor glasses lay in smithereens and grabbed up a couple of pieces and ran back to me. He only did such a foolish thing because he knew how terrible I felt about losing them. They were prescription glasses and I would never have bought them without his urging when we were in Santa Barbara. He had convinced me that I not only deserved the luxury, but would probably be less of a pain in the butt if I could see better on the bike--like read signs and road maps. Now I had lost them before we had even got back on the road. I was disconsolate.

That evening I tried to act normally, but I kept crying over the slightest things. Our friends were very kind. We all knew our departure was way overdue.

Then one morning it all came together. We had the damn green insurance card in hand for the Gold Wing. To save gas money while we toured the Scandinavian countries, we would have to leave my motorcycle in Holland (which I hadn't ridden for over a year!). We were going to the German Gold Wing Treffen which was practically on the way to Denmark where we were headed, and of course we hoped to meet some more Scandinavians there. Dirk and the other guys couldn't make this one for some reason, so we hugged and kissed them and said bye-bye and parted company.

We arrived in Wezel, Germany, at the Treffen around seven in the evening. We were mobbed by the curious and a few we knew and I realized I'd have to get used to all the attention all over again. Terence was in pig heaven--speaking all his foreign languages again and endearing himself to the throng. Few things made him as happy as being asked to translate German to Italian, Spanish to French or whatever they needed... In his element! He was at loss to understand why so few of the Europeans themselves didn't learn at least the languages across their borders.

After sitting dutifully at his side for an hour or so in the main tent, the smoke got to me and I retired. Terence was being plied with all sorts of drinks to keep him talking and before I left, I asked him if he realized he was mixing some pretty weird poisons in his system. "Oh, no problem, Gail," he assured me, "This stuff is harmless." The stuff was Salembuca, a clear, horribly sweet liqueur from Italy, and he was knocking it down with beer chasers. I figured he'd started with vodka and when somebody switched to the liqueur, his tastebuds had been dulled and he hadn't noticed the difference. Oh well, he was a grown man and could take care of himself.

At around eight in the morning, my grown man was heaving into the cook-pot and making such pitiful noises that even some of the toughest bikers walked over to see if they could help. The bike tour of the medieval part of Mezel was taking off at ten o'clock. The mayor and townsfolk were supposed to be dressed in 13th century garb to give speeches and welcome us all to the town's 750th birthday party. It didn't look like he and I were going to make it. It was raining pretty heavily anyway. I handed him a wet washcloth and thought about the trip a hardy few of us took to Asissi in a downpour during the Italian Treffen in Castigliano del Lago. Not one of our more wonderful moments. Terence looked up from his bucket, red-eyed and pale and said, "In weather like this, the mayor should come here!"

By afternoon, he was feeling much better. We were able to ride in the "Tour of Nations" where all the bikes line up according to country and fly their colors and get to stare back at the populace. This is the ride I always loved best and in Germany there are always hundreds of Gold Wings because the Scandinavians can make the distance for the weekend too, swelling the ranks with their proud and glistening steeds. It was no wonder the northern bikers had such gorgeous motorcycles. Snowed in so much of the year, all they could do was polish the chrome and dream of summer. And add hardware. So many beautiful Gold Wings. The guys had spent so much money and time for this moment of glory. People along the way, oohing and aahing at the perfect and shiny motorcycles, laughed and pointed at the big ugly black top box I was leaning against on Terence's Wing. I thought HA! If they knew there was a viola, a violin and a typewriter in there, they might show more respect. The family jewels.

Our fellow Wingers were all showing off their speaker systems by playing terrible American rock and roll and country western music. I leaned forward to ask Terence if he could do something about it and he slipped in a cassette of Joan Sutherland singing "I Puritani." I sang along. The roar of the engines disguised enough of my faults, I thought, and it was great fun. The crowd at the sides of the road thought I was wonderful. Especially when I let Joan do most of the singing.

The tour wound up at a locally famous Roman Ruin site that was frankly more reconstruction than ruin, but we meekly paid the 5DMs and looked around and took pictures. Every important-looking description was in German which was too bad for most of us in our group. At least half of the maybe three hundred bikers spoke another language. Time for Esperanto!

The rain held off while we packed up the next morning. I had had strange WWII-like dreams during the night I couldn't explain. A couple of Swedes offered to show us the way to the ferry to Denmark, but soon lost us because we were too slow pulling the trailer and they had to get home to work the next day. Terence was fuming because he hated to wear his full-face helmet and every time he would pull off the road and switch to the open-face to be comfortable, it would start raining hard again and he would have to repeat the performance and put on the heavy one again. We stopped for lunch in a lay-by off the autobahn and I made herring sandwiches. Terence must have been allergic to something very toxic there because his eyes began swelling up into two pink balloons. We jumped onto the bikes and by the time we had found a gas station he could barely see out of them. Seriously worried, I looked for a pill I'd been given by a fellow allergy-sufferer in California that she'd told me to give him for just such emergencies. I never thought I'd use it and certainly didn't expect to be able to find it when I needed it. We had no idea if it was wise for him to take it but he did anyway, and incredibly it worked. Thank the Lord for modern medicine. And good friends.

It was getting dark by the time we got to Lübeck, so we drove back into the countryside looking for a place to camp. Found a nice spot behind a hillock near a village. I thought it might be the city dump, but it was too dark to care.

Chapter Forty-One

ON TO SCANDINAVIA

WE TOOK a ferry from Germany to Denmark the next morning and then sped up the Danes' beautiful highway through a very strong headwind. It felt like any second my helmet would be yanked off, but otherwise the ride was exhilarating. Great fat clouds would slide under the bright sun and for moment our world would be dark and cold. Then suddenly everything was bathed in golden light again and I was dazzled by the purity of the colors. I didn't realize it then, but I was getting my first look in a very long time at truly pollution-free air; something we would see a lot of in Scandinavia.

After being properly scared to death by the Traveler's Health Insurance people in the States on the subject of the dreaded tick-borne encephalitis that was supposed to be so bad in the forests of the northern countries, we tried to get a prevention shot at a hospital in Copenhagen. We naïvely had thought it would be much cheaper than getting it in the USA. Maybe it was at one time, but no longer. The price they wanted for us to get it in Denmark, as tourists, was probably close to the cost of the cure for the damned disease! So we decided to take our chances.

Chapter Forty-Two

SWEDEN AND THE KINDNESS OF STRANGERS

IN ORDER TO get to the Esperanto Conference in Norway in time, we would have to skip seeing much of Denmark this time around. We drove to the ferry at Helsingør and sat there in line for about an hour waiting to go to Sweden. It certainly seemed strange to think that this was the only way by land (and some sea) for all of Europe to travel to Sweden and Finland. Perhaps there was a good reason for discouraging people who were trying to get to their countries?

Finally aboard, the fifteen minute voyage went by very quickly and rolling off in Sweden, we were feeling pretty good, when we were waved over by a lady customs officer and told the trailer would not be allowed on Sweden's roads! Gulp. We waited until something else took her attention and Terence shoved his helmet over his head and took off toward the gates. I followed. Other officers indicated rather weakly that we should halt, but he ignored them, pulling the heavy mud-splattered trailer over the huge ruts in the dirt road as if he knew that if he stopped, he might never get us out of there. The gates were still open, letting out the last of the ferry's passengers. The border guards seemed to be asking each other what should be done about us but when we had passed and they saw our nationality stickers, they must have figured we'd be O.K. in their country. Everybody knows Americans have lots of money to spend...

It was 10:30 at night when we found a forest road in the rain that looked promising. We were about thirty miles north of the Ferry landing and had tried in vain to find a tourist information office in any of the small towns along the autobahn. Cold and very wet, we ate whatever we could find in the little fridge and curled up inside the trailer tent.

We were greeted with more rain the next morning as we began to break camp. Tired and no doubt fighting his own demons, Terence chose aprés breakfast to launch into another speech about how disappointed he was in me because I didn't seem to be learning Esperanto fast enough. By this time, he said, he expected us to be talking together only in that language, in preparation for the conference in Norway that was fast approaching. He recalled that I had promised him somewhere back on the trail, that if he would stop hounding me to learn the language of each country we passed through, I would concentrate on just the one language and would be fluent by the time we reached the conference. Apparently, he felt he had kept his part of the bargain. Oh God, did I really promise that? Who'd have thought he'd remember? I think it was somewhere way back in Spain, for Pete's sake. No doubt it was one of those times when I was trying to piece together dinner in the dark, and he was firing verbs for me to conjugate and just to get him off my back I made a pact with the devil... It never pays. Anyway, I was in trouble now. I had broken a promise. And worse, he was saying, having no one good enough to talk to in order to improve his own skill would make it that much harder for him to be fluent when the time came. He stayed quietly furious after the lecture, and my pitiful excuses fell on deaf ears. I felt truly terrible about it. Not just about letting him down, but about the awful realization of knowing that I was probably not going to get any better at learning languages at least while I was on this ridiculous trip! Just staying upright was hard enough! I wanted to go home.

It poured. Dark woods loomed over us from both sides. It felt more like the middle of the night than a summer morning. We seemed to be alone on a road that was supposed to be the only artery to Stockholm. Straining to see the road in front of me through my streaming faceplate and windshield, I tried to decipher odd dark forms that would once in a while break up the long lines of trees. Was that a horse crossing the road? A moose? Am I seeing a lake on the right or is it simply a flooded field? Where is everybody? We rode on and on like a leaf in the current. It didn't take long before the poor over-worked Gold Wing decided to quit. All that moisture was too much for the weakened electrical system. Terence pulled off the road. While I sulked, still smarting from the morning's unpleasantness, he worked over the dead machine, rivulets of water coursing down the sides of his helmet to add to the lakes and puddles gathering busily in the bike's engine. Somehow, he got it started again, and had just turned the rig around to get back on the highway when we noticed that the trailer had a flat tire! Poor Terence. How much could he take? I was in such a blue funk I couldn't care less about his troubles. Our troubles. Let it rain, I thought gloomily, it matches my mood!

He unhitched the heavy trailer from the motorcycle without a word, and as he roared off into the storm with the tire under his arm, I stood disconsolately next to the crippled rig under a dripping tree at the side of the road. He came back about forty-five minutes later with the tire fixed. I was curious about how he'd managed to find a station and wondered how much it had cost, etc., but my pride and wounded feelings kept me silent. On we went, but the bike was in serious trouble. And it never stopped raining. Lunch time came and went and I began to feel weak. There were no turnouts, and the overpasses were designed so that no one could stop under them because there was no extra space and the shoulder dropped sharply into a drain thing. I thought it seemed a little mean. I remembered the friendly German overpasses where bikers could gather out of the rain underneath and chat and have a smoke and look over each other's motorcycles.

As the Gold Wing began to lose power once more and darkness was setting in--even though it was only around four o'clock--Terence decided to take desperate measures. He got out the Gold Wingers' membership book for Sweden and found a phone and tried to call somebody who lived in the next town (Norrahammar) to see if he could loan him some tools and hope against hope, a dry place to work on the bike. Not surprisingly, all attempts failed in that direction, and I was dreaming of a nice warm hospital bed in case I fainted and fell off the bike, when a nice young couple in a car waved us over and asked in English if they could help! Terence told them about trying to find a Gold Winger and because they must have been our Guardian Angels in disguise, they said they knew of a man who owned such a motorcycle and they would take us to his house! Swedish Saints.

The couple that came to the door did not appear thrilled when the nice folks explained our plight. They peered around them at us and we must have looked pretty bad sitting sad and sodden in the rain. But they were kind souls and although the husband did not speak English, the wife spoke some and had been born in Germany, so we were able to communicate clearly enough. The fellow rolled his spotless Wing from the garage into the storm while his wife bustled about clearing other things away so that Terence could pull our bike with its great monster trailer in there.

One look at my glazed expression and Monika Karlsson took matters in hand. While her husband Stig showed Terence where the tools and outlets were, Monika led me to a hot shower in the basement and my outlook on life began to change. Soon we were being served hot tea and cakes and cookies as if they'd been waiting for us all morning and ten-year-old Daniel chatted away in Swedish to us all about his latest soccer game and we smiled and nodded in what we hoped were the right places and we were just one big happy Swedish family having tea together and the day's horrors receded to a silly speck on the wall.

A couple of hours later, after Terence had worked his miracles on the motorcycle and I had festooned the Karlsson's basement with drying laundry, Monika called us to sit down to supper! This time the fare was open-faced sandwiches, cheeses and thinly-sliced ham, tomatoes, crisp wheat crackers. Life looked rosier. We were given the daughter's old room and after a very sound sleep and a fabulous breakfast the next morning, we were in a very cheery mood to ride to Stockholm. We took pictures of the kind family next to the rig and promised to send them some. (I did).

A surprisingly nice ride with little rain, although the wind was quite cold. All that fortification of food and warmth--not to mention the extended glow one gets from human kindness--made us both feel like road warriors again, able to slay whatever dragons the fates or foes should put in our paths. The first was just a little dragon--a sympathetic young miss in the Tourist Information Office outside Stockholm who said she was sorry but there was no campground open and we would probably have to stay in a hotel. Ah, but Sir Terence was not to be daunted. Armed with his trusty Gold Winger's address book, he located a lady biker we had met at a couple of the northern Treffens and we rode out to a Stockholm suburb to see if she could put us up for a couple of nights.

Kikki Bennaceur was originally from Finland, but had lived so long in Sweden she probably considered herself Swedish. An extremely independent young lady, she was one of the very few women we met along the way that could not only handle a big bike like a Gold Wing, but who actually rode and maintained it and even enjoyed being an active member of the Gold Wing Club of Sweden. She rode the several hundred miles down to the Treffens every chance she got --resembling a true Valkyrie in her white leather pants and jacket atop her matching steed. For all her toughness and boundless energy, Kikki was as friendly as she was spectacular, and she had meant it when she had told Terence we could stay with her in Stockholm and she'd show us around. While she worked in the city during the day on Thursday, Terence and I rode into town to see the museums and other sights, then the next day, June 21, Kikki and her friend Johnny, also a Gold Winger, took us to the mid-summer pageant on DjurgŒrden Island in the middle of the city, bought us a couple of horrendously expensive beers as we watched the locals revel and dance, and after returning to her apartment that night, treated us to a traditional MidSommer meal of several kinds of fish--including succulent salmon and boiled potatoes. She handed me a bottle of wonderful white wine while she and the guys drank beer and then we all toasted each other and the holiday with vodka. Booze is so hard to get in Sweden I had the feeling we were probably drinking her entire allotment for the year in that one night but it was obviously something she enjoyed doing and I wasn't about to complain. They both spoke English beautifully and we wished we could take them home with us... Forget home, at least we'd have liked them to join us for the rest of the trip. Alas, life is unfair.

The alarm went off at 4:45 a.m.. We'd hit the sheets about four hours earlier so everybody was snoring when I got up to turn it off. Terence and Johnny went to get the rig out of Johnny's garage while I made coffee and as I saw that T. had a nasty hangover, I took charge and packed us up. We had a ferry to catch to Finland! It didn't help Terence's foul mood to discover that somehow the thermostat had flipped to HEAT on our little fridge; thereby cooking his precious infrared film inside. !!@#*!!

We hugged and kissed Kiki and begged her to mount her beautiful Wing and join us to the land of her birth, but she had partied not wisely, but too well herself, and with a weak smile wished us good fortune and went back to bed. Johnny was in pretty good shape though, and insisted that he be allowed to guide us through the rush hour traffic to the ferry, and after a good look at my companion's green face and semi-conscious demeanor, I was grateful for his offer.

On the dock, we said goodbye to our new friend and as we sat in line with the other vehicles waiting for the massive doors to open into the ferry's belly, I could tell Terence was feeling better. Sitting a bit straighter in the saddle, he looked around and let out a great Falstaffian belch, and while Swedish faces grew even paler at the affront and I cringed inside my full-face helmet, an impish smile slipped up the sides of his Irish face and your man was feeling himself again.

Once on board the Viking Line "Amorella," we were tying the rig to the sides of the hold with thick ropes when a rather colorful Finnish biker walked up to us and lit a cigarette. He was all in very dirty black leather and must have been around fifty years old. He spoke English pretty well and told us he had just come back from one of his yearly trips south--this time to Turkey and had thought it a great place to see. When he heard that we were planning to ride all the way to the top of Finland, he felt it his duty to warn us about the various hazards of that part of his country. "Particularly by the lakes," he said. "MOSS-KEE-TOES..Terribly vicious things... They'll eat you alive!" He puffed on his ciggy and walked away.

After finding a fairly comfy seat among the hundreds of passengers that had boarded the big boat, Terence's head fell in my lap and he snored blissfully for most of the trip. I was glad he was conserving his strength, because he would be doing all the driving while I sat helplessly behind him and who knew what was ahead if it kept raining, and fewer people would be speaking a language that even Terence could understand... Not to mention--the vicious moss-kee--toes! Looking out of the salt-flecked windows of the great lounge where we sat, I could see lots of small rocky islands for miles out of the coast of Sweden. Each one seemed to have a little cottage on it with a tiny boat dock. Swedish summer homes! Children were chasing each other around the miniature blobs of land, mothers were hanging laundry--some didn't even have space enough for a wash line! I was entranced. Talk about getting away from it all! I supposed there were telephones, at least. And one could visit one's neighbors by popping in the boat and floating over to the other islands. Think of the fishing! And there were hundreds of them. A whole community. I wondered if there was a sort of watery bus service. Did any of them live out here year 'round? Lot of people live on their own island in southern climes, but way up here you'd have to be tough as a, well, Viking.

The ferry docked at the large island of Mariahama. Terence and I had thought we might get off and check it out but we discovered to our horror that in forgetting to turn off the fridge (perhaps T. was unconsciously trying to be sure his film would stay cold), it had sapped all the energy from the Wing's weakened battery and there was no way to start the bike. In fact, it was a real stroke of luck that it happened at that point in the voyage because we were able to plug the bike into one of the ship's outlets and even though we weren't able to get off and see the island, we thankfully weren't in anyone's way--hugging the inside wall as we were--and the crew was very understanding about our needing to use their plug and keep the rig on board while the hold was otherwise emptied of automobiles and trucks and then refilled around us later. The bike was rejuvenated in the couple of hours more to Finland, and we slipped off and past the customs officers without a hitch, and rode about four hours into Turku. More rain didn't help give us much of a good impression of that gray-looking city, so we just rode on into the forested country in search of a spot to camp and finally found a dirt road leading into the trees that T. turned into for want of anything else. The rain had turned to drizzle and in looking for a nice rock to put behind the trailer wheel, we came upon a small dumping place full of tin cans, condoms and to our amazement, a life-size plastic sex-doll thing--akimbo and with one leg torn off that was hanging over a near-by branch. She/it had been deflated (but I noticed the boobs remained intact), and her sad little Marilyn Monroe-style face stared wide-eyed up at the trees. I followed her painted gaze to a torn pair of lacy panties fluttering mournfully in the wind and I could only be thankful the thing had not really been human. Terence took a couple of pictures and then we put it out of our minds and ate dinner. While he studied the map, I wrote in my journal and after a very long day, turned in early.

It wasn't raining the next morning, but a damp fog found its way into our clothes, chilling our bodies and spirits as the motorcycle growled irritably beneath us. At one stretch in the road, the fog had lifted enough for us to see a group of people gathered around a car that had fallen into a ditch about 30 yards ahead. Terence automatically slowed, which may have saved our life, because we soon hit a large oil slick--no doubt the reason the car was in the ditch--and for a few moments (that felt like days), the rig slid all around the road completely out of control. I'm sure it was only due to Terence's superior skill and amazing strength that we stayed on the road. The little group of people watched us open-mouthed as the trailer sashayed around the road and the motorcycle tried to shake itself free from Terence's grasp. Nobody moved when the rig finally came to a stop down the road. I guess we were all in shock. I glanced back to see their reaction and my gaze was met with stony looks. Terence sat back, cursed a bit and started the engine up again. As we picked up a little speed, I began to wonder what the Finnish mindset could be about Americans--or American Bikers. I realized I had not done my homework on the subject.

Chapter Forty-Three

RASTILA CAMPGROUND, HELSINKI, FINLAND

Lots of space. Great facilities. No one bothers us, not even curious. It suited us just fine. We arrived in the early afternoon and after setting up, headed for Helsinki sans trailer. It felt great to be so unfettered after so long. We rode into the city and looked around. I was pleased at so much Art Deco architecture. The famous train station by architect Saarinen the senior, was particularly interesting and the shopping area smart in an old-fashioned way. The sky cleared above us and I found myself breathing deeply, trying to dry out my lungs. Returning to camp, we had a leisurely dinner and with plenty of light in the summer sky, we took a nice walk to the lake. Lots of bugs drove us soon back and Terence crawled in bed to study and I stayed inside our big extra tent to write.

The next day was Monday and museums were closed, so we busied ourselves at the local harborside market and found a rare bargain in tomatoes and bought a lot. Later, parked in front of a ladies' clothing store we were getting out the cameras when a fellow came out of the store to ask us the usual questions about our trip. His name was Mr. J. K. J. Tenkku, and he was the owner of the store. We three had a fine chat. We were told not to be afraid of the stories about radioactivity in northern Finland. (What radioactivity?) We should realize, Mr. Tenkku said, that the Cherynoble reactor was much further than we thought (Where is that thing, exactly?), and anyway it had been a couple of years already so there was nothing to fear. We should feel free to buy all the reindeer fur and antlers from the Finnish Lapps we wanted when we got up there. (What was the matter with the reindeer?) While we looked at each other with strange frozen smiles on our faces, the kind merchant ran into his store and brought me a little bottle of perfume as a bon voyage present. We thought it a very pleasant introduction to his country.

Later, I read that the Finns were in deep trouble thanks to the Cherynoble disaster. Apparently the fallout in 1986 had not only affected the entire reindeer population, but would remain in the lichen which succeeding generations of the animals would eat, and therefore the Finns weren't supposed to sell any part of their number one product--not skins and antlers to tourists, not even the meat for catfood--for export. Luckily, for the Finns, most tourists hadn't heard the news. Luckily for us, we couldn't have afforded such luxuries anyway. Knowing how expensive Scandinavia was going to be, we had loaded up on dried foods from Germany, and rice and potatoes and whatever canned stuff we could carry. If the water was affected, well, what the hell? You gotta die of something...

That afternoon we walked through Sibelius Park and saw the huge monument to the great composer. Afterward, we rode around the spiffy part of the residential part of Helsinki taking in the Art Deco architecture and we decided 1929 had been a very good year here.

One of the loveliest things about the Rastila Campground was its unlimited supply of hot water. Very hot showers had given me a new lease on life and I was able to get our clothes cleaner than they'd been for a long time. As I scrubbed over my washing in the laundry room, I began to notice a group of people that had been there since we'd come days before. In fact, they looked quite settled in their part of the camp. They were Gypsies. Gypsies aren't allowed in most European campgrounds. They do tend to take over and they're hard to get rid of once they're established. Apparently, things were different in Finland. I was fascinated by the women's clothing. Unlike in the southern climes, instead of many colors, these women wore black and white only. But what black and white! The skirts were long and made of black velvet! The women all looked fat for some reason--perhaps there were many underskirts. Then the blouses were dazzling white--and I mean dazzling. It looked like the material was a sort of satin--thick and shiny--and upon its surface was sewn all sorts of sparking things, such as sequins and rhinestones and whatever else one could put on a blouse--all white--a strict uniform. I would have liked to have been able to talk to the ladies. They seemed to have so much fun together. They loved to gather in the women's restroom and smoke and laugh. Just like Jr. High School. But none of them spoke English. We looked at each other and smiled and it was very frustrating. Strangely, the children and the men wore no such costumes. Except for their dark complexions, they looked just like the Finns and the men seemed to have jobs each day because they wouldn't get back until late and then all the big ladies would troupe out of the restroom and wrap white aprons around their velvet skirts and cook standing around in the mud between the caravans.

Before we left Helsinki, we attended the local Esperanto Club meeting. No one spoke anything there except Esperanto, so Terence was in heaven. I hung on by the skin of my teeth and probably understood about half of what they were saying. They were very nice folks and after a time I realized that we weren't the only foreigners. There were Swedes and a Czechoslovakian couple there too! It was quite an uplifting experience, really, and I wished I could have done better. As we were leaving, the president of the Club gave us a very precious gift. It was the Kalevala, the famous Finnish book of Folk Tales and Kantos, translated into Esperanto. It was very generous of him and all we could think of to say was that we certainly hoped he could come to California one day. We all said we'd meet in Bergen in July and it felt as if we'd known them all for years.

On Wednesday, the sun shone. We joyously dragged out everything damp and hung them over tree branches and over bungee cord lines hooked to the trailer and motorcycle. Terence took his shirt off and sat at the little table smack in the sun and did some homework while I sewed and studied Esperanto. Looking up to see the washline flapping in the sunny breeze filled me with a sense of well-being I wished I could bottle and cork for later. We both needed this day..because...

The next was dark and cold again. Back to normal. No wonder so many of these poor Nordics drink themselves to death. Brrrr. We forced ourselves to visit the Ateneum Gallery of Art in the city and were very glad we did. Nowadays, when I think of all the great art unsung, I think of that museum in Helsinki. So much fabulous art and we Americans never heard of them. Perhaps if more of them had made it to Paris... It's a shame. Still, their own country loved them and that's something. Their most famous son was undoubtedly Akseli Gallen-Kallela with Albert Edelfelt running a close second--both from the late nineteen century. I realized our precious book from the Esperanto Club was full of Gallen-Kallela's wood-cuts.

Sometime around two a.m. one night, I woke up to the sound of a motor running. Shook Terence awake and we looked out of our little tent flap to see one of the big Gypsy mamas sitting in an automobile--all by herself--counting a huge wad of money. The car's inside lights were on and the engine was running and she had parked right next to our trailer. We decided she had needed a spot away from the Gypsy camp to do something private, but why so close to us? We stood it for about fifteen minutes and annoyed, Terence noisily crawled out of the trailer tent and walked behind the motorcycle and relieved himself. She'd have seen him if she'd looked, but she never stopped counting that wad of bills. Over and over. After about twenty minutes, never turning off her car's engine, she pulled out and went away. Very strange.

The night before we were to leave Helsinki, we met a nice Welsh couple in our camp. Christine and John. We had been walking around the grounds and when we saw their national plate, we'd waved and they waved back. Later they came over to visit us in our big tent, and we got out a half-full bottle of Scotch we had found on the ferry after its owner had taken off without it. One does not sniff at half a bottle of Scotch in Finland. I believe it costs around $50 there--if you can find it. Terence and I don't much like the stuff, but we had nothing else to offer. Well, the Welsh folks loved it, and Terence had to keep them company, drink for drink, as the perfect host, and around midnight, he lost consciousness and crashed to the floor. Christine and John went right on with what they were saying as if this happened to them all the time. I pretended to ignore his prone body lying between us, for the sake of decorum myself, but was very impressed at their nonchalance. After another half-hour or so, as Terence began to snore so loudly as to drown out all conversation, they stood up and, over his sleeping form on the tent floor, we shook hands and hoped we'd meet again. I left him there and went to bed. He woke up enough to crawl into bed around 2 a.m.

It took him most of the morning to recover enough to decide we could leave that day as planned. I had packed everything and was eager to get on and finally, after a cup of tea, so was he. He dropped his poor abused body heavily into the drivers seat and strapped on his open-face helmet. Thank God it wasn't raining for once. If he'd had to wear the full-face one, I probably couldn't have budged him out of there. We paid at the office and headed east for Porvoo, 50 kilometers to the east.

The blessed sun came out here and there, and it made for a lovely ride. The village of Porvoo was full of cobblestone streets and old wooden stores and homes in a style that is fast disappearing from the area. The local church on the hill had been burned so many times throughout the centuries that we could see the levels of rebuilding in the stonework and the patterns of each layer of stone and brick provided a very pleasing effect.

A couple of nights too close to water (which is everywhere in Finland) brought us to the realization that we were indeed at the mercy of the dreaded MOSS-KEE-TOE. No matter what precautions we took, we were attacked from all sides every time we stopped the bike. Sitting on my little camp chair at dinner and completely covered, I thought I was safe until the next morning when I discovered welts in stripes on my behind, where the blasted buggers had stung between the chair slats--and through my jeans! They had no couth. We doused ourselves with strong anti-mosquito sprays, but wherever it didn't protect, they got us--especially in the face and hands. We actually began wearing our full-face helmets at all times to minimize the attacks. Terence became a nervous wreck. What good was it to be a dragon-slayer when an insect could bring you to your knees? Finland is called Suomi by the natives. Terence began calling it Suomp-land. And much worse. That crusty old biker we'd met on the ferry knew what he was talking about. We wished we were in Turkey.

Stopping at a beautiful old cemetery to take some pictures, we were impressed at how perfectly such places were kept in Finland. Each grave, no matter how old, seemed to have been fussed over--leaves cleared away and fresh flowers at the marker. Elderly women could be seen bent over the task, washing flower holders, raking, rearranging small objects at the grave's head. As we left the quiet place, we were startled to see a large ornate monument to the fallen soldiers of WWI near the entrance. "From a Grateful Germany," it said.

A stop at Ruotsinpyhtää to see the octagonally-shaped wooden church we'd read about, proved disappointing when we couldn't go in because of a church service. Really, haven't the Suomis something else to do when we want to see their places of interest? Instead, we walked along the banks of the river nearby and contented ourselves with taking pictures of old rowboats. Later, thanks to our guidebook, we found the truly charming old Pyhtää stone chapel not far away--full of frescoes and hanging wooden ships and a fabulous wood-carved pulpit consisting of overly-made up angel faces which we found most irreverent and completely charming. The 14th century frescoes knocked me out. Almost childlike in the drawing, but painted brightly and faces all eager and happy. Apparently the frescoes were discovered only recently after having been painted over in the Reformation period. Those must have been grim times...

After a (ugh) sardine and bread lunch on the road, we headed for the Russian border. Terence was all excited in case he might get a chance to work on his Russian. This was June of 1991, before glasnost, and the Russian guards were not amused when our dirty and decadent rig rolled up for a photograph or two. We were ordered away, and not being as dumb as we looked, we went.

So we rambled along. It was a beautiful day and the narrow road heading north was full of Finnish folks doing the same. The poor things had such a brief summer they had to grab the moment. We stopped for gas and a lovely young gypsy lady walked over with embroidery to sell. She was so fascinated by the rig that she forget to give us her "pitch" and Terence invited her to climb onto the seat for a photograph. With a big smile and a quick glance over yonder where some of her people stood, she picked up her long black velvet skirt and slid into the pillion seat. We took a picture and gave her a Polaroid one. When I discovered she could speak some English I questioned her about her costume. She told me that it was what every woman wore when they married. Each woman could sew whatever they wished on the blouses (hers was festooned with lace and embroidery), as long as it was white. She seemed quite happy with the plan--probably because marriage was every girl's goal in her world, and the dress announced that she'd made it. She also wore lots of gold neck-laces and her fingers held several large rings with stones that looked real. She loved her photo and as we rode away waving I found myself hoping she wasn't going to get into any trouble not selling us anything.

July first found us in the Lake region. "The mosquitoes are a terrible scourge," I wrote. "Terence needs desperately to study, but there is no place at all where we can stop without being plagued by the little beasts. Only in the middle of the towns are there few enough for us to be able to breathe without swallowing a couple. They never rest. Even during the day, if we want to stop to admire the scenery they come in swarms--with biting black flies joining the feast--if we foolishly stop to admire the scenery in this godforsaken land. Forget whatever beauty there may be out there beyond our helmet's visor. We want outta here!"

But first we had to see Savonlinna; after all, I'm supposed to be an opera buff and this town--draped over several islands in the middle of some lakes--had one of the most famous Opera Festivals in Europe.

The place was mobbed. Were all these people opera fans? Sadly, no.

Savonlinna also sported a pretty terrific castle with a juicy history--all about when Sweden and Russia came sweeping in and so on, and let's face it, Finland hasn't that many tourist traps outside of Helsinki. They were making the best of what they had. We took the tour of the castle where the operas were performed, but costing a hefty sixty-five dollars each, a ticket to actually hear one was definitely out of our reach.

Back on the road north, I reflected about how tough it was to find a restroom there. The only one for women was high in one of the huge castle's towers--four flights up a twisting stone stair-case. I had passed several women who were trying to get their breath and all I could think of was what if one was handicapped, for Pete's sake. Or pregnant, or maybe just with a bad cold? At sixty-five bucks a ticket for the cheapest seats, you'd think someone could be sent to dig a hole and put some walls around it at ground level. Shameful.

About 23 km west of Savonlinna was the village of Kerimäki, home of the world's largest wooden church, or so we were told. Indeed, it was big and was supposed to hold up to 3000 worshipers! The outside was pretty ugly but once in, you couldn't help but be enchanted with its faux gothic carvings and columns painted to look like marble. Everything was in colors of white and light gray and the tall surrounding windows were of clear glass. The colorful stained glass was used in the chandeliers and to very nice effect. Giant silver-chromed heaters stood spaced around and little pewter candle sconces adorned the walls and columns. All within reach, I noticed. You can't be too careful about fire when everything's made of wood!

A couple more days and nights doing battle with Finland's very effec-tive defense system, the Legions of tiny, thirsty vampires which neither rain, nor sleet nor heat of day could discourage--and we were begging for relief. Way behind in his Law studies now, with no help for it in sight, Terence grew silent and angry. The road was monotonous with pine forests on either side closing us in for hundreds of miles at a time as he doggedly pulled our rig north to the border to Sweden. I sat on my perch and looked up. There seemed to be something wrong with the trees. I am no nature buff, but I do love gardening and I can tell when a tree is sick. These were evergreens and yet all of them seemed to have lost so many of their needles and the trees themselves looked kind of black and greasy. I looked around at the things growing underneath. So little green and this was summer! Acid rain? There was certainly no industry this far north that I could see. Could it have been the fallout from the Chernobyl disaster?

Why not? As I sat on the speeding bike, I wondered if anyone had made a study up here about why insects seemed to thrive when everything else sickened. No way, I mused. That would be admitting they had a big problem in the first place. It wouldn't do to alert the World Community. No one would want to come to Finland and spend money--not to mention the panic of the Suomis themselves to learn that their country was poisoned beyond man's power to do anything about it. Good old mankind. We've learned how to destroy our planet without learning how to undo the destruction. I looked at the leather jacket in front of me-- hunched over in gloom. "Still, I'll bet at this point Terence would rather take a little long-term radiation poisoning than have to deal with short- term mosquitoes!," I mumbled inside my helmet. Each time we had to stop--to eat or sleep--they would be upon us with no mercy. Trying to read was impossible. Trying to type his homework as they crawled into his clothes and landed in platoons on his hands was torture. There were times when I wanted to scream and run around in circles when they wouldn't leave me alone, but then I would look at Terence's drawn face and know his troubles were worse. How would the Law School in California react when he told them he couldn't finish his third year because the mosqui- toes were bad in Finland? We had to get out of there.

At Kajaani, the biggest settlement in a very large part of rural Finland, we tried to send part of Terence's school assignments by the equivalent of "registered," but the woman in the post office couldn't understand what he wanted. So after a long search, Terence was able to find a copy machine and make two more copies and then he went back and sent two of them by regular mail, keeping one for himself. Still, I could tell he was worried they wouldn't make the trip to California. Being in town, we were blessedly free of mosquitoes and we relaxed a little and took some pictures of the wooden churches and prepared for the next leg of the trip which was up to Rovaniemi, the "Capital" of Lapland. We knew we had to spend the rest of our Finnish marks because we would soon be in Sweden, so once we arrived in that city, we went to the nearest market and bought some supplies. Rovaniemi certainly wasn't much to look at. Checking our ROUGH GUIDES TO SCANDINAVIA, we read that the town was completely rebuilt in the late 1940s after the departing Germans had totally razed the wooden Laplander houses during the Second World War. Hmmm. So much for a "Grateful Germany."

We crossed the border into Sweden at Pello and with a sigh of relief zoomed toward Norway. Stopped for lunch at a beautiful park full of little daisies on green grass and next to a rushing stream where fishermen were trying their luck. Somehow the breeze and the fast-moving water perhaps were keeping the insects at bay, so Terence whipped out the typewriter and on a convenient picnic table, began catching up on his homework. I took out a washcloth from my tank bag and walked downstream from the fishermen to do a little personal washing. The water was icy cold but so refreshing and it was so nice to be able to scrub off layers of dirt and sticky insect spray off my skin. I would have washed a few more areas on my body if I'd had some privacy, but I looked up to find a couple of the fisherman grinning at each other on the other bank, so I decided against it.

After about sixty miles of straight riding, we discovered to our dismay that we'd taken the wrong road and were heading to the Finnish border again. Instead of backtracking, we decided to just cross back into Finland after all because the road seemed to travel straight to Norway.

We called daughter Meredith in Santa Barbara, from a telephone at the border and were relieved to hear that things were O.K. at home.

Terence put the pedal to the metal. The way was long and flat and instead of forests, the land stretched away on both sides in marshes and lakes and what seemed to us, total desolation. The wind was fierce; I could tell Terence was concentrating hard on holding the rig to the road and I felt a kind of deja-vu as I held on to my helmet--remembering my beautiful sunglasses being ripped from my face from a wind like that in Holland.

Chapter Forty-Four

NORWAY!

WE BEGAN to see snow on some rather jagged peaks ahead. Norway! We sat up in the saddle and cheered. As the road began to climb, we began passing small log houses with smoke curling out of their chimneys and dogs playing out in front. Each one of the huts had stacks of reindeer furs hanging on wooden frames and Lapplander folk trying to wave us down. I would have loved to see the wares up close but Terence was never tempted by such places and I knew we couldn't have afforded anything anyway and would thereby only disappoint the eager Lapps who were running out of their little cabins when they heard the motorcycle coming their way. Everybody waved and we waved back and in my ignorance of such things, I thought they looked just like Eskimos. We probably looked just like Germans to them!

It was Friday, July 5th. We had no Norwegian money yet and there was no place to change it at the tiny border outpost in the mountains. We would have to wait until Monday. So after putting on our electric vests to keep warm we rolled up and down the snow-spotted mountains awhile until we found a fairly sheltered camp-spot next to a little stream and pulled in to stay the week-end. It was quiet and cold. But the sun shone well into the night and we put up the big extra tent and were nice and cozy inside. While Terence studied, I drew water from the stream and heated it up on our camp stove and washed clothes. During meals, he spoke to me only in Esperanto and I tried answering him in the same language. I hated it, but I was desperately trying to avoid another bad time for both of us. In panic, I couldn't think of anything to say so I stayed silent most of the time. This was not doing wonderful things for our relationship and it was beginning to scare me. I put my fishing rod together and while he typed cases, I tried the little brook outside. I had to face the fact that the stream had no fish in it--it was nothing but snow runoff and much too high up to contain fish, but just the attempt of casting and clomping about the rocks made me feel better. And the air...it was like an elixir! I wanted to call Terence to come out and take a deep breath but then I realized it would have to be in Esperanto and I was so afraid I would use the wrong tense or something I just gave it up (I should have tried anyway, I know.. "Venu!," I could have said... "Venu kaj enspiru la puran aeron!" But I didn't even know that much then..and it was just so daunting).

On Sunday, Terence heated water for about two hours and filled the big black plastic "shower" bag and actually showered! He said the mosquitoes didn't bother him too much. What a brave guy. I stayed dirty.

The motorcycle wouldn't start when we were finally ready to leave that afternoon. Not even with a push down a hill. And there was no way to push it back up again. Geoghegan, the resident electronic genius, fiddled with some aging wires and after much cursing and praying to the gods from PEP BOYS, he managed to bring it alive again and got the heavy rig back on the road. The mountains grew bigger and bigger. We headed for Tromsø. Somewhere near AndersŒl we pulled into a gravel pit to spend the night. A man in a tractor rolled by, but smiled so we relaxed. It was drizzling so we put the plastic tarp over the trailer tent. The air was sharp and very cold. All around us the dark mountains had lines of snow cut into their slopes, looking like zebra stripes. I made a hot meal and we looked at each other over our forks with widening eyes. "THERE ARE NO MOSQUITOES!!," we screamed at each other. We whooped and hollered and poured ourselves a congratulatory sip of our precious Apfelcorn which we were saving for just such an occasion. "To Norway!," we toasted.

We were loving this country. It took forever to get to Tromsø because we kept stopping to take pictures of wonderful things--hulls of boats by mirrored lakes, sod-covered huts and adorable goats and strange-looking cows with brassieres on their udders. Everything was amazing to us. Was it the air? I was reminded of Switzerland and yet there wasn't that attention to detail--the obsession to neatness that the Swiss seem to possess. For one such as I, the broken fence and the paint peeling off the barns made me feel so much more welcome. Like coming home.

Tromsø has been called the Paris of the North. Well, it is a city. And it is in the north... never mind... we liked it a lot. Several people spoke English and we were able to change our traveler's checks and get groceries. We found the public library and it had lots of reading material in English! We gorged on the news magazines and hated to leave after a couple of hours. While Terence was locating a copy machine and I was guarding the rig, a fellow struck up a friendly conversation with me and asked me what I thought of the Norwegian food. I laughed and confessed that the price of food up here was so high that we were pretty much sticking to what we'd brought from Holland. Terence and I had actually seen a head of cabbage a few miles back that went for about six dollars! He was a nice old guy and I believe he said he'd been to the States once and we compared the usual things about our countries and I told him how impressed I had been already by Norway and he seemed pleased. He left, and soon after, Terence returned, and told me where he had found a public restroom on the wharf and so while he guarded the rig for a change, I headed for it. When I came back a little boy ran up to us as we were putting on our helmets, and handed us a big sack. He said it was from a "friend." We looked inside and found a wrapped butcher-paper bundle of reindeer meat chunks, some cheese, some gorgeous salami, a can of tuna (oh well..) and a jar of the locally famous Cloudberry jam! I looked for the saintly fellow but he had disappeared. Welcome to Norway!

On the way out of town, a slim, leather-clad biker on a Harley kept us company at each stop sign. A long brown braid and an earring told Terence the motorcyclist was a "chick" but I wasn't so sure. At the petrol station on the edge of town the "chick" took off his helmet and walked over to us! He introduced himself as Arvid Mikalsen and he was very impressed with the rig and the map-story I had painted on the back of the top-box. He asked if he could ride along with us for awhile and we said "sure."

After a few miles out of town we were feeling hungry and waved Arvid to a stop and told him we would be looking for a place to camp soon. He said he was near his turnoff to visit his friends who were building a boat and would we like to come? We were game. How far could it be? We followed him all around a huge lake for over an hour and just as we were beginning to despair of ever reaching our destination, Arvid pulled up to a small boathouse where two men were indeed building a boat. It was beautiful and looked very much like a Viking boat--only without the shields on the sides. We were very impressed. We chatted a bit with the men while Arvid translated for all of us and then, feeling super hungry, we excused ourselves so that we could find a place to camp. Arvid said his parents shared a boathouse with a friend who lived nearby and would we like to camp near there and use a boat to fish on the lake? We were thrilled at such an offer. Both of us were dying to fish, and if we caught anything, it would improve our diet of reconstituted dry soups and tuna immensely. We thanked Arvid and invited him to dinner after we'd pulled the trailer into the place he'd shown us, but he said he'd have to be on his way and would come to see us in two days if we were still there. Ha! Still there? He should come back in a month or two and we might still be there! A real fishing boat. Whoopee! Terence was so happy he forgot to speak Esperanto and the next day we walked over to the boathouse and found the key Arvid had said would be there. Inside were nets hanging neatly from the rafters and several hooks lined up on the wooden work-bench. He had told us to use anything we wanted and swore we'd catch big fish with anything we chose. T. and I laughed at the clumsy fishing hooks--huge things on long thick strings that were wrapped around a sort of bobbin-thing. Very primitive. We were glad we had brought our own gear because we were determined to catch something that day and next to our delicate rods and state-of-the-art reels and large variety of hooks of all sizes (which we'd hauled around for the whole darned trip), Arvid's gear looked downright Stone-Age!

I'd made a lunch and we had brought books to read and we were so excited we could hardly stand it. We pushed the fiberglass boat (I was grateful it wasn't heavy wood) into the water and climbed in. While Terence rowed, I looked over Arvid's strange hooks and because I'd promised him I'd try one, I selected one of the smaller bobbins and dropped the big fat hook with a worm on it into the water from the back of the boat. The yank took me by surprise. Maybe I'd snagged some weeds? A bigger yank. "Terence! I think a fish has it!!" Terence looked skeptical. "So pull it up," he advised, helpfully. I awkwardly wound the thick line around the bobbin. This wasn't fishing, this was knitting! I had some sort of dead weight on the other end. Then a slow movement and suddenly I was staring at the snout of the biggest cod I've ever seen in my life. It wasn't fair. I had barely got the hook in the water. Terence's mouth dropped and he stopped rowing and reached for one of our rods. While he cast out the line, I brought Moby Dick aboard and got the hook out of his mouth. I prepared to knock it unconscious so that it wouldn't suffer. "Don't do that," T. said, "You may want to throw it back." "Are you nuts?," I shouted, "I've never caught such a big fish in my life!" But I let it flop. With the regurgitated worm from its mouth, I baited my big hook again and let it out from the spool over the side. I don't think it hit the water before I got a big jerk on the line. "Oh, NO!," I yelled, "This isn't even sport!" "Maybe I should give up on this rod and use one of those stupid things," Terence said enviously, when all at once the yank almost pulled him over the side. We both pulled in fish that were so much bigger than the first one that I picked the poor thing up by the tail and threw him back. "Grow up!," I yelled, and both of us roared with delight.

We didn't get to read our books. We didn't even get to eat our sack lunch. Two more giant codfish within minutes and we decided to return to shore. The wind was strong and the waves on the lake were choppy and it took both of us to row back to the boathouse against the strong current. But oh, how happy we were! It all had happened so fast. And we could go out again as soon as we wanted to. We giggled and hugged and took Polaroid photos of each other holding the four big fish.

We soon learned we were not by just any old "big lake." We were, in fact, camped by a real-live fjord, and squatting at the foot of nothing less than the famous Jaek'kevarri glacier looming around 8033 meters above us and the source of our drinking water. Arvid told us the water could be around 10,000 years old! The thought blitzed my brain as I cleaned the fish in the rushing stream. Big white sea-gulls floating on the air above me were very interested in my beginner's attempts to filet our catch. I threw the entrails up to them and they caught every piece.

Need I say dinner was superb that night. And the next and the next.

Arvid and his young boat-building friend and another biker dropped in as promised on Wednesday evening. They had brought beer and something they thought we ought to experience if we were going to get to know the real Norway. Seagull eggs and seal-liver pate. My mind recoiled in horror when I thought of cute little seals slaughtered for this stuff, but I had the wits at least to keep quiet until I thought it over as the men talked. Terence watched me carefully as I helped myself. He knew how strongly I felt about such things. It occurred to me that this was not exactly a case where giant Fur Companies were killing off the baby seal population for their furs and leaving the carcasses to rot, as I had seen in various wildlife magazines and films on TV back home. Arvid and his family lived way up here where a single cabbage cost $6 and reindeer meat might be radioactive. Fish and more fish was the only thing they could count on and if I thought I was sick of tuna, imagine what it would be like to have no choice your whole life? I ate the pate and it was delicious. The seagull eggs tasted the same as chicken's except the white part looked somewhat bluish and transparent, like skim milk. I had made some rice before they came and so we had a lovely feast. The beer was especially welcome and we all got jolly.

The boat builder went home, but the rest of us decided to climb the trail to the glacier. It was about eleven at night and of course the sun would not be setting way up here--even though there were clouds to hide it, there would be plenty of light. Arvid's long-legged pace up through the trees an over the spongy moss full of wobbly rocks almost did me in--I was shamefully out of shape from sitting inside the tent or on the back of the motorcycle to the exclusion of much else. Anyway, being far too proud to ask for a rest, I plowed on--with Terence giving me a hand now and then. He had the graciousness to say it wasn't easy for him either. A couple of American softies!

After a while we found ourselves on a plateau, looking way down at our lake/fjord. The runoff from the glacier made a wide river that seemed impossible to cross, but our intrepid Norsemen hopped across like bunnies over the rocks in their leather motorcycle boots while Terence and I slid and sloshed across in our huge rubber rain boots trying to keep up. Arvid showed us a hunk of reindeer horn stuck in a stump and pulling some fur from a bush nearby, he showed me how to rub it between my fingers to get an idea of how warm it was. He said his mother was a Lapp and she was up north visiting her people. (Farther north? How hardy can you get?)

We all lay on the soft moss and watched the Midnight Sun roll around the sky. Arvid filled a pipe with hash and tobacco and passed it around. (Ah ha! So that's what these people do to keep sane during those long winter months!) I tried to be one of the boys and took a puff. The first one was O.K. but the second burned all the way to my lungs and it was very painful and scary. I coughed and gasped and must have looked ridiculous. One puff was no doubt enough anyway, because when we had to walk over the next stream it seemed, to my addled mind, that the rocks were moving! The harder I concentrated on the one upon which I was to put my foot, the more it moved around to get away. So annoying. Who needs that stuff? I guess I'll have to face the fact that I may never be "one of the boys" after all.

The guys left around 1:30 a.m. for Tromsø. I asked them if they ever slept and they answered, "Not in the summer!" Poor guys. I suppose that meant they must hibernate in the long winters.

The sun shown pink and gold on the snowy peaks encircling the lake. Terence went to bed but I just couldn't have slept. I took a short walk by the lake. I seemed like noon.

Still at the base of "Old Jaek" by July 11th. Terence was typing like a madman to get the year's course of study completed so he could finally relax. The sun attempted to break through earlier, but failed and then the wind came up--sweeping down the glacier so the sweaters came on and the camp stove got fired up and we tried not to think about Santa Barbara in July. I was fashioning postcards for my loved-ones out of card board--pasted over with pictures of Norway from our tourist brochures. It was a sweet little life on that fjord, but we knew we had to move on. The thought of Bergen and the Esperanto Convention made me reach for my grammar book. Would enough of it really sink in by the time we got there? I doubted it.

On Saturday, we finally forced ourselves to pack up. But not until we'd taken the boat out for one more go at the fish. Again, it was no contest and we almost had to beat them off with the oars to keep them from jumping into the boat. It was about as sporting as buying them at the fish market, but at least we had plenty to eat for several more days. We brought the boat in and cleaned it and also Arvid's hooks and put the key back and rather sadly headed back to the campsite. I walked over to the stream to clean the fish while Terence tried to start the motorcycle. The battery on the GoldWing was completely dead again and there was nothing for him to do but hoist it under his arm and walk to someplace that had electricity. Luckily, a young man named Chris picked him up in his car and brought him back so it wasn't too long before we were on the road again.

We spent a humid night next to a giant parked snowplow battling midgies and mosquitoes, then rode into Narvik, where we looked up a pal we'd met at the German Gold Wing Treffen. Sven Rindstad and his girl-friend Ann were very sweet--showed us all around and insisted we stay in Sven's dad's home for the night so we could get a shower. His dad was out of town but they were sure he wouldn't mind. Much appreciated.

Well rested, we headed on down the road the next morning and in great good humor, absolutely adored everything we saw again. (It had to be the air!) The sights made Yosemite look pale in comparison. We camped by another lake and snuggled, warm and cozy, while a light mist dripped a soft staccato on our trailer tent roof. Life was treating us very well.

We stopped at Ye Olde Tourist Trappe the next day at what was touted as the "Arctic Circle," although I think there are as many "Circle" lines as there are enterprising locals up there. This was a big quasi-museum and Folk Art/Craft gallery (read stacks of reindeer pelts)--a kind of Shopping Center for the Gullible. The prices must have kept a lot of Laplanders in business. More power to 'em.

Outside the shop/museum, we read the terrible inscription on a large monument commemorating the German-held Russian and Yugoslavian prisoners of War that died while building a railroad on the frozen tundra up there. We placed a call to our friend Chris in Paris to see if he was going to meet us in Trondheim as planned. He wasn't. Boo Hoo.

At Lakforsen, we got some marvelous pictures of a long, flat waterfall. Later some more at a lofty and delicate church--painted stark white with lots of black lacy ironwork crosses in the graveyard surrounding. The Norwegian flag had been seen fluttering at half-mast for miles before we got to this town. We were told a famous local woman had died. At 93! The newest grave was hers--covered and surrounded with flowers.

Another night in a forest sharing space with too many mosquitoes--it was getting warmer as we rode south--and then we rolled into Trondheim. Sven's brother Rolf met us downtown and took us to his bosom. We were able to shower and even do laundry at his flat and the luxury was almost too much for us. A lovely wife and daughter and good food and new friends.

Rolf showed us the famous cathedral in Trondheim and later we hunkered down in the local library to catch up on the news of the world. That evening Rolf and his wife fed us like Kings and showed us a video of a sensational folk opera, written by two Norwegian women and called "Which Witch?" Rolf said he thought they were Norway's answer to Andrew Lloyd Weber and I was in no mood to disagree. I would love to hear more of their work.

Rolf was a steward on a Norwegian Airline and had to work the next day, so T. and I moseyed about the beautiful "Old Town" of Trondheim and as rain began to fall in earnest, we ducked into the Kunstindustrimuseum, a long word for the Museum of Art and Industry. We really enjoyed the Art Nouveau Room representing their most famous artist of the period, Van de Velde, who had even done the breathtaking stained-glass skylight in the museum's ceiling.

The second floor was taken up by scenes and trapping of Norwegian's royalty, which seemed to disgust Terence. I noticed the Norwegians were eating it up, however. Then there was various hand-crafts and furniture displayed by Norway's brightest and best, and enough fabulous contemporary and historical glass on exhibit to put Murano's museum near Venice to shame.

That evening we were treated to a stay at a handsome new hotel called Hotel Bakeriet where Rolf had a one-night pass from the airline to use up and insisted we use it! What good fortune! Rolf took us up to the gymroom where he showed us the free beer tap and how to borrow videos to watch in our room and we thought we'd died and gone to heaven. Hot showers in our pure white private bathroom, and free shampoo and soap, and all that free beer, and rain tapping against the curtained window above the goose-downed bed got me to wondering what such a room cost mere mortals. I really didn't want to know. We had discovered the garage alone was almost six bucks a night so of course, we left the rig in the street.

Back with reality the next day, we said goodbye to our new friends and rolled on down the coast toward Lesund where we had read the entire town was in the Art Nouveau style and not to be missed. We camped in some quarry and then left the heavy trailer chained to a pole near the ferry and so, unfettered, we were able to make the rest of the trip to the island town. The architecture, although of the same period as Nouveau, was definitely German--what they call Jugenstile--lots of knights and maidens and shields and steeds cut idealistically into the stone designs. Frankly, I love the stuff. You can't get too schlockly for me...

Even without the trailer we were stared at quite a bit by the other tourists. We must have looked pretty strange. Our clothes were becoming a little tattered by this time and that quarry had been pretty muddy on the boots. We zoomed back to catch the ferry and then hooked our trailer back up and pulled it up and around a couple of mountains until we came to the ridge above the Geiranger fjord and had to stop. The sight was so beautiful we couldn't speak. Way, way below us, a tiny cruise ship as white as the snow on the peaks above it, was gliding on what looked like a piece of teal-colored glass. It was so far down we couldn't see it move but just then a little plume of white smoke rose from its stack so we knew it wasn't just a poster we were looking at, but a real-live image of Norway the Beautiful...showing off.

As if to prove her great diversity, we were treated next to an almost free-fall ride down the side of our mountain--culminating in a dive into not one, but three freezing, cold and dark tunnels. It was like being swallowed by hungry beasts and the sun was blinding when we emerged. This country was simply nonstop performance. Meanwhile, the glaciers were melting above us and the long trails of water falling down the sides of the mountains looked like skinny lightening bolts. Hundreds of cute little goats were hopping around the rocks and we could see them begging from the tourist caravans stopped at every layby.

We took so many pictures of quaint little grass-topped cottages, grass-topped sheds, and grass-topped boathouses that I swore I'd take no more, and then that afternoon we saw another one on a mountaintop, covered with daisies. Get out the cameras...

Terence was drilling me in Esperanto. It seems that everything I said had to be corrected. I grit my teeth and kept on trying.

We had to pull into a church parking lot just outside of Bergen in a town called Knarvik. Terence's allergies had been kicking up again in Trondheim (as the air became warmer), and Rolf had given him something he had for his allergies that he thought would help. It may have helped somewhat, but the drug also made Terence very sleepy and it just would not do for him to fall asleep at the helm of the rig, so he thought he'd better take a nap. We opened up the trailer tent there in the parking lot and he crawled in and zonked out almost immediately.

Taking the wrong ferry to Bergen that afternoon was annoying, but we finally made it to a campground outside the city called The Paradise Tennis Camping and Caravaning site, which was actually nothing but a parking lot next to a Fitness Center. Terence was in a foul mood. I knew from experience that it was mainly the allergies, but we had other problems. We really couldn't afford the ten dollars a night for the space in the parking lot for the whole week of the Convention, but all our hoped-for "contacts" proved to be unable to let us stay with them--or even on their land, if they had any.

That afternoon, we went into Bergen (which charged a toll of a couple of bucks to enter the city!) to the Grieg Concert Hall to check in at the "Kongreso," and all the leads we had had for places to stay with Esperantists went dry. No one there cared to advise us about where we might camp outside the city, no one seemed even to know what was going on. And for this, we had paid quite a sum the year before to be allowed to attend. When we offered to help set up chairs and tables because the local Esperantists seemed to be rather unprepared for the influx of attendees, no one seemed interested in taking us up on the offer. Terence's mood worsened. On the way back to the motorcycle, he snapped, "I'm beginning to think Esperanto, as it exists today, is nothing more than a social club for people who can't get laid!"

I had to admit it was strange that there were no posters up anywhere, no one at the Tourist Information Office a couple of blocks away had even heard of the Conference, there wasn't even a sign on the door of the hall telling people who came all this way to the convention what time and where anything was happening. Terence had studied so hard for this moment and the Esperantists inside the hall had even spoken to him in English. He was smoldering with exasperation.

It hardly helped when we tried to reach my daughter Meredith by phone and instead got one of her friends who seemed to be living at our house in Santa Barbara rent-free. Just as the young woman figured out who he was, the telephone took a powder and she could no longer hear him. He gave up. At the Poste Restante, he got none of the mail he was counting on, including an important pair of riding gloves his father was supposed to send. He still didn't know if his Law school received anything he had painstakingly sent from Finland, and the one letter I had received from Meredith answered none of the questions I had asked her long ago about our financial situation at home. Perhaps not completely trusting himself, he stopped speaking to me and I was not about to open a possible can of worms. It got worse.

I think instead of going into very much detail about the week of the Esperanto Kongreso, I shall just say that it was a time I would rather forget. Terence finally found interesting Esperantists to talk to and became involved in almost everything. His hostility and anger with me because I couldn't keep up with him, drove me into a misery that made me appear even more like the dolt he was painting of my character. I often slipped away when I felt I was embarrassing him with my pathetic attempts at conversation. He stopped talking to me entirely, and became very thick with a beautiful young language teacher from Estonia. Seeing them together drove me to the public library a few blocks away where I nursed my bruised ego with periodicals and books written in the only language I could handle. I took long walks around the harbor and marveled at how beautiful Bergen truly was. The days were sunny and hot. Everyone said how unusual this was. I met some nice people in the parks and made some sketches of the old wooden store-fronts.

Finally, on Friday, the horrible convention experience was over. As we took our leave from the group, and I was saying goodbye in Esperanto, the Estonian's eyes grew wide and she looked at me and said, "Oh she can speak!" I wish she'd been right. The sad thing was that I knew the once beautiful relationship between Terence and me would never be the same again. It was if Terence might forget, but never forgive. And I would forgive, but never forget. Probably just as well.

Our first night away from Bergen was spent in a parking lot next to a soaring waterfall. Summer visitors were all but gone as we pulled in that evening and just coming back as we left in the morning. Terence almost lost his life crawling out on a limb for a photograph over the falls but he said it was worth it. We two had a long discussion over dinner about the previous week and the air was clearer, at least.

Trying to avoid the toll coming up on the main road to Oslo, we foolishly took a side road going in what we thought was the same direction. We should have known better after experiencing some pretty harrowing moments on what was Norway's only highway to Oslo from the west coast. Sometimes so narrow, even trucks had to back down when we met them on the curve--because our trailer made it impossible for Terence to be the one to give in and back up.

Anyway, we climbed a mountain or two over lumpy, holey roads and finally wound up at some sort of resort at the top, where we at first met only Norwegians who couldn't speak anything but their own language. (Like Americans.) Actually, we loved hearing the lilt and song of the language. We realized we hadn't heard much of it because so many people spoke English. After a while, we found some folks whom we could talk to and they showed us the way. However, not before insisting we take a large box of raspberries they'd been carrying. They said they had more than they needed.

The raspberries came in handy as a house present when we reached our destination in Oslo. Terence had met a charming young lady named Mariam Lund at the convention who had invited us (and several other Esperantists, as it turned out), to her parent's home in that city. The Lunds were very gracious and told us to feel free to place our trailer on their front lawn for the duration of our stay in Oslo. It rained each day, but we did lots of sightseeing in that marvelous city and each evening we would return to the Lunds to greet yet more Esperantists coming up the walk. Monika Lund, the mother, invited us to go mushrooming with her and it was a rare experience. She told us how wonderful it used to be to take walks around her neighborhood and pick mushrooms as a child. There were few houses in the area then and enough for everyone to count on the fungi as a large part of their diet. But now with the growth of the city bringing so many more people and also using up all the land, it was practically the end of the practice unless one drove a car to some distant forest. The variety of the mushrooms was endless. Some were quite colorful. The red one with white dots was one that I had thought came from the imagination of Walt Disney! Terence and I didn't trust ourselves to know one from the other but Monika patiently instructed and we three picked a large sack full that she cooked for the family that night. They were delicious.

On Monday, August 5th, Terence's birthday, he and I visited the City Hall with its immense murals. I gave him a book I had bought in Bergen--a pictorial dictionary in Esperanto--and that evening everybody at the Lund's sang Happy Birthday to him and Marianne and somebody else who played the violin joined with him and his viola in a string jam session far into the night and I think it must have been one of his favorite ways ever to celebrate his birthday.

We visited the National Museum of Norway and almost perished from the hot rooms. The heat couldn't have been all that good for the paintings in there. At the huge Vigland Sculpture Park, we ate our bread and cheese while looking up at the massive bronze figures that lined the bridge and path leading up to the embankment that held the amazing Obelisk. Gustav Vigeland was a Norwegian of world renown during the twenties and apparently gave most of his life's work to the city in exchange for a free apartment and studio. It's an incredible amount of sculpture in one place and is topped by a twenty-meter high obelisk depicting the cycle of human life, no less, and while I thought it a mite overwhelming, Terence adored it, and took roll upon roll of black and white and slides.

Returning to the Lund's house that evening, we discovered even more Esperantists gathered around the trough. We slipped away to have our dinner by the rig on the front lawn and then came back for dessert and song.

We ate our breakfast before the rest got up the next morning and then drove through the drizzle to the Viking Ship museum and on to the Kon-Tiki museum, which was really interesting. Took a few pictures of half-sunken boats out there, then drove all the way across town to the Edvard Munch museum where we discovered, to our chagrin, the entrance fee was about five dollars each. As we were turning away to walk back to the parking lot, a young man struck up a conversation about the rig and after answering the usual questions, I decided to mention that we weren't able to see the exhibit. Like Manna from Heaven, he turned out to be one of the museum's officials and insisted we be his guests. We didn't struggle much, and he took us by the arm and walked us back to the gate and into one of the best exhibits we'd seen in Europe. What a country! Later, eating our lunch in a small park, a drunken fellow asked if we would share and after such generosity shown to us, we were happy to pass on the favor.

We returned home around three. Monika Lund asked if we'd like to accompany her to a friend's house down the lane--for tea. Ingrid J. spoke flawless English and served us lemon pie! The view of the islands of Oslo from her verandah was thrilling.

By August 8th, it was time to move on. Rode over a hundred miles and passed by some interesting ruins of a castle that had been Danish, Swedish and Norwegian at separate times. Later, we camped in a farmer's field along with too many mosquitoes. I had a sore throat and blamed it on the cold wind I'd endured all day.

But the next morning it had developed into cold/flu from Hell. Terence tried to drag me around the city of Gothenburg which might have been interesting, but I was in no shape to appreciate it. I seem to remember waiting for him on the bike while he looked at things, and at one point I found myself sitting on a bench in some sort of Antique Warehouse burning up with fever and desperate for a drink of water.

We gave up on me around noon and rode back to the area where we'd locked the trailer to a post, and while I drooped over the seat, he hitched up everything,and pulled out of town looking for a place where I could crash. The only possible spot was in a parking lot for a nature preserve that had signs everywhere saying it was forbidden to camp there or spend the night, but we were desperate and at that point, I couldn't care less if the entire Swedish army descended on our little encampment, I thought I was going to die anyway.

I had thrown myself on the trailer bed with all my clothes on and I wasn't able to rise again until the next morning! It was a frightening experience. My fever raged all night--first freezing, then burning up. As a nurse, Terence made a much better mechanic, but at least he stayed nearby. I recall he had THE EUROPEAN, a thick newspaper written in English that he'd found in the city and from time to time, when my eyes would focus, I could see him sitting by the tent, reading. I know I asked him to keep my washcloth wet so I could try to keep my temperature down by draping it over my forehead and I was vaguely aware of him lying beside me during the night as the rain came steadily down. Poor guy. It couldn't have been pleasant having to sleep next to someone with the Plague.

Fortunately, although very head-achey and weak, I knew I could get back on the bike the next morning. The fever had broken and the present symptoms were just sneezing and coughing. I kept the toilet paper in my jacket pocket and blew my nose inside my helmet at short intervals while Terence drove us on to Varberg.

At Varberg, we snooped around the castle and its museum. A particularly fascinating exhibit was the "Bocksten Man" murdered with an axe and thrown into a bog in the fourteenth century, he lay in the peat for 600 years before someone found him and put him in a glass case in the castle. He was amazingly well-preserved. I couldn't get over how his hair was still flaming red and young looking after all these years. Perhaps if I added a bit of peat to my shampoo...?

Our Gold Winging friends in Helsingborg were waiting for us with open arms. I was fearful that I might give germs to their new baby, and did my best to keep away from the adorable tot, but the "Platis" Plateryds seemed to take no notice of my coughing spells and were as kind as could be--showing us the town and treating us to real home-cooked Swedish food and taking us for long walks around the countryside in the company of their two large German Shepherds. At dinner the second night, I had another bad coughing fit and excused myself from the table. When I came back, my host had warmed up some sort of Aquavit and told me to drink it down. Horrible stuff. It wasn't the burning going down that I minded so much as the strong peppermint toothpaste taste--in the middle of my wonderful dinner. Still, I suppose it helped the coughing and that's what mattered. I felt much better the next morning.

The next town down the road was Lund, a lovely college town with a handsome twelfth-century Romanesque cathedral right in the center. We popped inside just as a rain squall appeared and although dark and cavernous, the "Domkyrkan" had lots to keep us amused as the storm raged outside. We were especially fascinated by the crypt beneath the apse. The low carved pillars showed a lot of imagination for Medieval times. One pillar had a man gripping it with an expression of terror on his face--all carved in stone. Our handy guide book told the story of a giant Finn who lived near Lund when the new cathedral was being built. Hearing the new church bells, he rushed to the town to destroy the church that had disturbed him, grasped the first pillar, and was promptly turned to stone!

We made it into Malmö by late afternoon. We were tired of fighting the wind and rain and were ready to just get on the ferry to Copenhagen when suddenly we discovered we were surrounded by bikers. And not just any bikers. Gold Wingers! They insisted we allow them to show us the best sights in that harbor town and so we rode along wondering where they all came from and how they seemed to know us. Had some of them been at the German Treffen in Wezel when I wimped out and went to bed early-- leaving Terence to find Scandinavians on his own? He said he didn't remember any of them. After an hour or so of being shown the sights and struggling with the language barrier, we all shook hands and the mystery was solved when one of them told us that they had been contacted and were told to look for us by none other than "Platis" back in Helsingborg. Some syndicate those guys had.

The name of the fellow who spoke the most English was Paul Nielsen. He offered to lead us to the ferry and on the way show us the town's old fortress. The structure wasn't much to look at, but we got to know each other better and by the time we got to the ferry, Paul told us he could get us on the ferry for free because the ticket seller owed him a favor. We were certainly impressed and very grateful and the money Paul saved us was spent on two pretty expensive beers on the way over to Denmark.

Although it had been a short ride from the ferry, it was dark by the time we reached Copenhagen and the Tourist Info places were closed, so we rode around the outskirts and just took the first campground we could find. It was a large playing field and full of gypsies. Noisy, dirty and expensive, we slept fitfully and were glad to get away to look for another the next morning.

We arrived at Camp Absalon near Copenhagen on August 13th. We put up the big tent and rode into the city. Bought beer and lots of other things so much cheaper than up north. Moseyed around the harbor. Terence found a phone directory and looked up Jaegar, a company that made the world's best viola strings, according to T. He needed to buy some and hoped for a discount. We were shocked to discover the famous Jaegar factory was a tiny home manned by a rather elderly couple who looked rather frightened as they peeped out their back door at a couple of scruffy American bikers. Blessedly, they both spoke English and Terence talked fast and soon they were caught up in our adventure and wanted to help. Terence had told me he expected to pay around $40 for a couple of A strings if they'd let him have any. They explained how difficult it was to keep up with the demand. We certainly understood. I found myself wondering if the dear old things actually rolled the strings together on the kitchen table...

They invited us to sit in the living room and began grilling Terence as to what he really needed the strings for. He told them about the viola staying in the back of the bike and how he played it whatever chance he got no matter where we were and I had to admit that was true. They seemed to like that. They conferred in Danish for awhile as Terence and I looked sheepishly at one another. Then Mr. Hansen left us and returned with a handful of A strings--extras for good measure, he said. They would not hear of payment. Yea--Denmark!

Forcing ourselves to ride through the rain the next day, and see some-thing of the city, our first stop was the National Museum of Art. We had read that there was no entrance fee but that generous practice had recently changed so they were charging 20K to get in to see what our Rough Guides had called a "So-so" exhibit. We were trying to decide if we wanted to dip into our precious budget when a rather over-zealous museum guard asked us to do our deciding outside in the rain, as we were dripping on his marble foyer. That pretty well decided us to give the place a pass. Terence dropped me off at the main library and took off to visit another brewery.

One day we visited the grisly Medical History Museum and took the hour-long tour past straitjackets, amputated feet, methods of syphilis treat-ment, eyeballs and various displays of tortures for women going through the "madness" of their change of life. (Gasp!) The Museum of the Danish Resistance Movement later sort of restored our hope for mankind in a kind of twisted way. Later, we gobbled our sardine sandwiches too close to the dear Little Mermaid statue. I began to feel like a cannibal.

Of course we had to climb the outdoor spiral staircase of the rather kooky blue and gold spire of Vor Frelsers Kirke. The slanted and slippery steps were a challenge for the stout-hearted all right, but the view across the city and beyond were worth all the risk.

It was a nasty hassle trying to get Terence's slides taken care of. The Kodak factory in Copenhagen decided for some obtuse reason not to "mount" his slides--instead returning them developed but in a huge roll that made it all but impossible to see the images. We were told we would have to ride to another factory way west of our itinerary to get the mounts.

It rained all day Saturday so we stayed inside the tent and kept busy writing and reading. All night we listened to it come down in sheets. We forced ourselves to pack up the next morning and miraculously at around eleven it began to clear up so that we were able to pack some things semi-dry. Camped that night in a sort of picnic area near a lake on the way to Korsør and in the morning, rode through blustery winds to the Kodak factory. While we waited for the slides to be mounted, we rode around the seacoast town and sat on a little beach to eat our lunch. The spot reminded me of home.

Leaving the Kodak factory, we set out for the island of Møn where we were told we could find some fourteenth-century frescoes in the churches, and as if that weren't enough for one tiny island, there were supposed to be lots of fascinating Neolithic burial places as well! We chained the trailer to a post in a parking lot at Vordingborg and rode over the long bridge to Møn. The wind was very strong but the sun kept peeking out from the blazing white clouds and after we found the first church we remarked at how clean everything looked brushed and scrubbed by the wind. As we neared the door to the church, it was shut in our faces. The sign read that it closed at 5 p.m.. With the sun high in the sky. We were aghast. We turned quickly and hopped aboard the bike to try to reach the next one before it closed. We just made it, ran in and spun around looking at the amazing frescoes before the sexton indicated that he too would have to shoo us out. The third church was all the way across the island but we decided to go for it. However, we weren't going to kill ourselves. If it closed early too, so be it. We bought some string beans from a farmer's cart near the second church. No one was around and a sign over a can told us how many coins to drop in. We loved it.

On the way to the other side of the island we stopped by various prehistoric burial sites that really weren't much more than small grassy hills. We would have to take their word for it as being something impor-tant. Happily, the third church was still open and no sexton to be seen. We took our time strolling around the interior with our heads thrown back as we gazed at the marvelous use of color and line by the talented peasant painter. They were mostly of rural life--with Jesus and other deities tossed in among the farmers and fishermen like good friends. I'll bet Jesus would have liked that.

We read a nice description of them in English there on the wall which was handy, and it also informed us of a very special burial barrow nearby where apparently a Neolithic "queen" had been laid to rest. The wind was beating the long grass down around us as we walked over to it and the moaning sounds coming from the tops of the trees overhead added to the spooky atmosphere. The barrow was a long narrow mound of earth that had been covered with huge rocks that looked as if they'd been dropped from another planet. As the sun neared the horizon, its orange-gold light reflected off of jillions of tiny quartz-like particles in the stone and made the whole west side sparkle like a diamond tiara. And of course the east side would do the same when the sun rose. Not a bad act for a has-been, I thought.

By the time we chained the trailer to the back of the Wing, the wind was truly scary and I thought it would be the dumbest folly to try to cross the next big bridge leading out of Denmark. Terence wasn't deterred and we did make it to the other side but I was still so shaken that he realized it might be a good idea to turn off the road and camp while I still had some light to cook by, so my mood wouldn't get any worse. We found a nice quiet park off the highway and I cooked chicken breasts and rice and with the succulent string beans we'd bought off the farmer's cart on Møn, we had a meal fit for gourmets.

As we packed up to leave the next morning, the news came out of the motorcycle's radio of the "Putsch" in Russia. It sounded like the bad guys were winning. Poor Gorbachev. What a surprise! And what would it mean for two American bikers who wanted to cross that troubled country in a year or so?

Chapter Forty-Five

GERMANY AND THE NEWLY FREED COUNTRIES

THE NICE YOUNG policemen in the patrol car asked us a few questions as we found ourselves stuck in a traffic jam going into the German town of Lübeck, our first stop out of Denmark. They seemed relieved to know we weren't planning on staying long. Just doing their job, no doubt. The old part of the city was fascinating, medieval and largely rebuilt after the bombing in WWII. Being summer, it was mobbed with tourists and so hot that we began to feel stifled and were glad to push on to the countryside. Spent the night in a barley field.

On August 21st, we stayed at an expensive campground in Hamburg; fifteen bucks with electricity extra; a warring Polish family too close to us; father shouted continually, while wife and teenaged children cowered. His biggest beef seemed to be the way the three others had put up the tent. He hadn't helped except to scream as the others worked. Then, to our astonishment, the whole family spent the night sitting in their car instead of using the tent!

We saw the Art museum and various old churches, checked out the "Dom" Carnival area that night and walked along the notorious Reeperbahn street of hawkers and peep-shows. Smelly and seedy.

A French lady from Grenoble walked over the next morning to give us a tape to keep, Tchaikowsky's Greatest Hits. She had heard us playing Mozart's "Magic Flute" the night before. (Trying to drown out the screaming father a few feet away). She said she and her husband were rather tired of the tape and thought we might like something new. So kind.

The village of Lüneberger was celebrating its 1,000th birthday when we rolled through. Hard to believe anything's that old. Oompa-pa bands and sudsy beer flowing all around for the tourists and townsfolk alike and a great feeling of camaraderie and fun. We pushed our way through the streets to a copy shop we were lucky to find open. As usual, Terence had to have copies of his last batch of homework papers. While I waited by the rig in the street, a jovial young man who spoke pretty fair English, asked if he could interview me about our journey for the local rag. When Terence came out, he took over in German and although we asked that a copy be sent to us, we weren't surprised that it never showed up. That evening we discovered the sweetest forest glen ever to camp in. It was like something out of "The Midsummer Night's Dream," with its carpet of green velvet and tiny white daisies and fragrant pines clustered around. The almost full moon rising over the tops as it got dark reminded me of other such spots we'd enjoyed along the way. The best it gets.

As we drove toward Hannover, we spotted several cars parked in a large lot way out in the country. Curious, we pulled off and watched whole families descend from their vehicles to walk down a path and around a hill. After a bit of sleuthing, I discovered that they were taking a very popular "nature walk" to some famous heather fields nearby. Purple heather could be seen for miles and we were told it only grew in this one spot in all of Germany so folks came from far away to walk by it. One was not allowed to pick.

It was a damp gray Sunday in Hannover. We parked the trailer on the outskirts of the city and rode first to the Baunhauf for information, then to the Rathaus with its uninspired architecture. We took pictures of a sad, bombed-out church--now covered with ivy and obviously used by the homeless to relieve themselves in the corners. A dog was doing the same on a tombstone. A baby swung on a modern metal sculpture. After a couple of hours, we rode back to the trailer, ate some bread and cheese and hauled ourselves outta town to find a camping spot. Not a simple task that night. Very few tree clumps to hide behind and no roads to them, anyway. Much as we hated to, we opted to take a walker's path that just could accommodate the trailer, and sneaked our way up a pretty hill overlooking some farm houses. Nervous dogs barked below us and a too-thin row of trees hardly seemed enough to separate us from prying eyes, but we were too tired to care. After it got dark, the eastern sky began to lighten and a great big juicy full moon rose above the pines on the next hill. Two house cats visited--too late for dinner but great company for a bit. Around midnight, a brass band played something over and over and we heard the pop of fireworks and we wondered what was being celebrated. Perhaps the great August moon was enough reason to throw a party.

Rolling down the hill early the next morning we came upon an ancient farmhouse whose roof was being restored. No one was about and upon closer examination, we discovered that the job must have been abandoned years before. The place looked spooky and intriguing and we wanted some photographs. The stone walls looked so old they might have been there forever, and high above the skeletal beams of the roof was a little pine tree top. This tiny Christmas tree-looking object is placed on houses-in-construction by the Germans for good luck and is often festooned with colorful ribbons and paper. It must be powerful magic because we had seen it everywhere in Germany. This one must have been up there quite a while because most of its needles had fallen off and all its ribbons had been bleached white by the sun and were fluttering limply and sadly--leaving it looking like a tiny ghost...left to guard the roofless house into eternity.

As we rolled into Osnabrück, we became aware of a man on a Harley Davidson bike following us. There was a young child in his side car and when we stopped at the Information place he struck up a conversation in German. He was not a young man and I confess my first impression was not overly favorable. He just looked like another middle-aged fellow impressed with the American film "Easy Rider" and trying to show off how hip he was with his full leathers and fringe and big bad "hog." I looked away with impatience when he offered to show us the sights but Terence was more friendly--after all, he was a fellow biker, wasn't he? So we allowed ourselves to be dragged along to the cathedral while the "boys" discussed engines and the little girl and I brought up the rear. Mercifully, they had something to do after we'd seen the church, so I thought we were rid of them. But coming back to a parking lot after a tour of the Rathaus nearby, we saw that they were waiting for us. I understood enough of the language to realize he was telling us that they had called his wife and would we do them the honor of sharing their Sunday dinner in their home? Embarrassment and shame must have filled my face. Terence looked at me and knew he wouldn't have to translate. "Do you want to?" his look said. I summoned up my brightest smile. "Sure!" I said.

Dieter, Tina and Jennifer Hamm lived in a cozy apartment on the outskirts of Osnabrück and although I was still smarting with self-loathing for my unfair first impression, I was partially right in my assumption that he was a victim of the "Harley mystique." Posters and trappings of all kinds carried the H-D logo and the motorcycle was obviously at least as important as his wife who, it appeared, was quite pregnant. I asked her when they expecting this wonderful baby and she said "Yesterday!" I warmed to her fast.

Dinner was marvelous. First beer, then roast beef and noodles and gravy, mixed vegetables, more beer, and then for dessert, vanilla pudding with blueberry syrup, coffee and cookies. Yum! I was very sincere when I told them as we left that I hoped they would make it to my house in Santa Barbara.

We arrived at the cathedral town of Münster around four o'clock; happy to see the massive church still open for us. Lots of rebuilding but with much care. The new stained glass windows were dated 1961, but fit in nicely with the ancient decor. The rest of the University town was a delight too. I heard my first porcelain glockenspiel. The shopping areas under the heavy medieval arches were trés upscale, we noted. You could smell the money in the streets. These kids--wearing Gucci backpacks and Pucci belts--were certainly not the old stereotype of poverty-stricken college kids. Western Germany was doing all right. We spent the night in a small wood just outside the town. Had to beat off a steady stream of bicyclists on the path to get to it!

Chapter Forty-Six

I GET BACK ON THE ASCOT

BACK TO OUR good friend Dirk Kraaij's house in Holland. We'd have lots to do if we were going to make it to Greece before the winter set in. Terence came down with some sort of stomach ailment right after we arrived but, typically, wouldn't give in to it, and although whatever it was lasted for several days, he managed to accomplish some Herculean tasks on the bikes to get us ready. He repaired, replaced and restored stuff on the bikes and even made places underneath the trailer for the new tires. I washed clothes and helped him repack the trailer with some of the things we had stored with Dirk. Lots of mail had to be dealt with and my daughter assured us in her letters that things were all right at home.

Because I'd been showing interest in ethnic cooking, Truus, Dirk's lady-friend, cooked us something called "Brudder" for our supper that last night with them. We were told that it was what the local poor people used to have as an evening meal. Actually it was like a large pudding--made with a "self-rise" flour mix and an egg and some raisins and then she put the dough into a pillow case and the whole thing was lowered into a big pot of boiling water. She cooked it for an hour and 10 minutes. The resulting heavy, solid mass was plopped onto a platter and sliced. We were instructed to pour hot molasses mixed with margarine--on top. Terence liked it. It was certainly...filling.

The day came when I had to see if I could still ride the Ascot, and it was a great relief to realize that I still knew where the controls were.

Terence didn't push for once, he just got on the GW and let me follow him around Wormerveer at my own speed. It was a gloriously sunny morning and soon I was singing in my helmet and picking up speed behind him. There was nobody on the long narrow roads on the dyke-tops and we flew past the watery netherlands and windmills and we both knew we were ready to make the journey to Greece.

As we crossed the border into Belgium, we noticed by our Dutch AAA roadmap, that the prices for campgrounds were as low as they had been in France. We finally located the Municipal campground of Antwerp (without benefit of road signs), and for about four bucks, including electricity, we had ourselves a fine spot to camp. We hopped aboard the Ascot the next morning to take a look at Brugge, and as the fifty five mile trip was over some very rough potholes and mean streets, I was dizzy when I slid off the passenger seat. But the bumpy ride was worth it. Brugge was something of a northern Venice, with its many canals and careful preservation of the ancient structures. Seventeenth century instead of Byzantine and gothic, of course. The most obvious difference was the wheel, the cars and bicycles that competed for space in the narrow brick cobblestone streets. The crowds of tourists didn't seem to mind the crush. Sightseeing boats cluttered the canals and the cute shops were bursting with folks buying the lace and chocolates for which this little country has become so famous.

We shot quite a bit of film and then we rode east to see Ghent, where the summer crowds were every bit as big because Ghent was another ancient city in superb condition with no less than three cathedrals and a big Rathaus--all piled on top of each other in the old part of the city that also boasted a wide canal that twisted around fetchingly past carefully restored 17th century warehouses and shops. Ancient and adorable. Boy, these lucky Europeans. Who needs Disneyland? We drove back to Antwerp and while Terence studied, I prepared us a nice Happy-to-be-in-Belgium dinner of chicken and vegetables and fresh green salad.

We woke up early. Had lots to do and places to see before heading for the next Gold Wing Treffen in Luxembourg. Dashed downtown to see the big cathedral of Antwerp. On the way, we passed a rather dreary part of town where the "Ladies of the Evening" were working now as "Ladies of the Morning." They stood in their skimpy lace underwear behind storefront windows, sort of moving to their own silent music. Somehow the morning shift lacked pizzazz. A kind of "second team" feeling to their shabby sell. The harsh light of day can be cruel.

The giant cathedral was full of Rubens, de Vos, and other assorted heavies. Glory be. Spent too little time to absorb much. We yanked on our helmets and made for the Museum of Art down the road. Another pathetic stab at trying to see everything. That damn Treffen, I thought. IF IT'S TUESDAY, IT MUST BE BELGIUM...

We had to find propane for our cooking and heating tanks. After getting lost a few times, dodging trams and tracks in suburban Antwerp, we located the only place that would give us any, and after an hour and a half, because the guy didn't have the right fitting, one of our canisters was filled and we were charged $12! We were both furious--especially at ourselves for forgetting to ask the price first. Hadn't we learned anything in three years of travel? We said screw the other canister, paid the thief and departed. Way out of town, on the long stretch to Luxembourg, we found a gas station that was happy to sell us propane and we filled our other tank for two dollars! Live and learn.

The Treffen in Luxembourg had a very loud band. All weekend the booming bass made sleep impossible until they quit--about 4 a.m. It seemed to be what everybody liked. I began to feel very old. Terence manfully threw himself into the fray, making himself silly with beer and Jaegermeister and then dancing dirty with whomever or whatever didn't mind being seen with him.

For some reason, sitting pillion behind Terence the next day on the Wing (because of course my little bike was not allowed to show its face among the big brothers), the long tour around the countryside with all the other motorcyclists didn't thrill me as much this time and although I enjoyed seeing some people I'd met on earlier Treffens, I was glad when Sunday came and we could get away. I was anxious to see more exotic lands. I was finally coming to the realization that we might actually make it to Greece.

We stayed another day in Luxembourg--touring the countryside by ourselves and seeing the village of Vianden up close--with its fairy-tale castle--that we'd spotted on the Treffen tour. We spent the rest of our Luxembourgian money on some nice brandy for Norbert and Burga whom we planned to visit again on our way south.

On September 9th, we spent a long day in the saddle getting nowhere fast. No direct route to Norbert's house in Mainz/Kostheim. The day was passing slowly. On one steep downgrade near the Moselle river, just after having passed a hilltop American Air Force installation, Terence took a bad spill onto the road because he had forgotten to put his kickstand up at the last stop. I watched from behind on my bike, reliving the accident in Spain and as before, unable to help. I saw the Wing first twist to the right and hit the guardrail, then swing over again to the left--this time throwing Terence to the ground in an explosion of dust and dirt as the machine dug into the pavement and shoulder. The right wheel of the trailer seemed to roll over him, then roll back as the heavy mass slid to the middle of the road in a metal box-bashing-scraping-horrible sound. I left my bike at the side of the road and ran over to help T. who was incredibly already on his feet. We both pushed the crashed hot motorcycle--still connected to the trailer--to the side of the road. We were very lucky. No one had come by during our mishap. Terence spent some time checking the unfortunate Gold Wing all over while I checked him all over. Amazingly, he had only sustained three long scrapes down his back and assorted bruises. The bike didn't do so well. But he was able to get it running, and that night we made it to Norbert's.

Four days in the bosom of our friends while we patched up the shabby old bike and Terence's bruises healed and correspondence was taken care of, and we were on our way to East Germany! After a telephone call to the factory near Frankfurt, the saintly Metzler tire company said we would be allowed to get free tires when we got to Vienna. We could never have gone this far without those guys.

Chapter Forty-Seven

NOT EXACTLY A WELCOME MAT YET

CROSSING THE GERMAN EAST/WEST border where not too long ago freedom had been denied the poor souls on the other side, we were surprised to see no sign of anything very dramatic. A neat little brick border guard house with no one inside stood by the road and the fence had been neatly removed and it was quiet and peaceful. It wasn't until we'd climbed a hill--several meters farther on--that we realized that that had been the border guard house. The Eastern side was all and more than we had imagined. Scorched earth where the fences had been. A tall concrete tower whose every window was smashed and below--as high as a man could reach, the scrawl of angry-looking graffiti. Terence said he couldn't translate it, much to his chagrin. They were all words and sayings he hadn't seen in his language books.

Then the debris. Bottles, cans and tons of shredded papers blowing all over the acres of cement parking lots covering the earth as far as we could see. Two Snack Bars on wheels (Imbiss) were parked on each side of the wide road doing brisk business in wurst and fries. We stopped. Everybody stared. We stared back. Terence took some pictures of the forlorn tower and surroundings. It was tempting to stay and muse on what might have happened those last days of the fall of the Berlin Wall, but the natives didn't look too friendly. We pushed on.

The road was full of humanity in the hot, dusty September afternoon. Lots of cars--mostly the tiny pollution-puffing Ladas and Trabants, but some West German ones also. Too few streets for the amount of traffic. And everywhere, road workers frantically trying to repair and widen what few streets they had. So much to do here. Bottle-necks at every village. People in their underwear, sweating, hanging out the windows above the streets to watch it all. Our rig gets whoops and gasps. People point and scowl. Both children and adults on bicycles race in front of me to get a better look at the trailer and read the map I had painted on the back of T's bike. I had a rough time trying to avoid them all and keep up with Terence.

Bumping over the brick cobblestones was terrible, enough to knock out your fillings. And the semi-repaired places with stinky soft tar were the worst--they lay in mounds and pits and you never knew how deep or sticky they were until you were on top of them. The poor slobs fixing the streets had a lot of catching up to do. But the architecture captivated me. I hadn't realized what terrific stuff they still had in the East. I guess I thought everybody would be living in a Quonset hut, but each town had many once posh areas. It was a little hard to believe at the moment. Tall and still proud, their walls might have been peeling layer by layer, but no one could deny that their design and construction had been fine at one time. Many of them were so old I could see--past the layers of stucco and slate and underneath the molded plaster and carved cornices--bricks and half-timbers! Some of these stately homes had been just big barns! And had stood for hundreds of years! How beautiful they were. And what stories they could tell if they could speak. Most seemed to have had their faces lifted last somewhere around the '30s. Sure, that would be right. Before the second World War. When the world was jung. I wondered if they would be tearing those handsome structures down now that they were joining the modern world. Or would they have the sense to save them? It would be expensive. Yet one would never see their like again.

Snaking our way through the heat and noise, I noticed that there were no sidewalks. The cobblestones dropped off into a ditch right at the doorsteps. The streets were just too narrow for sidewalks. And yes, there were Quonset huts. Right at the outskirts of each town the things squatted--usually at the edge of a factory where a plume of black smoke rose from an ugly stack or two. The air was terrible--we were told it would be--and the lack of rain that summer turned the rivers to mud, and the dust was thick enough to chew. There seemed to be so many young men standing around with nothing to do. Perhaps the factories had laid them off. I saw old people hard at work in small gardens. What would happen if the young unemployed helped Granny make a bigger garden while the sun shone so brightly and the lads had their shirts off?

We had pulled over to eat lunch. Overhead, a NATO jet streaked by. Russian soldiers, looking sad and terribly young, passed by in a long line of tanks. "How do you suppose they feel now?" I asked Terence. "I think the East Germans probably spit on them," he said.

Leipzig had to be the Queen of the Terrible Streets. Just when I'd get comfortable again after avoiding a bottomless pothole, some sneaky trolley car would loom out of nowhere behind me and I'd have to choose among greasy tracks that looked like iron spaghetti in front of my tire, and pray I wasn't on the very path the clanging monster behind me was going to take! Hadn't anyone been on Cobblestone Replacement detail during the Communist years?

We really enjoyed seeing the Art Museum in this old city. A lot of very captivating Lucas Cranach paintings I'd never even seen in my art history books. But then, a walk around the small shopping center proved disappointing when there was absolutely nothing to buy. They just weren't ready for tourists, yet.

We played an exasperating game of "Ring Around the Rosie," trying to call friends in Berlin so we'd have a place to stay when we got there. The telephone at the campground no longer worked, the lady in the office told us, because it was full of coins and could not take any more. (We wouldn't have that problem in Los Angeles.) She said the phone company had to come and empty it out. We surmised that it had been like that for weeks. Maybe ever since Die Wall came down over a year ago. Showing unusual concern for others--for a person so recently Communist, the woman further explained that although there were phone booths on the way back into the city, they were only set up for local calls--only for Leipzig! Berlin might have been on the moon to these poor people. How to keep 'em down on the farm... We finally discovered a phone at the Bahnhof--the main train station--although it was a neat trick trying to race to one that worked, when everybody else in the city wanted it too! We might have saved ourselves the trouble. We were unable to connect with anyone on our list even after losing several precious coins down the neck of the nasty contraption. Depressed, we headed back to the campground to pack.

On the road the next day, Terence remembered a biker he met in Copenhagen the day I sat in the library while he toured the Carlsberg Brewery. The guy lived in Berlin. Terence found a phone that worked, just as we came to the outskirts of the city, and called him. We were told by his roommate that the fellow was way down in Munich partying hearty at the Oktoberfest but that we were welcome to come on over anyway. We pulled onto the congested autobahn and sat through stop-go traffic all the way into the city where the madness of too many cars in an outdated and over-populated Berlin made Manhattan look like a prairie. I was petrified trying to follow Terence through the mayhem as he kept changing lanes and his mind about where we should get off. A man in a delivery van leaned out his window and screamed obscenities at me--probably because of my frantic weaving around cars to keep up with Terence. I didn't exactly understand the language, true, but I was pretty sure it wasn't a greeting of welcome.

At last we arrived at the small apartment where we met Carsten, the roommate. He was as warm and friendly as could be, and on his way to visit friends for the weekend. He hoped we wouldn't mind too much being in the apartment alone. Hoop-la! Our luck was changing. For three days we played around Berlin. The huge Gallery of Art was divine. Sensa-tional. And...eat your heart out, Prado, free! We gorged. There were all sorts of other free museums around too. Even in the newly opened East sector, where the museum-goers in each room were outnumbered by the aged security staff--glaring from their chairs and shrinking away to dust in their faded uniforms.

Chapter Forty-Eight

DRESDEN

AFTER BERLIN, our good fortune continued. I wrote in my journal on Monday, Sept. 23rd that if I were a true pessimist, I would be able to find all sorts of reasons why our next camping spot wasn't perfect. We were on the outskirts of the city of Dresden where everybody hated Americans. It was night. Some one will see our lights and report us to the authorities, I thought. Maybe this time the ticks will fall from the trees and invade our brains. Maybe a rabid fox. The truth was, I couldn't believe our fantastic luck. We had rolled toward Dresden from Berlin in a fierce wind for about four exhausting hours. It was dark, and we couldn't find the campground the guide book promised was there. Terence was traveling very slowly looking for a road off the highway into the trees but I felt certain it was a study in futility. Every road leading into the forest on both sides was of a very fine white sand--making traction impossible for him pulling that heavy load and I sure didn't want to ride over the stuff. Also, there'd be no privacy. There was no underbrush to conceal us--just miles and miles of skinny pines in every direction. Finally, we stopped in a reststop where T. asked somebody where any sort of campground was, and as we turned off the highway to look for one someone had mentioned, Terence spotted a dirt road leading into a thicker wood and on impulse, yanked the trailer on to it with me trailing along behind with my heart in my mouth. The road curved and then went up a little hill and then down into a pretty little meadow. Our headlights shown on a ring of white birch trees circling around a spot that seemed to be waiting for us. The grass was thick but short and firm enough to ride over and we couldn't have been more surprised if there had been a banner saying WELCOME, GAIL AND TERENCE!

I made dinner and we sat back and filled our lungs with the cool night air. We snuffed the lights and listened to the crickets in the grass around us. The wind high above had chased the clouds away from our sky roof and a full moon rising like a hot air balloon appeared over the trees to our left to join the stars already performing for our amusement. The higher it rose, the brighter the white trunks of the birches shown until it seemed they were made of neon. We snuggled up. As I became sleepier, I felt I had been placed in a cozy nest made of white straw and the soft rustling of the tree tops that framed the sparking sky set me to dreaming my favorite dream of flying like a bird, floating above land and sea and...

Dresden. Oh, poor, sad Dresden. An example of the best in man and the basest. We rode through the city snarls of traffic and dirt to get to the other side where we had read the municipal campground was situated. Leering hulls of bombed-out buildings and rubble in the streets told of the horrors the British and my own countrymen had inflicted upon them. Yet unlike Berlin in the west, so little had been done to reconstruct and rebuild. It might have happened yesterday. We were glad to get out of the city. There were no signs at all to show us the way and we had to keep stopping to ask. Only westerners now could afford the campgrounds which once were practically free to the people of Eastern Germany, and who wanted westerners staying here anyway? For once nobody thought we were German. May you lose your way and leave us alone!, every face said.

The sour woman in the office wanted ten dollars for us to stay the night. We gasped. Obviously, these brand new capitalists hadn't learned the basic rules to making themselves rich. First you earn it, then you charge it. No one else was around and the place was a dump. There was no bargaining. The news that she was charging more than they do in West Germany didn't move her. She obviously loathed us and it was disturbing. We turned around, deciding to go back to the city for a quick look and then get the hell out of there. Back in the grim town center, we toured the hull of the Cathedral and dutifully read the pleas for funds to rebuild, that had thoughtfully been written in English. The Art Museum, which contained treasures hidden from the bombs, was five bucks each to get in, so we had to pass. We climbed on the bikes and rode east.

We spent the night on a hill, still in Germany, overlooking the border to Czechoslovakia. That country had been recently liberated too, but we didn't know what to expect, and could still remember the first time we crossed over when we were forced to change way too much money into their currency, and the rules about camping "wild" were strict and enforced. Even if they didn't like us, the East Germans would leave us alone when we camped in their forests. What would the Czechs do?

Chapter Forty-Nine

CZECHOSLOVAKIA: THINGS WERE CHANGING

WE HEADED TOWARD DOKSANY, Czechoslovakia. The crossing that morning had been a breeze. Nobody manning the border at all, as far as we could see. What a difference from two years before! We stopped to take pictures of an enormous monastery castle complex that had appeared like magic in front of us on the way into Prague. It looked 17th century, and no one had done any maintenance in at least the last couple of hundred years, but even though it was tumble-down and chickens roosted in the walls, it was still quite beautiful. Lining the street out front were several stalls selling home produce and used items and whatever these poor people could dig out of the attics--from framed pictures of grandma to broken farm tools. The people seemed more cheerful than when we'd been there before, and if I'd had any money to spend and any room to stash anything, I might have looked closer. We knew they were desperate for dollars and Deutch-marks and I thought it was rather a shame that westerners must be ripping them off by taking the family heirlooms from these people. Ah, but I probably would have had less conscience if I had had more money, and these brand new Capitalists seemed so happy to be free at last to sell whatever they chose to whomever...who was I to find fault with any of it?

We began to see people smiling at our rig again. It was a good feeling. Especially friendly were the young men in various types of uniforms. Two years ago they were staring with slack jaws and frowns. Now they seemed to be thinking, "Say, I might have one of those motorbikes someday!"

Chapter Fifty

THE KOTVA SPERTKLUB PRAHA ALIAS CAMPING BRANIK AGAIN

EVEN A FAX MACHINE now in the office. Things have really changed. No sign of the Russian supervisor this time. Price of a spot on their muddy river bank up to thirteen dollars so we won't stay long. We went into the city for our favorite dark beer and paid another triple price. They told us the opera tickets were out of sight for the Czech people, now, but there were plenty of tourists to buy them. And we saw the hordes of westerners in the streets of Prague. In the old town everybody was selling something, card tables on the streets, even out of the back of cars--desperate to get enough of that tourist money before winter set in and the cash cows all went home.

We were awakened early in the morning by a persistent fellow in a baker's white coat. We stuck our head out of the tent and he shoved three small but fragrant pastries under our noses and asked for 24 crowns (80 cents). They were marvelous. Up at the wash house I saw yet another example of the new market economy at work. Pasted all over the walls of the toilet cubicle were advertisements (in English!) about restaurants and places to shop. Very enterprising. What was next? Jolly jingles piped in the shower?

Terence got quite a blow that evening. He rode into town by himself to present Ludovic Balaz's father with some new strings for his violin. When he finally got an answer to his knock at the restaurant door--where two years before we had heard Mr. Balaz play that marvelous gypsy music--he was told by the people in the restaurant that the man had died. They had just buried him the day before! Terence came back ashen. He took a long pull from the Apfelcorn bottle. Later, we visited his son Ludovic and his wife. They seemed touched that we cared. It was such a rotten deal that his father never got much of a chance to play his instrument as a free man. Never even got to use some decent strings...

September 27th found us back with the Petzes in Wolkersdorf. Ten days repairing the bikes and running various annoying errands in Vienna that all seemed to take hours when they should have been taking minutes. Terence getting his slides mishandled again at Kodak...

At least we got to know the Tom MacCallums better. Lovely people. They had us to dinner one night and we were introduced to a real Scottish steak and kidney pie. Loved the steak part. A "Tipsy Laird" for dessert. Heavenly. That Sunday we went with them and their two small boys to the Kaiser's castle gardens in the heart of Vienna. Jolly good time.

Finally on Thursday, October 10, we made it out of the Vienna area around four in the afternoon. Much later than we'd planned but it couldn't be helped thanks to the usual hang-ups with film and motorcycle batteries. It was dark by the time we made it into Hungary, and the cheap sodium street lamps gave me a headache as I peered through the dusty orange gloom trying to follow the bouncing trailer lights ahead of me. We made it to Györ where the Campground officials were not thrilled to let us in so late, then the next morning, early, we rode out of that depressing city and realized that we needed gas. Mile after mile and no station and we knew we had a good 50 miles to go before we reached Budapest. We pulled off to think. I took some peanuts out of my tank bag and handed some to Terence. The wind was so strong it tore the shells off practically without our help. This was supposed to be the main highway to Budapest. We couldn't believe there were no gas stations. We had seen restaurants along the road--no doubt complete with singing gypsies, but not one petrol station. We realized that we hadn't been very smart. Other people must have learned to fill up at the borders. Terence took my bike and rode off to find some gasoline. I brought out my journal from the tank-bag and wrote. The day was bleak and gray. Dry corn stalks all around for miles. The people's collectives. The air grew colder and I smelled rain. Terence made it back before the drops began falling and he had found gas. We shared it and then put on our rain gear and rode to Budapest.

We had heard about a couple of campgrounds in Budapest being better than Hars Hegy, where we had stayed before, so we followed the Info

Tourist signs for miles around the city until they ended at a hotel! The lady at the desk said we would have to stay there because in the last few months, the campgrounds had all gone up to $35 a night! We almost fainted. We left her at her rather seedy hotel and found a campground in the south of the city on the road south--to Yugoslavia. It was all but deserted due to the lateness of the season, but still open and we were told it would be about ten bucks--three times what we paid in Budapest two years ago--and just not within our budget at this time. But at least it proved the old hag at the hotel was lying. We decided to move on and kiss off seeing Budapest again. We had loved that city so much two years earlier and we wanted to keep our good memories intact.

It was around four in the afternoon when we found ourselves riding through a very unusual-looking town called KecskemŽt. Lots of new paint on exotic architecture and even a handy Tourist Info office! Just before the door closed in our face, the ladies told us of a nearby campground so we relaxed. A group of boys who had been slobbering over the rig while we were in the Tourist office offered to take us to the Post Office so T. could mail some homework and then they pointed out a market so we could get some provisions. After some twists and turns, we located the campground and the young lady behind the desk turned out to be witty and friendly and only asked for four dollars a night from us, and we decided to stay awhile.

We stayed four days. Terence caught up on his Law studies. I washed clothes and wrote and read. We toured the charming city, and ooed and ahhed over the exotic Hungarian/Jugenstile/Peter Max architecture. This was a town that knew how to be nice to tourists--even if those tourists were almost all Hungarian and had little money to spend. There were gypsies selling needlework and crocheting but they didn't press us. We peeked into the churches--a Catholic one, a Lutheran one and an Evangel-ican one. The huge, once-splendid Jewish synagogue had been turned into a museum for some rich man's collection of copies of Michelangelo's sculptures! Very weird. The "Bound Slave" was there, the "Pieta," even the "Lorenzo de Medici" tomb group. All in what looked suspiciously like plaster. I couldn't help wondering what had happened to the synagogue's previous congregation. I was afraid I knew.

Autumn camping is my favorite kind. There's usually less rain and the breeze is balmy and the leaves are gorgeous and smell wonderful. There are fewer people camping and those that are still at it by October don't have children to chase around, they might be retired or young adventurers and have usually been to several exotic places. They often have fascinating stories to tell and make great beer buddies. If they are shy because they don't speak English, Terence soon puts them at ease using their own language--whether he knows it or not! He's so amazing. The other campers at KecskemŽt were mostly Western German, and we all had great times comparing notes on what they thought of Hungary and even Eastern Germany! The tales of the war in Yugoslavia were getting scarier and even though the east part of that country was supposedly free of conflict and were desperate for tourists, our new friends said it would be a good idea to stay out of that country for awhile. Worried, we wrote long letters to our loved ones.

Chapter Fifty-One

ARRESTED IN YUGOSLAVIA

AFTER A VERY HOT and sticky day of riding, we crossed the border into Yugoslavia. We found an office to change our money in, and learned from a German tourist in the parking lot that we could do much better on the black market. The trick was in finding someone one could trust not to report you to the authorities!

We rode into the setting sun as people in the vast cornfields around us worked at cutting and bundling the dry stalks. The standing bundles reminded me of Halloween and growing up in the country. Again my senses were assailed with the divine smell of burning leaves and corn stalks and turned earth, and the sense of flying through the wind--that being on a motorcycle can give you. How I wished I could have preserved that feeling.

We were again staying off the main autostrada--not just to save the toll money, but to get a better look at the real country. The road surfaces weren't nearly as bad as we were led to expect, but there were hazards. Chickens, dogs, people seemed to appear out of nowhere. As the farmers and their families began to come home in the dusk, we noticed there were very few tractors. Whole groups of dusty, tired-looking people passed us-- sitting in a cart drawn by a skinny old horse or two. No lights on the carts, so as it got dark, I began to worry about hitting them--as there were no streetlights either!

Despairing of finding anything resembling a campground (Didn't anybody want to make any money?), we finally pulled into a cement factory lot by a river just outside of the village of Becej. During the night it rained. We tumbled out and hurriedly put on the tarp because our tent was becoming so threadbare it just was no protection anymore.

At 5:30 a.m., we yanked on our boots and made coffee so we could be out of there before the factory workers showed up for work. We were too late. Men were standing around in clumps staring at us as if they'd seen their first spaceship. I refused to panic. Besides, I was hungry and who knew when we could stop again. I poured some ghastly choco-puff rice substitute cereal we'd found in Hungary into a couple of bowls and we stood around wolfing it down. Terence's old wooden camp chair given him by a sweet old fellow in Hastings, England, had finally given up the ghost. We were hoping to find something cheap to take its place in this country. Yeah, right. Mine was all wet so I joined him in standing and drinking the welcome cup of coffee before we headed out of the slimy swamp to the road.

We were stopped after a bit by a police barricade. They asked to see our passports and wanted to know when we had come into the country. When we told them we were just passing through, they let us go.

As we rode south, we began to notice the long lines of cars waiting for the gas stations to open. Some men were pushing cars and trucks into the lines. We stopped to ask when they thought the stations would open and they said maybe six hours! We moved on, a little concerned now, because the thought of being stranded in a country at war was not funny at all.

The campground we'd been heading for in Belgrade was closed and by this time we were becoming anxious about our own fuel situation, so we decided to get on the main toll road where all the rich tourists and businessmen would be driving--in hopes that we might find a station open. The mile-long line at the first open station we came to on the toll road worried us quite a bit, but fortunately, although we did have to pay a toll, the next one had a much shorter line and no one at all at the UNLEADED pump! Blessing the Biker Gods, we filled up both bikes plus two huge plastic jerry-cans that Terence very wisely thought to buy when we were in Czeckoslovakia. Those big ugly containers saved our bummies. Without them, we might be there still.

Greatly relieved, we got off the autoroute at the next opportunity and finding a grassy knoll, pulled off the road to have lunch. Stretching our legs a bit, we strolled down the road to have a look at two strange wreaths we'd noticed when we had passed them earlier. They were apparently memorials to the dead; two separate car accidents had occurred at the same spot, and the custom in this country was to erect an elaborate display at the place of death and then just leave it there to wither away and fall apart. We were fascinated. We had seen markers at such tragic spots in many of the countries we'd visited, but nothing on this scale. A kind of easel held the wreath, with a table spread before it. The life history of the deceased was placed in the middle of the wreath, complete with his picture and encased in plastic so it could be read by the passersby. Various offerings were on a neat white tablecloth on the table--flowers in a vase, opened bottles of Coke and beer, candles in a small soup can, sweets, cups of espresso--that sort of thing. Not a bad idea for awhile, I suppose. However, when a couple of weeks go by-- maybe a month, the stuff looks truly macabre. The wreaths turn brown and lose whole chunks, and the gay plastic flowers wired into them fade in the sun to a greasy gray. The liquid evaporates in the Coke and beer bottles and closer inspection reveals masses of tiny bodies of flies and bees who had crawled in for their last taste. The candles in the soup can melt in the hot sun and resemble large white worms oozing down the sides of the can and onto the cloth. Yuk. Maybe it's all part of the plan. To remind the living that everything decays and one better grab life by the short hairs? Probably not. Around this humorless land, the message is probably more like "This is what will happen to you if you don't take that curve slower."

The day was sunny and warm and the side roads we were taking afforded us some very appealing views of the countryside. As the sun began to set and turn the cornfields to crimson, we stopped at a particularly photogenic location on a little rise and took some pictures of some really fantastic haystacks--all hunched together like a huddle of giants. A woman came out of her farmhouse nearby and let us know that we could not take pictures there. Terence was putting new infrared film into his camera at that moment--sitting on the ground with his arms in his black changing bag. He decided she was just some grump and ignored her. I was across the street giving some old gent a Polaroid picture of our rig because he had been kind enough to allow me to take his picture. It seemed to amuse him. After we got on the bikes and down the road about a hundred yards, we noticed a sign in several languages that indeed said "No Photograph Taking," which we thought very odd because like why not?

A couple of miles later, a police car pulled us over--blue lights flashing. Soon, two more cop cars joined him and they all indicated that we should follow them to the local station in Kraijevo. They understood none of Terence's many new languages.

Four hours later we emerged, sadder (and hungrier) but wiser. Our crime being that we had taken pictures too close to a train tunnel or trestle or something (which we never saw), and as the country was at WAR, we were turned in by the ever-watchful citizenry and then interrogated by both the local police and the military--after they finally found an inter-preter--a lovely young lass who soon liked us and was very sorry about the inconvenience. We were asked over and over what we saw and took pictures of, and everybody was obviously very disappointed at our short and boring list concerning haystacks and horse-carts. After going around in circles for hours and having some "face" to save, no doubt, it was decided that we would be released if we either (1) exposed the film in our cameras in their presence or (2) left it with them so they could send it to the lab in Belgrade to be developed, whereupon the military could have a look at it and then cut out the "offending" frames, and then someone would presumably send it on to our Embassy in Belgrade whereupon someone else was to sent it to our address in California! Sure...

We agreed to comply with the former idea. At least we pretended to. "The nerve of those morons," Terence mumbled. He was not about to relinquish a single slide. Interestingly, in four hours of questioning, no one had asked us how many cameras we had. Nor did anyone think to look in our saddlebags or tankbags! We were allowed to go out to the bikes, which were being guarded by a bashful young policeman who hadn't been filled in on what we were supposed to be doing out there. He looked away as we took out our cameras--Terence switching cameras right in front of the lad and putting in a fresh roll of infrared and then shooting at nothing to make it look like pictures had been taken...Then we walked back into the station and in front of our interrogators, with doleful expressions, took out and exposed the film. I had only taken the one shot of the old man so it was no big deal giving up my roll. Strangely, the Chief Inspector seemed embarrassed and apologetic later. Hah! Wait 'til he finds out the Croats will win the war after Terence sends them his exclusive photos of the clas-sified haystacks!

It was dark and very cold when we were finally released, and we asked the Inspector, through the interpreter, where we might be allowed to camp for the night. He conferred with the military who conferred with the desk cops and they all decided we could be allowed to camp by the river just out of town, and we were given directions on how to get there. Terence thought to ask if they thought any more policemen or citizens would be stopping us, and they assured us that it wouldn't happen again. We were safe to proceed all the way to Greece, the interpreter said they said.

So we walked out of the station, thanked the kid watching the rig and climbed aboard and rode out of there, leaving a goodly audience standing around, probably hoping for the entertainment of a public flogging at the very least.

The spot by the river was the city dump--which was insulting at first until we realized every place by the river was a dump of some kind. The thoughtful police had probably picked one of the cleaner areas for us and we should be grateful. We pulled the trailer close to the underside of the bridge to make it less conspicuous and I made us some dinner. We were just cleaning off the dishes when a patrol car came bumping down the dirt road. We stood frozen as the bright lights blinded us. Two cops we hadn't seen before--one in a trench coat, one in uniform--emerged and walked up to us. Again the language problem. Terence tried Esperanto. They demanded our passports. After a while we understood they were asking about the whereabouts of the third member of our party. "What third member?" Terence asked in German. "The man that rides that motorcy-cle," the guy in the trench-coat snapped in Serbian as he pointed to my Ascot. Terence pointed to me. "She rides that motorcycle," he said. They looked at me. Then at each other. Do the Americans think we are fools?, their looks said. I put up my hand for their attention and then very slowly so they wouldn't think I was reaching for a grenade or something, I got out my International driver's license from my jacket pocket and showed them the stamp allowing me to ride a motorcycle. They held their flash-light on it, turning it this way and that and studying my photo on the first page. Then they began to laugh. They laughed so hard they had to sit down but there was only my little camp chair so the trench coat sat, while the uniform put his hand on his pal's shoulder and tears streamed down his face. Terence and I forced a smile, hoping they'd go home and although they seemed to want to stay and talk about it some more, there was that language barrier. They gave us a wave of dismissal and still chuckling, went back to their car and drove away. I told Terence he was slipping. Look at the trouble he'd gotten us into. He'd already been in Yugoslavia a day and a half--and he hadn't yet learned to speak Serbo-Croatian!

We forced ourselves to get up at dawn again. Still, we were the late ones. Figures in the fog were crossing over our bridge, as I tried to find a place to pee-pee underneath. Silent and shabby, the gray faces looked down at us without interest. Others emerged from the paths along the river, passing us without a word or a glance. Each one looked so sad. They were all headed in one direction. Probably another cement factory.

We packed up and warmed up the bikes. Terence gunned the Wing pulling that heavy trailer up the sharp embankment and over the curb to the street--narrowly missing the zombies now in great numbers like a gray tide, oozing their way across the bridge. I followed, slipping here and there in the muddy ruts because I was afraid of hitting someone if I rode the bike as fast as I needed to to get up there without losing control. Happily, I made it and caught up with him after a bit and began to feel a nice warm sense of freedom to have put that nasty bit of adventure behind us.

We rode for a couple of hours without making very good time because the roads were bad and too narrow to pass when we'd get stuck behind some black exhaust-belching vehicle or herd of goats or whatever. We stopped to look at an old monastery and while I sat on my bike, Terence snapped a couple of pictures of the place and then we went on. Coming down from some mountains, we joined a line at a gas station that seemed open for business and while we stood around, a car came to screeching halt beside us and we were again told to follow it to the local police station! Either taking pictures of a monastery are also forbidden, or someone was following us to see if we took our cameras out again. In any case, we followed the group of uniformed men into a very shabby building and were told to sit on a bench in a dingy hallway and wait while they handed our passports around to everybody who could write or use one finger on a typewriter to copy it all down. Lots of Important Telephone Calls were made. Someone was determined to get a promotion.

We weren't afraid this time, just angry. We were beginning to see this happening over and over as we tried to get to the Greek border. Terence was near to breaking some heads. This time there was no interpreter and no one smiled. I stood up and walked down the hall to a large window where I could see people reading our passports over and over and typing the information laboriously on archaic machines. They looked up and saw me. I tried to look them all in the eye, one by one, in my best patrician manner--as in: "What is the meaning of this!," but it was a little tough in that I probably looked as if I'd spent the night in the city dump, which of course I had.

After two hours, we were told that we must not take any more pictures in Yugoslavia. They handed back our passports and then one of them got in his car to escort us through the crowded streets to the edge of town. There, he waved goodbye to us real friendly-like and I found myself wondering why weren't all those men at the front?!

We rode fast after that, anxious to get away and to clear our heads of the ugliness of the recent experiences. We had about four more hassles--"security" checks--while oily-faced officers of many uniforms and descriptions searched through my saddlebags--especially the one with my underwear in it. One even asked me if I carried a gun! Terence was asked if he had any drugs once, but incredibly, nobody ever asked him to open his saddlebags! Just mine. The brains of the outfit!

We passed through some gorgeous country. Mountainous with rushing rivers and giant oddly-formed rocks. New England-style autumn leaves and fragrant tilled fields. We passed a dead cow on its back in a shallow river, bloated with its feet up in the air. Somewhere in the Islamic south a skinned goat was drying high up on a telephone pole. Terence said it might be an advertisement for a local butcher shop. (We took no pictures, however). And everywhere pieces of mangled cars. Sometimes a fender or a door was used for a gate or fence. I even saw pieces of cars cleverly used as terraces to hold back erosion in front of hillside homes.

The terrain became hot, dry and flat. We kept passing men wearing embroidered little caps, on their knees by the side of the road, praying to Allah--with their empty gas cans at their elbows. Some of them had their wives and children sitting on a ancient tractor waiting. If a truck came in view, they'd jump up and wave their cans in front of it, trying to get it to stop. Once, when we had stopped to check the map, three urchins about 8, 10 and 12, ran barefooted across the field and up to us to beg. First they wanted our stuffed bear mascot we had tied to Terence's antenna. No way. Then they mimed for anything sugary. Being a mean old bitch (and slightly terrified), I tried to ignore them, but Terence thought I should give them the rest of the candy bar he knew I had in my tank bag. I dug it out and gave it to the biggest child, thinking of course he'd share it with the younger children. Nice work, Gail. There was a scuffle between the three like hungry seagulls. After stuffing the whole portion into his mouth, the oldest boy walked to my bike--with me sitting on it--and shoved his hand into the tank bag! Without thinking, I cuffed him on the side of the head and yelled "GET OUT OF THERE!" He did.

Skopje was a place we had hoped to explore, but it would have to wait. We crawled through the snarled traffic and muddy streets and were stopped by the police again just at the outskirts of the city. This time one of the officers spoke English and as he could see how anxious we were to get to the border, he didn't even look at our passports, but waved us on. We began to breath easier. Night came upon us too early as usual and we just had too many miles to go to reach Greece, so we had to find one more place in Yugoslavia to camp. We found a new section of the highway being built parallel to our road, so we rolled onto it and prayed the dark would shield us from anyone in authority. There was hardly anyone using the main road anyway this time of night and we planned to get up early. The recent rains had turned the newly dug road into a quagmire of mud. Trying to make dinner as my boots sank and made horrible sucking noises when I pulled them out, was something new in the Culinary experience!

Up before the sun rose, we looked up from our coffee cups to see a rather rustic fellow walk out of the thick fog near us, pushing a wheel-barrow with a small saw inside it. He kept his eyes straight ahead. Before we rode away later, that same man appeared with his wheelbarrow full of young tree branches and logs. We reasoned that that must be why the whole south of the country was denuded of trees. We wondered where he'd found this one and how far he was going to have to walk to get home. What were all the people going to do for heat when there were no more trees? And their winter was just beginning. With a shudder, I packed away the last of the kitchen stuff and putting my shoulder to the trailer, helped Terence drag the heavy thing out of the muck it had sunk into and soon we were on our way.

About eleven in the morning the fog started to burn off--its icy white fingers clutching the mountain tops behind us as if it still wanted to try to snatch us back from freedom.

Chapter Fifty-Two

JUNE, 1992. GREECE

HOO-RAY! We were finally in Greece. Was it just our imagination that the air suddenly became warmer as we rode from the border? We stopped at the first little grocery store we came to after changing our money and bought bread and cheese for lunch. Then, because it was the only place with any shade trees, we parked at the nearest cemetery to eat. We had become very fond of cemeteries due to the lack of privacy of late. As we began to relax, a car came off of the sweltering road and skidded to a stop in a cloud of dust. A young man jumped out and walked briskly down the path to a grave. He seemed to adjust something in front of the headstone-altar thing and then he left just as quickly. After our repast, we ambled down the path ourselves to look around. All the graves had little window boxes where one could change the contents around on shelves. Like Yugoslavia, there were lots of half-filled bottles, often soft drinks of every kind. One jar in common with all the other offering places puzzled us. It had a top screwed on and what looked like cooked cauliflower sat in some liquid inside. I still don't know what it was. I never asked anybody.

We arrived in Thessalonniki on October 18th. After rolling into the ancient, crowded city through narrow streets clogged with polluting and battered old cars, we finally found a place to park. Terence needed to go into the local Taekwon-Do studio and talk with the master there, Mr. George Stylianides. I waited outside and guarded the rig. T. had decided that this place would be a good place to stay the winter because he could probably find work teaching at the large gym Mr. Stylianides owned and at the same time, study with other high-ranking Taekwon-Do masters in preparation for his next level of rank. But we would need a place to stay inexpensively for a few months. Terence was told they would see what they could do for us. Then we rode out of the city to the only open camp-ground at Agia Triada. They wanted eight bucks a night which wasn't too bad, except we knew we couldn't keep it up and besides, it was 20 miles of solid traffic jams to get to the city.

While we lingered there, the weather seemed to be apologizing for its nasty temper of the weeks earlier. Balmy and breezy, it was just the way we liked it best, and the Aegean Sea sparkled nearby and the calico-colored leaves of the poplar trees above us drifted down and lay about the muddy ground smelling luscious. We were in no hurry to leave. There were no other campers in the hundreds of spaces around us--too late in the season, the manager told us. A sweet little black and white kitten adopted us and we were a family.

For the first three days it was very pleasant. We made forays into the city for food and Terence looked for a job. Saturday night, the night turned hot and windless. Mosquitoes began to feast. Terence's foot began to hurt for some reason. As we dragged ourselves out of the trailer-bed in the morning after a pretty sleepless night, the air began to move around us and in just a few short hours, it had turned into a full-on Mistral, Greek-style. The wind began to shred our poor trailer-tent and tempers. We had tried to save money by not putting up our main tent which they would charge extra for here, so the dirt and sand began to get into absolutely everything--we were chewing it on our bread and drinking it with our coffee. We took a walk along the edge of the sea to cool off and another stray cat followed us back. Oh no! Please, Lord. Not more starving animals. I went into the block house that was the Ladies's restroom and washed four pairs of jeans by hand in the small sink. I was grateful for something to keep my mind off the wind and hungry cats.

The dust storm raged for four days. Then it turned cold. Rain then, and lightning and thunder. I had never seen so much dramatic weather changes in one week in my life. The two cats moved in. By Thursday, we couldn't take it any more and put up the big tent and paid the extra fee. The cats were delighted. Terence and I felt much better, too.

We introduced ourselves to the top man in the local American High School in the city. He was very nice and said he'd try to find us a place to stay and said anytime we'd like to be guest speakers for his classes, we'd be more than welcome. However, there would be no money in it. Georgio at the gym hadn't come up with anything either. Of course, why should he? I was beginning to feel like a homeless bum again. Let's face it. I was a homeless bum again. We began to panic as the weather became colder. I was reminded of the same situations earlier in the trip, in Toulouse and Palermo. No prospects, little money and winter approaching. This was even tougher because we couldn't speak the language. Back at the campground Terence tried to study. I knew it was hard on him when I worried, so I tried to stay out of his way.

The wind howled. As I made the trek to the Ladies's room, I noticed how gorgeous the full moon looked again. Only this time, instead of being a harvest moon, it looked more like a snow-ball up there between the swaying trees. The campground was painted in black and silver and I could see that it would be the last night for any leaves left on the Poplars. I could hear the waves crash on the beach. Just a few days ago, the sea was an emerald green. Now, during the day, everything seemed to be in icy shades of gray under the thin sunlight. Didn't anyone have a little shack we could hole up in for the winter? I wanted us to go farther south but Terence reminded me it would cost too much to take the whole rig and so far we had no place to store anything. Also he wanted to practice his Taekwon-Do with the Thessaloniki black belts. I understood, but golly, that city was unappealing. After several earthquakes throughout the centuries, cheap and fast housing had gone up everywhere, ugly concrete blocks of apartments with little or no plan. Constantly snarled traffic in alleyways that should have been widened before the buildings went up but hadn't and now it was too late and everyday more cars. No room for sidewalks of course, and the masses of pedestrians had to take their chances moving around automobiles that enclosed drivers with nothing but their blasting horns to relieve their frustrations at not being able to move faster through the maze.

The days pass. Terence studies. I am given things to type for him--to keep me busy. Still no word of a shelter for the winter. Weather blows, drips, fogs.

Things livened up a bit when two Austrians, Alex and Verena and two Brits, Amanda and Adam, and an Aussie named Steven Bell moved in all in the same day. Because it was so cold and we had the only big tent, everybody popped in for a spot of tea and warmth by the stove, only it was more like a spot of cheap ouzo and wine. I was glad for the diversion and sat like the Lady of the Manor with the two cats on my lap while we all swapped stories and complained about the weather.

The young Austrians invited us to dinner. They had been only away from home a week and expected to travel a year in their van which was already breaking down! Terence took a look underneath and did what he could to help--mostly in experienced advice, but the lack in Greece of repair shops and auto parts was not in their favor. They would go on anyway. Ah, the courage of innocence...

Dinner was a sort of hash--made from wurst and potatoes. They had also bought two large wine bottles, one a Greek retsina which tasted like tree sap and the other a cloyingly sweet red. With ouzo between.. Gasp...Certainly the best way to keep me sober. The Greek taste in booze surprised me. Was this what was served at all those Bacchanals? Wine was supposedly invented here. It must have become a lost art.

That afternoon we had discovered a dead German Shepherd in the wash-up room. Foam covered its mouth and various fluids streamed from its inert body. It was a large dog and a pretty horrible sight. We all complained to the Reception desk, who promised it would be cleaned up by morning. It wasn't. I began to wonder if the whole pack of stray dogs that I was constantly shooing from our camp, might be infected with rabies. The manager was sure it was no doubt poisoned by the stuff they leave out for the rats. As I wrote about it in my journal, our little black and white kitten lay curled up in my lap purring and truly believing she had found a good home forever. The other one, a pale beige and white and black calico--the color of the fallen leaves around us--licked herself on the tent floor. Her tail had been badly mangled by what? A cruel boy, a dog, a car wheel? It oozed and bled. The plight of my little furry friends broke my heart. It was hard not to imagine the fate of those two cats and all the others we had seen on the trip. Terence said we could have a hundred when we returned home.

October 31, 1991--Halloween for the Homeless. We had heard from Georgio about an apartment for rent for around eight dollars a day near his home on the other side of Thessaloniki, and we were desperate enough to go for it. It too was inconveniently far away from the city and we had hoped for something cheaper. But the cats were driving us crazy, several more were scratching at the tent walls for food and warmth, and the mud on everything from the rains had helped remove the bloom from Paradise. It had taken the manager three days to remove the dog-- and only after Terence shook them up in the reception office with tales of animal corpses blowing apart from their own bacterial gases and worse. Somebody finally phoned someone to bring a truck and remove it. And just in time too, because that afternoon a Swiss camper drove in and spent the rest of the daylight washing his very large RV with a small rag and several buckets of hot, soapy water. He would have disliked having a dead dog to step over in order to draw his water, we decided.

Trying to "skirt" the sprawling city of Thessaloniki to get to its west side was a mistake. Still, after two extra hours of getting lost, we found the village of Methoni, a rather sad-looking cluster of stucco houses on the Aegean, with a short strand obviously built up for summer tourists and which now, in the off-season, looked pretty shabby and forlorn. Small fishing boats lay about the dirty beach and appeared to have been there for years. If the stories about the pollution problems of this part of the Aegean were true, it would explain why nobody was ever seen fishing anymore. A small oily surf pushed by the wind slapped the sand leaving clusters of brown foam clinging to the black seaweed on shore. Terence and I found the small apartment building. It was a no-nonsense two-story structure obviously built for the tourist trade. The sign out in front only advertised

"Zimmers" and "Chambres," so we presumed the Greeks must spend their summers elsewhere.

We were shown into a freezing cubicle that was the kitchen and, without much ceremony, we paid the black-garbed woman for a month's stay. After she drove off in her car, the silence closed in and we walked into the tiny bedroom to part the curtains and look over the water below. We could see the dark strip of land across the bay which had been our old campground and were uncomfortably aware that we missed it and maybe should have brought the cats.

The rain came and stayed. We were glad to be inside, although the walls were so damp they wept all day and formed little puddles on the floor. The village seemed deserted. After forcing ourselves out for exercise and a change of scene now and then, we discovered a bakery and were happy to be able to buy fresh bread. Villagers who were standing inside the shop when we arrived, stared and looked uncomfortable. The baker was positive we were German. We announced loudly that we were actually American. They didn't believe us. Lying Germans, their looks said.

Terence studied hard to get his "school year" over with in a hurry so we could figure out what to do next. I tried not to bother him but the cold and damp and depressing environment was getting me down. We were paying eight dollars a day to live in a tomb and trying to feel grateful to Georgio who found it for us. Who knows what he had to do to get the woman to open her doors for us out of season! But there was no hot water so it was very difficult to get the mud out of our clothes. Everything seemed greasy and cold water just couldn't do the job. Terence was taking his showers at the gym where he worked out twice a week. I took "Sailor baths" for awhile until I gave in and let him rig up that horrible black plastic bag in the bathroom into which I poured water that I had boiled on our camp stove. The bathroom was a tiny windowless closet with a chipped-marble floor that was like walking on ice cubes and always wet because every pipe in the room leaked--the sink, the toilet and the shower contraption which was nothing more than a hose on a hook with a shower nozzle. There was a drain-hole in the middle of the floor. During the summer, the water flowed past the solar panels on the roof and presumably came out at least warm, and one could shower in the tiny room and not only wash the body, but everything else--sink, toilet and floor. Instant janitor service. In the winter, those same solar panels had frost on them and so the water was icy and not very pleasant, but then, I reminded myself, the place was not supposed to be open in the winter.

We went into the big city for supplies twice a week--the same days Terence worked out with the black belts. We took the Ascot to save gas. It was a bumpy cold ride and took about forty-five minutes each way but it was a good way to break up the short winter days. We'd shop for groceries in the street markets in the morning, then eat our bread and cheese lunch in a park or down at the rather drab harbor and then while he worked out in the gym, I walked around the downtown area to study the architecture and peer in the windows of the shops, and usually wound up at the wonderful little American Library and read for a couple of hours. Thanks to a little white lie born of desperation about my "permanent" address, I was able to convince the librarian I was trustworthy enough to be allowed to borrow books. They saved my sanity.

We made up our minds to ride south at the end of the month and try to find work or at least a better place to live. The cold and damp was simply something Terence hadn't planned on when he had decided we could spend the winter this far north. We were so naïve. Wasn't Greece supposed to be sunny year 'round? Maybe he could find a viola job with an orchestra in Athens! Our spirits lifted, we began to enjoy our walks around our little village. We took pictures of the rotting fishing boats on the beach. The couple of small restaurants along the water that had remained open for the winter always had the same one or two customers. Maybe family members. Sunday afternoons was the day the place came alive, although just barely. Local families would have Sunday dinner at the two restaurants and the sound of their laughter floated up to our window and almost made the place seem like a real village. We found a few stunted berry bushes by the road above the village and T. helped me pick ones that looked edible and I hoarded them and cleaned them carefully from all the road dust and we had them on our oatmeal for breakfast once in a while as a great treat. We finally met a real Greek person who could speak English and he became a good friend. His name was Thanasis Pantelis and although he lived in the city, he rode his motorbike out to Methoni to check on his parent's summer house from time to time. We three were thrilled to find each other. He thought we were crazy to be doing what we were doing and he was extremely keen on doing the same one day. But sadly for him, it would have to wait because he was going to have to serve a term in the Greek army for a few years first.

One evening as we came out of grocery store in Thessaloniki, we noticed with dismay that my motorcycle was covered with bird-droppings! We looked up into the branches of the old tree overhead and were surprised to see hundreds of small birds--puffed up like fat little balls on the branches--sound asleep! Every one. Completely motionless. We couldn't see their heads which must have been tucked under their wings. They looked like soft brown tennis-balls strung along a wire. The really amazing thing was that this was in the heart of Thessaloniki--at a very busy intersection, where buses even stopped next to the tree and people shouted and the street and shop lights shown garishly bright. City birds. The pollution alone should have been enough to knock the poor tiny things to the ground. I couldn't get over it.

On December seventh, Terence got up first after a very cold night to listen to the Voice of America on our little short-wave radio. I could hear the announcer talking about a gasoline strike in Greece. "That's all we need!," I mumbled. I was staying in bed to keep warm and was debating how to get breakfast and stay in bed at the same time when he burst in the bedroom and ran to the windows and yelled, "Gail, you've got to see this!" I reluctantly pulled myself from the blankets and peered out the little clearing he'd made in the fogged-up window for me to see. He was looking through a taller one and whistling in amazement. Snow! My jaw dropped to the floor. Methoni was covered in snow and lots more was blowing past. I had to admit it was a beautiful sight. We looked at each other and both of us ran to the kitchen to look out at the motorcycles and trailer in the back of the building. We could hardly see them anymore. I ran to get my jacket and boots on and grabbed my Polaroid camera. In my haste, I slipped on the ice on the stairs and went down hard on my knee. It really hurt but after I found I could still walk, I just decided to forget about it. Long ago and far away was any place I could get it looked at. I suppose I cracked the knee-cap or something because it took two years and some months before I could stand any pressure on it in kneeling. Anyway, I limped back up the stairs and Terence made some coffee. I seem to remember we both made the decision at the same time. "Let's go home for Christmas!," we two babies screamed.

We spent the day making plans and as soon as the streets were cleared enough to get to the city, we found a travel agency that spoke English and bought the only plane tickets we could afford--Yugoslavian Air!! (Uh oh). The plan was to return to California for six months and then come back and just take the GoldWing to Turkey to save on gas money and then return to Greece and get my bike and zoom up through Bulgaria and Rumania and over to Vienna in time for the next Esperanto Convention.

Although it wasn't easy, we were able to convince Thanasis's parents that it was a terrific idea to keep our rig in their garage in Methoni while we were in California. They didn't seem thrilled, for some reason. Georgio and his family helped us get to the airport--with our usual luggage of several giant boxes, and we boarded the small plane that was to land in Yugoslavia to connect with a big one. Walking off the Greek plane in the Belgrade airport, we were ordered to stand in line with other foreigners so that our names could be checked by computer to see if we had ever been ARRESTED IN YUGOSLAVIA!!! Our worst nightmare. We thought this was it! But luck and the marvelous caprices of Yugoslavian technology prevailed and the computers were down and couldn't be fixed in time for the next flight so they let us go! Whee-ew!

Chapter Fifty-Three

WE RETURN TO GREECE

I̶T̶ ̶T̶O̶O̶K̶ It took us every bit of six months to get back again. We worked and saved our money and unsnarled various problems with the house and put my daughter back in charge again. Somehow I had developed a bone-spur on my heel, but I was sure it would go away after awhile.

We flew to Terence's dad's in Connecticut for a short visit. Had some difficulties getting insurance for the Gold Wing again, but by five o'clock on Saturday, May 30th, 1992, we were on the road to New York--T.'s folks driving us in their truck. At the airport, Terence struggled for thirty minutes trying to get us a flight. The latest news was that new sanctions were in place for Yugoslavia so none of their planes were flying. Our round-trip cheapies were duds. Somehow he softened somebody enough, that we were given two places on Kuwait Air, on a 747 to London. Olympia Air was then supposed to fly us to Athens and somehow on to Thessaloniki. We kissed the folks goodbye and found the last two seats on the plane. T.'s head fell on my lap for three hours and while he slept like a baby, I dozed fitfully.

This time Heathrow was a miserable experience. Very long corridors and too few signs to follow. Some of the automated walkways didn't work so we had to carry our heavy things miles. At least we were fortunate we spoke English. Anyone who didn't was simply out of luck. The British simply don't care. "Let'm learn English," is their motto. We were ferried by airport buses to other long corridors. The computer had lost us. We

showed them papers from the JAT folks in New York and out of the goodness of their hearts, we were allowed to "stand-by," and after a tiring hour,
we were told to find seats on some plane going to Athens. It was crowded,
but I found one in the smoking section and Terence another way in front.
Three Greek businessmen next to me were polite enough to ignore me but
smoked. Terence seemed to be in an even worse cramped space, but at
least he had cleaner air to breathe. I enjoyed a Bloody Mary after having
slept through the take off! Then, thanks to the generosity of the Greek
gentlemen, I also had a glass of white wine with dinner. Ahhh. And a great
meal it was. Four large slabs of smoked salmon, served cold, fresh and
with a juicy hunk of lemon. Then superfluous roast beef and little potato
balls and a delicious sauce. I pecked at the salad and wished I could take
such food with me.

We landed somewhere outside of Athens. The waiting room for
Olympia Air was crowded and smoky. JAT's demise had inconvenienced
everyone, and getting a new ticket for Thessaloniki was no easy task. After
some long hours, Terence wrangled two tickets on an AirBus just leaving
and we were fortunate to find the two last seats. On my immediate right
was a plump businessman, fingering his prayer beads.

The stewardesses had just started to serve some orange juice when the
plane started bouncing around alarmingly. They soon gave up and
buckled themselves in their seats and for much of the rest of the trip, the
plane was tossed around the clouds and I was really scared. Terence
squeezed my hand hard while my other neighbor rattled his beads. After
we landed, everyone clapped. We were loaded into buses and taken to the
terminal where nasty-looking soldiers glared at us from behind a glass
partition. They seemed to be looking for fugitives from justice. Perhaps for
the notorious American Haystack Photographers! We averted our faces.

It was close to midnight. We had our bags and boxes stacked high on
two trolleys and finally faced the problem we both had been dreading
since we first decided to go home for the winter. What do we do now?! We
had been so determined to get back, that we just figured things would
work out once we arrived one way or another. We hadn't felt we could
impose upon Giorgio again. We attempted to call Thanasis's parents to get
the key so we could get our rig out of their garage, but nobody at that end
could speak English and Thanasis himself might have been off somewhere
in the Army! We thought about sleeping in the Airport Waiting Room but
the fierce-looking soldiers were the only people around now that everyone
else had been picked up and we knew we looked very suspicious in our

un-Greekness and with all those heavy boxes on the trolley looking like they contained rifles.

We walked out of the Airport as if we had some purpose, and were looking for some grassy knoll to perhaps sleep upon when we noticed a city bus sitting at the curb with no one on it except the driver. Terence asked how much it would be to take us to the train station in downtown Thessaloniki and the guy said about a buck-fifty--for both of us! We grabbed it and rode about twenty minutes to the station and then we hauled all our stuff into the waiting room where we found a nice naugahyde seat to settle in for the night. But there's no rest for the wicked, as my mother used to say, and some self-important looking dude walked up to us when our heads began to nod, and told us in German that the room would be closed in a couple of hours and we couldn't stay the night. So after we were kicked out at 3 a.m., things got really uncomfortable. The foot that had begun to bother me in Santa Barbara began to throb and swell. I occurred to me that I had probably developed a bone-spur from wearing other people's cast-off shoes, but I had hoped ignoring it would make it go away. It hadn't. We found a place on the floor in the outer waiting room among several students and other souls already sleeping. I noticed there were benches all around the walls but each and every one of them were taken by the city's homeless--true bums, not train passengers who just couldn't afford hotels. These men seemed to have taken up residence on their benches...probably never left them all day so they could lay claim again at night to the same bench. It made me angry. We were so tired..and still had a long way to go. Terence looked like he was going to drop and the bums had all the seats! It was a long night. I couldn't find a comfortable position for my stupid foot and the floor was very dirty.

Around 6 a.m., a couple of motherly Greek ladies walked over to us and one handed me a fresh circular roll--covered with sesame seeds. She had two left for the other lady and herself--she must have bought three at the cart near the Taxi stand on purpose--to share with us. So very kind. It was incredibly delicious. All warm and soft. We had seen the things hanging in bakery shops, but they looked like pretzels, so we thought they would be too salty. Wrong. Bless that lady.

About a half an hour later, we pulled ourselves up to get in line for tickets. Rather, we joined the shoving horde that constitutes a Greek "queue." Terence managed to get us two tickets on the train for Methoni, where our bikes were imprisoned, and they cost only four dollars for both, which was a relief.

The race to the correct train had to be one of the worst experiences Terence must have endured in our five years on the road. I was practically useless with my sore foot, but I managed to carry a few small things, while a frantic Terence lugged all four of the giant boxes--one by one--in a mad dash to beat the train's departure. People stopped and stared, incredulous, but no one offered to help. Our conductor was not pleased at how much stuff we had. He knew he'd have to hold up the train when we got to our stop for who knew how long and it made him irritable. But when we got to Methoni, I leaped out with the cameras, tank-bags, camera bags and the viola case, while Terence threw out the chair, his jackets, etc., and while the Conductor was holding up the train, Terence slammed and slid those four monster boxes out the door all by himself and onto the pavement in a matter of seconds. The conductor said something admiring, I think, with a big smile on his face as he climbed back on the train. He wasn't the only one who was impressed with such strength and determination. I never ceased to be amazed at my companion.

Georgio Stylianides was something akin to the local Don in Methoni. Owning the biggest gym and health club in Thessaloniki besides being a high-ranking Taekwon-Do black belt must have impressed everybody around. He had built a big house on a hill overlooking the village and seemed to know everybody. We still owed him for convincing the landlady she should rent to a couple of crazy Americans in the dead of winter. He obviously liked us and we would have loved to get to know him better but he spoke very little English and of course our Greek was non-existent. Terence had called him about our return to Methoni and he generously offered to pick us up at our landing place next to the tracks and take us to his house where we would be able to store our big boxes for awhile and wait until we could contact the Pantelises about getting our rig out of their garage. He pulled up around noon with his two teenaged children, and he and his son helped Terence put the boxes in the van and then they brought us to their immaculate new house and we unloaded them into his garage. We were given cool drinks in the living room and at that point, I passed around the little gifts we had bought in Santa Barbara for them. Struggling for words seemed to embarrass everybody and breaking the silence of non-communication, Georgio said something to his wife and kids, and then ordered Terence and me into his van. Bewildered, we climbed in and were driven to one of the little seaside restaurants we had ogled on our walks the December before. Georgio sat opposite us and as if forewarned of our visit, waiters began bringing out huge dishes of fragrant seafood that one could die for. Noticing our drooling faces, he asked, "You like fish?"

Feeling a little silly, we tried to determine the Grecian way of eating so much at once. I waited for Terence to move. He didn't. Georgio smiled and helped himself to only one morsel at a time, so we followed suit. There were mussels fried in batter and tiny fish also batter-fried complete with heads and tails that, after seeing Georgio do it, were obviously meant to be eaten whole. No problem. Another large platter held big tomato chunks and green peppers and other salad stuff--also to be stabbed one piece at a time, I noticed. Our host sliced a plate of octopus into bite-sized pieces and passed it around. He knew we'd have trouble with that one. It had been roasted in olive oil with peppers and onions and was simply divine. A sort of tempura-ed squid tasted heavenly in its crunchy-oiliness. An imported beer was poured into our glasses and it was the perfect accompaniment. The Aegean sea was green and blue again, holiday-makers were playing on the sand which looked much cleaner than we remembered, and I supposed our little apartment house up the street was full of French and German tourists.

About halfway through the meal, as all three of us were trying to think of things to talk about in our limited knowledge of each other's language, Georgio's son came roaring up on a scooter to the edge of our table and excitedly informed his dad about some sort of crisis or other. It seemed to have something to do with a broken water main at his local school. Or maybe the school cistern had run dry--we could understand only that it had to do with water and school. Anyway, as Georgio was the most impor- tant man around, everyone seemed to expect that he must be able to do something about it. In any case, he excused himself and indicated that we should stay as long as we chose. Of course, the bill was taken care of.

Terence and I lingered at the table for some time. There were several other diners. What a difference from the wintertime, when no one was around and we had stood on the sand beyond the railing, taking pictures of icicles hanging from the edge of the table umbrellas. We enjoyed stuffing ourselves to popping and then thought we ought to at least leave a good tip, 'though who could say whether that had been taken care of too...

We walked up the long hill to Georgio's splendid white home--with its shiny new red-tiled roof and azure swimming pool. The family wasn't there now, but we had been told to feel free to come in, so we let ourselves in the big gate at the foot of the driveway and allowed ourselves to be slobbered over by the dog before entering the house. We both took fitful naps on the plush couches in the living room and then about six o'clock, Mrs. Pantelis called. Terence couldn't understand what she was saying but just in case she was actually in town and over at the house, he decided to walk over and see. Fortunately, that's exactly what she was trying to tell him and he was able to get the Gold Wing out of their garage and then came over to pick me up at the Stylianideses. A son a little younger than our friend Thanasis was with the couple and could speak a little English so with his help, we all had a fine chat and the little gifts we had for them from America seemed to be much appreciated and that made us feel very good. Mrs. Thanasis served some very strong coffee--rather like the Italian espresso but in larger cups. I tried hard to get her mind off my appearance, which must have looked surprisingly like a middle-aged woman in a thread-bare leather jacket and jeans who had spent the last two days sleeping on floors and jumping off trains. She warmed up right away, bless her, and with the help of her son, we discussed motherly stuff and became bosom buddies. And Terence did all right with Mr. Pantelis, even though that gentleman had obviously been less than delighted to have our rig in his garage the last six months. And he was going to have to have mine in there for a bit longer while we were in Turkey. He had never met an American before and I hoped he had an open mind about such dubious ambassadors as we.

We yanked the Wing and the huge old trailer out of their yard and onto the street to the yelps and shrieks from the village boys on their bicycles who were circling around and around in glee by the big motorcycle. I hugged Mrs. Pantelis and wished I could have really talked to her about how much T. and I loved Thanasis and how we appreciated what they all had done for us, etc., but they understood and everybody waved as the kids in the street led the way to the campground which was about a mile out of town.

Open for the summer now, the Methoni campground served the usual international set on their way to Greece's northern border who couldn't afford hotels or who just preferred traveling in their RVs. No Greeks, of course...just as there were never any Hungarians in Hungarian campgrounds nor Sicilians in Sicilian ones. It was located on a gentle slope above the beach--a small area, but not full. Pine trees that sighed in the breeze carried a two-part harmony with the sound of the surf below us as we set up camp. We began unloading the big metal box on the back of the Gold Wing so we could clean it out and put the viola and typewriter inside. Suddenly Terence drew back. "It's alive!" he shouted, and I looked inside. Things were squirming and jumping out of the mess at the bottom. Mice. The sheepskin for the bike's seat had been stored in there. It was completely soaked with mouse-urine. I lifted it out slowly and gingerly shook the little poops off and dropped it onto the grass to be washed later. One of his helmets had a large hole in the foam rubber lining and two plastic sacks of papers had been totally chewed up to make nests for no doubt several generations of the tiny rodents. We couldn't remember what sort of paperwork was in those sacks. Maps, maybe. There was no way to know anymore. Terence carefully scooped the nests up and out and placed the wriggling mass at the foot of a nearby olive tree that had a lot of leaves at the base. We hoped the little mouse-mommies could take care of them there--many were newborn. What a mess. I suddenly felt dead-tired and with a headache that meant business. I begged off cooking dinner and flung myself onto the trailer bed and slept for nine hours. I vaguely heard a thunderstorm during the night and was glad Terence had insisted we put the tarp over the trailer's roof. Welcome home!

Chapter Fifty-Four

TUESDAY, JUNE 2ND. THE STORY OF BUGGER THE DOG

WE WENT over to Georgio's the next day to pour through the boxes we'd left in their garage. Mrs. Stylianides and her daughter Elena were trying to help and apparently it made them late in catching the bus to the city, because they seemed frantic all at once and ran down the hill together and their antics excited the big German Shepherd puppy whose name sounded like Bugger to us but we couldn't be sure. He was an expensive dog, we'd been told, but somehow we didn't think they were paying for brains. Also, he was badly in need of training--eager to please and all over you and not getting any smaller, if you know what I mean. Innocently, Terence opened the gate to get the bike in to pack it, and immediately Bugger dashed down the drive and out. Terence called and whistled but that pricey dog was gone. It occurred to me then that the reason the Stylianides were so paranoid about that gate was not security but to keep that dumb dog in. Terence ran after it of course, but soon returned, saying that it was obvious the dog had a particular destination in mind, as it had galloped away without so much as a glance backward. We felt awful and naturally, responsible. What to do? We found the elderly caretaker who was mowing the great green lawn in front of the house, and pantomimed the problem and he did a head-slapping OH NO! gesture and pantomimed back the theory that the dog, no doubt, had run after his mistresses and knew the way to the bus stop on the other side of town. We grabbed the dog chain and took off on the Gold Wing, deciding we'd find that damn dog if it took all day. We rode through town and just as we got to the bus stop, the bus was pulling away! Hey, is Chevy Chase in this movie?

We followed it to the freeway just in case the women may have taken the dog with them. But he gave up after a bit and in case the Bugger might still be around the village, we began cruising along the beach and waterfront where all the best doggie smells are--fish and garbage and other mutts. We stopped to ask a man if he'd seen the beast. We'd learned that skilos meant dog, so we felt confident he'd understand. But it wasn't until we mentioned the name Stylianides that the man brightened with understanding and with much energy, he described in careful detail how we could find the Stylianides house. Uh..thank you, sir. We rolled on..looking down every alley and even into doorways. The dog was probably well known in those parts. Riding slowly past the string of restaurants by the waterfront, the waiters waved and shouted hopeful welcome noises, no doubt remembering we'd been down there yesterday with the Don and figuring we were ready to grace their tables again. Alas, no dog.

We rode back to the house where the caretaker was waiting for us. When he saw us poochless, he shook his head slowly and walked back to this lawn mower. Just then, a young man rode up on a moped, waving and shouting to the caretaker. Apparently, the dog had been found, and as everybody for miles knew whose dog it was, we could have saved ourselves the trouble of searching. The kid had been dispatched to ride to the manor and tell somebody it was tied up and waiting to be taken home. We got back on the bike and followed the boy all the way across the village again and close to the bus station. Some men untied it and handed it over, probably disappointed the Don himself hadn't appeared but had sent over his German servants instead. We knew "Thank you" in Greek and said it several times and then Terence snapped the chain onto Bugger's collar. While I sat in the passenger seat on the motorcycle, Terence put the huge animal in my lap and told me to hang on to him while he drove. I put my arms around it and began frantically scratching behind its big ears to keep it calm. Riding as slowly as possible, we passed the villagers in their doorways with wide expressions of disbelief on their faces. Ol' Bugger was trying to hold on, thank God, and seemed to love the lavish attention from my fingers. Every time he saw a cat or thought he heard something interesting, the big black ears would swing forward and I quickly covered his eyes and petted him furiously. At the top of the hill with the long dirt road to go, Bugger realized he was almost home and began trying to jump off. It was too much for me. I told Terence to stop and let us get off. T. could ride the bike to the house and I would walk with Bugger on the chain. The damn dog pulled and strained all the way to the gate, causing me to run and inflict nasty punishment on my sore heel, but we got him home--hot, tired and dirty but safe. So was the dog.

We made one more trip to the big city--for food and to cash Traveler's checks and to give Terence one more workout with the black belts in the Stylianides gym. Our friend Thanasis appeared and treated us to a beer in his favorite pub. We were going to miss him. Then we rode back to the campground and packed the last few things and while Terence did some studying, I planned us a route through the rest of Greece and part of Turkey. We had a lot to see and in order to get to Vienna for the Esperanto Conference in July, we had only five weeks in which to do it.

Chapter Fifty-Five

MONASTERIES IN THE SKY

SATURDAY, June 6th. A very warm day. Left Methoni around 11 in the morning and began a long hot ride up mountains and through dusty villages. Stopped here and there to take pictures of stork's nests and stuff. Made a rare intelligent decision not to take the shorter but thinner route on the map to Kalambaka. The "better" road became all but impassable in several places, especially in the mountain villages themselves. Terence had to yank and shove the rig up--with me pushing from behind-- back and around the rutted trails several times--to the amusement of the villagers who were probably hoping we'd flip spectacularly over the edge of the cliffs so they'd have something to talk about for a change in the tavernas.

The heat became fierce. We said to hell with the hot leather jackets and just wore T-shirts and slathered ourselves with 30% sun-block cream but we still got such a burn we soon learned to cover ourselves and endure the discomfort of too much clothing. By evening, when we had reached Meteora, we didn't bother to bargain or look for the cheapest campground in the popular area. The first one we came to had a pool, and we were so hot we didn't care. I even donned my 15 yr. old bathing suit and swam and walked around in the body I had sworn I'd never show again. Some things take precedence.

Before the sun set, around 8:30, we rode out to snap a few pictures of this amazing area. Then early, to beat the heat, we arose early the next morning and went back for more.

Meteora is a place of asceticism and prayer. And of course, tourists. Still, it is so far off the beaten path with no pretty sea coast nearby, that it remains fairly unspoiled and it is a mind-boggling place to see. A forest of giant rocks, some as high as mountains, rises from the Thessalian plain between the Koziakas and Antichasia mountains. For hundreds of years, monks have lived on top of those rocks and built their monasteries and fasted and prayed and became guardians of the sacred letters and arts of Orthodox Hellenism. At one time, there were twenty-one monasteries perched high in the sky and at the present, with fasting and silence perhaps not as popular among the young men as in the past, there are just six left. Still, these six holy structures in the clouds are a tribute to the power of faith. They are awe-inspiring to see. You can't believe men could have built them without wings! Even the abandoned ones are magnificent as ruins. Terence and I rode up the mountains on the bike to the ones that could be reached and had a glimpse of some of the views the monks had every day. They surely must have felt they were sitting on the right hand of God up there.

Went back to the campground around noon. The heat was awful. Our poor little fridge puffed away, gasping under its cover. We gave up trying to read and write and instead, jumped into the pool--This time with half the town's male youth. No females. Obviously, the camp manager was ignoring the signs that said FOR CAMPERS ONLY, perhaps it was an act of kindness to keep his friends cool. Perhaps his palm was greased. In any case, there was little room in the water to do anything but stand for a minute or too before being smacked in the head with a rubber ball or a flailing foot and I soon felt like a being from another planet and stepped out. Walking, still wet, back to the rig was pleasant but too soon my skin was dry again. Soon, Terence gave up trying to find room to swim in too, and we sat under a tree swatting biting black flies and grousing together about the temperature. Terence read from a newspaper that people in Athens were being hospitalized due to the heat. "Ye Gods. Already?" I groaned. It was becoming increasingly clear why we had planned to see Greece in the wintertime in the first place, but it was a little late to do anything about it now.

That evening we met some of the other campers. There was quite a mix. A shy Danish biker was right next to us and a wild bunch of Dutch bikers on the other side. Conveniently for us, they all spoke English and we had a beer together on the dry grass. The rather anorexic young lady with the Dutch group had the Rough Guides book for Greece and I contemplated killing her for it. She saved her skin by loaning it to me and while the guys drank another beer, I read as much as I could about where we were headed before I had to give it back. The fellas were hot to get answers about how to travel in the USA on motorcycles, and Terence, in his element, held court until about one in the morning.

On the flat plain towards Delphi the next morning, we were dismayed to see tons of trash dumped all along the side of the road. Winds had blown it everywhere--in piles against houses, caught in the branches of trees, stuck in the ditches by the road. We spotted a large gypsy camp in a valley. It was the first time I had ever seen the gypsies's area cleaner than the environment around them! A large cloud cover stayed with us most of the day for which we were very grateful. The humidity was extreme, but it wasn't quite so hot. About three in the afternoon we began climbing. Curiously, the trash level dropped with the tree level and as we got higher, the view of rocks and brush reminded me of the American West. It felt and smelled the same, too. We gassed up in a rather dreary small town between mountains and then climbed some more until we passed under a huge banner that said in English: "WELCOME TO DELPHI." How...quaint.

We passed a large campground that looked full, and rode into the village which is obviously solely supported by the ancient tourist attraction. The little house-shops all clung to the rocky slope with one purpose in mind. To part the visitor from his money. There being only one way to get from one end of the village to the other and that being an extremely narrow street full of people, beasts and machines, one was trapped and reduced to a snail's pace--forced to read the garish signs on every inch of space and to endure the sales pitch from every side to buy or at least stop for a meal. We were especially vulnerable of course, being on a motorcycle and as exposed as a baby's behind, with no windows to roll up or steel doors to protect us from the begging palms and voices. Welcome to Delphi. Unfortunately, when we reached the other side of town, we saw that there was no campground of any sort there, so we had to find a place to turn around and go back through the Purgatory of Dante again to reach the one we'd seen earlier. It was almost entirely full of Dutch RVs, with one Canadian and a smattering of Germans rounding out the spaces. We were lucky to grab one of the last spots--on an ant-hill but under a couple of skinny but welcome pine trees on a slope. My heel hurt a lot. The day's ride in the heat had made my foot swell, and the long walk to the women's room was agony. But the camp was pleasant, otherwise. The many pine trees helped to keep us cool and the view down the mountain to the valley below was pretty terrific. There was a swimming pool on the grounds that Terence splashed merrily in. It was unheated and seemed to be made from ice water and none of the other campers wanted to use it. I sat on the edge and put my throbbing foot into it and began feeling much better.

At the famous site at Delphi the next day, we were stopped at the parking lot and asked to buy a ticket for $5 each to walk among the ruins. It was more than we could afford. My foot couldn't take the walk anyway, I decided. "I prefer my architecture in one piece, anyway," Terence said gallantly. We left for other adventures.

The streets got even narrower in the smaller villages near the base of Parnassos. Everybody stared as Terence yanked our great caboose around fruit stalls and narrowly avoided men on rusty scooters. Once on flat land and among the trash heaps again, we pulled over to eat lunch. A hot, dry and dirty wind blew the nearest garbage against our legs. The bread we had brought was like chalk in our mouths. I tried to make it more edible by putting pieces of sardines with oil on top of the bread but it didn't help much. A truly terrible repast. We lost our way several times thanks to the Greek habit of not bothering to place road signs in strategic places. We spent hours climbing mountains and twisting through grimy little villages. The men, dressed in filthy clothes, stood on the sides of the road, mouths agape and seemed to have nothing to do. We had learned to ask the children for directions. They seemed so much sharper than their elders. We wondered between us about what might have happened to people's brains out there as they become adults. Hopelessness and boredom played a part, no doubt.

Chapter Fifty-Six

ATHENS AND BEYOND

WE FINALLY FOUND THE "DAPHNE" campground on the west side of the sprawling city. It was expensive, no pool and not very clean, but this was Athens and they really didn't have to try harder. Fearing from the horror stories about ghastly traffic and of tourists dropping from the heat in the notorious city, we waited until evening to venture forth and have a look. Surprisingly, even at ten at night, the congestion was extreme. We didn't know where we were going, but we sort of followed the flow. I was giving directions to Terence with the queerest notion that I'd been there before. It was a very strange feeling but I was enjoying it hugely. The night was clear and we rode up one of the hills in the city to look around. We came upon a parking lot full of lovers walking hand in hand in the balmy night air and getting serious inside their cars. The view of the city was lovely. Even through the smog. We rode down again and then through the city center. I observed from some of the smarter shops that some people had plenty of money here. Yet it must be damn few compared to the rest of the country. There was some marvelous architecture, most of it 19th century and crumbling. Anything earlier already gone, and there was lots of neo-Greek classical stuff. The Greeks copying themselves. The air was absolutely poisonous, just as we had heard it would be. But nothing seemed to be happening to change it. Trucks, buses, old wrecks--anything and everything was allowed to belch black gases in the packed streets of Athens. Most of the ugliness of the city was due to automobiles. Tires thrown down every slope, pieces of motors rusted and ancient--lying in sidewalk and drives. For some odd reason, car doors of every color were everywhere. Even on balconies of apartment buildings. Oil puddles and stains on walkways and driveways alike. The whole city looked like one vast garage and repair shop.

We made the obligatory visit to the Acropolis the next day. There was a very interesting "old" section of the city at its base. It reminded me of the gypsy flamenco borough at the foot of the castle in Lisbon. Rich people were fixing up the houses. It had obviously been a wealthy area a very long time ago and then, as these things go, fallen into disrepair and abandoned to the poor. Now the old structures were getting a major face lift and it was no doubt going to be the "in" place to live again.

My heel announced that it could not make it up the long path to the Acropolis. I really didn't mind. It would have cost $7 for me; Terence was able to use his (somewhat doctored) student card and got in for $4. I spent the hour he was gone, on a bench under a tree and enjoyed myself looking at all the interesting people taking the tour. I could see the Parthenon and several other interesting pieces of the famous site from where I sat so I didn't feel too deprived. Still, a small but nagging voice was asking me if the darn heel was going to get much worse and what the heck could I do about it? Even if I could find a doctor to operate on the spur, there would be all that recovery time we couldn't possibly afford. No, I would simply have to tough it out for the four or five months more it would take to finish the trip. It wouldn't kill me, and anyway tough old Terence was used to doing all the physical work anyway. I would just try to keep my part of the chores running smoothly and try not to bitch when it hurt.

For some reason, it was difficult to find bread. We never saw it at the street markets. After almost giving up one afternoon, we asked a lady in her car at a stop sign if she could point out a bakery. She said to follow her and up she drove to one of the hilltop suburban areas of Athens with us riding behind. After a bit she stopped in front of a kind of Mom and Pop store with no signs at all out front. She pointed, smiled and drove off. Terence and I found the best bread we'd eaten in Greece inside that little store.

The "Disco" next door to the campground went on until four a.m.! It was a very hot and sultry night with no breeze. The glaring neon lights from the women's room nearby never went off. The sounds of the trucks on the nearby freeway changing their gears and the two-stroke motorbikes screaming to get their riders to work early the next morning induced us to cast our votes for the place being one of the worst campgrounds we had experienced in our four years of travel. Terence groused that the kind of Greek dance music they were playing at the Disco--a sort of monotonous whine with a tooth-loosening beat in the bass--definitely pushed our all-time winner, the garbagey campground in Sables d'Olonne during the sandstorm, right off the charts. We were glad to get out of there the next morning.

We rode through Athens to its bustling port of Piraeus and tried to buy tickets for the island of Santorini. They would sell us the passenger tickets, but refused to take the responsibility for deciding how much we would have to pay to get the weird-looking rig on board. The clerks stood at their window looking at the trailer on back of the Wing and shook their heads slowly. The ferrymen at the dock were not thrilled to have to make the decision, either. They decided we owed them fifty dollars over and above the price of the passenger tickets to get the rig on. It was piracy but we had no choice. We paid up and pulled the rig onto the ferry and tried not to think of the more civilized countries that had sometimes allowed us to put it on free of charge when they could find no category for it.

It was hot and dirty on board. Full of students, mostly American, who immediately rolled out their sleeping bags on all the deck chairs and necked or went to sleep. We got out our dinner of bread and cheese and watched as Athens slipped back into its smog. Down below we finally found chairs in a non-smoking section--the sign being ignored by some pretty serious smokers. Terence, at one point, tried to enforce it himself but only succeeded in pissing off the staff. I attempted to placate everybody, afraid that we just might have another Pompeii experience, Greek style, but Terence calmed down and started studying his Law book and had soon cooled off. I knew he was still smarting from being ripped off about the rig. So was I.

Around 1 A.M., he went down to the trailer in the hold and got out our sleeping bags, so we were able to catch some sleep for a couple of hours the way the Greek folks were doing around us--on the floor wrapped like mummies.

At 5:15 A.M. we arrived at Santorini. We grabbed our stuff and ran down to the hot pit where the huge lorries around us had started their engines--even though there were signs everywhere saying NOT to until the hold door was opened. The deck was filling up with carbon monoxide. We frantically untied the ropes holding the rig and I began to cough and get frightened. The truck drivers had their windows rolled up and were watching us--not giving a damn if we asphyxiated or not. Terence yelled for me to get out of the area--to run to the other end where the cargo doors were opening and I could breathe. I limped to the doors, wondering if Terence would be able to make it himself. The big trucks started to move off at last. Terence came barreling around them to get out and into the air. He tore down the ramp with the ferrymen glaring at his nerve in pushing ahead in the line. He would have been last if he'd waited and might not have made it at all but it obviously wasn't their problem. Pushy Americans!

It was just before dawn. The islands forming the big crater were purple against the dark blue of the dying night. The passengers around us haggled with the islanders over prices for lodging. We pulled the rig over to the edge of the dock and got out our cameras. By the time we came back to the motorcycle after filming some pretty exciting sunrise-over-Santorini shots, everybody else had disappeared and the great ferry boat was pulling away. We started up the zig-zag road of the volcanic cliff to the village in search of a campground.

The first one we came to seemed deserted and with no manager in the little office, even though a sign in the window stated in several languages that it was open. Terence got tired of waiting for someone to show up, so while I waited next to the unhitched trailer, he zoomed away in search of another place.

The sun came up in a cloudless sky. It looked evil and made me aware that there were precious few trees on the island. Terence came back to announce that there were two more campgrounds; both with awake managers, so we headed for the first one which happened to be nearest to the main town of Santorini. Too tired after sleepless nights of Disco noise and sleeping on decks, we didn't bother checking out the other one and just paid the guy and set up the trailer top and tried to take a nap. There was no shade. Several baby trees had been planted around the area but they were as yet too small to help much. It felt like we'd been placed in an oven under the plastic lid of the trailer. We gave up trying to sleep and tumbled out to have a look around. There was a pretty little swimming pool and a snack bar where we discovered we could get an omelet for $1.50! Things were looking up. After that very welcome bite of breakfast, we walked back to the rig to change into our bathing suits. We were shaken from our good mood by the first blasts of Oh-no-give-us-a-break--Disco music! It came from the pool area we had just left. Ah quaint and curious Greece. Land of the infernal sun and constant noise!

Terence decided to get our passports back and try the other campground. He promised he'd keep his temper. He didn't, and also didn't get our passports. The manager insisted we had to pay for a whole day's stay. He couldn't for the life of him understand why we weren't enjoying the music. He told Terence we couldn't possibly find a campground without it. "What has the world come to?" I groaned, feeling old. How we wished we could "wild" camp. But not only are they very strict about it (all that money lost), but nowhere in Greece had we seen a place to hide. Not even the gypsies could find places. One saw them here and there, semi-legally parking next to buildings or paying a little rent to Greeks with vacant lots. We endured the noise and resolved to leave the next day. I wrote some postcards to put it out of my mind. There was a postal strike at the time. I hoped they hadn't heard about it on the island. Silly me. I found out later that few of the folks I wrote to as we traveled around Greece ever got my mail at all. The cards and letters I wrote in Santorini are probably still in the post boxes where I dropped them.

We hitched up the trailer, paid the nasty manager and took off the next day for the other end of the island where the campground called "Perissa" was located. It was full of very tan young people from Northern Europe and America, all romping happily on the nearby beach and drinking lots of beer. It reminded me of "Easter Week" on Balboa Island when I was in high school. We pulled up under a rather spindly pine tree and I made us a lunch of ham and tomatoes and cheese with that chalky bread they sell in Greece--if you can find bread at all. Afterwards, we hopped on the bike and explored that part of the island. It was a nice ride--with the breeze cooling us off and the sea on both sides of us a rich dark blue. We stopped to take pictures of old windmills and abandoned villages. Apparently, earthquakes had really done a number on the architecture through the centuries. Here and there, the people had just built right over the rubble. In other places, they had given up and left it and built a short distance away. I sat on the passenger seat of the bike a lot while Terence took short hikes for his pictures. The heel wasn't getting any better. Would I have to finish the trip in a wheelchair? After we returned to our beach camp, Terence went swimming in the deep blue sea while I remained on the beach sitting on my camp chair and soaking my foot like an invalid.

I cooked a chicken that evening that really lifted our spirits. We were beginning to settle in nicely at Perissa until about 9 o'clock when the noise level began to rise and by ten, we were being subjected to not one Disco's decibels but three, and each one louder than the other. Plus the boom boxes thoughtfully provided by the American kids which, as I recall with uncontrollable shuddering, emitted mostly Rap, which threatened to turn us both into a kind of two-headed Jack the Ripper. Terence seemed worse off than I for a change. He announced that he would be leaving at crack of dawn to try to book us on a boat out of there as soon as possible. That would be fine with me.

The hot wind the next morning made it hard to think. The three bands had played all night and when they finally stopped around 5:30 a.m., the kids had straggled to their tents shouting and laughing. They were having a wonderful time. We realized, as we talked about it over coffee, that we were greatly spoiled having been at so many of the greatest places off-season, or at least where there had been rules. We remembered the campground in Pannonhalma, Hungary. Thinking about the 10 o'clock curfew there made us downright wistful. Of course, the "no-rules" policy must have been the great draw here for the rich western kids. And as long as they paid exalted prices for it and bought the touristy junk in the local shops, the Greeks would turn a blind eye. We had noticed that, unlike the disco next to the campground in Athens, the music had been all American-Adolescent last night. Not a single Grecian song. This place was strictly for westerners. The Santorinians made the bucks any way they could in the summer months and could look forward to their peace and quiet (or at least their own music) during the long winter.

We rode into the main town to get our tickets for Rhodes. Aware that the price to ferry the trailer would be prohibitive now, we would have to skip Crete. Terence was convinced that it would just be more of the same anyway--tourist kids in the camps, loud music and Greek indifference. My throbbing heel and I selfishly agreed. For some reason, we were not overly surprised when we were told about the two-day strike the ferries were going to have, starting the next day. *What's next to strike?*, we wondered. *Campgrounds?* Staying on Santorini and waiting out the strike, we had to have a place to camp for at least two days. There was only one place left. The little lonely one that we tried first after getting off the ferry.

Before we rode back to it, we toured the village at the east end of the island called Oia. So Terribly Charming it had to be the one on all the posters for Greece one sees in the travel agencies in the States. It was awfully hot among all that blinding white stucco, but we managed to get a few pictures at least. Then we rode over to the larger town of Fara, which sits high above the little harbor where the cruise ships of the privileged dock at Santorini and deposit folks who pay a lot to sit on a donkey and be led up the cliff to the town above.

On Wednesday, June 17th, we arrived at the Kamari campground in Santorini. The sign was in English. It read: "PLEASE SAVE WATER." And yet, everywhere I looked, it was being wasted. All the toilets leaked and were constantly running. Hoses dripped into overflowing buckets and of course few of the faucets could be completely turned off. Perhaps the sign was in the wrong language.

It was blissfully quiet. Nobody else around. Terence decided it was unpopular because it didn't have a Disco! Ha Ha. He studied, and I cooked another chicken to have it cold for the trip to Turkey. Who knew but that food sellers might strike next! While I cooked over the little camp stove, flies of every description dive-bombed and nipped at me. I'd swat one and two would take its place. It was still windy. A fellow was digging at a large hill of cement not far away--not caring that the stuff was blowing all over my cooking, my hair--everything. I gritted my teeth. Grittily.

That night we went to a movie. The local Cinema Paradiso. Real Santorinians sat around us in the outdoor courtyard and the screen was a whitewashed wall. Very nice. The movie, alas, was American. Some horrible super violent flick whose title I have blissfully forgotten.

We left Kamari at noon on Friday. The ferry was to leave at midnight, so we had the rest of the day to kill. We took the trailer down the zig-zag trail to the ferry dock and lock it up and hopped back on the Wing to ride to the only spot we hadn't explored on the island, a nice old village that hadn't been rebuilt much since the earthquake of 1956. The people had simply slapped more paint on the rubble and moved back in. There were some incredibly beautiful old buildings among the ruins. We got some good shots.

Around 6 p.m., we rode back down the cliff to where we'd left the trailer. One thing can certainly be said for the Greek people. They don't touch stuff that doesn't belong to them. We opened it up while the dock people watched, and I made macaroni and cheese for dinner. Some guys in a truck stopped and walked over to us with a fabulous green melon. We were glad we knew how to say thank you in his language. Terence called my attention to a raging fire a couple of miles down the coast near the town of Thira. Huge flames were leaping up the side of the cliff. It was spectacular. I imagined it must have looked something like that when Santorini was born from a volcano eruption. We turned around to see the reaction of the other people on the dock and nobody was watching it! Not even the other tourists. I couldn't understand it. T. and I shared our little binoculars as we stood at the end of the wharf exclaiming at the sight. Everybody else just watched us! As it got dark, the glow from the great fire shown across the water like red-orange moonlight--an amazing picture. And still we were the only ones who gave a damn.

Finally, I asked a Greek couple what it might be and after they talked it over for a word to use, she came up with "Dead." Dead? This is how they take care of their dead? Nah, that couldn't be what she meant. We decided it had to be a controlled fire of some sort--perhaps the city dump. But what a show.

The ferry was an hour late and we were irritable. When the boat people saw the big trailer behind the motorcycle they freaked out, of course, and several of them talked at once with lots of hand gestures. First they told Terence he would have to put it on the deck above the trucks--where the automobiles would be. Then, at the last minute they signaled him to stop and wait and then motioned him to go last--in front of the trucks--on the bottom deck. But because this boat only had one opening, he would have to come down in the middle of the night when they landed at Crete and move it out so the trucks could get off and others come on and then he would have to ride it on again after the trucks from Crete got on. Or something like that. Terence blew up. I felt, personally, that losing his temper at these simple sailors who were already annoyed at us for bringing something from Mars onto their boat, would only make matters worse, so I intervened and told the fellas in the white uniforms that it would be O.K., we understood their (Byzantine) instructions and the rig would be moved at Crete. Terence glared at me with hate and said under his breath that he thought it more important that they understood that we really thought that they were all a bunch of ignorant, incapable, and worthless peasants! His choice of terms focused mainly on their genitalia which I was sure would only serve to piss them off so badly we just might find ourselves left on the dock and Lord knows I didn't want to spend another night in Santorini. Did he?, I asked.

We finally extracted ourselves and went up on deck. As we leaned over the rail, Terence told me that he really couldn't understand why "in every situation" I wound up "Kissing ass." Hurt, I told him that I didn't understand why he so often had to play "macho-man" and lock horns over the slightest things with other men. Then he said something about how I had "Kissed ass all my life and he was the first person in my whole life whose ass I didn't kiss!" Oh really? I didn't know how to respond to that strange attack. I didn't even understand what he meant. All I could do was sulk, so I took my sleeping bag and curled up on a chair a long way away from him and while he slept soundly, I kept myself awake because I'd promised the officer (whose ass I apparently had kissed), that Terence would be down there to move the rig around in circles for their amusement when we docked at Crete. I could understand why Terence was angry. But what choice did we have?

I tried to make him take the tickets when I woke him at 4:30 a.m. in case they asked for them, but he was still seething, and snapped that that was a pretty dumb idea because no one would ask for them because he wasn't getting off the boat to stay, (and then they did ask for them which only made him angrier). After he got back to our deck, he went to sleep in his bag again and this time I dropped off too, until we were both awakened by the barking of a small dog some fool had tied to the railing before disappearing--sending the poor animal into a frenzy of fright. Everyone who wasn't Greek was furious. I forced myself up and limped down to the desk where three of the staff in Officer whites manned the desk while they listened to loud music. I explained the situation with the dog and they only seemed slightly amused. I gave up and hobbled back above decks and had a chat with the young German fellow who had been sleeping in the lounge chair next to me and waking up now and then to polish off a very large bottle of wine. He had been pretty visibly disturbed by the noise too, and so he and Terence walked over to the dog and untied it--to the dog's great delight. And mine. After a bit, we heard it barking from the deck beneath us. Terence guessed it had been tied up again. The German got up again, went downstairs and untied it again! Stout fellow!

At Karpathos,the next port stop, Terence, his jaw hard, had to run around the track again. This time he took the tickets with him...and they wanted to know why I wasn't there! "Morons!," Terence exclaimed as he came up the stairs. I began to think we'd never make it to Rhodes.

The sun came up. The heat with it. We docked around 4:30 in the afternoon. The sight before our eyes was as wonderful as it was unexpected. Instead of the usual starchy-white stucco boxes on rock heaps we'd been seeing in every port, we were greeted with lots of pine trees and medieval walls encircling a very large old castle and absolutely fascinating Venetian, Moorish and Turkish architecture all along the wharf. We were going to like this place! We rolled off and I could feel Terence relax. We first went to the convenient Tourist Info place and found out that the only campground was way out of town but we didn't care at this point. When we got there it was practically deserted--no doubt too far for the kids to get to, so they probably gave up and stayed in town. It was expensive--11 dollars a night, but there were trees, clean bathrooms, a swimming pool and even a little store. There was no hot water in the tap for dishes or wash however, and we had to pay extra for the electricity to keep the fridge cold. A padlock on the toilet paper roll and a long list of rules in English made me wonder what their problem was. On the other hand, why weren't the other campgrounds this frugal? First time I had seen small hand sinks for the children. Nice idea. Benches and hooks in the shower. We hated the bright lights lining every path all night, though. Wished they'd save their money on that!

After the bummer of paying a very stiff price for two tickets to Turkey, things began to improve the morning of Sunday, June 21st. There was lots to look at and take pictures of and I decided to hell with my heel, I could walk long enough to enjoy the sights and pass out later. We had become smarter about the heat. I wore two scarves. Both soaking wet. One around my head and one around my neck to keep from getting burned.

Museums were supposed to be free to the public on Sundays. The canny Greeks counter that bit of nonsense by thinking up reasons to have them closed when you get to the door. Jolly plump Greek ladies sat at the door in barely concealed amusement, telling the cheap Sunday museum-goers that, for some reason they could not explain in any language but their own, the museum would not be able to open today and everybody would have to come back the next day. So we busied ourselves elsewhere. We burned up the film rolls. I was taking color prints to  draw from, and Terence was shooting slides and black and white. Pigeons on minarets, exotic squares, walls, doorways. Flowers growing from unlikely places, Renaissance Turkish carvings, copper and brass in the old market..a distinct lack of Greek-ness. We loved the place.

By early afternoon though, I was tired and in a lot of pain and climbing back on the bike, swore I wouldn't get off again until we got back to the campground, but then we rode by the island's most popular beach, and the sight of the bare breasts stopped Terence in his tracks and of course he had to reach for his camera. I couldn't blame him, it certainly was a spectacular sight for those of us who came from a land of the cover-up, and as he was fishing around in his camera bag I became aware of the sensational colors of giant beach umbrellas all over the place and decided to get some shots of my own. We must have looked a pretty pair--with him sneaking up to women who were wearing half a bathing suit, and trying to look casual in his motorcycle boots and photographer's vest with lenses and bulky film in all the pockets--and I no better a sight as I limped along the sand, dressed in a shabby cotton frock and two wet bandannas and taking pictures of people's umbrellas when there was all those beautiful bodies to shoot. Mad dogs and Americans go out in the noon-day sun...

The day we chose to go see the famous town of Lindos started out hot and windy. I even soaked my dress along with my scarves so that I could stay cool longer. It worked for the first few miles until everything was dried and once again I baked. After paying 200 drachmas to park the Gold Wing, we raced up the side of the mountain to see the famous castle at the top. We had overheard someone in the parking lot say it was going to close by noon because it was Monday!! The winding path was covered with red-faced and puffing tourists like ourselves trying to reach the top in time. It appeared no one else had been informed in time of the early closing either, and the atmosphere was one of panic. Blocking half the narrow path were the village lace-sellers smiling and sweetly calling to all of us in German. I seemed to remember reading how they hated the Germans in this part of the world. Oh well. My heel was screaming at me to rest. Terence was determined to make it and hell, so was I for that matter. What a dirty trick to encourage all these people to spend their money parking and buying lace and all the while knowing that the most important sight in Lindos would be off-limits by noon. Monday my eye! They probably do this to people every day! Getting even for the war...

We sped past the Lace Ladies and elbowed the slower tourists out of the way as we ran to the finish line. At 11:45 we stood at the gate gasping for breath, only to be told by a smirking guard that the gate was now closed--Fermee and Geschlossen--as he let out a trickle of folks who had known to come much earlier. We were furious. My heel gave me no peace. I looked around at the international set around me--perspiring and incredulous at the announcement that the site was closing. The heat was intense and several of the people had tired children in tow as well as babies in carts that they'd pushed up that terrible mountain path. How could these Greeks be so cruel? Of course, if they'd put up a sign at the bottom of the mountain, the Lace-sellers would miss out on their prey. I wanted to slap every tourist that stopped to buy lace on the way down!

Without much interest, we took a few pictures of the village--along with everybody else, and then boarded the bike for the next place on our list--a small mountain village with an interesting church. The church was O.K., but the true point of interest was the painter tied to one of the bell towers. He was busily engaged in painting very good trompe l'oeil tiles and even ventilation holes! There were real ventilation holes on the lower parts of the church and his version looked exactly the same. Well done. I determined to look more carefully at Greek churches thereafter.

As we were putting on our helmets, a terrible-looking old wretch in black stopped near us and sat down with a great moan on the low wall in front of the church. She was very small and dirty and seemed to have a layer of bloody skin over the whites of her eyes. No teeth and so pitiful a figure that I couldn't stop myself from pressing a 100DR note into her hand. She didn't seem surprised and it occurred to me that it might really be a thirty-five year old in makeup. Naw...Anyway, just in case she had some pride, I asked her if I could take her picture for the sum and she agreed. I wasn't looking forward to seeing the results later, however.

It must have been 110 degrees in the shade as we rode across the island. At each watering hole, we soaked our bandannas and splashed water on our clothes. I began dunking both my socks and shoes in the water because as we rode, the wind cooled my feet and the one with the monster heel attached was especially grateful.

Somewhere on the north side of the island, we came across a canyon that had been advertised by big signs in English for several miles. The Famous Beautiful Butterfly Canyon. We got off the bikes and I asked the gentlemen at the kiosk how long a walk it would be before one could see any butterflies and they decided it would be about two miles and would cost us 200DR each. Terence said he had no interest in another long hot walk after that fiasco we'd experienced running up a mountain to see nothing--earlier in the day and my heel was in accord and so I made the fellows scowl over their cash box when I told them we wouldn't be buying. Before I got back on the bike, I read the back of one of the post-cards for sale and discovered two interesting details. First, the main attraction was moths, not butterflies, and second, this was not the time of year when the dear furry things hung around this particular canyon! I was getting smarter. And I suspected there also might be ladies selling lace all the way to the-canyon-with-no-butterflies-in-it as well! We quit the scene.

On Tuesday, June 23rd, after a sleepless night boxing mosquitoes and gasping from the heat, we packed up and pulled out of the Faliraki Camp-ground and rode to town to pick up our tickets for Turkey. We were furious to discover we had to pay a Port Tax of fifty dollars each. Some-thing new, and designed to discourage travelers from leaving Greece and taking good tourist dollars to the enemy, Turkey. (We were to learn the practice was abolished a couple of weeks later...)

We had several hours to kill so we paid 2 drachmas to go underground and see the extremely depressing aquarium. (I still think a lot of the fish were plastic. It was the first time I'd seen fish with green algae all over them). Then we shot a few pictures in a curious Muslim cemetery that was right next to the Bare Boobies Beach and yet strangely deserted and quiet-- as if it were a thousand miles into the desert. Tall and dusty eucalyptus trees drooped overhead, giving welcome shade and so we dug some provisions out of the bike and had a beer and petted the graveyard cat. Then we rode over to the very old part of the harbor and got some arty shots of rusting hulls. Terence took a dip in the water to cool off but it didn't look too clean and I just walked around at the edge to give a soak to my heel.

Finally it was time to grab the boat to another country. We were very excited and none too sorry to leave Greece. Terence put a call through to his father in Connecticut and then went to retrieve our passports at the Customs office and all hell broke loose!

Three men, one in uniform, had decided we had to be detained. Greek law said motorcycles had to be out of the country in six months, and of course because we had had to go back to California in December we were overdue. Never mind that we tried to forestall just this sort of thing from happening by getting stamped permission in Thessaloniki. (Also never mind that we left another motorcycle in Methoni...!) Terence and I couldn't possibly see what the big deal was but the Greeks were shouting and treating us like terrorists. We became very worried. The boat to Turkey left without us.

Finally they gave us back our passports and were told to return the next day to the Customs office. We pooled what was left of our Greek money and found we had just enough for another night at the Faliraki campground. We hauled ourselves back and told the manager what had happened and perhaps to make us feel better, she related much worse horror stories than ours that had happened to other "guests" in the past who had had the audacity to try to leave Rhodes (with their wallets intact).

We were pretty dejected all evening. The night proved hotter than ever but Terence had been smart enough (over my objections) to spend eleven dollars for a small fan that afternoon, and, fastened to the pipe-strut that held our little trailer tent together, its noisy breeze pushed the heavy air around and even shoved the mosquitoes to the side so that we got a pretty good night's sleep.

Armed for bear the next morning, Terence took off for the city. He didn't want me along because he said it might complicate things and being of little courage after yesterday, I was just as happy not to have to go. Indeed, it might have been one of those circumstances where ass-kicking, not kissing was required. But I paced around the site, biting my nails and wondering if he was going to lose his temper and wind up in jail again. After a couple of hours he was back--thirty precious dollars lighter. It had been a shake down after all--what a surprise. I suppose we should have been happy it wasn't more. But our tempers were getting shorter and shorter in that country. It was time to leave.

Back to the city again pulling our old gypsy wagon. The same travel agents re issued our tickets and wanted our passports again for the Customs officers. Terence explained slowly and carefully about seeing the officers that morning and paying the extra "tax." The agents insisted we hand them over. This time one of them spotted that I had another motor-cycle in Greece. Oh no!! Terence quickly lied that it was being repaired in Thessaloniki and the Customs officers in Rhodes knew all about it. The young man didn't smile as he put my passport on top of the pile for the Customs officers to look at. My knees felt watery-weak.

Four o'clock. I stood by the rig trying not to look worried while Terence went into the Customs office and talked to a completely different set of officers to get our passports. After showing them the receipt from the morning ripoff, they begrudgingly handed them over to him. Taking no chances, Terence walked fast to the Wing, slammed his helmet on his head and commanded me to keep people out of his way.

The ferry was very small and it was obvious the Turks were not thrilled to have our cumbersome rig aboard. But Terence was in a hurry and had such obvious control, they stood back in admiration as he jammed that sucker aboard. I tried not to think about the itty bitty dinky piece of board they'd put down to bridge the gap over the water from the boat to the dock. Terence was so determined to put Greece behind him that I think he would have made it with nothing but air between the two sides!

We were so happy to be on board we were laughing to tears--not daring to believe we were safe. And sure enough, we weren't! One of the Turkish sailors found us on the top deck and said to Terence: "Why didn't you go through Customs? You must go to Greek Customs!" He pointed to a self-important figure standing on the dock who had apparently just finished chewing him out for taking the rig aboard. Our jaws dropped. Un-be-fucking-leeevable!

Terence went down with heavy heart and faced the next dragon. The other passengers stared at me as I sat in shock. I didn't dare go with him in case the guy spotted the Ascot on my passport. Terence told me later the guy was not impressed--or probably didn't know what to make of the piece of paper the earlier Greek officials had given Terence. It was probably bogus. They knew we couldn't read it and the bribe was shall we say--unofficial at best.

The Turks were anxious to leave but they knew they couldn't possibly ride the rig off the boat themselves. They glared at me and babbled amongst themselves but were probably used to such delays with these Greeks with whom they held an uneasy truce. I suppose they were lucky to even be allowed to dock at Rhodes once a day.

After much discussion, the man made new paperwork for everybody, stamped yet another entry into Terence's passport, crossed it out with a hand-written date, stamped a new EXIT mark, and hand-dated that. Thank God the rig was aboard. If Terence hadn't forced his way onto the little ferry when he did, we'd probably still be in Rhodes. What a thought!

Chapter Fifty-Seven

WE TAKE ON TURKEY

THE FERRY RIDE seemed much longer than two hours because T. and I had to take turns holding onto the rig as the little boat pitched and rolled. All around us people stared, mute, knowing who to blame if the boat was late getting them to their loved ones or if it should, Allah forbid, sink with the unwieldy contraption on board.

But once we were safely on shore, this new country surprised us with a very unexpected warmth and friendliness. After the huge rig was rolled onto the pier, the custom agents actually smiled under their handsome mustaches, waved us over to the desk, quickly stamped our passports and in a group, stood around the rig complimenting us on our fine machine and trailer. Now that was better! A slow ride through the seaport town because of the traffic, proved also good for the soul as Turkish men of all types waved and shouted "Welcome to Turkey!" over and over. Signs were written in letters we could read again and as I sat behind Terence looking around at the friendly crowd, I realized how much I had missed seeing people smile.

The Beck Campground was just outside the city but it was almost dark when we arrived. A tall fellow welcomed us with hands outstretched and seemed to have been waiting for us. He personally walked us around the site and explained in English where everything was, etc. Terence pulled the trailer in and unhitched it under a large tree in hopes that we could get some shade the next day. I made dinner and very tired, we went to bed early. As our funny little fan clacked and whirred above us, we compared notes on the day's adventures. With it all behind us, we could afford to laugh about it. We fell asleep with silly grins.

Trying to beat the heat, we went into town early in the morning of the next day and rode around running errands and checking out our new country. Even without the trailer, the GoldWing was an unusual sight to the people and of course, with the three big metal boxes Terence had built on it, they probably had never seen its like even in the movies. Young men clustered around the same way they had in eastern Europe, but this bunch was a much more jovial sort. Much more physical too, which was a new one for us. Hands would touch the motorcycle and actually reach for the levers, which was unnerving to Terence, because no one to this point had ever had the nerve to do such a thing. We both knew that nobody meant any harm. They were very much like children and so happy to see us and be allowed to get close. Even when the men lightly touched my arm or dress, I didn't feel threatened in any way. It was a sort of over-enthusiasm born of curiosity and frankly, after the hostility we'd experienced in Greece, this new experience was O.K. Still, I searched in vain for a female face. Such a shame.

We spent about six dollars on a nice lamb and salad mixture in Pita bread with three beers for lunch. We were the only customers for some reason--sitting at a table in the middle of a long river of identical tables on what must have been "Restaurant Row." Men and boys begged and cajoled from every doorway as we made our way past the first several outdoor eateries. Hoping to snag a customer or two, the enterprising owners had covered the sidewalks with their chairs and tables, so if you had to get out of the street fast--fleeing from oncoming cars, you were caught in their little webs and a menu was thrust into your hands before you could get free. And that's what happened to us. Our owner rubbed his hands in glee when we decided to stay, and I tried not to see the envy and disappointment of his neighbors still standing in their doorways with eyes sweeping the street for another customer. The food was filling and very tasty and not a bad introduction to Turkey. It occurred to us that this was what Greece must have been like before they got so spoiled with all the tourists. Turkey was number two and trying harder. With so many of its people speaking English and German--and with an alphabet most tourists could relate to--making it all so much easier, it had to just be a matter of time before they caught up to their neighbors on the other side of the Aegean.

Meanwhile, the difference was truly refreshing to a couple of jaded bikers like ourselves. Back at the campground, we had meant to clean out the trailer, but the heat was so oppressive we simply turned on the fan and sacked out for a couple of hours. We couldn't move. Later Terence walked down to the shore to swim and I went with him with the same intention, but after seeing all the broken glass in the water I changed my mind. All I needed was to get a nasty cut or two on my feet and along with the bone spur, it'd be wheelchair time! I went back to the campground and took a shower and sitting wet on my towel felt a little cooler at last. We met two nice Brits in their van. They gave us their old magazines and we traded with our old THE EUROPEAN newspaper. They had lots of advice about Turkey and the other countries we'd be passing through on our way north and it was pleasant to be with people from our part of the world again.

We left the next morning for Pamukkale, leaving the bustling seaport of Marmaris far below as we wound our way up the pine-spotted mountains. At first the ride was quite a joy, with spring-fed water fountains every few miles where we could stop and drink our fill and soak our bandannas and splash at each other. But once over the ridge, the road entered a long very dry valley. No trees. No water, and by the time we reached the very popular tourist spot, we were so parched and uncomfortable, we had little patience with the pushy young men trying to sell us lodging and post-cards, and the hands that were thrust our way almost got bitten off in our frustration at not being able to find any sign posts for the campground T. had read about in our guide book. Our bandannas had dried long ago and we were so thirsty we felt faint. There was no way to ask directions--no one spoke English beyond "You buy?" and we were afraid if we stopped, we'd be mobbed and suffocated by the eager merchants. After going around in circles for awhile, Terence decided to go down a road that had a sign saying Camp with Swimming Pool. To our amazement, a real live woman was walking toward us. A glance at the advertised swimming pool explained it. All the men for miles around were splashing happily and shouting to each other. No women allowed in the water. She didn't speak much English but enough, and led us to the only shady spot in the area. When we asked her the price, she was stymied. Apparently, she could be trusted with just so much and no more. She called for her young son who seemed about eight years old. Maybe ten. He decided on two dollars. All--

right! Later, what must have been her husband came around to be helpful. I had the uneasy thought that while $2 might have been the price for most people, he would have liked to ask a bit more from rich Americans. But he didn't and before we left to go sightseeing, he brought us two cups of coffee. This time it was the real thing. Two tiny cups of thick and foamy stuff that putting milk in would be a sacrilege and that one could only drink half of because the rest of the cup was the grounds. Wild. We loved it.

Thus buzzed, we climbed aboard the Wing to visit the famous site of great lime cliffs of Pamukkale. We first passed the ancient city of Hieropolis, which lay scattered about the crest of the mountain looking more like a construction site than the remains of a city thousands of years old. Great neat stacks of carved and hewn stone stood at the side of the road as if men through the ages had gently placed them there intending to patch up the damage from earthquakes and wars and rebuild and perhaps add new temples to the gods. There was a small museum that had once been thermal springs baths for the Emperors of Rome, and contained whatever was left after all the centuries of robbers had helped themselves. Everything being in Turkish made it a little difficult to learn much about the place. We walked down the road to the lime cliffs.

Pamukkale means Cotton Castle. It is a dazzling white plateau, almost 400 feet high, consisting of hundreds of pools and stalagmites in varying levels, filled and formed by the limestone-rich water fed by the thermal springs of Cal Dagi. Being the height of the tourist season, there were so many people taking pictures and splashing merrily in the pools, that the spectacle was easier to see on a postcard, but still remarkable for all that. My foot was giving me so much pain that I told Terence to go on without me and get some good pictures while I sat by one of the warm pools and soaked my heel. It might have been rather pleasant, but the locals wouldn't leave me in peace. I and every other tourist in the area were fair game. Especially those of us that stopped moving for some reason or other. I watched as other tourists would try to take a picture or maybe blow their nose. They were immediately set upon by the sellers of lace or embroidery or post-cards and if they didn't keep walking, the beggars would descend in greater numbers until the poor soul had no way to break free--like a buzzing fly in a web. The more he'd resist, the tighter the bond of humanity would press. And there I was, obviously lame and not going anywhere soon. After the hundredth time of firmly saying no, I gave up trying to rest and pulled myself up to limp around and find Terence--several of the more persistent sellers following along--no doubt hoping I was simply trying to find the half of the couple with the money bags.

Terence was glad to find me--he'd been looking for me and probably worried that I'd limped my crooked way off one of the steep cliffs without him to hold my hand. We rode back to the gorgeous ruins of Hieropolis to get more photographs. For some reason, the beggars left us alone there. It was 6:30 p.m. and still broiling hot. After about an hour, we boarded the bike for the ride home and were half way there when a taxi driver excitedly waved us over. We naïvely thought he needed help by his frantic demeanor, but it seemed he only wanted to invite us home for tea. We had read in some guide book or other that to refuse such an invitation in Turkey would be bad manners and not knowing how to get out of it, we accepted. Terence had made the mistake of speaking German and as the man spoke no English I could do little else but go along for the ride. We followed him to a dusty concrete block among other such dwellings in the village and were waved inside with much pomp and smiling. We took our shoes off at the door and while Terence and the man sat on the floor, I was allowed to sit on one of the beds in the room. The wife came in and we all shook hands. She then seemed to back into a sort of doorless closet and sat on the floor. The man brought out stacks of his wife's embroidery to show us and I thought how nice that he appreciates his wife's work when suddenly the look on Terence's face told me we had been ensnared in a classic con job. I listened carefully to the man's German and realized he was saying that we were to choose those we wished to buy! I said through gritted teeth to Terence that I didn't want any of the darned things and wanted to leave but it wasn't that easy. T. translated for me that he was saying how hard life was with three kids and a lousy job driving a taxi and working as a gardener at some hotel. My heart remained hardened. He wanted thirty dollars for the large scarf I had made the mistake of admiring just to be polite. I told Terence to offer him five dollars and no more no matter what, and the man pretended to faint. I felt myself getting angrier--especially looking at that poor woman in the doorway who resembled the family dog more than the artisan who had slaved over all those useless pieces of cloth. I wondered if she actually had to eat her meals out of a bowl on the floor. Terence seemed as though he might give in and buy the sad offerings to get us out the door and that made me even madder. Who's kissing ass now? I thought. I decided to cry and see what the Turk would do. I must confess that it worked. (Probably the first time he'd seen a "German" cry). I was so furious at the setup and with the heat and my foot hurting, crying was easy. The man became rattled and quickly told Terence to forget buying. Everything was cool, he was assuring us-- we'd have some nice hot tea and be friends. He ordered the family dog to bring it to us. HOT TEA, IS HE CRAZY?, my expression must have said. Terence was actually smoothing things over while I sulked and when I noticed the wife was not going to be allowed to partake--and instead had sat back down on the floor in her closet to watch us, I really flipped out. It seemed to me Terence looked just a little too comfortable on the floor with his male chum as they chatted brightly in a language neither the wife nor I could understand. Grrr.

I stayed frosty until we could leave and then hoped the poor woman wouldn't get a beating or something because we hadn't bought her pathetic needlework. We rode back to the campground and wordlessly ate some cheese and cherries and pieces of cucumber for dinner. Then, feeling sticky and wanting to wash off the whole taxi-driver experience, we decided to jump into the not-too-clean pool. After splashing around awhile, we started up a conversation with two French ladies and a Turkish fellow who were having dinner at a table near the pool. They were the only other visitors as far as I could tell, and we all enjoyed meeting each other. The owner came around and put two small teacups on a tray with a sugar bowl and tiny teaspoons and floated it over to us in the water. Our spirits lifted.

After paying the princely sum of $2 to our host the next morning, we rode on down the road through the small village of Denili and out into the searing flatlands. At a sort of ancient burial ground just outside of Cardak, we stopped to take care of personal business and shoot some pictures. I found a tall weedy area where I could have some privacy and watch the women work in the fields way in the distance. I was pondering the lot of such folk and thinking about what a hard life the women led here when I heard rustling in the weeds next to me and almost jumped out of my skin. It was just a large tortoise making its way to the little stream nearby.

On through Isparta to the rather touristy town of Egirdiz by a lake. Terence was looking for a place to change traveler's checks but the bank was closed. Among the curious onlookers was a small boy who was smiling shyly at me. I smiled back. He wiggled his way past the bigger boys and handed me a string of little prayer beads and ran away before I could thank him. The older guys laughed at my surprise and gestured that I must keep them. I was delighted. A man who had been looking at the Wing asked if he could help and took T. to a hotel where the manager asked for American dollars. We had about $100 and the exchange was far better than we'd gotten with the checks but it was all sort of under the table. We wished we'd had more dollars, but of course carrying money around wasn't a very good idea either. While Terence fended off a gang of carpet sellers, I found a place to buy bread and cold soft drinks. Ascending the mountain just out of town we spotted a turnout and pulled off to eat lunch. We had bought cherries earlier from a very cranky old man who had insisted we buy two kilos for 40KTL. About six dollars. Terence gave him 10KTL and he angrily took out one kilo from the sack, leaving us one kilo for one-fourth of the price he had demanded. We were learning.

Coming down the mountain, we passed several miles of planted pine trees then past a large reservoir and then into the dusty town of Konya. No signs indicating any campgrounds. We stopped at a small market to buy milk and vegetables and even found some cookies. But no one had heard of any sort of legal place for the likes of us to spend the night. We pushed on. Got gas at the edge of town where "Full Service" included a small tray of two glasses of real lemonade!

The road was hot, dusty and flat, flat. Small tufts of grass kept the sheep alive, I decided, because there were almost always flocks in the distance--being tended by young men in tattered clothes walking slowly over the hot sand. I began to despair as the red sun sunk in the west. No trees or rocks to hide behind. Nothing but flocks of sheep on the desert. I told Terence I really had to go pee-pee and there was nothing to do but stop the motorcycle on the road and try to hide behind it. A large truck containing three Turks came to a stop behind us as I was attempting to relieve myself and the men jumped out--all smiles and delighted to be able to welcome us to Turkey! As I hurriedly pulled up my pants, they surrounded Terence and began asking the usual questions about the bike. I was furious and embarrassed but the men obviously couldn't guess why. I was only a woman, after all.

After a bit, we were able to shake the Happy Truckers and get back on the bike and ride away. It was getting dark and we were resigned to having to camp in the open somewhere. We had heard it was dangerous to drive in this part of the country at night. Terence pulled off the road and we rode on some gravel for about a hundred yards before we decided the terrain wasn't going to get any better and so we stopped and set up camp. We were tired and dirty and a little frightened to be so exposed. T. told me to start writing in my journal to keep my mind off the danger, while he made some macaroni and cheese. It was delicious. And the strong vodka drinks he mixed with some sort of fruit juice went down very smoothly. Soon we were giggling and playing music tapes to full volume. We could see the headlights on cars far away on the highway but they became fewer as the hour grew later and the vodka gave us courage. Who could possibly see our black motorcycle and trailer on this moonless night once we'd turned off the lantern? We fell into bed and were deeply asleep in no time.

Chapter Fifty-Eight

A RUDE AWAKENING

SOMEWHERE AROUND MIDNIGHT, bright headlights were streaming into the open flap of the trailer-tent. I bolted upright and tried to wake Terence. I could make out about four men--two soldiers and two in officer's uniforms standing in front of the glaring lights of a sort of truck. Terence wouldn't wake up. He'd had a lot more of the vodka than he should have. One of the officers was asking me questions in Turkish. I could now see the rifles in the hands of the soldiers trained upon us. My mouth went dry and I became uncomfortably aware that I had on a very thin T-shirt.

I shook Terence hard until he opened his eyes and sort of waved at the guys and went back to sleep. I swear one of the young soldiers waved back. I was afraid to dig under the pillow for my passport unless absolutely necessary because (1) it might have been construed as a "furtive movement" which would earn me a bullet at close range, or (2) the officers might want to take it to the nearest telephone or communications center-- nearest being around 100 miles away--and I might never see it again. So, drawing the sheet up around my neck, I pretended to look cool and said, "Americanski. uh..Americani. AMERICANISHE."

"Ahh," said the leader in what looked like a trench coat. He gestured to the others and including himself, announced "Turk-ish!" "Really," I said, hoping I was showing the right amount of admiration and wonder. "Isn't that nice?" We all relaxed. The two kids in camo didn't put down their weapons, but they were smiling and seemed to be enjoying themselves.

The other two looked over the bike and jabbered to each other and said lots of things to me but soon realized it was useless. None of us had a word in common, the only linguist amongst us was snoring blissfully at my side. The foolish grins on the soldiers made me uncomfortably aware that I was not exactly in competition for the latest look in fashion. Hair dry, dirty and windblown, a mass of greasy mosquito lotion slathered all over my sunburned face, and with the glassy gaze of the just awakened from a deep slumber. I realized later, after they had gone, to my horror, my threadbare T-shirt I liked to sleep in on hot nights, was on wrong-side out and read, "7891 GNIDGNIW REMMUSDIM SGNIW REDROB." No wonder it took them so long to figure out what language I was speaking! And here I had been thinking they were staring at my perfect breasts. Oh, well.

After a short discourse on what could have been anything, and then what sounded like a brief fatherly lecture on maybe the perils of camping wild, they waved and left in a spray of sand. I crashed back onto the bed in relief--waking my Lord and Protector who mumbled something about how that had to be the last of them, and then he was snoring again. How could he do that?, I wondered.

As I attempted to relax into sleep, a tremendous wind came up. I couldn't believe it. What next? It whipped around the trailer and howled as if it wanted to devour us! The slope side of the trailer roof--right next to my pillow, bumped and rattled with the empty extra gasoline containers Terence had strapped on the other side. He had placed--not secured--my bike cover over the front of the Gold Wing to keep the reflectors from showing to the highway beyond, and the thing was flapping like a sail. I knew I should get up and tie it down or take it off. If it freed itself, it could blow across the plain and over the horizon during the night and we'd never find it and we really couldn't afford to lose that cover. But the sober thought of getting out of bed in my undies and into a dust storm with who knew who else might be watching us from the highway dampened my best intentions and so I just lay there like a coward waiting for the storm to blow away. Every time Terence turned or breathed differently, I asked hopefully, "Terence, are you awake?" But he never was.

The last time I looked at my watch it was 5 a.m. and the Sirocco was still in full blast, but I must have finally dropped off because the next thing that I heard was not wind, but the distant sound of sheep bells, and coming our way! Terence woke up alert, finally, and realizing I was not about to make him the full-on breakfast in the middle of a flock of sheep

(Oh where is my sense of adventure?), he agreed that we ought to fly out of there before the welcoming committee arrived. We almost made it, but not quite, as the two young shepherds ran to catch us before we could roll.

Again the welcoming gestures and the open mouths at the sight of the rig. Their flocks forgotten, some of the woolly ones were walking down the highway by the time we could maneuver through them and I think the guys must have had a sweet time gathering them up again. No dogs, we noticed. How could they make do without dogs? About ten miles down the road, we stopped to eat our hard-boiled eggs and cold coffee with boxed milk substitute and cherries and cheese. Not a bad breakfast, considering.

Later that morning, we stopped to take pictures of a large herd of black goats that seemed to be exploring the rather romantic ruins of an ancient mosque. We were so pleased to be getting some exciting pictures that we felt generous and offered to take a Polaroid photo of the two men who were tending the goats. Bad mistake. After we handed them their picture, the older one began to badger us for a roll of film! He was very persistent and things became ugly. To get away, T. gave in and gave him a cheap roll of B & W. We pulled away from the scene with another bad taste in our mouths. The goatherd would probably try to sell it to tourists... Would we ever learn?

I can't describe the landscape of Cappadocia without reading somewhat out of the guide book. It tells us that some thirty million years ago there were three volcanoes. Over million of years, their eruptions covered the land with a type of stone that was soft and easily worked. A few million more years of erosion turned the place into a dream landscape that attracted the hermits of early Christianity, then just other folks who found their own funny rock towers to dig holes into and live in. Some of the rock forms are the shape of bananas or very tall mushrooms or even human forms. More than a few are amusingly phallic and those seem to have been the most popular to carve houses into. Other are so huge that they give the appearance of whole apartment houses and reminded me of the charming soft-cornered surreality of the architecture of Antonio Gaudi in Barcelona.

Once we had unhitched and settled our dusty prairie wagon into a campground in Göreme, we immediately rode out again to have a look at this fascinating region. The Cappadocian Valley is made for motorcycle touring.

Terence and I went nuts with our cameras. There were masses of other tourists too, but the valley is so gigantic and there are so many endless vistas that nobody could feel crowded. For days, we packed our lunch and rode out to see all we could before we had to push on. In one of the villages in the Göreme Valley, Terence went down into an ancient underground village (dug to beat the heat?) while I opted to tour an old Byzantine church above ground. After he came up, we took a chance on stepping into a tiny bakery along with the locals, and bought a round yeast bun that had a small piece of feta cheese and tomato in the middle. It was big enough for two and really delicious. And thirty cents!

One afternoon we passed through several desperately poor mud villages where men and children and even a few mummy-wrapped women waved hello. Everyone so friendly, but we couldn't help but be glad we were just passing through. Shopping for groceries was difficult-- even in the larger towns. Even without things to sell, the men and boys would surround us and the same old pattern would begin. First the super-friendly hello and welcome. Then the questions (in German) about where we came from and how much the motorcycle cost. If we were at all friendly (and we tried), the questions would come thicker and faster and soon the demands from the younger boys who couldn't contain their excitement would begin. They would reach for the levers and tell Terence to play the radio or cassettes. Once when I turned around from taking a picture a few feet away from the bike, I saw the kids wearing our helmets! Terence had allowed them to try them on --not thinking about nasty stuff like lice. I really wish I didn't have to either, but that we didn't need. Each stop was the same. The kids just seemed to materialize out of nowhere. Maybe out of the ground. The grown men were only slightly more hesitant. Once I went into a place to look for a newspaper. When I returned about five minutes later, T. and the bike were swallowed up in a large crowd of men. I had to push my way through. Then they all wanted to help hoist the old lady onto the seat. Arggh. And forgive me, but they smelled terrible. Terence asked, "Whatever happened to the Turkish Bath?"

A great black cloud was raining on the scene way ahead of us as we barreled over the high plain. On both sides of us lay more of the pock-marked canyons where humans had carved little dwellings for themselves for centuries. All empty now. Great slices of golden light slid across the cave faces as thick clouds were blown across the sun overhead and the air became suddenly cooler. As we rode down into the canyon and turned around a bend, we heard first a clap of thunder and then the muezzin's call to prayer in the village below. We stopped the bike above the cliffs to look. The cloud-edged light from the sun shown over the wet roofs and minarets of the little village like spotlights and played on the cave-dotted cliffs above as if it were some painted backdrop. The ageless chant continued from its tower and we looked at each other close to tears. Times like these made the hardships truly insignificant.

Coming back to camp, we noticed the rain had hit hard and fast there. Muddy runoffs were gurgling down the streets and furrows were half full of water in the fields. We considered ourselves very lucky that we had missed the cloudburst.

That evening we went over our timetable. We had been dawdling here in this wonderful valley too long. We decided that if we left the trailer in the Göreme campground, we could ride fast one whole day and find a cheap hotel in Kâhta, where we could spend the night and go on a special guided tour to the famous mountaintop of Nemrut Dag in the east, something we really didn't want to miss. That evening we met a charming French couple also on a motorcycle, who were planning the same trip to Nemrut Dag. We all planned to meet in Kâhta for dinner at the Pension the next day.

Chapter Fifty-Nine

A REALLY TERRIBLE AWFULLY BAD DAY

WE LEFT Göreme around 7:45 a.m. Drove around in circles awhile, there being no road signs again. Why do they do this to tourists?! Finally found the right road and did the light fantastic to Malatya in about five hours where we stopped for lunch at a little cozy-looking hole in the wall in the center of town. Men sat around eating and drinking tea and watching Belly Dancers on TV. We were ushered past them and up some narrow stairs to a curtained loft. Where the lepers and women were fed, no doubt. We tried to tell the waiter we wanted something like the stuffed pita bread we had in Marmaris. He seemed to understand. He brought forth a plate of pita bread cut into tiny triangles. Then a platter of salad--tomatoes, cucumber slices mostly. Then, puffing up the stairs (serves him right for banishing us to the attic), he carried two dinner plates of super thin sliced lamb over hot rice. Not bad. The meal plus two warm cokes plus tip cost us five dollars.

In Göreme, Terence had found a tourist place that went over the map with him and although there was a shortcut to Adiyam near Kâhta, T. had been advised to ignore it because, the woman told him, it was mostly gravel. Now, looking at the map in our little restaurant, we talked it over. We were running late, thanks to the lack of road signs. The Wing was big and strong, we were tough and what the hell, we didn't have the cumbersome trailer to hold us back. It wasn't even raining. How bad could it be?

We had to ask several times of course, how to find the famous shortcut.

Finally, we seemed to be heading in the right direction, up a steep red-pebbled mountain and down and up again for what seemed like hours. Occasionally, we spotted a small child with a few sheep and we wondered what on earth they found for the animals to eat up there. There wasn't another sign of life in all those rocks and the heat was really intense. After the road would dip down into a dry little valley, we would find more people to ask the way, then up again we'd go with the red pebbles getting larger and larger until it was like riding on a dry river bed. A time came when we realized we'd made a mistake taking this way--but then, we asked each other, how much farther could it be?

Up and down, up and down and around. Now the valleys we rode into were flooded in places. We saw whole families trying to dig out their crops that were submerged by the mud. It looked bad. Their faces showed such anxiety I felt so sorry for them. For once, boys didn't shout greetings to us as we passed. Everyone was too busy trying to dig away the mud. After a bit, our "road" began showing signs of the same catastrophe. Several times I had to get off of the bike so that Terence could maneuver through the cracks and rivulets in the road without the extra weight. Some of those eroded places were dangerously close to the edge of the cliff. I began to get worried. It got worse. Steeper. Rockier. Hotter. I was telling myself I couldn't complain because I had agreed the "shortcut" would be a good idea and anyway, Terence was doing all the work while I sat back there gnashing my teeth. Oh, but my rear was getting sore!

Riding through a particularly dirty village on the side of a mountain, we were hailed by the men sitting outside their cafe and asked to join them for ay (tea). We waved at them and forced a jaunty smile and kept on. Just outside their village we came to a fork in the road. No signs of course. Only one of the roads was paved, and with a sigh of relief, we took it. It was heaven being on a paved road again. But after about 15 miles, I leaned forward and mentioned to Terence that we seemed to be going west instead of east and that couldn't be right. He stopped the bike and looked at the map. A little farther on we saw a group of men standing in front of a house. We showed them the map and pantomimed our confusion. They seemed thrilled to be asked. They passed the map back and forth between them, turning it this way and that and all came to the conclusion that yes, we were going in the right direction. So we went on. Terence decided after a while that they had to be wrong. He said they probably couldn't read...and that they thought that because we were hot shot westerners on a dream machine, we must know what we were doing and so the polite thing for them to do would be to simply agree with us. He was furious. I was suddenly in great discomfort. My aches and pains wouldn't stay ignored any longer. Everything hurt and I was scared. Somewhere along the long road to nowhere, the realization had come to me that the people around us and in the muddy fields weren't Turkish anymore. Kurds? What had we been reading about in the last newspaper we found about the war between the Kurds and the Turkish? Something recently about an ambush by Kurdish rebels that wiped out a whole local police station? Ohmygod, that was why the truck in the middle of the night and the drawn rifles! If they'd have thought we were Kurdish in the dark, asleep in our little flapping tent in the middle of the desert and decided to shoot first and ask later.... Stupid, that's what we were. And very lucky. Forget American Embassies and Consulates attempting to locate us months later after our worried relatives staged hunger strikes on their steps in Ankara. We could have disappeared without a trace, the flotsam and jetsam of our disassembled motorbike home dangling from hooks on a hundred mud walls from here to the Iraqi border.

My companion was feeling his own adverse effects of the long day. He was in his Fear and Loathing mood and decided to take his disappointment in the whole world out on me where it did not sit well. Just as we were losing complete control of ourselves and screaming at each other, we saw a truck with two men and with a motorcycle in the back! Nothing less than a Deus Ex Machina--way out here where they call the wind Mariah. Biker to biker, Terence calmed down and asked them for help in finding the right direction and they seemed to understand what route we needed. They said they were on their way to Celikan and we should follow them. That was the dirty little village where the friendly tea-drinkers had tried to flag us down--over an hour ago! There was nothing to do but turn around and follow the sports. As I feared, we were led to that signless fork in the road where we had chosen the paved road over the dirt one and made our fatal mistake. The two men leaned from their truck's cab and gave us what sounded like very heavy advice in Turkish and we couldn't understand a word. Now that the experience is over, and I'm writing this down, I'm sure what they were saying was "FOR ALLAH'S SAKE, DON'T GO ON THAT ROAD BECAUSE IT ONLY GETS WORSE AND I WOULD NOT SEND MY WORST ENEMY THAT WAY NOW THAT THE STORM HAS WIPED OUT MOST OF THE PATH so why don't you come into Celikan with us for a cup of tea? But as you know, we didn't understand the language.

On we pushed. At yet another rutted fork in the road, we asked a farmer the way to Adiyaman and he pointed up. Up and up and the gravely path got thinner and the falling off edge got closer and the streams eroding ditches across the road every few feet got deeper. I took a couple of pictures of mighty Terence doing his Iron Man thing across a particularly bad stretch and thought about how great they'd look in say, the National Geographic--especially if I caught him just as he was sliding over the cliff to the rocks way below.

The sun was going down. We realized we were not going to be able to meet those nice French bikers at the Pension Restaurant in Kâhta after all. We probably weren't going to meet anyone ever again if we didn't get out of this God-forsaken series of gorges-from-Hell! Terence sweated and strained. The big bike fell over once or twice in the soft rocky gravel but we slid on...there was certainly no turning back at this point. The only thing that kept us going now was in hoping things would improve just around the corner--coupled with the other thought that the only worse experience would be trying to find our way in the pitch dark!

Stuck at a three-fork crossroad, we picked the most important-looking path and coming around the bend, found ourselves in the middle of a road construction zone. T. asked an elderly-looking fellow the way to Adiyaman and looking rather frightened, the man gestured wildly for us to go back the way we came. As we made a "U" in the soft dirt, a guy came running out of a shed, putting shells into a rifle and pointing it at us! Terence yelled at me to duck down behind the top case of the bike while he careened us out of there. We heard a crack as the rifle went off and skidding around the bend I prayed there'd be no pursuit. A long way from an invitation to tea, for sure.

Three more times we tried different paths from the fork and were met with only failure. One went to a rushing river. It looked like it had once been the right road. One went around a hill on a truly terrible rock path that only T. could have traversed, and then it circled back to the stupid crossroads! And the third led across a stream and up a long slippery grade to a newly-built bridge whose approach road had been totally washed away, leaving a gap of about fifteen feet between the new bridge and the mountain! Glumly, Terence pulled the laboring motorcycle around in the rocks and we headed down once again. But the banking had been all but washed away and as we tried to get around a curve, the poor bike simply sank in the gravel and rolled over on its back like a dying elephant--sending both of us flying into the large rocks of the mountainside. I pulled myself out in some pain but I didn't think I'd broken anything. Terence was shouting at me to hurry up and help him turn the bike over before all the gasoline drained out.

Somehow, thanks once more to Terence's astonishing ability to summon the strength of two men when he needs to, we were able to right the huge machine and as we were attempting to assess the damage, an elderly farmer came running up the hill to help. He mimed that he'd seen us tumble and was very concerned for us. Really kind. We mimed back that we were O.K. and then incredibly, from another path out of nowhere, a small white car full of people rumbled down the hill from the direction we'd just come. More hand gestures and they agreed to show us the way out of there--if we'd follow them. By this time, more dark men had emerged from the shadows and all seemed anxious to help. Because, as it turned out, the only road to Adiyaman was through the river that had apparently washed out the road in the last storm.

In the failing light, the rushing water looked like Niagara Falls. The men mumbled to each other on the banks and shook their heads. I said no way was I going to go across on the motorcycle and T. said fine, he didn't want my extra weight anyway, so I stood on the bank with everybody else who said it couldn't be done and we all waited to see bike and rider fall over in the current and go bobbing down the river, and Lo and Behold, that Gold Wing took him across as if Moses himself had parted the Red Sea!

The men and I cheered. Then they looked at me. My right foot was beginning to swell from my recent landing in the rocks and I figured it might feel good to soak it a bit and anyway my shoes were crap so no harm there, so I walked through the river, which although moving fast, was not as deep as it looked.

Everybody waved goodbye as I boarded the Wing behind the Fearless One and we were almost safe. Somewhere, as we were coming down the mountain, a small group of boys though it fun to throw rocks at us and one hit my helmet. Terence was serious about turning around and throwing the little darlings off the cliff but although it was tempting, I felt we'd had enough display of machismo for one day, and talked him out of it.

Everything after that was easy, even though it had gotten dark. After riding down one more mountain and then through the long-sought town of Adiyaman, the next little dusty berg was Kâhta where amazingly, we saw our French friends walking down the main street. They had missed us at dinner and were on their way to their hotel where they had been charged an exorbitant price for a room. The cheaper Pension that we all had read about in the guide books was no longer in existence. The natives were getting smarter. Dead tired and hungry but unwilling to pay what the poor French couple had had to cough up, T. and I rolled around the grim little town until we found a sort basic one-star hotel called Mezopotamya West where we were shown a large room with three single beds with a balcony that overlooked what seemed to be a wild celebration of some kind. It was a team of soccer players and their fans--all men of course--who had just come from what seemed like the game of the century between the home team and their favorite rivals from the next town. The manager promised us that the music (?) would stop at eleven, but we really didn't care. After our experience on the scorching mountains of Hades and the passage through the River Styx, the revelry of screaming fans and Dervish band music would sound like a lullaby. We bought a couple of beers from the manager, finding food would be too much trouble at this hour and anyway, we were past being hungry. After a blessed shower, we leaned over our little balcony railing and watched the party below. The rituals seemed so strange to us. No women anywhere. Men dancing with men. The drunker they got (Islams drinking booze--such rebels!), the more sensuous the dance...writhing and hip thrusting against each other..bump and grind..then suddenly the music stops and everybody goes back to their beer and cigarette.

We crashed and slept soundly. I was vaguely aware of a minibus being loaded with American student tourists around two in the morning. It was the touted "Sunrise Trip" to the famous Nemrut Dag summit that we too had come to see. The word was that the best time was at rosy dawn, when the effect was supposed to be "magical." Uh huh. I went back to sleep.

On Wednesday, June 31, we woke to a blinding sun coming over our balcony wall. It was only 6:30 a.m. and already hotter than Death Valley at noon! "Yuk," I said, and went to look for an uninhabited W.C.

Auntie Gail's Handy Hints for Ladies on Surviving Third-World toilets: have I mentioned that I've discovered the Western solution to getting in and getting out of certain water closets without losing your lunch? Well, the secret is in holding your nose--not your breath. DO NOT BREATHE FROM YOUR NOSE UNDER ANY CIRCUMSTANCES. Just breathe with your mouth--in and out--as if your nose didn't exist. Wave away some of the flies and squat. As you are doing your business, turn on the water faucet that has been placed ever so conveniently on the floor and fill up the (usually) provided plastic water pitcher. Do not look at what may already be in the pitcher. Finish personal stuff (you did bring toilet paper, didn't you?) and attempt to stand. The paper goes in a receptacle provided, so I'd been told, but I never saw one, so throw it in the horrible hole and let them worry about the plumbing. Draw on clothes and then bend down and pour your filled pitcher of water around and into the hole; making sure you don't leave any paper around because the next person in there might be a Turk who would see it, and being unacquainted with toilet paper, might become alarmed that perhaps the person who was before him had dropped his or her grocery list or the odd love letter. Exit with your head held high.

The breakfast included in the bill consisted of two glasses of the usual hot ay then a very long wait for food while we haggled the price of a ticket to the famous Mountain Top with the Tour Director. They were all in this together, I reasoned. The eternal wait to be served might have been cleverly calculated to weaken us into submission and force us to pay the higher price. Who could tell? After we agreed to pay the Director 75KTL each, about $23, we were served a small plate consisting of a thin and greasy triangle of one stirred and set egg, and three tin foil wrapped items: a tiny pat of butter, one of processed cheese and the third containing something that resembled apple butter. There had been a big basket of bread, but an American college girl who sat down to chat was steadily helping herself to it and T. and I were so hungry after our adventures the day before, I brazenly asked the waiter for another rather than snatch it from her.

Back in the hall after breakfast, I had to rebuff the what sure seemed like amorous advances of the hotel manager. It had been so long since I'd had to play that game, he caught me completely unaware and for too long I just thought he was being super friendly. I realized later that the thing to have done was to give the signal to cease and desist at the very first sign of, well, whatever one feels is improper or simply uncomfortable. But being a friendly sort of person (especially where rather attractive men are concerned--so sue me), I figure a little teasing won't hurt and in America we all know the rules. Well, there I was in a strange country with all its ambiguities--where straight men dance seductively with other men, the broadcasts from the minarets in every village wakes you at 4:30 a.m. to pray, and men prize their sheep more than their women and all the talk of morality-- so holier than thous of the rest of us. Why is manhandling the tourist suddenly O.K.?

Well, no harm done. Once I realized what was up (so to speak), I let him know I wasn't interested and pretended to have heard Terence call me, and took off....And thereafter avoided the man like the plague--with him looking at me sulkily from doorways. What the hell did he want from me, anyway? There were all those nubile college students running up and down the stairs. Maybe it's "hands off" the possible virgins here. Maybe it was the tattoo on my ankle or the motorcycle mama look. Maybe from past experience he's discovered older women love it--he wasn't bad looking-- and are inclined to slip him some extra money for the "compliment." Actually, he probably thinks all western women are whores.

While we waited for our tour to take off--we were going on the "Sunset" tour, at what seemed to us like the much more civilized hour of two in the afternoon--we decided to ride around Kâhta and look for a bank so we could change some traveler's checks. We were happy to find one after only a few wrong turns, and I sat on the bike nursing my foot while Terence went inside. The usual crowd began to gather. I looked around at the squalor of the buildings and pretended not to be unnerved. I was actually getting used to the stares by this time. The guys meant no harm. I was sure they had no idea they were annoying or scaring me. They seemed a lot like a bunch of children whose parents had taught them a totally different set of manners than what we were used to. Apparently, respecting another person's privacy was not high on the list of how to make the visitor comfortable.

As I was contemplating this profound bit of wisdom, a handsome gentleman with gray hair and twinkling eyes handed me a rose. A rose! In the middle of the desert. I couldn't have been more surprised nor more pleased. As quickly as he appeared, he disappeared, and I was left wondering if I'd imagined the thing in the noonday heat except that I still had the beautiful flower in my hand. I looked around at the audience. Smiles everywhere. Damn, I wish I knew some Turkish! And as if that weren't amazing enough for one day, an actual woman stepped out of the crowd! She was swathed in black cloth and elderly, but she was obviously respected by the others and after ascertaining that I was an American, she indicated that there was a person in the vicinity who could speak English and she would go and fetch him. I watched her cross the street while the mob watched me trying to get more comfortable on my black leather seat. It was terribly hot but I felt safe sitting there and the thought of limping around to find a seat somewhere in the shade while watched by the multitudes gave me pause. She walked up to a thin young man who was reading a book in front of a shop and took him by the arm and dragged

419

him across the street and the crowd parted for them. He looked terrified, but indeed spoke enough English to ask the usual questions which I dutifully answered, and he translated to the mob's great delight. The poor kid had the worst speech impediment I'd ever heard...rather like the unkind stuttering act that Red Skelton used to do on television in his bit about the punch-drunk prize fighter. The town was obviously very proud of him. The matriarch in black told me he was studying to be a doctor. Ah..good luck. Although why not? He was reading a book when we interrupted him, wasn't he? How many other people in this baking village could read? He'd probably make a great doctor.

At two p.m., we were picked up at the hotel to be driven by minibus all the way up the mountain to see the famous ruins of Nemrut Dag. We were happy to see that the couple from Liverpool that we'd met that morning were coming too.

Our driver was a surly young Turk who spoke no English and seemed to dislike his job (or us) from the beginning. Maybe he was Kurdish. Churlish is more like it. Before getting on the right road, he first tooled around the village picking up friends and dropping them off and generally seeming to be trying to put off the distasteful task of what he was being paid to do--namely, get us up the mountain by sunset.

What a ride! We had been discouraged from taking the Wing--they said it was too rough and after our ordeal over the mountains the day before, Terence was all too willing to let someone else do the driving. And rough was what it was. Especially in that our driver, who couldn't care less about our comfort and was probably trying to make up for the time lost in playing BUS for his fellow villagers, careened and bounced our little minivan up and around the mountains so perilously close to the cliff edge that we all were hanging on for dear life--hoping that Mr. Hostility didn't want to die anymore than we did. He came to a dust-blown halt in front of (big surprise) a restaurant halfway up the mountain, indicating that we could have ten minutes to swallow an overpriced beer before boarding again. Chewing dirt, we all did as we were told and were soon aboard for more of the same torture. Somehow we arrived in one piece.

Nemrut Dag is the mountain peak where Antiochus I is buried, in case you've always wondered. Colossal stone statues carved sometime around the first century B.C. face both east and west--hence the hype about wanting to be there either for sunrise or sunset. All the giant heads of the huge statues have fallen off and the resulting effect is really pretty spectacular. The place is becoming more and more popular with tourists and although the Turkish may have been a little behind with the amenities at first, they're finally catching on as to what a little gold mine they have there and if the few bad guys could stem their enormous greed, there ought to be money aplenty for muddy villages for miles around as the tourist influx swells. When we were there, everybody had their hand out and the sneaky Tour Director who pocketed the "tour" money back at the hotel had carefully avoided mentioning the various "entrance" fees along the way, the stiff twenty-minute walk from the bus park, and the refreshment stand--leading up to the summit where the stone heads were. As we all climbed out of our little buses, we were immediately surrounded by dozens of donkey drivers dressed in rags, chomping at their bits to greet each unwary visitor who might blanch at the long hot walk to get to the top. The little animals were really more like miniature burros and as usual I couldn't help but think what an awful life they must lead. Spying an American woman with a limp made all the drivers see dollar signs and it was so embarrassing to be closed in by the smelly men and beasts slathering to be chosen, that I decided to tough it out and walk the whole way to the top. Terence was no help in getting rid of them. He thought I should take them up on their offer, probably because I was so slow and would be holding him back. I was sorry, I told him, but I just couldn't.

I toughed it out and made up my mind to definitely have surgery on that foot as soon as I got home. At the top, several busloads of eager viewers got in each other's way trying to get the best photos and there was no way to take pictures of the wonderful heads without someone walking past and spoiling the shots, which I thought a shame, but Terence said he was happy with ones he took, and after we all oo-ed and ahh-ed at the pinks and golds splayed over the western decapitation site by the sinking sun, everybody started down the long path to the waiting vans. My foot was throbbing. Once again, the burro-drivers clustered around me like vultures. Terence haggled and for two dollars I was placed upon one of the pathetic little donkeys. Humiliated and feeling terrible about the poor animal in its travail, I let the driver yank us down the mountain. We went not on the path, but on what was supposed to be a shortcut--over great sharp stones and straight down so that it took all the strength I could muster to hold on with my knees so that I wouldn't fall headlong over the animal's head and onto the rocks. A nasty experience and I could have murdered my burro-driver, who obviously thought my yelps of fear hilarious.

The maniac at the wheel of our van gave us a ride down the mountain in the dark that made my ride with Maurizio Oldani in Italy seem like a kiddie carousel.

One more night at the glamorous Mezopatamya West, and at 6:30 a.m. Thursday, we were ready to beat it back to our campground at Göreme.

Passing through some city whose name escapes me, we decided to stop and have lunch. Just looking hungry was enough to set the café owners on our heels and one extremely persistent boy of about twelve, practically strong-armed us into his father's restaurant before we could get our helmets off. We were shown how to pick and point at sample dishes behind a glass partition and we got about the same stuff as in Malatya. Along with the obligatory warm cokes. It was all very tasty but then we had a big shock at the cash register. The boy, who spoke the only English in the place, had charged us 200,000 TL or about thirty dollars. Terence said no way could this be possible and the cook was called and came out with a calculator! He found the kid in error to no one's surprise, and indicated that we really owed about ten dollars--twice what we paid in Malatya. Still far too high but we'd been conned and they wouldn't go any lower. We were aware that the boy knew what he was doing and had hoped that we wouldn't know any better. We paid up and at the same time lost our blind trust for the Turkish. From now on, we'd be very wary and ask that all prices be written down first, which is probably what the guide books had suggested, if we'd read them properly.

Back in our cozy camp, nestled among the stony mushroom-shaped "fairy chimneys" of Göreme, we had supper and a great night's sleep-- allowing for the usual rude awakening of the 4:30 a.m. call to prayer. "No wonder these people are warlike," Terence mumbled in the dark from his pillow.

Chapter Sixty

ANKARA

Before we left Göreme, we made certain to join the line of tourist buses to the "open-air" museum, where there were over two dozen Byzantine churches, hollowed out of the cliffs and standing stones by monks in the 8th and 9th centuries, and complete with stairs, tunnels and windows. Some had beautiful frescoes on the walls. Then we rolled out to the main road and passed many a black, smoke-belching truck to the sprawling ancient and modern city of Ankara, arriving in the late afternoon. It had been a filthy, hot, and frustrating ride, with all of eastern Turkey using the same narrow road because there was no other. No directional signs for the weary stranger, of course, and once we had reached the giant metropolis, the pollution among the swarms of rush hour drivers made breathing more like trying to digest a heavy meal.

Finally locating the Tourist Information center, we discovered that the only campground was fifteen miles back the way we'd come. Why were we not surprised? But then, the campground itself, once we'd found it, was surprisingly beautiful. It was named the Bayindir Baraji. An oasis of green and cool. We thought we might spend a few days catching up on things, until we met a couple of uniformed campground officials with clipboards who seemed to see us as rich Americans who needed to be fleeced. Terence was truly ticked off when they decided to overcharge us for the electricity to run the little fridge, and I was likewise angry when there was

423

no hot water even though we were paying for it and the "managers" kept insisting there was.

On Saturday, we elbowed our way into the city of two million people to find the American Embassy to get visas for Bulgaria. It was closed. So was the American library which really made us grumpy. We had hoped to get some news about the earthquake we'd heard had occurred in California the week before. We tried the bookstores in downtown Ankara (after tons of fun trying to find a street going in the right direction that wasn't being torn up or repaired). As we peeled ourselves off of the hot motorcycle we'd parked near the shops, some Anatolian clod who spoke a little English laughingly asked Terence if I was his wife or his mother which sent me into the depths of depression, especially as I was rather painfully aware of how terrible I was looking. For some reason, I observed hotly, Terence always looked younger, the dirtier and shabbier he got, but I just looked older. There's no justice.

The next day we packed up and left, stopping first for a look at the famous Museum of Anatolian Cultures. We both agreed it was sensational. Small, but filled with such treasures of the distant past that it definitely served to ease the pain of not being able to spend more time in this amazing country. The very best of the ancient sites had been brought here and we felt enlightened and inspired and our appreciation for Turkey soared. At least ancient Turkey. There was another less than wonderful scene as we returned to our rig when a man calling himself the parking lot attendant demanded a high price for the spot the trailer had occupied. As usual, no signs at all about such a charge. We haggled. We paid. We left.

Eager to get away from that grim city, we yanked the trailer northwest heading for Istanbul. The scenery changed dramatically from dry and barren stretches--with people of all ages everywhere you looked, to green fields and actual forests and streams--still, however, with the crush of humanity absolutely everywhere. I noticed with some alarm an awful lot of dead animals in the road--chickens, dogs, sheep, a baby donkey with his whole head smashed flat and most amazing of all, not twenty yards from what looked like a very well-attended soccer game in a nice stadium, a very dead full-grown horse! It was horribly bloated, with its feet sticking up in the air and even stranger, a young donkey standing by the corpse! No one seemed to notice! Whole families going to and from the stadium-- buying food, eating, getting in and out of cars... Terence said the horse looked as if it could have been dead for days! We weren't in Kansas, Toto...

The road to Istanbul was as perilous as any we'd experienced. We'd heard about the risk of driving in this country, but so far the roads we'd been on had been fairly free of cars. We had enjoyed the friendliness of the Turkish man in the street so much, we were just not prepared for the Mr. Hyde that the Turkish Dr. Jekel became once he closed the doors of his car or truck around him. I thought about our rotten minivan driver in Kâhta. Such a mean disposition and a terrible driver and yet he seemed surprised when none of us tipped him later. Tipped him! We were ready to complain to the management and get our money back or maybe sue for psychological damages! Anyway, here was our Terence, having to play Every Man for Himself the whole way to Istanbul on that two-lane excuse for a highway. I hung on and yelled encouragement when I wasn't closing my eyes in fright. Overloaded trucks billowing black smoke out both sides were lined up nose to tail most of the way like a herd of ambling elephants. The trick was to try to get around them when you could find a space in the oncoming traffic and then find another space between the trucks to slip back into before you cashed in your chips dawdling in the passing lane. Nobody wanted to give. Not the oncoming Turks who wanted to claim the center as their own for all time, nor the truck drivers you had to pass to get anywhere...or simply to breathe! Once in a while, after you've decided you're stuck forever, some bloke becomes inattentive for a moment and you have to go for it. Terence would wait for the tiniest shaft of daylight and pull out as fast as he could--and so would all the cars behind us-- honking and trying to push us out of the running by passing us as we passed the truck in front of us! It had to be the Turkish way of keeping the population down.

A taxi, passing in the oncoming lane, veered way over into our lane. Terence yanked the rig as far over as he dared without turning us over in the moment he had to react, and the taxi grazed the side of the trailer. It was quite a thump. We looked back to see if the taxi driver stopped to assess his damage but he didn't.

There were almost as many overturned and smashed vehicles along the way as dead animals. I really think this "Will of Allah" thing can go to far. I was very grateful I did not have to ride my motorcycle through this country. Probably if they noticed I was a woman, they would have aimed for me!

We were dead tired and aching when we reached the city. To save money we had had to take the back roads instead of the tollroad, which probably added a couple of hours, but at least we knew we were in the right direction. Still, no one had put up signs to tell us where the campground might be, and we spent a lot of time inquiring as to directions. It was dark by the time we rolled over the last big bridges and the smell of the sea and the lights of the great city from the bridge reminded me of San Francisco.

Camp Atakäy was all the way over at the far west side of Istanbul. It was 10 p.m. by the time we arrived, but being a big international campground, no one cared; we were processed efficiently and we settled in quickly.

Chapter Sixty-One

ISTANBUL

HEAT, mosquitoes, and smog thick enough to slice. But also excitement, history and enough architecture to thrill even the most jaded. Istanbul reminded me of Naples. Lots of beggars--mostly small boys. And an endless stream of humanity in a hurry. We took a bus from the camp-ground early Sunday morning to hop a boat for a half-day tour up the Bosphorus to the Black Sea and back. It was a great way to get a look at the huge city without being crushed to death by the multitudes. I loved the Ottoman architecture on some of the old palaces by the water. We splurged by having lunch in one of the small cafes in the fishing village where the boat docked near the Black Sea. We ate what everybody else had--grilled mackerel--a thin, very crisp offering, and absolutely delicious. On the trip back, I sat on a bench on the deck next to a black chadored lady. We looked at each other, and all I could see of her was two very frightened eyes. Shoot, she though I looked scary...what about her? I mean, dahling, black is just wrong for July!

Of course we toured Aya Sofia. Being 99% Islamic, the locals were happy to collect the entrance fees, but short on upkeep on the sad old once-Christian church. It was dark and dirty and little remained of the mosaics. Someone at some time obviously decided to paint the designs in the places where the mosaic tiles had worn off. A serious mistake, espe-cially in that persons of little talent had done the job. Perhaps on purpose. The "Blue" Mosque across the street, in contrast, was as colorful as Santa

Sophia had been drab. Laden with carpets of many colors and designs--warm and welcoming. Hundreds of tiny light bulbs swam under the intricate geometrical patterns painted (with obvious skill) under the domes high above. We were asked to leave our shoes at the door. (Guess who had a hole in her sock).

Returning to the motorcycle we'd parked outside of Aya Sofia, we were alarmed to see it surrounded by policemen! I counted them. Fourteen! They looked serious and seemed to be looking for the owners. (gulp) Around them, a dense crowd of Turkish men, curious as always and waiting for something interesting to happen. We made our way through the crowd and "owned up" as we unlocked the metal boxes to put away our cameras. At first the cops just stared, then they all broke into smiles and the usual questions began. Greatly relieved, we answered every one carefully. My foot was aching and I know Terence was eager to get away but we didn't get on the bike until we figured it was polite and shall we say...prudent? We found Turkish police super nice everywhere we went. And they were everywhere.

First thing in the morning, July 9th, was a foray into the famous Covered Bazaar. I was actually intending to shop for once. But the Turks wouldn't let me. Every store had its young boys to soften you up. Always the friendly beginning. "Hello! Where are you from?" We had learned to ignore the little darlings. Then the bigger guns were deployed and older brothers or fathers or uncles took over calling to us to come in. "Madam!" they yelled at me. "Madam, come back and look!" They didn't actually grab at our clothes, but it felt like it. I wanted so badly to look here and there, but if I dared, I was pounced upon immediately. "Do you like that?! Come in and I'll show it to you! MADAM WAIT!!" I wanted to scream. As I said to Terence, if I saw the item of my dreams, I'd never know it. The salesmen made it impossible.

We headed for the Topkapi museum. Bought a chocolate icecream cone on the way that had the consistency of rubber cement. I couldn't eat mine and gave it to Terence. He thought it was awful too, but ate it anyway.

The Topkapi museum had a lot to see. A fabulous emerald collection of the Sultan and some rare Chinese blue porcelain. A bunch of other collections. The most famous item, the notorious Topkapi Dagger was on loan to a museum in Memphis, Tennessee! We entered the sacred rooms displaying among other things, Muhammad's sword and sheath, tomb soot (!) and a piece of his beard. Lots of the chadored faithful in there, so Terence and I had to stifle our reactions and remember our manners. There was something for everyone. One of the display cases contained the forearm of John the Baptist. We seemed to recall seeing that bone at least three other times on our travels. Either it got around a lot or John had more than two arms. (All the easier to baptize you, my dear!) Of course we made the obligatory visit to the Royal Harem, where all those lovely young women romped and played and took baths all day and practiced Belly Dancing for the amusement of their lords and masters.

Chapter Sixty-Two

THE PATHS OF LEAST RESISTANCE

ON FRIDAY, July 10th, we left the campground and headed west for Greece. We were not terribly sorry to leave Turkey, even though prices were lower than anywhere else we'd been and the people were super friendly and there were lots more sights left to see in that country. Our biggest problem was the lack of privacy. Being so vulnerable on the motorcycle made every stop a nightmare. It was a shame. If we could have escaped into an enclosure such as a van or even a car now and then, it might have made all the difference. And the poverty everywhere. Who could ignore it? So many people. Never enough room or money or food for all those masses of humans and every day more are born to already large families. The Turks just don't want to face that problem. Their frightening religion. Their non-women. Black-covered creatures pulling little children along. Only men to talk to. Fifty percent of their population doomed to a lobotomized existence.

As we rode by the sea to the border, I noticed rows of newly-constructed condominium-type buildings. Mile after mile of them--all brand new and really quite handsome in their design. At first I though they must have been built for rich foreigners as summer homes, but then I noticed that unlike the Costa del Sol in Spain, for instance, all the signs were in Turkish. Could it be that Turkey had that many rich people? I felt I was leaving this curious land knowing less than when I entered. I would have to do some studying.

Crossing the border into Greece showed a marked contrast. Suddenly we were back among the claptrap concrete boxes--cheaply thrown together and left unfinished...looking like they had just survived a strong earthquake and were waiting for the next one. It was getting dark so we had to stop in a kind of resort camp on the way to Thessaloniki. It was rather posh for Greece and very popular. Full of families. As we rolled into our appointed space, a lady from across the path walked over and offered us a "frappé," which was really instant coffee, whipped with water, then sugar and milk added to taste. So nice of her and truly appreciated. She was Greek and her husband was Italian, so we were able to talk in Italian. I was experiencing my usual hangup about how could I reciprocate such kindness when later they asked if they could use our camp stove because their electric one was on the fritz. We were delighted to loan it.

Saturday morning we phoned the Pantelises from somewhere, to let them know we needed them to unlock their garage again in Methoni so I could get out my bike. We arrived in Thessaloniki around 3 p.m. and just made it to a grocery store before they closed till Monday! Then we rode into our little campground in Methoni and relaxed at last with a hot shower and THE EUROPEAN newspaper. Ahhh.

Sunday was spent washing clothes and puttering. Terence completed three cases of his law school homework and at 8 p.m. we rode to the Pantelis' home in the village. The whole family was waiting for us. Except for Thenassis. But two brothers who spoke some English were there, plus two grandmas, mom and papa, and two friends of the oldest brother. We socialized awhile, then while Terence got the Ascot running again, I presented the family with my drawing of the Methoni church (to which I'd added some watercolor). They seemed pleased. We were sorry to miss Thanassis. Apparently, he was off serving his country somewhere near Athens.

Monday, we had to ride into Thessaloniki to change money--most of which would go to shake down fees at the border because the bikes had exceeded their six month limit. We were glad to be leaving Greece, however the next couple of countries would hold no great allure at this time either. With the war starting in the Balkans, we felt we'd be lucky to get to Hungary in one piece!

On July 14th, we left in a drizzle, with the sprawling city of Thessaloniki looking dirty and gray in the smog behind us. We tried to call daughter Meredith several times at likely-looking places and finally got

431

through to her message machine, which was not exactly satisfying. We told the machine we were safe and heading for Bulgaria.

We were coldly received at the Greek side of the border and after standing in a long line for some while, we were taken to another office where people coming in Greece were being processed. We were left there at the counter while two Hellaneous Officiali with cigarettes dangling from their lips helped other people in front of us, around us, and behind us--to get over the border from Bulgaria. It seemed that it was easier for them to deal with who should be allowed in their country than who should be allowed out! We were convinced that all the garbage put into our passports by those idiots in Rhodes was hopelessly confusing to the customs people here and no one knew exactly what to make of it. We certainly couldn't understand it. And of course nobody spoke English nor anything else but Greek. One would think that at a popular international border...oh well, forget it.

For a change, Terence was calm and I was fuming. It was just so stupid! Finally, after I complained loudly to another lady tourist--making sure the men behind the counter could understand the words "Greece" and "never again!," accompanied with appropriate hand gestures, one of the officials went to get someone from a back office to talk to us. He appeared, shuffling and swathed in his own cigarette smoke, and walked over to our part of the long counter and without looking at us, read and reread our paperwork and with his eyes red and watering from the smoke of a cigarette which never left his mouth, he tallied the charges we would have to pay before we could depart his precious country. We paid up and waited for sometime again while someone "processed" the pointless paperwork and finally it was finished and we climbed on our bikes and pulled the rig over to the Duty-Free shop to spend our last drachmas. Just as we started for the door of the store, there was a commotion back at the station and out of the smoke-filled office that we had gone to first--ran several men in uniforms along with the first clerk who had taken us elsewhere to get the proper papers. They demanded we halt and return immediately to show everybody on that side of the building what our new paperwork looked like! It felt like Rhodes all over again. More stamping and scribbling Greek things into our passports and then wonders of wonders, we were at last allowed to leave.

The Bulgarian officials at their side of the border seemed like family in comparison. No hassles, no problems. Not even any charges! We were waved on through after showing our visas and riding past verdant fields and cool forests, we allowed ourselves a great sigh of relief to be out of Greece and starting a new adventure.

The young woman managing the campground outside of Sofia was super nice. She even took Terence back to the gas station where apparently he'd been ripped off, and got him back his money! We explained that we simply needed a spot to camp in. She explained with a good sense of humor that if we allowed her to write "bungalow" on her report to her superiors, we could sleep in our own tent if we wanted to or in the bungalow itself. If we didn't want the key, then she would have to write "tent" on her report, and she would have to charge us extra. Ah, the mysterious East! Naturally, we took the key to the bungalow and after inspecting the funny little hut, decided to spend the night in it after all. It was like a children's play house, with just enough room for two army-issue metal beds whose springs sagged to the floor when any weight was applied. But it was clean and a different experience and private, and that's what I'd call a different experience!

During the evening, we met a few of the other campers. Terence actually found an elderly couple speaking Esperanto! They invited us for tea at their bungalow and conversing in that language, we discovered that they were a married couple who had met at an Esperanto convention. He was Dutch and she was Bulgarian and neither spoke the other's language! A real Esperanto success story. They were going to be at the Esperanto conference in Vienna, too. They offered to show us something of the wife's country but alas, we had only a "Transit" visa instead of a "Tourist" one because in our ignorance at the time, it was cheaper and we didn't know anything about Bulgaria and were running rather late to get to Austria. A sad mistake.

Another interesting couple were a Turk from Cyprus and his wife, an Englishwoman. He told us he was so crazy about America that he had named himself U.S.! Even had his bracelet engraved in those initials to prove it. Of course, as we were two representatives from his own special idea of heaven, we had a tough time keeping him from falling to his knees in adulation. As it was, he hung around like a puppy. I should have let him do the dishes.

The next morning, bundled up for winter, we rode through thick fog to the Bulgarian/Yugoslavian border. At the Bulgarian version of a Duty-Free shop, we bought five hand-made and painted wooden boxes for gifts because they were so incredibly cheap. Came to about fifty cents apiece...exactly the same price as a can of orange Fanta soda! How sad and unfair, I thought, and wondered where I could get a bracelet engraved with the initials of my country...

Nervously, we approached the Yugoslavian Border guards--after no problem whatsoever with their Bulgarian counterparts. To our amazement, the Yugoslavs waved us through as if they were almost glad to have us in their country. This, from a people at war at the time--with American warships in their waters!

Chapter Sixty-Three

FOR WHOM BELGRADE TOLLS

TOO SOON WE found the answer to the "Open Door Policy." Just two weeks before, a new law was passed demanding road-toll payment of all non-Yugoslavians. (They were learning from the Greeks, perhaps?) For us motorcyclists--$110 plus gas coupons of $18! We were subsidizing their war! Still, if we'd tried to ride through Romania, our only other choice, we'd probably not make it. The horror stories we got from other campers in Sofia convinced us it would be way too dangerous for us--being so vulnerable on the bikes. The English wife of Mr. U.S. had told us they had waited six hours to cross a bridge while people who paid the asking bribe of about twenty bucks were let go to cross immediately. Meanwhile several waiting in line were robbed at gun point. No thank you. So, burning from yet another blow to our budget, we stepped on the gas and flew across the eastern part of Yugoslavia. It would take about a whole day if nothing went wrong and both of us had sour memories of delays and worse from when we'd traveled in that country the year before. As our motors droned on and we started to relax in the sun which had just come out, I was surprised to note how pretty this part of Yugoslavia was. Travel brochures love to use the words "A land of contrasts" and this part of the world certainly fit the bill. A beautiful four-lane highway most of the way with few other motorists on it. (Not surprisingly. Who could afford it?) Tall, still-green cornstalks and brilliant yellow sunflowers in field after field, clear water rivers and old red-tiled roofed villages whizzed past. A recent downpour had washed everything to sparkling and the scent of it was heavenly. Great white clouds, plump and puffy sat on the horizon looking satisfied with themselves. And yet, just over those innocent-looking mountains to the west, there was a war going on...with people killing and maiming their neighbors. Bodies lying in the streets, unburied and unclaimed. Who could believe it? A land of contrasts.

We passed a large Yugoslavian Tour Bus that had stopped by a cornfield. A bunch of people of all ages were emerging from the cornstalks-- zipping their pants and straightening skirts. A Yugoslavian relief station. At least in Turkey, I thought to myself, the tour buses had the good sense to stop at restaurants or cafes along the way where one could wait in a long line for a stinking hole and buy postcards and over-priced soft drinks. Hmm. Actually, the cornfield did have its charm...

We shook in our boots every time we passed a police blockade. Strangely, most of them were on the other side of the highway. We got stopped only once. We were asked if we were tourists and where we were headed. It was nice not to have to accompany the officers to jail this trip. Needless to say, we did not take our cameras out of the bikes once!

There was a terribly long line at the border with Hungary. People looked like they'd been there for days. We naïvely thought the problem must be cranky Yugoslavian custom officers. But the fact was, it was the Hungarians--having big problems with all the Yugoslavian refugees fleeing the country. After sitting in the hot sun in line for two hours, some nice fellow told us we should drive to the head of the line and we would be allowed through, being westerners. Terence didn't believe the guy and didn't want to lose his place in line, so I was elected to ride up to the officials and ask if we American tourists on two "motorads" might be allowed to pass through and they said "yes!" We could have been out of there two hours earlier! Aiyeeee! I wound my way back on the bike to Terence and he pulled the big rig out of the line and as we waved to all the poor suckers still waiting in line--some of them pushing their cars forward to save gas, they smiled and waved back. No hard feelings.

Thanks to the stupid wait at the border, it was dark as we rode the last few miles to our favorite Hungarian campground at KecskemÉt. There were no street lights at all, but a great full moon was rising from the direction we were facing and as it flooded the land with light, it seemed the very nicest of welcomes.

A big difference at the campground from when we were there in October. This time it was the height of the summer season and the place was jam-packed with every manner of RVs and cars. It was almost midnight. We found a tiny spot under a tree and wiggled ourselves in between the sleeping campers. They must have had quite a surprise when they woke up. We stayed about three days while Terence caught up on his studies. The days were hot, but cooler under our tree. A Dutch family with two small spoiled boys were much too close for comfort. An ex-East German family were sharing our tree. The teenaged daughter seemed to have a bit of a crush on Terence. Her eyes kept following him around. How could she not? When he wasn't at our camp table typing on his portable typewriter plugged into his big black motorcycle, he was striding around half-naked or ruggedly adjusting something on the bikes, or whirling around in various martial attitudes as he studied his Taekwon-Do, or showing a sensitive side, practicing his viola with eyes closed--a cowboy bandanna wrapped around his head to keep his dark curly locks out of his eyes. To her he must have looked like he just stepped out of decadent Hollywood film! I had a bit of a crush on him myself.

The closer we got to Vienna to attend the Esperanto conference, the cooler Terence became. My fault, I supposed, because he knew I was going to keep my vow about never attending another conference after the miserable experience in Bergen, Norway. That meant I had to stay in the campground and busy myself while Terence went by himself to the event, which was O.K. with me. The campground we chose--the one closest to the conference center--was treeless and expensive, but clean and with lovely hot water. I was able to wash our clothes and sleeping bags--even my kitchen pots and pans--really clean for the first time in a long time and it was good for my soul. I took trips on my bike around Vienna and spent some time in the American library while Terence spent the days at the conference. He found some Esperantists to play his viola with and was having such a good time that he soon got over his disappointment that I wasn't attending too.

On August 5th, soon after the conference was over, I made a big paper cake-card for Terence's birthday and we celebrated with a last look at the town. We visited the excellent Kunst Museo Vien that contained lots of Hundertwassers, an artist we had come to love. We were best friends again and it felt good.

Chapter Sixty-Four

BACK EAST AND THE BALTICS

WE LEFT VIENNA ON AUG.7TH. Stopped somewhere in Czechoslovakia after the sun went down, but couldn't find a campground. Not a good idea to try to camp wild in that country, so we shelled out eight dollars for a room in what appeared to be a sort of youth hostel. Not bad. The room was clean if Spartan and contained four single beds. We supposed we might have to share the room with others, but nobody else showed up. No hot water in the shower but the air was very warm and we felt so dirty that we took cold ones. Slept well and woke to a very hot sun baking through the windows. Before packing up and checking out, we took my bike and rode through the town. Bought staples at a grocery store. Very little offered and many lines. A street market in the square with produce that looked like it had been found in trash bins. Rotten carrots and overripe tomatoes. Clothes of many strange and pathetic styles that thrift stores in L.A. wouldn't have taken. Very long lines at the gas pumps. We went back to our hotel and paid and packed up. Riding toward the border to Poland, we noted how much alike these Eastern bloc countries were. Beautiful forests largely left alone for some reason. Outstanding older homes here and there, left to rot or just so full of squatters and strangers who haven't the means nor interest to keep up the maintenance, that the once-lovely property was deteriorating around their ears. Then the horrible concrete government buildings housing the rest of the population as if they were criminals. Factories in each village--largely empty now. The ex-factory workers on the street selling whatever they can get their hands on. No wonder no one smiled.

No trouble at the Czech-Polish border, although we had to fill out a money form stating how much we were carrying in. We lied. Got to the campground at Cracow around 4 p.m., August 11th. Still baking hot and the air smelled foul. Found a thin tree to park under. Met Italians, French and Dutch campers. There seemed to be plenty of Poles also for once, but we couldn't speak their language and they seemed to know no other. No hot water again. We took showers anyway. A big old factory loomed from the east side of the campground. Windows broken. Abandoned.

Who'd have thought there could be a heat wave in Poland? The heat was so intense, my foot swelled painfully. Still, I didn't want to miss anything, so I hobbled along with Terence to check out the old city. Touring the Museum of Art, we paid an extra 75 cents to view the rather underwhelming "Laocoön" of El Greco, on loan from the USA! The canny museum folks forced visitors to walk through a warren of rooms full of Polish artifacts before getting to the international stuff, but that was O.K. because we were interested. They consisted mainly of the trappings and toys of Royalty of days gone by. Necessities of life for the rich while the Polish peasants paid for them. We toured the craft bazaar in the center of Old Town. We were delighted to see at last some real art being done by the people. Lots of talent. However, no bargains. Everything really good was western-priced. Can't blame them. We had a hamburger-clone and a warm coke for three bucks total. I dreamt of ice cubes. Terence and I agreed that the first thing we'd buy when we got home would be a refrigerator that makes ice cubes! Tried to find a zipper repair place to fix our thrashed tank bags. Failed. Tried to find a Polish/English dictionary that didn't cost thirteen dollars. Settled for a really crummy substitute and then realized that even if we had the right word, we didn't know how to pronounce it. Should have bought the Berlitz in California. Suddenly Hungarian looks easy!

The heat reminded us of the "Sundowner" in Santa Barbara, when the wind becomes as hot as a furnace and the risk of fires starting in the dry hills above would become acute. We dragged ourselves back to the campground and flopped on the trailer bed and gasped. Not until the sun went down around 8:30 p.m., could I bestir myself to make dinner!

The next morning around 7 a.m., thunder woke us and it started to sprinkle! Hooray!! We dashed out and put the rain cover on over the trailer tent and lay back to enjoy the storm which never materialized. Oh well, it was cooler at least and Terence actually got some homework done.

The next day we toured Auschwitz. Grim but not as frightening as I'd expected. It's been cleaned up by the Poles and prettified, I'm sure. Lots of tall green poplars wave in the breeze between rows of clean and neat brick buildings that used to house the prisoners. The trees couldn't be over forty years old. Even the movie they show you is tame. I've seen lots worse of the horrors--in films brought back by our military. The exhibits staffed by non-Poles in each country's separate museum--of human hair and collections of the prisoners' shoes and combs, etc. were a lot more chilling.

The following day, we visited the Wieliczka Salt Mines. Talk about chilling. For someone with a touch of claustrophobia, this was not the best idea. As you may recall, I let him go alone into the underground villages in Turkey while I stayed above. Still, I didn't want to give in to my stupid fears, and the French campers had told us this was a great place to visit. To me, it seemed like another Auschwitz. Only underground. Brrr. The guide only spoke in Polish, there was no other choice. We must have walked for miles down there and then had to stand while he lectured--never a bench to rest on. I suppose we should have been grateful we weren't handed a pick! I almost croaked after a couple of hours abusing my heel. Terence's back was giving him a lot of pain also. Standing for a long time on hard surfaces is always rough for him. We decided that the only thing worse than having to work in the damn salt mines was having to tour them! Ha ha. I had tried to be so brave during the long tour down there--and not think about how it was like being buried alive and how I couldn't possibly get out if I wanted to and no one spoke English and would understand if I needed desperately to come to the surface to breathe... Terence tried to keep my mind off my panic by being funny and pretending to translate the droning of the guide in the ribald way that he loves so much. It helped. The other tourists kept looking over at the silly American woman who was giggling at the back of the crowd. They must have thought they might have missed something funny about what their guide was telling them. Or, far more likely, that the strange foreigner was just crazy. The "famous" salt carvings were a disappointment--not only because they were the same old subject matter for followers of Christ and done by amateurs, but because we had expected them to be all salt-sparkly and instead, everything was a kind of wet-black. Apparently, the stuff had to be refined to be white. Duh. We really couldn't understand what our French friends had seen to like so much. When the tour was finally over, the guide told us there was no room for us on the elevator the Polish tourists had packed themselves into. We would have to ride up with him on the "staff" elevator, and he waved us into a tiny wooden closet and turned out the lights! I thought I would die! As the stuffy little box creaked and bumped its way to the surface, I reached for Terence who put his arms around me to reassure me or maybe to keep me from falling in case I fainted. I didn't but after it was over, I expected at least a medal for such bravery. Two weeks later, we read in THE EUROPEAN that the famous mines were becoming flooded with a leak in the walls on the lowest levels and they didn't know how to keep the water from coming in and had to stop their very profitable tours. Oh boy. We got out just in time.

That night we went to the movies in Cracow. For $1.50 each we got to see "Basic Instincts" in English, with Polish subtitles. Lots of sex and naughty words. I wondered if they translated the strongest stuff. I bet not. After all, this was the Pope's hometown. Another evening we went to see the comedy "Hot Shots" with Charlie Sheen and loved it. We laughed until the tears streamed down our faces and turned around to look at the rest of the audience. Stony expressions. It must have lost a lot in the translation.

Two more days there, with Terence catching up on his studies. I washed clothes and wrote in my journal. At one point, about 55 French teenagers rolled in on buses and, although they were nice kids, the noise and annoyance was too much for someone trying to study, so we pulled up stakes and headed for Warsaw...

It turned out to be a six-hour trip but a lovely day for riding. Traffic light and drivers polite. We only stopped for our cheese and bread by the side of the road and to get gas. Nowhere could we find a place that could put air in the shocks. None of the gas stations had air and when we finally located the special mechanic's shop, they had a compressor but the hose was broken! Jeeze. Later, I got stung on the neck by a bee that had flown into my helmet. A hummer Bummer.

We pulled into one of the Warsaw campgrounds that had been touted by the Polish Camping Guide as "the best bet." The GROMADA. The price was twice that of the one in Cracow and filled to the brim with mostly French campers. There was only one small building with toilets and several of the those stalls were "out of order." No hot water, no place to do laundry and we were told that the water from the few spigots was not to drink! The only place we could fit the trailer and the two motorcycles into was under some weird tree that dropped sticky things and the dirt underfoot was covered with the stuff. We pulled in anyway. As soon as we turned off the engines, Terence walked away to talk with a Norwegian couple he'd noticed on the way in. That left me with dinner to prepare and having to fend off the too-friendly curious at the same time. I was tired. A thick dust was on everything and there was no way I could keep it out of the food when the breeze kicked up. Never would I travel this way again, I decided. The camper vans of my neighbors looked like heaven to me. I was stricken again with the irritating thought that so many people think it's O.K. to bother a person cooking dinner--or even brushing teeth!--if the person is in the open. How would they like it if I walked into their campers to chat unannounced and uninvited? It got dark. Still no Terence. I sat in the dark, hiding from the curious throngs and ate my dinner in a blue funk. After awhile, he came back, hungry and bushy-tailed. He knew I'd be pissed off, but he'd had such a good conversation with the Norwegians, and was all apologies and sweet. He made some vodka drinks and I stopped sulking. Later, we walked over to their van and they made some wonderful coffee to share. He was right. They were a delight to talk to.

On August 18th, we rode to Warsaw's Old Town and saw the famous movie about the Nazi's destruction of Warsaw in 1944. Pretty heavy stuff. Then we walked around and watched mostly Japanese tourists buying amber in some very posh shops, and took lots of pictures of the beautifully restored town square and had chili con-carne next to some Danish folks in an Irish pub! It felt like the International Village at DisneyWorld. After hours of looking, we found a place that was able to fix the zippers on our tank bags. Driving back to our charming campground, we noticed that it was bordered by the city dump! I guess that explained all the dirt, the undrinkable water and the sticky stuff on all the trees. And as if that weren't enough of a grim find, as we rode to the place where we'd put the trailer, we found it surrounded by our old buddies, the 55 French teens we thought we'd left behind in Cracow! Zut, Alors! Oh well, they really were nice kids and we didn't really mind that much. It was a good way to practice our French, and later in the evening, I heard them singing camp songs--some of which I sang myself at Girl Scout Camp years ago. Awww...

As we packed to leave for Lithuania on the 21st of August, I decided to experiment and see if I could get my filthy tennis shoes clean by the next stop. I filled a plastic bucket half-full of the non-potable water and added wash powder. Dropped the shoes into it and then put the bucket in the center of the stack of tires that was tied onto the top of the trailer. I thought maybe with a day's sloshing in the bucket back there, I could get out the awful greasy dirt we'd picked up in that City dump they call a campground. It was worth a try. It meant I had to stuff my swollen right foot into my old cowboy boots because I didn't have anything else to wear. The injury from falling into the rocks in Turkey wasn't healing as well as I would have liked, either. Terence would have to help pull them off me later.

We wild-camped that night, and by 11 a.m. the next morning., were waiting in line at the Polish border to Lithuania. We would have made it earlier but something went amuck with an inner tube in a trailer tire and Terence had to slave away at it in a garage for hours. A young "helper" punctured the new tube Terence had just bought for six bucks and I really had to admire the way T. kept smiling as he looked for the patch kit. Amazingly, the kid had another tube the right size in his trunk! But no one could find a patch kit. The boy went to buy one somewhere while Terence put the new tube into the tire. When the guy got back, T. paid him for the kit and the two of them patched the first tire which the boy put into his car. Sometimes, I'm so glad I'm a girl.

At the border, we talked to some Dutch people in a camper who said they'd been in line for twenty five hours! But everybody told us that motorcycles were allowed to go to the front. Did I say I'd like to trade my bike for a van? Bite my tongue. We rolled by hundreds of cars, trucks and vans. People who'd been waiting for days were sitting in little groups in the fields with a bag of apples and a loaf between them. They looked so resigned. They were probably used to it. Young guys in gray border guard uniforms motioned us over to the side where bicyclists and motorcyclists were gathered. They strode around arrogantly and refused to look anyone in the eye when questions were asked about why everyone was being detained. They were just boys playing soldiers, ordering people around without any idea why. Following a superior's orders without question was so much easier than having to think.

Terence and I felt lucky. We had food and could sleep in the trailer if we had to, but why the delay? No one could find out. He wanted to try handing out the condoms he'd brought from the states. He'd heard stories of them working wonders as bribes. But the thought embarrassed me and anyway who was in charge? I had visions of the things falling out of the kids pockets as they strutted around with silly grins on their faces and then still doing nothing to help us. We should wait for Mr. Big, I told him.

At one p.m., a tough-looking young man with the top half of his clothes a sort of uniform swaggered by, and with a gap-tooth grin and upraised fingers informed us assembled bikers that it would be 10 p.m.

when we would be allowed to leave. We all looked at each other. Did he really know that? I groaned and wrote in my journal:

"At the moment we've got a group of ten guys clustered around our bikes. Some of them are fascinated by my writing. Lord, how they smell in the hot sun. IF YOU CAN READ THIS, TAKE A BATH OR AT LEAST USE DEODORANT! One of the men has a T-shirt that says CROSS THE BORDER in English. He doesn't understand when Terence and I laugh about it. Terence translates by using his Russian. Everybody understands now and are laughing too. A good joke. A lot of the other shirts around us have English writing on them too. Apparently it's the fashion. How strange to be wearing words you can't read. Now we are watching a fracas involving Polish police who just rode up in a van and grabbed some poor German guy who had been waiting in line. They're hitting him with a night stick and nobody seems to care. Oh well, after what the Nazis did to Poland in the last war, I guess they try to get even any way they can. Suddenly it's over as fast as it began."

Mr. Almost-a-Uniform, with the missing tooth, had just finished what looked to our untrained eye, a very shifty transaction involving motorcycles that had just came in over the border and someone running up from the forest with sacks of what Terence said looked like motorcycle parts which were then put into their sidecars before they zoomed off. The guy then turned around, and with his arm around a girl he'd picked up somewhere, he ordered Terence in Russian to allow him to sit on the Gold Wing and go varoom varoom or something like that. Terence would have rather punched out his lights, but we still weren't sure if the guy had anything at all to do with our ever getting across the border, so he begrudgingly assented. It was fairly obvious the little man wasn't sure if the big bike would fall over, but he had his pride and covered it well. Terence was seething--afraid the jerk might do something stupid to his bike--especially if he tried to pull the heavy trailer around, but things ended well enough when the guy decided the young lady was suitably impressed--and got off the Wing. Before taking off with his moll in a cloud of dust, he indicated with his dirty little fingers that we might be allowed to cross at 5 p.m. for being such good sports. I shall not repeat what Terence said.

As we were trying to push the rig a little further off the road to avoid getting hit by passing trucks coming in from the Lithuanian side, a long train of Wedding party cars roared up past us, and waving best wishes to the happy couple who were no doubt honeymooning in Romantic Poland, made a screeching U turn around us and tore off to return to their own country--leaving us under a heavy cloud of dust! Damn! I hated being so dirty. It was now 3:15 and I was beginning to hope the pseudo-Caligula in the army shirt was right about 5 p.m.! But that hour came and went and we sadly realized that our little dictator was no one in authority after all. Probably just the local smuggler king. We were making all sorts of friends with other hapless bikers and bicyclists who were stuck also. We all wondered what on earth could be the plan. A wealthy-looking Danish businessman was foaming at the mouth near us. This sort of thing had never happened to him before, he shouted, and he did not intend to stand for it! But he had stood for it for three hours already and nobody had paid him any attention. I wondered what he had given to get his car into the front of the line. As we talked to him in English, we all came to the conclusion that perhaps the Polish were trying to make things uncomfortable for people leaving their country for the same reason the Greeks did it to us. Namely, to try to keep the tourist money at home--and out of the pockets of their rivals in the next country. There never seemed to be any problem in letting people in. But the Dane said he'd even tried to bribe the soldiers. No luck. I was glad we hadn't given away the condoms.

I watched a family of four sitting under a billboard nearby. The father had ripped away the pretty little sunflower that had been growing there. At first I thought he had done it in anger and frustration. Then I noticed they were eating it! All four members of the pathetic little family were eating the green seeds out of the slaughtered flower. I guessed they must be starving. Should I open the trailer and pass out whatever food we have? I looked at the long line of waiting cars disappearing into the distance. So many people. If the Poles did want us to spend our tourist dollars in their country, you'd think they'd have snack stands at the borders. Were they just being monsters?

Around 8:30 p.m., a very kind young Pole who spoke some English befriended us and told us he'd try to get us across. He told Terence to follow him to the kiosk up ahead where someone was in charge. (In charge? Was there someone in charge?) Terence told me later that the young man pleaded that we and the German bicyclists should be let through, and around nine, the children in uniform heard voices from on high through the little walkie-talkies pinned to their shirts (along with their names and addresses, no doubt), and waved us through. We never did find out why they were keeping the border closed. We didn't stop to ask. The sun had gone down and the road was full of potholes we could hardly see to avoid. On the Lithuanian side, everything was chaos. Terence waved for me to follow, and we barreled past the surprised guards and ran into the office to get our passports stamped, ran out and tore outta there without looking back.

No lights on the streets, the roads truly dreadful and we didn't know where we were going. A moonless night. The last lights we saw were on kiosks selling vodka near the border where men seemed to be buying cases for the road. Oh fine. They'd be fun to share the dark roads with... Two Polish motorcyclists had warned us earlier not to try camping in the wild here in Lithuania because we'd get our throats cut for sure! Swell.

We rode for miles in the dark--our bikes's puny headlights hardly making a dent in the blackness ahead of us. The road was covered with sand from the encroaching shoulders, and was a hazard I could have done without. The first town we came to was Alytus, and with the help of a man on the street who could understand Terence's Russian, the two of them woke up a night watchman in a hut in a fenced-in parking lot and he kindly gave us permission to pull in and camp there. It was hardly a pleasant place to spend the night--on asphalt among rows of trucks and cars--but at least we figured we wouldn't get our throats cut there. The fellow was nice enough, charged us about 45 cents and went back to sleep.

No toilet of course and worse, no water to wash with because Gail had not hooked the bungee cord correctly around our water container and we lost it somewhere fleeing from the border. So we used the soapy dirty stuff at the bottom of the plastic bucket that my shoes had been swimming around in for two days--and glad to have it! At least we got the worst dirt off of our hands and with the last of the drinking water we'd bought in a bottle, we rinsed them. Sticky and smelly but so tired we did sleep. But at 6 a.m. we both voted to be somewhere else and so we took down the tent and bailed out of there.

Came across a little forest just out of town where we ate some black bread and cheese and then rode on again until we came to a stretch of gravel that seemed to go on and on. I was sure glad I didn't have to pull that trailer. We passed tiny, old, but quite pretty farming villages with their brightly painted and carved wooden window frames and doors. On through the summer countryside until we arrived at the campground outside the village of Trakai near Vilnius. A young soldier guarding the gate let us in and I wondered, "Lord, if he lets in the likes o' us, who does he keep out?!"

The camping platz was an ex-soccer field, surrounded by beautiful old trees and near a lake. Later, we came to understand the place had been one of the many retreats or camps for Communist Youth in the bad old days. Now, such places were deserted unless someone thought to open it up for western business.

After we set up camp on the soft green grass--what a pleasure not to be living on dirt for once, two Americans on bicycles showed up. Californians, in fact! Leslie and Brian Bowen. They had some wonderful stories to tell about their trip so far in the Baltics. A bit later, two Swiss motorcyclists who had overtaken us on the road earlier were eager to make friends and spoke English, so we all had a party. It began raining after dinner and because Terence and I had put up the tarp, we played host to our new friends, and we chatted until about 11 p.m. when our yawning must have clued them in about leaving. The hot water in the showers was a luxury that was almost more than we could bear.

The next day Leslie asked if I could use her old shoes, size 7, because her husband Brian had just bought her a new pair--better for bicycle-riding,and she really had no room to carry her old ones. Sure, I said, and put them on my feet. The relief my lame foot felt was immediate. I couldn't believe what a difference a good shoe made. I thanked her sincerely and decided to put her into my will.

The restrooms have to be described. Clean enough. But so strangely constructed I wondered if some of the young Communist campers had built them for a craft project. They were inside an old building so the ceiling was O.K., but the walls separating the men from the women and between each toilet stall and shower were made of eight-inch "textured" glass blocks. So the men washing their hands could sort of see the women showering--albeit fuzzily, and the women at their sinks could see the distorted images of other women sitting on the toilets. It let in a lot of light of course which was nice... The floor in both rooms was covered in a linoleum in good condition, but it hadn't been tacked down and didn't really fit at all, so that one was left with the feeling that someone cut it hastily or just unskillfully, and threw it down in a hurry to cover god-knew-what underneath. Maybe the local factory just made glass blocks.

Walking up a weedy hill near to the soccer field, and looking almost romantic from a distance was the old toilet block. White stucco with a curved roofline and sort of leaning. Doors akimbo. I had to have a look and discovered to my great horror that it had nothing inside but six holes in the ground--on both sides--no basins--and the holes actually had crusted poop around them!! Dis-gusting! Interestingly, after I got over my shock and revulsion, I noticed there was no smell. Probably hadn't been used in years. What? No camp project to clean them up?

Rode into Vilnius the next day, the capital of Lithuania. Not much left of once handsome buildings. Communism and the Occupation had taken their cruel toll. The Parliamentary Building was surrounded by barbed wire and cement blocks--the Lithuanians desperately trying to show they meant business about getting rid of the Russians and being independent. Of course, being independent meant no more help of any kind from Mother Russia. We wondered how they were going to fund their poor economy now? A look at the faces of the people told us they were asking themselves the same sort of question.

We tried to find a restaurant for lunch. Nothing. We ate a scone and had a beer at one of the gypsy-wagons. Amber was extremely cheap here but looked it. Nothing polished or set in silver as in Poland. Just small hunks and odd shreds strung for necklaces.

We rode away from that glum city and headed for Daugavapils, Latvia, in the east. The closer campground in Kaunas was no more, some policemen told us. We could tell they were happy to have us move on. Way out in a forest, we found the Daugavapils campground thanks to Terence being able to speak Russian to a passing woman in a horse cart. We'd been going back and forth on the road where we were sure it was supposed to be. It seemed someone had taken down the sign. We decided it was the camp manager because when we got to the gate he had to stop fishing in the lake and let us in. This was obviously one of the deserted ex-communist People's camps that wasn't set up for westerners. He refused any money but Latvian, which was not like the rest of his countrymen, who would have much rather had Deutchmarks or dollars or even yen, for that matter, but in truth, he was probably just trying to get rid of us. There was nothing for us to do but turn around and ride all the way back to Daugavapils where we found a bank that was more than happy to exchange a fifty-dollar bill for Latvian rubles. The town was full of people walking in the evening twilight. Men unsmilingly stared at the motorcy-cles and drew closer when we stopped. We went to the hotel where our American bicyclists had stayed, but we were told they could not promise the rig would be safe in the night, so we knew we'd have to go back to that camp in the forest. But first, we found the town's only restaurant in a base-ment where a sort of thug-doorman said he'd keep his eye on the rig while we ate. A long corridor let to a ugly dark room where several diners were drinking vodka at their tables. After quite a wait, a piggy-faced waitress left off talking to a male friend at another table and deigned to toss us a menu we couldn't read. Terence asked her in his college Russian to bring us a "hot meat" dinner with two beers as they had no wine. She seemed disappointed that we didn't want vodka with our meal but realizing we were foreign--what could we know about taste?

The "hot meat" was pounded pork and tasty enough. We also got potato things on the side and a salad of sliced small tomatoes with a flowerette of cucumber and a stack of very sour bread that Terence actually liked. A loud mock Rock Band came on soon after we were served and we were trapped. It made digestion very difficult. Perhaps we should have ordered the vodka. We paid and left and rode the long trail back to the now pitch-black forest and miraculously found the camp again. Perhaps the old fellow admired our gumption or simply ran out of ways to discourage us, because he seemed friendlier when he let us in this time. (Also, he could hardly fish in the dark). Anyway, he charged us only 50 rubles (25 cents) to occupy a bungalow on the premises. He really was living in the past. Though I noticed he didn't go so far as to unlock a restroom. No big deal. We were used to coping with that problem. The bungalow was damp and a little creepy, but it had started to rain and we were grateful to be inside. Sometime in the night Terence woke to an owl's screech and leaped out of bed not really awake and ran out to the rig in the rain before he realized no one was there. He had dreamt that someone was breaking into the trailer. I think it was all that Russian he was speaking.

It was still raining when we packed up and rode out of the woods the next morning. It took us most of the day to get to Riga, Latvia's capital. We got some splendid photographs on the way. One sight was a stork's nest high up on an abandoned farmhouse's chimney. Lots of unspoiled scenery--when nobody has any money it's hard to spoil the natural scenery...We drove around the cobblestones and trolley tracks of the big city trying to find a tourist information place. Impossible task. But we did find a map and located a campground south of the city on it. But when we finally found the place, it was not in business, so we had to ride all the way around the city again, getting lost several times, until we found the other one several miles north of the city. It was on a pine-covered slope leading down to a pretty lake and open for business. The manageress barely looked at the muddy rig behind us and held out her hand for 1000 rubles or five bucks. They learn fast in the city. Another bungalow and the same WWII army beds, but we were getting used to them. I thought for that price the restrooms might even have hot water but the only "relief station" was right out of Stephen King. The smell alone almost felled me on the path from yards away. And the sight of the interior made the old blockhouse at Trakai look good. One hole with two bricks for your feet. The feces had built up practically to the surface so I could see swarms of maggots wriggling around the top. I almost threw up in the doorway. Back to the woods.

There was a washup place near our cabin and we were assured the water was clean, so I played Lady MacBeth and washed and washed until that "damn spot" of a latrine began to fade from my memory. We unpacked some stuff and then locked up the trailer and covered it and unhooked the Wing and rode out to where we'd passed some enterprising guys cooking meat and onions--to sell--on metal sticks over a fire. They had the barest of cooking needs--a small grill and a board where they were cutting the onions. A couple of jars of mustard and a bowl of what must have been their "secret sauce" completed the offering. Martin and Andrea, a biker couple from Germany we'd met at the camp, came with us and the four of us stood around at the side of the road and chowed down on the good food. They even sold beer. And we had thought we were never going to see meat up here. That little industry seemed to be springing up all over Latvia. Maybe a Turkish import. Good for them. A traveler could starve up here without them.

On August 28, we left the trailer covered and locked to my motorcycle, and rode the Gold Wing into Riga to have a look around. The amber jewelry was plentiful and better looking than in Lithuania, so we bought some for gifts for the folks back home at embarrassingly low prices. We rode around the old part of town gawking at the Jugenstile architecture, had a dry pastry with a 12 cent beer and then went back to our campground in the pines. Around dinner time we attempted to find a restaurant in the vicinity. Rode around knocking on doors of likely places--some of which had people eating inside. But no one would unlock the door. Very peculiar. One place had an open door, but when we walked inside, everybody stared and the woman behind the bar told us they didn't serve food which was obviously untrue. Just not set up for the Western trade.

So we rode back to our friends at the Sashliki Bar-B-Que down the road. We liked the food so well there we were kind of glad the Latvians hadn't wanted to serve us.

During the following night, we listened to a soft rain falling on our bungalow roof. It was nice to be warm and dry. But we had to push on. Time was getting short. After we gave back the key, the mangeress tried to sell us a few pitiful things out of her cabin. Small jars of caviar and some unidentifiable objects made of green yarn. We declined, which turned her frosty. I felt no guilt, being sure she had charged us far more than the other campers as they seemed to be people she knew. We were glad to be back on the road. The clouds parted and the warm sun shown on some luscious scenery. Every so often we came across a family picking mushrooms, but because they had had to drive a long way out of the city, that luxury could only be afforded to the few Latvians who owned cars and could afford petrol. Probably only Russians. There was so little traffic therefore, that the road was a dream for us motorcyclists. Around 2 in the afternoon, we found ourselves in a pretty large town and Terence, who never gives up, pulled over in front of what certainly looked like a restaurant in business and went inside to ask. There were no signs in front and I sat on my bike waiting for him to be thrown out, but he turned in the door and waved me to come. We were stared at again, but the women behind the counter seemed resigned to serve us the order of the day which was the same for everybody. We were given a bowl of watery onion soup with greasy bits of wiener floating on top, and two pieces of sour bread. I also had a cookie and the two of us had a bottle of mineral water each. All for about a dollar.

A way down the road, we met our two motorcyclists from Switzerland who seemed a little nervous because they couldn't make themselves understood anywhere. They asked if they could stick with us for while and we said sure. The four of us crossed the border into Estonia with no hassles and soon found the campground in Tallinn, which was actually a hotel that had opened its gates to campers and let them stay on the surrounding lawn. It was pleasant enough and after settling in, the four of us rode into the city to try to find a place to eat. We actually located a place that served a pasta dish of a sort. Although the menu on the walls seemed to have a nice variety, we were told they were out of everything except this dish. No surprise. We were getting used to the same old story. We were all hungry and happily ate whatever we were served.

We stayed on the hotel's lawn for three days. We spent most of the time riding into the capital. The old central part of Tallinn was a joy to film. Soft oranges, pinks and yellows painted on baroque architecture gave the northern city a warm look. The old Hanseatic city had known many foreign influences in its time and the atmosphere reflected it. The Estonian people didn't stare at us--they seemed as if they had seen it all before, and for a change, we didn't feel like creatures from Mars. I took far too many pictures of gabled roofs and church spires but I just couldn't help myself.

The nooks and crannies and narrow cobbled lanes seemed to be inviting us for a closer look and when we did, we discovered bits of history dating back to Renaissance and Medieval, and even earlier, and lovingly preserved.

During the night before we left, a tremendous electrical storm jolted us awake. I had never experienced such a terrifying few moments. We clutched each other and waited for it to pass over. As the worst of it came through, the lightning was almost constant and seemed to sizzle around us. The rain flooded down upon the trailer top and the wind almost tore our flimsy little tent from our grasp. Terence seemed more fascinated than frightened, but I thought it was the end. I was glad to see it finally fade away.

Chapter Sixty-Five

SEPTEMBER 1ST. THE EVIL EMPIRE

WE PACKED up in the morning's thin sun. Everything was damp again but we didn't care. We were going to Russia! An elderly gentleman who played the piano in the hotel lounge, had warned us the previous day to be extremely careful. "I know of a whole family who recently drove to St. Petersburg," he said. "They disappeared without a trace!"

Roads were fairly good. Great long stretches lined with pine trees. Around noon we saw a truckstop kind of "workers" cafe and stopped to take our chances. Again, it was cafeteria style with a couple of heavy matrons in dirty white uniforms dispensing the menu du jour: greasy, watery soup with a plate of small boiled potatoes and apples lying under a thin gravy that may have contained minuscule bits of ground meat. A salad consisted of a small cluster of unripe tomato slices with a teaspoonful of sour cream dolloped onto the middle. A glass of sweet, red-colored water accompanied the Grande Repast.

Boarding the bikes again, we noticed the road ahead was thick with smoke. It smelled like a forest fire. The other drivers barreled through it so Terence and I buckled on our helmets and hoped for the best. Fortunately, it wasn't as bad as it looked, and we managed to ride on through it without passing out. Emerging, I felt uncomfortably warm. It wasn't the fire, just an exceptionally hot day for this part of the world, and after last night's storm, hard to believe.

We nervously approached the border. This was it! The Evil Empire! So much had happened since the year before when we had been rebuffed at the border between Finland and Russia. The Estonian guards waved us through. The Russian guards waved us over. Terence had all sorts of papers to show, including an "invitation" to teach Taekwon-Do in Moscow, which he and Master Tom MacCallum had thought to acquire while we were in Vienna. We figured that's what made things easier. They only insisted upon a complete list of how much money we had and the value of our amber jewelry we'd bought in the Baltic States, plus the same for our watches, etc. It helped of course, also, that Terence was able to converse in their language. He told me later that he'd fibbed about what we had in the trailer in case a sly telephone call might alert someone down the road who wanted to play Robin Hood to the rich Americans. I thought he was being a bit paranoid.

We rode past wood-carved cottages, painted in primary colors with picket fences bright with contrasting colors! The effect was of a children's park and I was enchanted. I would have loved to bag some of them with my camera but the sun was sinking in the west and we sure didn't want to travel in this country at night. We might disappear without a trace!

With no signs to help, we immediately got lost when we entered the outskirts of St. Petersburg. We knew the campground was supposed to be at the north end of the city, but in the gray gloom of dusk, we couldn't get a bearing. Terence began asking people the way. We were lucky to get a gesture of understanding and a wave in some direction. The center part of the massive old city became our worst nightmare--the streets nothing but a series of joined potholes between trolley tracks. I couldn't remember anything worse. They had to have been better in Peter's time! Getting dark now, Terence frantically asked help from any likely source. At a stoplight, a young man in a car offered to lead us out of the megalopolis to the right road. We had little choice but to trust him. The trailer bumped high and hard over the horrible tracks and into holes in front of me as Terence tried to follow the swift little car in the dark. It was all I could do to hang on to my handlebars myself. I tried not to think of the damage it must have been doing to our poor bikes. I realized we were crossing bridges. Then at last, the man pulled over and pointed to a sign. The International symbol for campground! Before he could drive away, Terence got off his bike and walked over to him. With a joyous look the young man accepted the gift of four little boxes of condoms.

A guard waved us into the campground. Again I wondered just who he was supposed to be keeping out. Inside the gate, we rode slowly by what looked like the mud-splattered finalists of a giant 4-wheel drive rally. All representatives of western countries, of course. They must have been celebrating and staying at the big ugly hotel on the grounds. We could hear the noise all the way to the R.V. and tenting area some eighty yards away. As we pulled in to a site for our rig, we found Martin and Andrea, our Bavarian friends from the Riga camp--right next to us! We were really glad to see them. But they had bad news. Apparently, some of their clothes had been stolen from the wash line while they slept the night before. We all decided nothing was safe here in Russia so we planned to take turns watching each other's stuff for a couple of days. We loaned them some sweaters and T-shirts. What a pain. It meant that while one couple rode in to see St. Petersburg, the other would stay in camp. Terence was tired and cranky. His back hurt from that roller-coaster ride through the city and he didn't feel like searching for the manager to tell them we had arrived. After all, it was the manager's job to greet you and do his paperwork. The Germans were paying fifteen dollars a night and we found out from a Dutch couple that they had paid thirty dollars by pre-paying from Holland! What might they decide to charge Americans?

I was happily surprised to see the toilets and showers were clean. There was hot water and bits of soap at the sinks and even toilet paper! Definitely set up for the Western trade. We could see they wouldn't be wanting our rubles. Martin and Andrea agreed. Everything here was sold for "hard" currency only. So...it seemed that now that Communism was no more, no Russian would be able to stay at this campground for awhile. The poor Slavs.

On Wednesday, September 2nd, Terence and I took the first shift guarding our friends' things while they toured the city. It seemed a little silly to be so paranoid, yet during the next night, after the four of us had partied in our big tent with some vodka and stale cookies and gone to bed, we all were robbed!

As often happened, we'd made friends with the local stray cat, though this one was obviously loved and spoiled and well fed, for a change. Anyway, Boris (he had to be Boris, didn't he?) was lying across our feet while we slept in the trailer. We had one flap open for air because the night was so warm, and sometime during the night I felt Boris rise off my foot and pad to the opening of the flap and look out. Semi-consciously I noted that he was soon curled up and relaxed again and I figure it must have been the very time when the thieves were robbing us of whatever they could feel in the dark and make off with; Boris had heard them and looked out to see what was happening. Hey, maybe that cat was part of the gang!! The Look-out!

Around 7 a.m., we all woke to discover the dastardly deed. Martin ran over and told us of their losses, and trying to remain calm, T. and I tried to think what we had left outside the trailer. The robbers had not unzipped the big tent, so we still had most of the cooking stuff and clothes and thank god, the helmets. But whatever had been on our little camp table or on the ground next to the trailer had been taken. Terence had been studying there and I writing, and feeling safe in that the table was so close to where we were sleeping, we had simply shoved things into our tank bags and under the table instead of stashing them in the zipped main tent. We lost both tank bags. Among things I lost were my riding gloves, a very large post-card collection that I used to make drawings from, my special drawing pens, all my makeup and other ladies's necessities, and truly irksome, a stack of just-finished newsletters for our friends back home. But the most important loss was Terence's. They had taken the current Law book he was using plus all of his finished assignments that he was ready to turn in for the year! Without those assignments, he would not be passed. He would not graduate. Even if they were late, the outcome would be the same. Four years of studying and work for nothing! We had to turn around. There would be no fax machines here nor any way to get a new book sent without it being stolen in the mails. He would have to race back to Poland and try to get a book and re-do his homework and get it sent to California by the due date, October 14th. It seemed impossible.

All four of us sat stunned at the little table. We drank coffee and talked about it. We knew no one at the hotel would care. T. and I still hadn't seen a manager. For all we knew, the guard at the gate did it. Or the lady who cleaned the restrooms. We were in a lawless and godless and desperately poor land. Martin slammed his coffee mug onto the table and announced, "The next time I come into this country, it'll be in a Panzer!"

Angry, and hating Russia, Terence and I reasoned we should at least see the Hermitage Art museum before we split for home. We'd been looking forward to it for so long. So the next day our friends stayed guarding our campsites while Terence and I took a quick look at St. Pilfers-burg. We dragged along the halls of the Hermitage and glared at the famous paintings and I was stricken with deja-vu--remembering how we had felt the same way in the Prado Art museum in Spain a couple of years before. We had just received the news that our renters in our house at home had not been paying the rent and we would have to postpone our beautiful trip and return to California. Still, then we were sure we'd come back to finish. This time, with our money running out and the motorcycles falling apart before we even got started on the road across the vast wasteland of Russia, and now the realization that we would probably be continually robbed and perhaps worse, we were mournfully aware that it was all over. We weren't going to make it.

Chapter Sixty-Six

"WHEN THE GOING GETS TOUGH, THE TOUGH GO SHOPPING"

We walked past the young men selling trinkets from card tables outside the museum. Terence bought a few medals with the red star on them to give to friends back home, and I found a black-lacquered box for my sister. We began spending the last of our money because suddenly it was "Why not?" People watched us from all sides. Nobody smiled. Nobody said "Welcome to our country!" the way they did in Turkey. Hostile stares and hungry looks like wolves. We looked for a store to buy some fringed Russian scarves all the women were wearing. The main department store was big, to be sure, but there was very little to buy and every counter had long lines. We figured we had time, so we joined one in front of some scarves on an otherwise bare shelf. When we got to the front of the line, we made our selection. The young lady in the white uniform wrote out a ticket. We were told to join the line to pay for the items at the cashier. So we stood in line for the cashier. A very long line. We paid the sum written on our paper and were handed it back with a stamp. We then had to stand in the line for scarves again so that we could hand the proof-of-payment note with the stamp on it to the woman behind the counter who proceeded to get the scarves off the shelf and hand them to us wrapped in butcher paper. After that experience, I was weak and hungry. We found a sort of donut shop next door to the big store. Stood in the line in the street until we were belly up to the counter. A large, red-faced woman in a soiled once-white uniform didn't ask what we wanted. She simply poured a milky tea from a huge samovar into two tiny teacups and placed them on a tray that already had two little doughnuts on a plate, and pushed it over to us with her plump hand out for the money. Everybody got the same thing. One tiny donut each and one cup of tea. Not having the correct change pissed her off, and as she opened the cash register next to her, we were soundly chastised to the amusement of the long line behind us. Their stares became smirks. Terence said he had no idea what she was saying. It was just as well. We followed the examples of our fellow snack-barites and stood at a tall and grimy round table where we dunked our doughnuts into our sweet milky tea and were glad to have it.

Becoming sharper at this shopping business, Terence braved a food store while I guarded the Gold Wing. He went in for milk but found a roast chicken instead. He said he got the last one and the people behind him in line were terribly disappointed. After bumping over the streets to home, I used the cheese we'd found in Estonia and made a macaroni and cheese dish which we served along with the chicken. We had asked Martin and Andrea to dinner. It was all very convivial, and later, the two men rigged up a very elaborate series of trip cords and ways to trap the burglar if he should come again during the night. None of us got much sleep for listening all night for sounds of the intruder, but no one appeared. Boris the cat didn't even show up to spend the night with us. I strongly suspect he was the brains of the outfit.

Because Terence had lost his important Class Assignment page as well as his Law book, we knew the trip was over. Yet even if he could have found a way to get the necessary paperwork finished by the due date, there were several other reasons for us being dead in the water. Obviously, trying to get across Russia with bikes in bad shape and no money would be pretty stupid--especially in such a climate of unrest and chaos. We'd read about two previous trips on motorcycles Westerners had recently taken--with trucks of petrol and food bringing up the rear, and helicopters flying overhead for security! And they had trouble making it! Even if we opted for the Trans-Siberian Railroad, we knew now we would have to constantly keep an eye on the trailer--if we would even be allowed to be near it. That trailer had become an albatross.

After saying goodbye to our German friends, we all boarded our bikes and roared out of the campground and past the "security" guard who dutifully raised the gate boom as we passed. With our still owing for our three night's lodging. I decided he must have allowed our robbers to pass just as nonchalantly. Terence and I bumped and banged through St. Petersburg. The Gold Wing was dying again. Every time we stopped, it expired, and I had to pull over and help him start the engine with my bike's battery. We were using two sets of bumper cables but they were small and took forever to work, so while half of St. Petersburg crowded around, I had to sit on my bike gunning the engine while Terence slaved to get his motor started. It was a great show for the Russians. I don't know what fascinated them more...the huge bike attached to the massive trailer or the incredible fact that something American breaks down. In any case, we stopped traffic and if we'd been there much longer, no doubt all of St. Petersburg would have come to watch.

I was in a foul mood. They glared, I glared back. So many drunks, and every man, woman and child with a cigarette that seemed to grow from their fingers. Gaping, pocked faces...like zombies with no place to haunt. As I raised my head to try to get at cleaner air I saw faces from a bus squinting through the dirty panes to get a look at us before the smoke-belching thing that contained them lurched over the trolley tracks and pot-holes and away. Their eyes looked hard and hungover.

Finally we were out of that maze of blackened concrete. Just outside the big city we passed an enterprising couple under an overpass selling meat. A pig, freshly slaughtered, was stacked in big chunks on a small table to catch the eye of the passersby. It sure caught mine. They had set the head against the pile of meat so that we could see it from a good distance. The poor thing actually seemed to have a ghastly smile on its bloody face. "Lord of the Flies."

The scenery became green and we began passing farm villages again. Everyone looked healthier and I began to understand the Russian art of survival--at least in the country. They don't have much--with their one cow and their shabby old clothes. They've probably looked much like that for centuries, and yet if you've got a cow you've got milk and cheese and if your neighbor has chickens you can trade for eggs and meat and if there's any land at all, grain and corn can be grown and with apple trees too, you're rich! Bartering. That's what country people have always done and if governments would leave them alone, they might do nicely, thank you. To get money to buy things you can't grow, you sell your surplus. Every house had a bucket of apples placed in the street to sell. No signs, no frills. If you stopped to look, someone would come out to sell them to you. Each bucket was identical. The same size bucket with the same stack of green apples with the prettiest ones on top. Was there a law about uniformity? Why not apple sauce in front of Mrs. B's house, and apple juice in front of

A's? Apple-faced dolls? Apple tarts? Apple butter? Nothing but the apples themselves from the tree in everybody's back yard. Commune-ism. Terence stopped to buy some. He didn't want the whole bucket at 120 rubles. (70 cents). The aproned housewife wouldn't let him take less. Later, when we had stopped and looked at our apples, we saw that they were all rotten except the few on top for show. We guessed every bucket was the same way.

We needed gas. To our horror, we found the petrol stations in Russia would not accept our rubles because we were "foreigners." We were supposed to have bought coupons at the border for our gasoline needs. Of course, no one at the border had mentioned it. Perhaps the idea was to get the westerner in the country, have him break down and while he was looking for gas, steal his vehicle. I had become suspicious of everything in this country. What could we do? We were close to empty and a long way from the border. After buying some coupons from a sympathetic truck driver at one station, Terence attempted to use them for gas but the mean old "Babushka" in the kiosk said they would not do, because they were "truck" coupons! T. just barely caught the truck driver in time to get our money back.

Help came in the form of a lanky young man in a long blond ponytail. He'd been circling our rig admiring it and he came up to us to tell us not to worry. Gasoline was everywhere if you knew how to look for it. Go back to the road, he said, and watch for people with petrol cans sitting by the roadside. We'd seen such people, only we thought they were out of gas and waiting for someone to come along and help! Aha! So that's what you do. We got back on the bikes and rode for awhile until we saw a sort of Army tanker-truck parked with its nose in the trees and two guys standing next to a hose sticking out of the back. Our petrol station. No prob-lem. They were happy to give us all we needed--including filling our reserve container on the trailer. Thirteen gallons for 1000 rubles or $5.50. Great relief. They probably filled it up each time from the gas station that refused us! Maybe they made a few cents on reselling it. It couldn't have been much. Maybe the "Babushka" was their mother! Maybe Boris ran the whole operation!

It was dark and we were still far from the border. Terence spotted a rusted Campground sign and we followed the arrows. It was just south of the large town of Pskov. Another recently defunct holiday spa for Commu-nist Workers. A lot of weeds and wooden temporary housing on wheels sinking into them. Really depressing. A woman coming out of one of the structures waved us in after we had sat awhile in front of the locked gates. She said we could stay and she would watch the trailer while we went into town for food. We locked everything up securely and boarded my bike for Pskov to try to find a restaurant. We were pretty sure we had enough rubles left for a Russian meal. But there was nothing in this sad little city that resembled a restaurant. No signs. Nothing. It was about eight in the evening. We went up and down the streets. We saw long lines that seemed to terminate in dark doorways for something or other but we would never know what because there never was a sign to tell us. Rather desperate now, we knocked on the door of what looked like a hotel restaurant, but were shooed away by a very gruff bouncer-type in a stained brown suit who answered Terence's questions with "THERE ARE NO RESTAU-RANTS!" We believed him and went home. It finally dawned on us that there probably were no restaurants in all of Russia open for the public at this time. There was no assurance for chefs that there would be food available when they needed it, the currency was a mess and the people didn't have any money anyway. We had been very naïve.

As I cooked dinner back at the campground, two young men appeared and indicated they wanted Terence to drink their vodka with them. I felt like their mother as I handed out three cups. They were very disappointed when Terence declined further drinking. He was hungry and wanted his dinner but they seemed to think him a wimp to quit, so they left.

We weren't quite finished eating when we were joined by a young woman supporting a great deal of makeup and dressed for a night on the town, who said she was the proprietress of the place. I rose to clear the dishes and offered her my chair and she planted herself upon it and babbled incoherently in several strange languages that even my resident linguist couldn't name. She had brought her own bottle and cigarettes and between swigs and puffs kept calling me "Madam" over and over until I wanted to smack her. Her agitation was so extreme we both knew she was on more than booze. Another young woman joined her after a while but didn't say much. Terence gave the newest arrival his chair and tried to move away from all the smoke without seeming too impolite. Our "proprietress" was saying that the people living in the wooden boxes on wheels were gypsies and therefore beneath contempt. We'd met a man coming out of one earlier and he seemed nice enough. But he was just one of many people on her shit-list and after a while I made motions about retiring early and Terence was showing signs of fatigue as well and the ladies finally got the hint and took their bottles and left, to our great relief.

Waking to a morning thick with fog, we drank some bitter coffee--we hadn't seen milk since Estonia--and folded our tent. One look inside the open door of the latrines confirmed my worst suspicions, so I took care of business under a tree in the fog. Then we rode toward the gate where we were met by a surly fellow in a old suit who told us that he owned the place, and to follow him to his cabin to pay the fee. "Whatever," we said, and followed and paid up.

Nervously, we approached the guards at the Russian-Latvian border. Terence chatted up an assortment of uniforms, ranks and ages, trying to keep their minds off of wanting to look inside the trailer. They wanted to see our cameras. I suggested to the most important-looking officer that I would be happy to take a couple of Polaroid pictures of them in front of the rig, (hoping that by giving them one I could have another to show our friends back home). They kept both pictures and solemnly waved us through. Oh well.

The Latvian side of the border had even more soldiers and officers, but they were lots younger and more relaxed and in a sort of miscellaneous collection of uniform styles. Terence could only speak Russian, but the guys didn't seem to mind and of course they had been taught the hated language in their schools during the occupation so they understood him, and when he told them how glad we were to be out of Russia, we got big grins all around. Encouraged by his audience's reaction, he then told the eager listeners how we'd been on the road for five years without having anything stolen (not quite true) and then it was mean old Russia where we were robbed big time in just two days! They loved it. They slapped Terence on the back and howled with laughter at the story. We really liked those kids. They stood around us with their plaid shirts showing under their army-issue jackets. A bunch of Minute Men, trying to wrestle their country back from the Bear.

We resumed our journey across Latvia. We were headed for Daugava-pils again, to the same sleepy campground, because Terence had left his precious Swiss Army knife in the bungalow there and he wanted it back. I remember thinking he had to be nuts thinking anyone there would be so stupid as to return such a prize.

Crossing a bridge over great piles of slag and other junk in some gloomy factory city, one of the trailer's shocks broke, and Terence had a few horrible moments as he tried to gain control of the Wing and bring it safely to the side. Shades of Malaga! He managed it, and just as he crawled underneath the trailer to try to hold it together with a plastic band, it started to rain. I grabbed my old yellow slicker from one of my side-boxes and yanked it on, and with one hand, began handing him tools while waving cars, trucks and even two police cars (!) around us with the other so they wouldn't run over his legs in the rain. A kind man stopped a little farther on the bridge and ran back to us to ask if he could help. Terence asked if he could show us the way to a welding-shop. He said he could and he slowly led the way, with Terence dragging the trailer along behind and I bringing up the rear, musing about what a darn shame it was that this hadn't happened somewhere in the middle of Siberia!

There were about seven men in threadbare suits, standing around laughing and drinking glasses of beer as Terence regaled them with nasty stories about Russia. The trailer had been rolled over a rectangular hole in the ground inside a garage, where a small man stood welding the shocks together underneath. It was taking all afternoon. I was hungry and feeling sorry for myself. I had not been offered a beer, and indeed had been completely ignored because I couldn't speak Russian and because as often happened when Terence was concentrating in a different language, he would forget to introduce me as someone also on the trip. The drunkest one had been eyeing my bike and when he realized I had the keys to it he began asking if he could ride it. I thought he just wanted to rev the engine around the garage yard so, forcing myself to be friendly (maybe they'd pass me a beer), I let him sit on it and foolishly turned the key for him. He took off like a shot and bolted out of the gates and into the busy street before I could stop him. Terence came out of the garage with his entourage around him and was furious with me. He thoughtfully translated what the men were saying about my being a stupid woman, and I wanted to kill somebody.

The drunken fool made it back after a while, but by then I was so upset I kept away from the men and found a chair in an adjacent garage and sat in it in my fat yellow space suit, hungry, hating everybody and feeling ridiculous. I decided not to tell Terence that there was a huge poster of Bresnev in there on the back of the door and he was perhaps telling his dirty Russian stories to Russians, not Latvians. After a while one of the men brought me some food from his home--a big piece of boiled meat and a hunk of brown bread. I was touched by his kindness and understanding and felt much better.

The welder wouldn't take any money, so Terence gave him a bottle of vodka and some condoms, and also passed the precious little things around to his eager audience. They were hugely delighted, the beasts.

It rained hard all the way to the little forest campground and this time the road was treacherously muddy and slippery. We found the manager in a cottage way down by the lake--drinking with what looked like a wedding party. He gave us the key to the same moldy bungalow we had before and was very sorry, but he knew nothing about a Swiss Army knife being found there.

As we were unpacking in the rain and trying to get some dinner started, we were ambushed by two young Russian couples who were not only totally sloshed, but completely insensitive to our fatigue and desire to be let alone. They put their arms around us and shouted about our being "brothers" and that we must all drink together. "Is this all these people do?," we asked each other. Terence explained in their language that this was not the moment--perhaps after we had had our dinner, we might join them (no doubt counting on the fact that they would surely be unconscious by that time). I kept silent and tried to collect what I needed from the trailer's kitchen box and drag it into the cabin with them trailing after me and shouting ever louder in Russian--things I couldn't understand but felt were getting progressively more hostile because they didn't like being ignored. Terence finally shouted at them to back off, and with much grumbling and angry looks and assorted gestures, they slunk away.

Fortunately, they weren't around when we were ready to leave at dawn the next morning. A different manager in the office who at first said he hadn't heard anything about a knife, had his memory refreshed when Terence offered the princely sum of ten U.S. bucks as a reward. He miraculously located it in his desk drawer, and I was happy for Terence that he had been so persistent and had gotten his trusty knife back.

On Sunday, Sept. 6th, we had a long and uneventful road across the border into Lithuania, and then through a cloudburst to our previous campground in Trakaj. A handsome young blond soldier let us in and opened a Bungalow for us as the rain pelted down. He only spoke Lithuanian, but we understood the proprietors would not be around until the next day and we could settle up then. We were a little nervous about how much the bungalow might cost us because the camping spot alone had been 1,000 rubles when we were there last. However, as the weather was being completely shitty, and we were on the way home, as it were, we decided to bite the bullet once again. It was cozy and warm in the little A-frame. Lovely to have the rain outside instead of on us. Feeling dry for a change, and hospitable in our little Baltic chalet, we invited the kid to share a glass of cheap Russian vodka we'd brought over the border. He and Terence finished the bottle and the soldier went back to his kiosk to sleep it off. The next morning, I walked over and handed the young man a cup of strong coffee before he was to be relieved, and he seemed grateful. Later, we rode the Ascot to Vilnius to take another look at the amber. This time we had better luck. We found some great buys and were able to afford a beautiful necklace for my daughter Meredith that would have been way out of our range in the States. Terence was pleased to find some leather passport-holders for gifts--again for a song, and a couple of new language dictionaries for his collection. We even stumbled across a kind of cafe that purported to serve pizza, so we sat down at the counter and ordered one each. They turned out to be sort of pita pancakes with tomato sauce on top and a lake of mayonnaise in the middle, upon which floated a small piece of melted cheese. Still, they were cheap, and we were hungry and no longer very discerning after a couple of months in Eastern Europe.

Returning to camp, we met two nice Dutch bikers, Jeroom and Menno, who spoke English and had been admiring (or at least curious about) our trailer. After gabbing awhile, we four decided to look for a restaurant in Trakaj. The lakeside village had obviously been a resort town at one time, and we could even see signs of what must have once been several restaurants for wealthy (or much-decorated or whatever) citizens, but there was only one left in the town which would serve us. I can't remember if it had a name.

Again, it seemed in the best tradition of let's-let-the-kids-decorate, with a sort of "Undersea" theme. The light from long strings of florescent tubes overhead filtered through thick and seaweedy plastic strips and blobs of green and blue translucent plastic, giving us the slightly suffocating feeling that we were being seated to dine or be dined upon, on some ocean floor. A Musak-type tape of watered-down Torch-song Hits of the Forties in English played over and over with about six or eight selections, also added to a feeling of drowning, and we learned from our waitress that we could have anything, as long as it was Hungarian wine and the Specialty-of-the-House, sometimes called the Menu of the Day.

The Hungarian wine was the best part of the meal. After making it quite clear that there was nothing we could order from the menu, and if we wanted food we would have to trust her, the impatient waitress brought us our plates consisting of two slices of tough beef fried in rancid oil with a side-dish of pickled beets and carrots and things that looked like french fries but were really fried dough made to look like fries. The two Dutchmen were happy to get anything. Without Terence speaking Russian to soothe the waitress's feelings of insult when we questioned the lack of choice, they would have starved in there, their bleached bones left on the sand after the tide went out.

After we got back to camp, I made us all some coffee. Terence poured some brandy in his that he'd bought at a kiosk in St. Petersburg. Nobody else wanted any. I thought the coffee tasted awful but Jeroom and Menno, being polite, pretended it was fine. I asked Terence if he could taste something terrible about it through his brandy and he thought about it and agreed. I checked the water bottle I'd used and Terence realized it was the one he had put battery acid into earlier in the day and forgotten to rinse out! I'd filled it with water from the camp faucet without knowing any better. We were drinking coffee-flavored battery-acid!! There went my prize for Best Hostess of the Year! Luckily, the Netherlanders had a great sense of humor. We could only hope it wouldn't kill us. I made a fresh pot.

In the morning I noticed that nothing had dried on my washline draped all around the bungalow, so I had to just throw everything damp-- into the trailer when it was time to roll. Terence went up the hill to pay the manager and was stunned to find we owed only 200 rubles! His Russian had improved so much in the last few weeks that the person taking his money for the bungalow (who was not the same person who had been there before) had thought he was Estonian! And we had paid 1,000 rubles as Americans for only a place to park a couple of weeks earlier! Elated, we pulled the trailer onto the muddy road and headed for that horrible border crossing with Poland where we'd had such a nightmarish wait before. It was a dark and drippy day.

As luck would have it, the long line was on the Lithuanian side this time, and Terence made the decision early on that he was going to be more assertive than before. We'd learned a lot in a couple of weeks about the Soviet mind. We'd been robbed, lied to, cheated and shortchanged, and now that he had been forced to leave their hostile countries, he just wasn't going to take any more of their bullshit. The least they could do was let him out! The Gold Wing was staying alive by a mere thread--every stop killed it, and so Terence gunned the engine and we swept past all the poor truck drivers and automobiles growing old in line, and while I leaned over from my bike and kept the Wing's engine accelerating, he went up to see if he could bribe anybody. They asked if he had any American cigarettes. Nope, didn't believe in 'em. But if they would be so patient... He walked back to the rig and dug out his stash of Condoms-for-trade. He gave the High-Ranking Ones six each--he told me it brought smiles to their faces.

Then, as we were waved past the underlings in uniform--who probably had more use for them--he handed out a few more. The boys really laughed when they realized what they were.

A short wait exchanging smiles with a few Polish motorcyclists who spoke none of Terence's six or eight Most Useful Languages In Europe, and suddenly we were free to barrel down the highway to civilization.

Chapter Sixty-Seven

ON OUR LAST LEGS FOR THE LAST LEG

WE HEADED in the direction of Gdansk. Bought milk and staples in the first town we came to. Then a long day's ride into the sunset. Just before it got dark, we saw a campground sign and following the arrow, took the dirt road through a thick forest until we came to a muddy knoll with a two-story house in the middle, encircled by a wire fence. The young couple with a baby in their arms looked astonished to see us approach. Nobody else about. We guessed September was a little late for campers this far out. We haggled a price and set up in the area for tents. It was creepy to be out there all alone in the dark but rather nice too. No children, dogs or boom-boxes. We slept well.

Having paid the night before, we were able to get an early start in the morning, and as the sun parted the rain clouds on the eastern horizon, we were bumping over the Polish potholes that, filled with rainwater, felt bottomless. Something was seriously wrong with my motorcycle. I signaled to Terence to stop and have a look. He discovered that my bike's frame was broken! No wonder it felt like it was falling apart. It was. We had no choice but to ride very slowly until we came to a town large enough to have a welder. Not a word was understood between us, but the welder could see what needed to be done as soon as T. took off the Ascot's seat. Fortunately, he was pretty efficient and in about a half-hour, the job was done. He waved away offers of payment, but Terence had another bottle of Russian vodka to give him and he seemed pleased. I gave him a

Polaroid photo of himself working on the bike with the big rig in the background so he would have something to show his friends.

On the trail again, we were just wondering what to do about lunch when we spotted a German-style snack bar by the road. Looking at the posted menu, we saw that everything was crossed off except the last item which we ordered. It turned out to be a sort of tripe soup and very tasty and even served with a roll. The older couple cooking were friendly and the place was spotless. I donno...I kind of missed the massive matrons in the dirty white uniforms. One gets used to those things.

We made many stops to revitalize the Wing and check the rest of the equipment. With the constant rain, everything was beginning to give up the ghost at once. We had asked so much from our machinery in the five years we'd been on the road, and the bikes were not new to begin with. It really was time to go home.

At the outskirts of Gdansk, a policeman pulled Terence over and asked for his insurance papers. I think T. was almost happy to have to dig them out. After all that trouble getting them in Holland, it was nice that someone cared. The cop was satisfied. Terence asked him about a campground in Gdansk but couldn't understand anything except something about a road to Helsinki and we got royally lost trying to find it. We located a very seedy-looking camping spot in a questionable part of town and were just turning around to leave when the manager came running out of the gate begging us to stay. I believe he was speaking German. Terence used our well worn fib about making a mistake and having to meet friends who would be waiting for us at the other campground (wherever it might be). We drove back to the center of Gdansk, rubber-necking at some rather spectacular architecture rising from the dusky gloom and in spite of several wrong turns and absolutely no signs to help us, we finally found the right place. The manageress told us there were signs about her campground all along the way. All we had to do was be on the right road! A Polish joke?

First thing we did after breakfast was to go to the Tourist Information place but the sweet young thing was worse than no help at all. She hadn't a clue how to FAX, or where, or even what it was. No idea how to send or receive a package, and was positive there were simply no express mail offices or anything resembling such an animal in all of Gdansk. She also gave us the wrong address for the American Express office. Luckily, we found it on our own and the woman there was very helpful. Terence was able to use her fax machine, and after several telephone calls from the main Post Office in the Old Town, things were cleared up with his Law School in California, they promised to send the right books and papers and it looked like he might graduate after all. I was able to contact my daughter at my home and she assured me all was well on that front. We breathed a long sigh of relief.

The days slipped by as Terence feverishly studied and typed to catch up. We were snug in our bigger tent, but the weather had turned mean. It was hard to believe how unbearably hot it was in Poland only a few weeks before. On September 16th I wrote: "Five times I've put up damp clothes on the line as the sun pokes out of the racing clouds, and five times I've run out to retrieve them when pellets of raindrops smack against the flapping tent. Terence and I are trying to stay calm. The last sunny day without rain and wind was six days ago and we're tired of it. We tell ourselves it's better than riding in it, but oh my, home sounds better and better. Terence says he wants a cat on his lap. I want a chocolate-chip cookie...and a cat on my lap."

After knocking out several weeks of lessons in nine days, Terence needed a break. We rode the Ascot out to Malbork (Marienburg in German). Sliding off the bike, we spotted a nice display of amber on a small table and ran over to it. This time we didn't hold back. "Why go home with any money?" said T. The pretty lady almost fainted with joy when we kept buying the stuff. Still, it was dirt cheap compared with the States.

The famous castle of the notorious Order of Teutonic Knights was impressive indeed, especially in that it had been completely restored to its former glory by loving hands. We saw a black and white photograph of the place right after WWII. Not much left. But somebody had pumped big bucks back into the project and it is beautiful today. I was so glad we had taken the trip. Many of its hundreds of rooms held exhibits--all tastefully presented. One included sculpture found on the site, another had several illuminated books dating from the times of the Knights! They had restored the kitchens and banquet halls in one part of the castle and if you listened carefully you could almost hear the clinking of goblets and the clanking of swords against armored thighs. In another wing they had a large Amber Museum which had been one of the reasons we made the trip to Malbork. On display were fabulous old pieces as well as lots of contemporary exhibits which were fascinating. I was delighted to see what the Polish artists of today were turning out. All of this was included in the small three dollar price of admission.

Back in Gdansk, Terence finally had caught up with his studies and mailed them off with a heavy sigh. We stayed long enough to climb the tower of the big church in the old town and see the splendid view. Terence was suffering from a nasty bee sting that he'd received while putting on his sandals that morning. It was his second in two weeks and this one was twice as painful. But he made it up the zillions of wooden steps to the top and said the sight was worth it. Another Polish casualty of WWII, Old Gdansk was rebuilt methodically and carefully to resemble the town during its heyday in the Renaissance. From our tower, the new bricks and tiles and sharp-sloped roofs were softened by the early autumn leaves of the trees far below and with the modern ship-building harbor in the distance, you could feel a marvelous sense of history and Polish pride.

On Thursday, Sept.24th, we packed up and rode west out of Gdansk-- hugging the coast for awhile before heading down to Germany. As the day wore on it got darker and darker and when I saw drivers coming from the other direction with their lights on, I knew we were in for trouble. Some-body had swiped my little digital clock off the dash (for the second time) and I supposed it must be around 6 p.m. But it was really only 4 p.m.! Just as we entered a village near the border to Germany, the rain started to fall hard. We pulled under a tree and laboriously pulled on our rain gear--me gritting my teeth because my stupid "rain" pants didn't fit at all and were never meant to be used on a motorcycle. The crotch seam wasn't rein-forced so it had split; allowing the icy water to flow freely inside and form large, cold puddles I had to sit in. Obviously, the damn yellow slicker was designed for nothing more strenuous than standing in the street and holding up a stop sign so children could cross the street! Terence sat ahead of me cursing because he couldn't turn off the engine or it'd die. We were quite a pair.

The rain got lighter and we pushed off again and the border crossing into Germany was so easy I can hardly remember it. I seem to recall seeing the usual truckers and folks having a smoke outside their cars and thinking about how amazingly relaxed everybody was where not long ago innocent people were shot or arrested for coming anywhere near the place.

We had filled up our tanks on the Polish side which was a very good thing because there seemed to be nothing on the East German side but forest for miles and miles. Somehow we suspected it might be that way. We were too far from Berlin to make it before dark and the poor Wing's battery couldn't hold a charge for the headlight so there was nothing to do but stop somewhere in the forest to camp. We took a small road leading to some village and then turned into a farmer's dirt road that wound around a sort of dump where we were able to turn the rig around facing the way out before the Wing expired.

We didn't sleep well. Worry about the motorcycle and the pain of his latest beesting kept Terence tossing and turning, and sometime during the wee hours of the night, an animal knocked the plastic sack with the garbage off the camp table and as it hit the ground a glass jar inside broke with a terrific crash and scared us to death until we'd realized what had happened. We were glad to get going early in the morning.

It was a short ride to Berlin from the forest, however, and we would have been in the campground by noon if the directions we got from the woman in the Tourist Information Center at the airport had been correct. But, thanks to her, we were two hours looking for the place and by the time we found it the poor Gold Wing was so weak it completely died at the gate and couldn't be revived. We pushed it in, trailer and all, and the campers standing around watched and shook their heads. We were lucky to find a spot left to put the rig because it was the Berlin Marathon weekend and the campground was full of runners and fans. While I washed and wrote stuff, Terence rode the Ascot to the Brandenberg Gate to get some pictures of the races. Later we visited a museum featuring Prague Jugendstil exhibit and really enjoyed it.

Monday, Sept. 28th, and we were still in Berlin. Terence was typing lessons. I was remarking about how lovely the September days were. So much like home. Golden leaves fluttered down from high Poplar trees. Thin bands of sunlight shown across the paths. The noisy bunch of New Zealanders had left, leaving us much relieved. For two nights they had partied 'till midnight playing their tapes so loud they had to have heard it all over the campground. On their vacated site, trash and garbage lay in the grass and dirt. Terence called them "Piglets."

Through sheer desperation, Terence found a way to revive the big bike enough to get us to our friends in Holland. It took us two days, with an overnight near the Dutch border in another deserted campground. Dirk and family welcomed us warmly as always and as I began deciding what to take home and what to leave, Terence got on the phone to shipping companies and airlines to find a way to get the rig home. After three days of trying, he had to concede that we could not possibly afford to keep our beloved old rides. We would have to leave them in Holland. And we had had such hopes about making a coffee table out of the Wing's engine!

Chapter Sixty-Eight

THE END OF THE ROAD

WE ARRIVED in Santa Barbara in time for my son's twenty-sixth birthday, October, 20th, 1992. Terence passed the California State Bar examination the next Spring and has jumped into the legal fray with the same passion and wild abandon he once showed on the motorcycle, and although he hates not being able to use all his languages at this time nor find much time for riding, he has found a new way to slay dragons and he seems content with that.

I picked up pen and paint brush--very happy to be indoors again with a toaster and hot water and even a garden to tend out back. My motorcycle was sold in Holland and beautifully restored by one of Dirk's friends. The big trailer was pulled to Romania by Dutch Gold Wingers and given to some very grateful folks. Terence's tired old Gold Wing was repaired by loving hands, it now has a new alternator and is in Dirk's garage to be loaned to any Gold Winger who might need it. Terence plans to ride it again one of these days.

THE END

Gail and Terence at the remnant of the Berlin Wall

ACKNOWLEDGMENTS

I want to thank my children, Meredith and Lucas, for encouraging me to follow my passion for adventure while they were still in college discovering theirs. In addition, I am forever grateful to my niece, Laurel Standley, who took it upon herself to turn what was a crazy jumble of drawings and pages into a real book for folks to enjoy.

ABOUT THE AUTHOR

Gail Lucas is an artist, singer, and author living in Santa Barbara, California. Graduated from UCLA in 1960 with a degree in Fine Arts and a minor in Music, Gail embarked upon an acting career in Hollywood and New York, appearing on "The Andy Griffith Show", radio, and stage productions. Ms. Lucas is the author and illustrator of the children's book, *Trevor the Traveling Tree,* and has illustrated several others. In 1993, Gail won the Santa Barbara Writer's Conference Mystery Writing Contest.

SPAIN

74090139R00270

Made in the USA
San Bernardino, CA
13 April 2018